CONSPIRACY to RIOT

In Furtherance of Terrorism

CONSPIRACY to RIOT

In Furtherance of Terrorism

The Collective Autobiography of the RNC 8

Edited by Leslie James Pickering

Foreword by Tom Hayden

Preface by Betsy Raasch-Gilman

arissa
media group
PORTLAND • PHOENIX

Library of Congress Control Number: 2011932801
International Standard Book Number: 9781936900183

Cover design by Keri Rosebraugh, www.kerirosebraugh.com.
Cover photo by Susan Micks.
Editing by Ariana Huemer.

Printed on 100% recycled, post consumer waste paper.

 **green press** INITIATIVE Arissa Media Group is a member of Green Press Initiative, which means we meet GPI's environmental criteria and support their efforts to reduce the social and environmental impacts of book publishing. For more information, please visit: www.greenpressinitiative.org.

Arissa Media Group, LLC was formed in 2003 and focuses on producing literary works that promote political and social justice, human rights, environmental and animal protection, and positive social and political change. For more information, bulk requests, catalog listings, submission guidelines, or media inquiries please contact:

Arissa Media Group • Tel: (866) 476-0964
info@arissamediagroup.com • www.arissamediagroup.com

Contents

Foreword

I am not an anarchist, but more a participatory democrat with pragmatic and anarchist tendencies. I was not present during the 2008 Republican National Convention in St. Paul, where the events in these pages unfolded. That summer I attended the Democratic convention which nominated Sen. Barack Obama, who became not only the first African-American president and a candidate pledged to end the war in Iraq.

I kept my eye on St. Paul, however. I knew some of the young anarchists planning to "welcome" the Republicans with a threat of street disruption, erupting wherever the powerful gathered since the shutdown of the World Trade Organization in Seattle, 1999. It was a worthy cause to give the Republicans hell in bluest Minnesota, I believed, but I didn't want to relive my own history one more time.

The so-called Welcoming Committee, including those who became known as the RNC 8, was invoking historic comparisons with the Chicago Conspiracy 8 of the Sixties, myself included. In particular they seemed to be imagining themselves as 21st century incarnations of Abbie Hoffman, Jerry Rubin, and the Yippies.

I knew if I showed up in Minnesota, the press corps would barrage me with distracting questions about the comparisons between 1968 and 2008. Pointing out the differences – the greater carnage of Vietnam, the draft, the voting disenfranchisement of young people, the uprisings from ghettos to college campuses - would require a virtual teach-in and divert attention from the issues at hand.

Of course, the similarities between the Nixon and Bush administration were real as well. Karl Rove, a modern master of dirty tricks, had been a leader of the College Young Republicans circa 1968.

But the pattern that drew my attention had developed

more recently than the Sixties, during the Seattle protests of 1999, which I attended as an eyewitness and writer. I was astonished at the sudden birth of a new, creative, and small-d democratic movement of young people in the streets. So were the Seattle authorities, the FBI and the hundreds of global trade officials trapped in the city's downtown hotels.

As a result of those demonstrations, the WTO was crippled as an institution and the corporate-dominated global trade talks were derailed. For the elite, Seattle was a stunning repudiation of their reputations, their undemocratic mechanisms of control, and their Ayn Rand vision of capitalism unbound. At the same time, rival visions of democratic economic development were on the loose, especially across Latin America. The slogan "Another World Is Possible", initially invented by an editor at Le Monde Diplomatique, began inspiring a new generation previously instructed to submit to the gods of the Market.

For a time, the unregulated freedom of anarchism seemed to mirror its enemy, the unregulated freedom of capital. The platform of the New Deal – collective bargaining, decent wages, health care, social security and other protections – had become too radical to tolerate for the banks and corporations operating globally, and therefore too weak and timid for a growing legion of dispossessed dissidents. The reforms of the 30s and 60s generations were being circumvented by corporate bureaucrats seeking cheap labor, investment havens and servile governments.

In these crises, the authorities started giving lip service to reform while cranking up the apparatus of police control. After Seattle, for example, President Clinton – an architect of the WTO plans – was at the Seattle podium commending the protestors for demanding more democracy, accountability and transparency. Attaching labor and environmental standards to future trade agreements became the talk of the Beltway, as if leaving democratic processes out of the trade protocols had been a bureaucratic accident.

After Seattle, there were more Seattles, in Washington DC (2000, 2002, 2007), LA (2000), Quebec City (2001), Oakland (2003), New York (2003, 2004), Miami (2003) in Cancun (2003), Los Angeles (2004), and in cities across Europe, Latin

America and Asia. All of these events preceded the so-called Arab Spring of pro-democracy movements in 2011.

In this context, in the absence of significant social reform, the FBI and police were wired and hired to over-react, thus building a climate of public fear, increasing their surveillance powers, and, not insignificantly, obtaining about $50 million in federal funding for each local threat-suppression exercise. This repressive apparatus mushroomed with the decade-long global "war on terrorism" which began two full years after Seattle.

This was the pattern and recipe for what occurred in St. Paul. When a group of radical activists, many of them self-styled anarchists, put out a call for protest at a national event, it was greeted as the equivalent of the Communist Manifesto (Here a clarification is needed. While the Communist Manifesto became more legendary, it was Marx's rival, Mikhail Bakunin, who became the ancestral patron of modern anarchism. Marx allowed for parliamentary politics in his vision of change, while Bakunin rejected the notion altogether.)

In virtually every "Seattle" occasion, the FBI declared that an anarchist threat was descending on local citizenry, with the wild estimate of 70,000 black-clad, bomb-carrying radicals often invoked. Wiretapping, informants and provocateurs were liberally employed. The alleged ringleaders were rounded up before their menacing actions could take place. The preventive detentions were followed by sweeps and arrests of thousands of peaceful demonstrators who, it was claimed, harbored dangerous elements in their midst. The round ups were accompanied by press conferences where dangerous anarchist tools were placed on display. (In Boulder/Denver in 2008, where virtually no protests took place, the police still claimed that bricks were suspiciously available around construction sites – and for their efforts, they took away the usual $50 million.) On the FBI's advice, large cages were erected in which protests would be allowed, though none were used, the protestors saying that free speech could not be caged. Again and again, severe restrictions were imposed on permits for peaceful assembly. After the crises passed, in virtually every instance the conspiracy, felony and misdemeanor charges were dismissed, plea-bargained out, or rejected by local juries.

The script was followed precisely in the Twin Cities, though few if any citizens knew the game plan. Led by a politically-ambitious Ramsey County sheriff and prosecutor, an activist office and apartments were raided before the convention, resulting in the eventual RNC "conspirators" spending convention week in jail. Eight hundred were arrested during the subsequent days. The use of gas, riot batons and tasers was perpetual. Undercover agents entrapped one individual activist into testing a Molotov cocktail while another informant drew two others into fooling around with gasoline bombs. As far as I know, Republicans and local citizens were inconvenienced, but few seem to have been assaulted by raging anarchists. A Google search shows that an 83 –year old Republican did suffer breathing problems when a protestor snatched his GOP credential, but how could that be blamed on a conspiracy.

The conspiracy charges were issued nontheless, more specifically, "conspiracy to riot in furtherance of terrorism." Two years later, after a prolonged local legal defense effort, charges against three of the eight RNC 8 defendants were dismissed. One accepted a plea-bargain, and served three months in county jail. The other three took various misdemeanor charges and served no jail time after the convention. This was not exactly McCarthyism or the repression of Guantanamo, but those nightmare scenarios were prevented by the massive crackdowns, the prosecutors claimed. In city after city. The conspiracies were prevented from being implemented, the public was told, because they were uncovered. No one seemed to notice that the numerous conspirators across America were released without jail time, free apparently to resume their wicked ways. In truth, they were pawns.

In retrospect, one can certainly have legitimate questions about the viewpoint and tactics of the RNC 8, as I do. For example, the "satirical" movie trailer of anarchists lighting up Molotov cocktails was sure to justify police repression and sew confusion amidst the public. Is it just a sign of my aging that I am asking myself, what were they thinking? In addition, the activists' ethic of open decentralization and pursuit of all tactics literally and naively invites agents and provocateurs. The anarchist goal of provoking and de-legitimizing state authority was perhaps ironically offset by the RNC's reliance on so many liberal-progressive reformers who stepped up for the tasks of legal defense, fund-raising, petitioning and press outreach that ultimately protected the defendants' liberty. As for the consciousness-raising lesson in these events, when can we pass from exposing the state to reforming the state, or is that interim objective ruled out by anarchist ideology?

Anarchism, and its kindred nineteenth century ideologies, is one attitude among several towards insufferable conditions in which there are no institutional avenues that promise radical and rapid reform. Its tenets require updating to the modern world of on-line communication, future-threatening environmental crisis, the power of nonviolent protest, and the urgency of immediate reform for the world's starving. As for myself, I believe all the 19th century "isms" should be the subject of deep scrutiny and debate by all progressives, with care taken that they become heavy baggage on the minds of the new.

In any event, this shocking chain of events in St. Paul was not an isolated instance in our modern times, but part of a growing pattern of police buildup and overkill. The events described here will play out again and again. We can all learn of the dangers to democracy contained in the case of the RNC 8, thank them for their courage and fortitude, and look forward to following the defendants' journeys ahead.

- Tom Hayden

Preface

September 27, 2006: The mayors of St. Paul, Minneapolis, and Bloomington, Minnesota, announced with excitement and pride that they had lured the 2008 Republican National Convention to our cities. The bid had to involve all three municipalities, because none of them alone had the facilities for such a mammoth production. The 15,000 reporters; the 4,000 delegates and alternates; the 10,000 volunteers; and the 15,000 staff, family members, and guests would stay in hotels in Bloomington, attend endless parties and entertainment in Minneapolis, and conduct their official business at the Xcel Energy Center in downtown St. Paul. This event would be "a boost for the economy," our mayors intoned over and over. "It's about business, not politics," they insisted. And indeed it was. For instance, Qwest Communications got millions of dollars for wiring the convention center (a hockey arena) for high-tech communications, and then unwiring it five days later.

The Democratic mayors had quite the selling job: they had all been elected by their solidly liberal voting public, and the sitting administration of George W. Bush was highly unpopular, even among "independent" voters. Reaction came swiftly from local progressives. We couldn't believe that the party that had started the "war on terror," invaded Iraq under false pretenses, denied global climate change, wanted a wall along our southern border to keep immigrants out, and displayed utter indifference to poor African-Americans during the devastation after Hurricane Katrina would be partying (pun intended) in our cities!

Anarchists and anti-authoritarians began organizing among the very first. As the stories in this book lay out, the points of unity for the RNC Welcoming Committee went out broadly early in 2007, along with the slogan "Because we live here."

Anarchists have, in fact, lived in the Twin Cities for at

least 100 years, since the founding of the Industrial Workers of
the World. In my own lifetime, I've participated in four separate waves of anarchist political activity. The first, in the 1970s,
started an impressive network of worker-run co-ops: selling
food, clothing, bicycles, housing, and even repairing electronics.
(Most of them had short lifespans, and those that survive are now
indistinguishable from upscale grocery stores – except that their
profits still go to the shoppers, rather than to private investors.)

The second wave of anarchist activity in the area largely
expressed itself in cultural ways: punk music, zines, and radical
gathering spaces. However, that soil provided a fertile bed for
Earth First!, which played a significant role in opposing the first
invasion of Iraq in 1991. The anarchist cultural scene also supported Animal Liberation Front actions throughout the 1990s.

The third wave of anarchist-motivated activity sprang
up in response to the widening of a highway to the airport in the
late 1990s. Highway 55 had stirred up controversy for some 20
years already, because it threatened either quiet neighborhoods
or a popular park. Just when the state Department of Transportation thought it could finally begin construction, an assortment of
young anarchists occupied the condemned area. The Highway
55 encampment lasted for an incredible 18 months, through two
bitter Minnesota winters, and drew traveling anarchists from all
over the country to its tents. The encampment also raised issues
of native sovereignty, as Dakota peoples recognized several
sacred sites in the highway's path. Dakota activists erected tents
and a sweat lodge alongside the anarchists' huts.

Each of these anarchist waves left some building materials for the next one: bookstores, theater companies, performance
and gathering spaces, bands, collective households, and cooper-
atively-run projects like Food Not Bombs. The RNC Welcoming
Committee (wave number four) made use of this infrastructure
and set a goal of strengthening it. We envisioned starting collectives and affinity groups for the protests that would outlive the
Republican extravaganza and build capacity for ongoing resistance to the State. Given the prosecutions which followed the
RNC, we had less success in this regard than we had wished for;
our post-convention energy mostly went into outwitting the legal

system rather than into more positive channels.

The track record of protests of political conventions is not terrific, and certainly led me to wonder over and over again (during my 18 months in the Welcoming Committee) why I was putting so much effort into something that would probably be only a blip on the screen of social change. The 1968 protests of the Democratic Convention in Chicago are legendary (and resulted in a long legal battle like ours). I didn't even remember the protests of the 1972 Republican convention in Miami until a well-wisher sent us a yellowing copy of their tabloid! The protests of the 2000 Republican convention in Philadelphia still stir up deep divisions between anarchists and faith-based peace and justice activists there, while the 2004 protests in Boston (Dems) and New York (Reps) had mixed reviews even at the time. (Protest pens? Why on earth would anyone cooperate with those?!)

Even knowing all this, progressives in the Twin Cities couldn't not protest the 2008 RNC. Anti-war activists announced a permitted, legal rally and march a year-and-a-half in advance; that had to be a record amount of lead time. (They spent much of it struggling for the permit and parade route, and ultimately suing the city of St. Paul to get them.) Mainstream labor unions made plans to protest, as did immigrant rights and anti-poverty advocates.

All modesty aside, the Welcoming Committee did some of the most thorough organizing, as the stories in this book show. One aspect I want to highlight – because it had lasting benefits – was the St. Paul Principles. These agreements spelled out a way for the major players to cooperate (or at least, not compete), with respect for a diversity of tactics.

The basic problem was this: the peace and justice groups wanted to march on the opening day of the convention. Like us, they had planned to draw a big crowd from all over the country, and they wanted to avoid arrests and police attacks. The anarchists and anti-authoritarians wanted to prevent the convention from even opening that day. (Labor Day, insultingly enough!) Blockading the streets and bridges, holding street parties, disabling delegate buses, and all kinds of disruptive tactics were considered. While many peace activists sympathized with the goal of keeping delegates out of the convention center, they drew the line at property destruction and generally feared provoking the police. Anarchists and anti-authoritarians wanted freedom to do whatever they thought might be effective, and they intended to defend themselves against the police. Everyone wanted to be in the streets at roughly the same time.

The St. Paul Principles allowed us to accomplish this small miracle. The WC and the local sponsors of the permitted, legal march hammered them out in some uneasy negotiations, neither group trusting the other terrifically much. However, they got written, and at a planning conference for the protests in February 2008, representatives of ANSWER, United for Peace and Justice, and the Troops Out Now Coalition affirmed them. WC members, touring the country to stir up interest in the RNC protests, explained these principles to their largely anarchist audiences. While we could hardly require that everyone abide by the St. Paul Principles without being authoritarian ourselves(!), we did stress the groundbreaking nature of this coalition, and that we would have to deal with the consequences if the principles were violated. Again, "because we live here."

These were the St. Paul Principles:

1. Our solidarity will be based on respect for diversity of tactics and the plans of other groups.
2. The actions and tactics used will be organized to maintain a separation of time or space.
3. Any debates or criticisms will stay internal to the movement, avoiding any public or media denunciations of fellow activists and events.
4. We opposed any state repression of dis sent, including surveillance, infiltration, disruption and violence. We agree not to assist law enforcement actions against activists and others.

Law enforcement got nervous about our intentions early on, and this statement didn't make them breathe any easier! A satirical trailer the WC released in August of 2007 got the attention of Ramsey County Sheriff Bob Fletcher. (Ramsey County contains St. Paul; Hennepin County contains Minneapolis.) We didn't know this at the time, of course – documents released in court and press statements later tell the story. One segment of the trailer shows a black-clad, masked anarchist running down an alley, lighting a Molotov cocktail, and tossing it over a garage roof. It lands in a barbeque grill tended by another black-clad, masked anarchist.

Law enforcement doesn't have a great sense of humor. They took that sequence and others in the trailer seriously, and Fletcher sent two deputies and a confidential informant to our meetings shortly afterwards. All innocently, we accepted the infiltrators into the WC, though some of us grew suspicious of them over time. They stayed involved right up to the demonstrations. More damaging yet, the FBI sent its own confidential informant to our meetings, and few of us had suspicions of him. He managed to entrap one activist from Michigan into testing out Molotov cocktails; Matthew dePalma is now serving 42 months in a federal prison because of it.

Andrew Darst, our FBI informant, was bad enough. The investigation of the WC overlapped with another investigation of anarchists in Austin, Texas, where the FBI employed a former activist named Brandon Darby. Five Austin activists drove with him up to St. Paul for the RNC, and on the way Darby persuaded two of them to experiment with gasoline bombs. Bradley Crowder and David McKay are also now in federal prisons now because of this.

Did we leave ourselves open for this infiltration? In fact, the WC organized openly. We put our plans on our website and invited people to check out our meetings. We intended to host thousands of anarchists and anti-authoritarians coming to town for the convention, and we needed all the help we could get. Most of us expected to play support roles during the actions: in the communications center, the legal office, the health clinic, and the kitchen buses. The WC itself made no action plans, although a few members put together their own separate action groups. We encouraged protesters to come with an affinity group and a general plan for stopping the delegate buses. To help them, we provided maps and as much information as we could about the delegates' transportation routes on our website. We consulted the city's own traffic flow maps to divide downtown St. Paul into sectors, and asked affinity groups to take responsibility for making a sector (or part of one) impassable. We didn't ask, though, what any given group planned to do, nor did we make suggestions.

As the stories in this book lay out, the Ramsey County sheriff attacked preemptively on Friday night and Saturday morning of Labor Day weekend, 2008. Deputies attempted to close our convergence center (legally rented and paid for); seized literature, computers, and cell phones from people there; raided houses of several WC members and carted away questionable evidence; and arrested eight of us. Thus, the RNC 8 spent the entire week of the convention in jail, while those of us at liberty dodged the police and held together our infrastructure for the protests.

The anarchist-led blockades delayed the start of the RNC for about three hours. The media hardly mentioned this, however, because the Republicans themselves cancelled their opening ceremonies that evening! As Hurricane Gustav barreled down on New Orleans, party officials realized that it would create the wrong impression if they were whooping it up at one end of the Mississippi while people on the other end were drowning. Delegates did attempt to get to the convention center on Monday afternoon for registration and preliminary business, but the gavel didn't fall officially until Tuesday night. (Gustav did not do as much damage to the Gulf Coast as everyone had feared.)

That freed up 15,000 reporters to cover the protests in the streets, which they did gleefully. Ten thousand people rallied and marched in the legal, permitted protest. Mere blocks away, tear gas canisters flew, concussion grenades boomed, and projectiles bounced around as police tried to escort delegate buses through the crowds. They arrested over 200 people on Labor Day, although most got tickets and were released. The next day at the Poor People's March, the police started using Tasers, riot batons, and other weapons. On the final day of the convention, as John McCain accepted the presidential nomination, police scooped up another 400 protesters. During the week about 40 journalists shared their fate, including Amy Goodman and members of her Democracy Now! news team. All told, over 800 were arrested.

As the Republicans left town, the RNC 8 got out of jail. Originally, Ramsey County Attorney Susan Gaertner charged them with Conspiracy to Riot in Furtherance of Terrorism. Later, she added more charges: Conspiracy to Commit Property Destruction in Furtherance of Terrorism; Conspiracy to Riot; and Conspiracy to Destroy Property. All of these were felony counts. At the worst point, the defendants each faced a possible 12 ½ years in prison. Sheriff Fletcher and Attorney Gaertner held the investigation into the Welcoming Committee open until June 2009, and Gaertner continued to threaten more prosecutions.

For all of us who'd been involved in the Welcoming Committee, (which disbanded the day after the convention ended), the next two months were nerve-wracking. Sheriff's deputies visited our homes, schools, and work places; lawyers told us that anything we said could come back to haunt us in court; and the media pestered us for interviews. An official commission investigated police conduct during the convention, while the mayors gamely repeated that it had all been "good for the economy." Even the mainstream media questioned that.

With more than 800 people facing court cases, we had a new organizing challenge. The defendants formed the Community RNC Arrestees Support Structure (CRASS) to track court appearances, index hours and hours of videotape, raise money for lawyers, share knowledge of the legal process, find housing for defendants who had to return to town for court appearances, and – of course – deal with the media.

The vast majority of the charges were misdemeanors, prosecuted by the city attorney, though 18 people (in addition to the RNC 8) faced felonies in the county system. After seven activists fought their misdemeanors before a jury and were acquitted, the city quietly dropped the bulk of the remaining misdemeanors. All this took months of attention, however. CRASS recruited and trained court watchers for every court appearance for more than a year.

Counter-suits flew, too. Activists sued both the city and the county for police brutality, invasion of privacy, seizure of personal property, and warrantless searches. The American Civil Liberties Union sued the sheriff's department for confiscating our anarchist literature from the convergence center on the grounds that it suppressed freedom of expression. That suit is still in progress, as of this writing. Most of the rest were settled with small awards paid from the city's and county's insurance policies for the convention.

The Committee to Defend the RNC 8 organized separately from CRASS, in recognition that fighting charges of terrorism would take much longer and require much more money. For those of us who'd been in the Welcoming Committee, the political landscape changed entirely when the target became the court system. In the WC, we had a strict policy against giving interviews to mainstream media or answering questions at press conferences. Now, we quickly learned how to give interviews to anyone who asked, including the local Fox News affiliate. In the WC, we paid little attention to electoral politics. Now, we realized that Susan Gaertner's ambition to run for governor gave us a pressure point. In the WC, we flinched at the idea of raising $25,000 for the protest infrastructure. Now, we set a goal of raising $250,000 for court costs.

The St. Paul Principles held! Organizers of the legal, permitted march did not criticize the anarchist-led blockades in retrospect, and in fact helped with our efforts to get the charges against the RNC 8 dropped. Even groups that hadn't agreed to the St. Paul Principles (like Veterans for Peace) supported the RNC 8 now. The huge police presence during the convention (at least 3,500 officers, borrowed from all over the region), the volume of chemical agents they used, the arbitrary closure of bridges that ordinary people needed everyday, the entrapment techniques employed to clear the streets of peaceful protesters, the walls of officers in riot gear, and most of all the house raids swung liberals solidly behind us. An example: until the house raids, we had a shortage of community housing for protesters from out of town. Two days later after the house raids, our online housing board had many more places available than we needed. Sheriff Fletcher sure solved that problem for us!

The Committee to Defend the RNC 8 consisted of a few holdovers from the WC, parents of the defendants, dedicated activists against police brutality of all sorts, and representatives from CRASS. Defendants frequently came to our meetings, though they could only give us the broad strokes of their legal strategy, or the evidence against them. The defendants and their lawyers determined the legal defense, while the DC worked on the political defense. Just as the WC had organized for almost two years before the convention, the Defense Committee operated for two years after it.

The stories in this book tell what the defendants went through much better than I can. For the DC, it was a long, slow slog and a disappointing ending. (See the final chapter of this book for the story of what happened.) Along the way, however, we had some real highlights:

- We collected over 13,000 signatures on a petition to the county attorney to drop the charges against the RNC 8. Supporters wrote from Europe and Australia.

- Andrew Darst indulged in a drunken brawl at a house in a wealthy western suburb, and pled guilty to assault and breaking and entering. We saw the notice of his sentencing hearing and showed up with a newspaper reporter. Neither he nor his FBI handler interpreted this as court solidarity! The judge put him in the county workhouse for three months. Given that none of the RNC 8 had anything similar on their records, we figured it wouldn't help this key witness' credibility in front of a jury.

- We dogged Gaertner's appearances in

her campaign for governor, and peppered her
fundraisers with flyers. When she went to Chicago to receive an award, a crowd of supporters
of the RNC 8 met her there, too. At one of her
fundraisers, a party official whispered, "You
know you're tanking her campaign, don't you?"
(To which we could only reply, "Aw, gee whiz!")

• Supporters in the Duluth (MN) Labor
Council (AFL-CIO) passed a resolution con-
demning the charges in March, 2009. A few
weeks later, Gaertner dropped the terrorism
charges, claiming that they were a "distraction."

• Members of the state Senate and House
of Representatives spoke on behalf of the RNC
8, including at public forums we organized.

• We staged a number of creative actions.
As the full picture of the police infiltration of
the WC came together, we wrote and produced
a satirical skit about it, which is online. We did
street theater when Gaertner appeared at the
State Fair to campaign. When she complained
that we would turn the courtroom into a circus,
we appeared outside the court house with a stilt
walker, a juggler, and two clowns (one Bob
Fletcher, the other Susan Gaertner), to show just
where the circus really started.

• We reached out to the press with probably more than 100 interviews, press conferences,
and press statements.

• We raised $128,000 toward the defense,
through online appeals, major donor requests,
rummage sales, dances, and dinners. Some activists contributed funds from the settlement of

their own legal cases. The most amusing contribution came from a settlement completely unrelated to the RNC: six or seven people dressed as zombies had been arrested in Minneapolis for walking down a main shopping avenue during the holiday rush, protesting the brainless consumerism there. They sued the city for wrongful arrest and won. Even zombies supported the RNC 8!

• In all of our efforts, we contextualized the charges against the 8: this is nothing new in our "liberal democracy," and many people are currently in prison because of their political activity. The "justice" system is anything but fair and impartial, as can easily be seen by the percentage of African-Americans, Latino/as, and Native Americans in prison and under court supervision.

One of the most unfortunate consequences of the long legal battle is that the Welcoming Committee never got a chance to review and process our organizing, to pull out all the lessons we had learned. Those of us who had not been arrested were potential witnesses in the case – we might be called by the prosecution, the defense, or both. Anything we heard from the defendants regarding their activities before the convention, or even their opinions about those activities in hindsight, could come up on the witness stand. Now that the cases have been settled, we can evaluate, although we've also lost a lot of the impetus for doing so.

This book might be the closest we ever come to doing that. In that spirit, I offer some of my own reflections.

First and foremost, was this worth it? Even before the 2008 political convention season, doubts about the effectiveness and wisdom of pouring movement resources into mass mobilizations had been growing. Personally, I attended eight mass mobilizations in three countries between 1999 and 2007, providing nonviolence training for protesters and participating in the actions. None of those were protests of a political convention, and I wouldn't have bothered with the 2008 conventions either, if one had not come to my backyard. ("Because I live here!")

In practical terms, protesting a political convention does not achieve much. The candidates and party platforms are settled long before the convention; even stopping the convention entirely wouldn't affect the electoral steamroller. By way of contrast, stopping the WTO from meeting in Seattle in 1999 actually prevented the world corporate elite from doing business; they expected to get something done at that meeting! In Miami in 2003, I heard trade representatives of Brazil, Argentina, and Venezuela say that our protests in the streets helped them significantly, in opposing provisions of the Free Trade of the Americas Agreement inside the concrete barriers around the meeting. They told us that the Caribbean nations felt bolder in standing up to the U.S. and Canadian governments because we were outside shouting. Those mass mobilizations helped shape the outcome of the trade negotiations. (The FTAA got so watered down in Miami that the U.S. pretty much gave up on it and started negotiating trade agreements country-by-country. That was definitely not their first choice! We basically won that skirmish in the struggle against neo-liberalism.)

Mass mobilizations, like any tactic, make sense in some situations and not in others. They make sense in some movements, and not in others. They make sense at particular junctures in those movements, and not at others. Many of us critique the formulaic rallies and marches; mass mobilizations run the same risk of being knee-jerk and predictable when they are used without strategic consideration.

That said, political conventions are a logical target for anarchist organizing. They offer opportunities to focus attention on the farce called democracy in this country – a process completely bought and paid for by wealthy individuals and corporations. (Remember those millions of dollars Qwest received for wiring the Xcel Energy Center in 2008? Guess who made one of the biggest contributions to the RNC Host Committee in St. Paul?) How do mass mobilizations against political conventions really make our point, though? How does chaos in the streets really show what democracy looks like? (It surely does show what repression looks like!)

Anarchists have a vision for a kind of democracy that could be more satisfying, empowering, just, and meaningful than voting every few years; how could we put that vision up next to the hoopla of a political convention and make our version of democracy look more appealing than their farcical version? What about flash mobs of anarchists appearing in different locations where convention delegates are known to be during the week of the convention? For instance, at a fancy restaurant where a reception is in progress, a flash mob demonstrates what a democratic food distribution system would look like. Or at a sex club, a flash mob shows what democratic sexual behavior would look like. If I have one wish for activists in Tampa and Charlotte for 2012, and other unfortunate folks later on, it is that they think creatively about the problem, and whether a mass mobilization will really advance their issues and ideas.

Because I live here, I know the downstream effects of a political convention. Every St. Paul police officer now carries a Taser, bought with us in mind. About 300 additional street cameras record our ordinary movements. The fusion center set up to coordinate the dozens of law enforcement agencies who came here (some of which we'd never even heard of before!) can be revived at any time. Political conventions are supposed to demonstrate our wonderful freedom to an envious world. In some very real ways, they destroy the freedom they say they're showing off. Maybe that reality is something anarchists could focus on – and get some real local support about, too.

The Welcoming Committee's commitment to a diversity of tactics got law enforcement all riled up. That's not surprising: when serious revolutionaries really challenge the power structure, whether they do that nonviolently or with arms, they can expect a savage reaction. Ask any democracy activist in Syria or Libya! The question in my mind is whether using a diversity of tactics against the RNC brought more suffering onto us than onto the power structure? The few broken windows, the couple of trashed police cars, were easily repaired. Rather than bringing down the state, that property damage just brought the state down on the heads of those who did it – and of those (like the Welcoming Committee) who refused to discourage it.

The pros and cons of diversity of tactics have been argued a lot – maybe over-argued – in the last 10 years. Even as a life-long nonviolent revolutionary and religious pacifist, I can't say that using a diversity of tactics led to a disaster for us. It didn't. I am struck, though, with some of the consequences, and would take them into consideration before working on an action organized in this way again.

First off, naturally, is the long court battle we've been through. The folks who led the permitted, legal march on Labor Day and the Poor People's March the next day were done with the RNC at least a year before we were. They could move onto other things. The Poor People's Economic Human Rights Campaign, for example, started some dramatic resistance actions against home mortgage foreclosures.

It's a truism, and our experience showed it again: government agents encourage activists to take riskier actions. Not only the FBI informants Darst and Darby, but also the Ramsey County sheriff's confidential informant (Chris Dugger) dared, prodded, and advocated for others to build incendiary devices. If the WC had put out a list of approved tactics, instead of our informal, though genuine, disapproval of Molotov cocktails, we probably would have been more suspicious of Darst when he raised the idea. As it was, his hints about having "a really red action" in the works made him seem like a more serious revolutionary than anyone else and built his mystique. He wormed his way deeper into the WC instead of being watched warily. The romance that connects destruction and even violence with revolution and effectiveness gave the State a foothold for further repression of dissent.

Security culture didn't keep us secure. We removed our cell phone batteries for most meetings. We set up vouching systems for all our national gatherings. (Brandon Darby breezed right through because of his long history of activism; no one suspected that he'd switched sides.) We checked out people's backgrounds; I'm sure I, being older, was checked out repeatedly! We were thoroughly infiltrated anyway. The sheriff boasted that he followed our tours to 67 cities. Security culture only gave us an illusion of security.

I'm not sure my friends, the RNC 8, would agree with all (or any!) of these conclusions. In the following pages, they speak for themselves quite eloquently. Their stories give a fascinating insight into the complex world of social change, lived ideology, and inspirational organizing. I feel deeply privileged to have worked so closely with them for so long. Enjoy getting to know them as much as I did!

- Betsy Raasch-Gilman

Introduction

On November 6, 2003, Luce Guillén-Givins invited me out to the Twin Cities to speak about the Earth Liberation Front at Macalester College, where she was then a student. Having been spokesperson for the Earth Liberation Front Press Office, my past experiences speaking at colleges had lowered my expectations of the ability of student groups to effectively organize and promote public events. As I stepped out of the car, I was hit by the bitter cold of Minnesota November and the thought, "Nobody is going to show up in this weather."

There was a sandwich board out front of the building directing people in, and Luce and accomplices had virtually covered the campus with posters (featuring a Hummer torched by the Earth Liberation Front) advertising the event. She explained how hard they had worked to get people out, not only from within the student body, but from across the Twin Cities. I was impressed, yet still skeptical.

Luce had reserved a stage at one end of a large student cafeteria, explaining that they decided to hold the event there at mealtime to potentially attract students who had just come to eat. They had arranged more seating than seemed necessary; behind the rows of chairs were a number of lunch tables with additional seating, and a mezzanine above overlooked the stage from every angle.

Sometime in the middle of my talk, I remember looking out over the audience and noticing that every seat was filled. There were so many people standing that I couldn't see the cafeteria tables. The size of the audience really hit me when I looked up to the mezzanine and saw that it was completely lined with faces looking down upon me. From the faces in the crowd, it was obvious that in addition to students, a decent number of non-students from the Twin Cities had showed up. There were so many questions and comments afterwards that the event dragged on exhaustively long after its scheduled ending. Luce was clearly an extraordinary event organizer and I made a point to stay in touch with her.

We made plans to meet up a week later in Miami at a counter-convention protest against a meeting of the Free Trade Area of the Americas (FTAA). Two carloads of young activists from the Twin Cities showed up for their first national protest, which everybody was hoping would be something like the World Trade Organization (WTO) protest in Seattle four years earlier.

Before the protests had even begun, a group of us were walking along a downtown street when we were suddenly surrounded and detained by police demanding to know where the "missile"/"projectile" was. Eventually we figured out that they were looking for a coconut that one of us had briefly picked up from under a tree a few blocks back. We had been under surveillance as we walked, and when the coconut was picked up, orders apparently went out to arrest us. By the time we were detained, the coconut had long been left behind.

We were about to be arrested anyway, until a large and increasingly angry group of union men emerged from a theater across the street shouting, "Let them go! Let them go!" The police acquiesced. Unfortunately, the coconut incident was to be the only really empowering event for us during the protests, and our friends from the Twin Cities would be denied any experience vaguely resembling what many of us had created at the WTO. Miami police far outnumbered protesters and were equipped with a terrifying arsenal of the latest anti-riot technology. They erected a fence around the entire FTAA meeting area that protestors could not breach, despite their best attempts. The measures taken by police to castrate the protest became known as the "Miami Model," eventually to be mimicked many times since. The event left me with an overwhelming feeling of defeat.

On December 7, 2005, arrests for a series of unsolved Earth Liberation Front actions commenced under the FBI's "Operation Backfire." On the one-year anniversary of these arrests, Luce, Rob Czernik, Scott DeMuth, Carrie Feldman and accomplices organized a "Twin Cities Fights the Green Scare" panel discussion at their Jack Pine Community Center and invited me to take part. Again, it was a well-organized and attended event, one which inspired the formation of Earth Warriors are Okay! (EWOK!), which was central in laying the groundwork for a strong and unified community against the repression that would come down as backlash against the protests against the 2008 Republican National Convention (RNC).

On November 30, 2007, I was warmly welcomed back to the Twin Cities during a book tour by Rob, Scott, Carrie and others. The environment and mood was unlike what I had witnessed before. My hosts were neck-deep in organizing around the upcoming RNC and the whole scene felt strongly reminiscent of Eugene, Oregon in the late '90s.

Impressively, the locals were organizing against the possibility of a Convention even before it was announced that the Twin Cities would be the host. There was a lot of energy and tension, and I really got the sense of the inevitable confrontation as the clock ticked down to the RNC.

On January 31, 2008, the RNC Welcoming Committee stopped in Buffalo as part of their "Crash the Convention" promotional tour. Luce, Garrett Fitzgerald and Eryn Trimmer arrived in town in a car with an artistic paintjob. The event went well and built local enthusiasm for counter-convention organizing that was happening halfway across the country. They were well organized, yet open and flexible to local conditions. Buffalo was no hotbed for radical organizing but the crowd was diverse, passionate and very participatory. It was this tour stop that spurred people from Buffalo to participate in actions during both the RNC and the DNC.

In the middle of the night after Luce, Eryn and Garrett had left town, we found them unexpectedly knocking on our door once again. They had been detained and searched at the border on their way to an event scheduled in Canada and refused entry. For hours, they reorganized their things, trying to piece together what information the authorities had collected. The combination of the car's paint job, their appearance, the fact that they were trying to cross the border in the middle of the night, and likely a trace on the license plate number virtually guaranteed that they wouldn't make it into Canada. We were glad to see them again, regardless of the circumstances.

Months later, my family and I flew into the Twin Cities for the RNC. Large vinyl advertisements promoting the Convention and welcoming those attending plastered the walls and floors of the airport.

We met up with others who had come out for the convention and were assigned to a household that was participating in the "Adopt an Anarchist" program, graciously hosting out-of-town protestors. Our hosts accommodated us with food, lodging, and even a tour of their city. It may be true that we got special treatment, but I got the feeling that our friends at the RNC Welcoming Committee, which had been working to organize logistics like these for well over a year, had really done a quality job. It was a sharp contrast with the WTO protest experience of 9 years earlier, where shards of glass clung to my clothing for the entire week because I hadn't brought a change of clothes, lacking any real place to stay.

The first thing that we learned when we got into town was that there had been a series of preemptive raids and Luce, Eryn and Garrett (and probably most of the other Welcoming Committee organizers we knew) had been arrested before the protests had even begun. This immediately changed the entire tone of our stay and participation. While we did go to a handful of the mass demonstrations and made our way though a number of skirmishes between police and protesters, we spent most of our time and energy on jail support for those who soon would come to be known as the RNC 8.

Although I saw a handful of other local organizers still on the streets during the early part of the convention, they all seemed to have the looming feeling that they could be snatched up at any moment--which is exactly what happened. The first time we saw Luce, Eryn and Garrett was when they were brought out from the holding facility for their arraignments. By the time they were released, the RNC was essentially over and it was nearly time for us to travel home.

While the drama and excitement in the streets outside the Convention was reminiscent of many of my earlier experiences, including the WTO protests, I couldn't help but question what had been accomplished at the RNC. In Seattle in 1999, protesters had not only shut down WTO's meeting, but we wrecked the city. An estimated $20 million in damages to multinational corporations invested in globalization-- including Banana Republic, Bank of America, Gap, Key Bank, McDonalds, Nike, Old Navy, Starbucks, US Bancorp, Washington Mutual Bank and many others -- was left in the aftermath of the protests. A precedent had been set that there was a force against globalization, and it was a force to be reckoned with.

In contrast, the 2008 protests left the RNC relatively undisturbed. Although the protests had not been entirely defeated as they had been during the FTAA meetings in Miami in 2003, many of us wondered if there was still hope for national counter-convention organizing.

I left the Twin Cities predicting that the most significant aspect of the anti- RNC organizing might very well be outcome of the case against the RNC 8. Not surprisingly, my Twin Cities friends went to work as hard at organizing the defense of the RNC 8 as they had the demonstrations against the RNC or anything else I had known them to work on. As a result, the RNC 8 case garnered national attention and support almost immediately.

On December 7, 2008, I was brought out to the Twin Cities again for the 3rd anniversary of the Operation Backfire arrests and yet another well-attended, organized and promoted event. What I remember most about this visit were the meetings I witnessed of the RNC 8 Defense Committee and the way that the defendants had bonded together into a tight unit to resist the criminal charges that had been brought against them as individuals and as a community.

There has always been and there always will be state repression. The RNC 8 case is not an isolated one by any stretch of the imagination. Throughout the late 1990s and into the current millennium, there was constant state repression in response to the significant resistance against corporate globalization, environmental devastation and many other forms of institutional oppression. Elements of rioting, street fighting and property destruction were incorporated into national protests. Environmental offenders suffered scores of devastating guerrilla attacks, and many of the perpetrators of these actions remained unknown. Eventually, some people were captured and convicted of crimes relating to a spree of Earth Liberation Front actions, but not before an example was set of contemporary revolutionary guerrilla warfare in the belly of the beast, gaining worldwide attention and inflicting hundreds of millions of dollars in damages.

What the state was really attempting to do in the case of the RNC 8 was a preemptive strike against a potentially threatening revolutionary struggle. With very flimsy cases, using new legislation that tramples basic human rights, the system singled out individuals whom it recognized as having the potential to be vertebra in the backbone of a promising revolutionary movement. In the big picture, It didn't really even matter to the state if these conspiracy charges led to convictions, because if we are too busy fighting for the rudimentary rights to gather in public spaces and voice our opinions, we will never even reach the level of struggle necessary for systematic change.

In 1969, twenty-one Black Panther Party members in New York City were brought up on conspiracy charges as laughable as plotting to blow up the Bronx Botanical Gardens. After the longest political trial in the city's history, the jury found the defendants "Not Guilty" on all counts in just 45 minutes of deliberation. By the time the trial was over, however, the Party had been "neutralized" in New York by the FBI's lethal and illegal Counter Intelligence Program (COINTELPRO). As a result, a number of the Panther 21 opted to continue the struggle by joining the underground revolutionary struggle.

In the case of the RNC 8, the big picture is not that eight people have been charged with felonies and terrorism enhancements because they helped organize legal demonstrations against an aspect of this country's political apparatus. It's not about an isolated violation of civil liberties, which have never truly been available in the real world anyway. What is really happening in the case of the RNC 8 is a disguised attack against the perceived future leadership of a freedom struggle still in its infancy. We must fight back.

A book titled, *Look for Me in the Whirlwind; the Collective Autobiography of the New York 21* was published in 1971 featuring brief, interwoven autobiographies of a number of the defendants, allowing readers a glimpse into the personal experiences that brought them into the freedom struggle and made them targets of bogus conspiracy charges. This book is produced in the same spirit.

- Leslie James Pickering

1
Chapter
UPBRINGINGS

The RNC 8 (pictured) from left to right: Rob Czernik, Erik Oseland, Monica Bicking, Eryn Trimmer, Luce Guillén-Givins, Garrett Fitzgerald, Nathanael Secor, and Max Specktor. Photo: Susan Micks.

Garrett Fitzgerald

Growing up, I was told that I was born during the last episode of the TV show M*A*S*H*. It was my parents' favorite show and, for my birth, my father had to miss it to drive to Minneapolis from where they lived in Mankato, Minnesota. I was born slightly premature, which is why my mother had to be hospitalized in Minneapolis instead of Mankato. Being in a hurry to get on to the next phase has been a theme throughout my life.

Mankato is a small farming city. Across the river, in the next county, is North Mankato. For all practical purposes, North Mankato and Mankato function as the same city. Children from North Mankato went to Mankato schools and one of the major employers in the area was in North Mankato. Folks who wanted to inflate how urban the area was would call it the "Little Twin Cities." Otherwise, folks would include all the little satellite towns and call it the Mankato area.

Mankato's biggest claim to fame is that it is the site of the largest mass execution in American history. Thirty-eight Dakota warriors were executed for their alleged role in the Dakota Uprising. Now at the site of this uprising sits the local library. There are a few plaques and statues but, like most of the normative population of America, Mankato residents tend to view the past as unrelated to the present and the mistakes as naive errors of our ancestors who this generation surpasses in enlightenment. This view of history allows the people who benefit from brutality to ignore that the privileges they hold today are a direct result of the atrocities of their ancestors, and allows a historically narrow view of their actions that creates the illusion that modern disparities of privilege are blamelessly inevitable.

My mother and father both grew up in the Twin Cities metro. My mother's father (Pop Pop) was from Alabama. He died when I was in middle school. When I hear about his life and remember things we did together, I wish he could see the person I've become and share his stories in this context rather than that of my childhood. He grew up rural poor. The stories I remember

him telling of his youth mostly seemed to involve things like
stuffing a frog's mouth with BBs and watching it jump and
land on its face. During World War II, Pop Pop was stationed in
Alaska. This was where he met my mom's mom. He was into
photography and took lots of pictures of the Alaskan wilderness
and some of his courtship with my grandma.

I never really got to know my mom's mom. She died
of cancer when I was old enough to have some memories of
her, but I never really knew her as a complete and independent
person. When we would spend nights over at my grandparents',
she would help tuck me in and sing "My Bonnie Lies Over the
Ocean."

My dad's dad was a chain smoker. He died in the early
seventies before I was born.

Grandma, my dad's mom, was a child when her family
emigrated from Germany. She has pretty much lived in the
Twin Cities since then. Her story seems like a classic case of
the (white) American dream. She lived through the Depression
and WWII, raised my father and aunt, and worked as a secretary
when her husband died. She owns her home and goes to church
every week. She likes to buy me new pants and haircuts, and has
a hard time understanding why I'm generally not interested in
either.

My mother and father both grew up in Ramsey County.
The way I understand it, my mother's experience involved
spending time with family members who were her own age. She
had a sister and a cousin who were within a few years of each
other. The cousin lived just down the block, so the three of them
were best friends by default. However, my mother has spoken
of how their play often involved two of them deciding to cut out
the third. My mother has summed up her gender socialization
stating that she loved to climb trees and play outside but was
discouraged away from "boy stuff." She went to college and
graduated with a degree in social studies education with an
English minor. When she graduated, she got a job at the St. Paul
Open School.

My father was one of two children. He and his sister
went to separate boys' and girls' private schools linked to their

Catholic church in St. Paul's Highland Park neighborhood. It's my understanding that during that Baby Boom era, there were always plenty of kids around and they ended up having free rein of the neighborhood. The picture that I have of my father as an adolescent and young adult is going to school, hanging out in his mom's basement listening to records, playing guitar, and working at a grocery store and later at an ice house. In college, he and a friend played guitar in clubs and cafés. Most notably, he's told me stories of playing at the old Cedar-Riverside Café in the Cedar/Riverside neighborhood (a.k.a. The West Bank) of Minneapolis.

He was attending the U of M studying mathematics at first, but later switched to education. He was student-teaching at the St. Paul Open School, where he met my mother while writing and directing a rock opera for the students. Over the summer, my father went to England. While he was there, my mother received a job offer, also in England. They met up and my father decided to stick around and delay going back to school.

In England, my parents worked together at a half-way house and later at a school. My father also spent some time working for a bookie while they lived in Wales. When I was a teenager, I went with them to Wales, where they showed me a school they worked at and told me how they would go on picnics around the coast.

When my mother returned from Europe and my father finished college, they moved to Puerto Rico, where my father worked as a teacher. When they returned to Minnesota, they got married. My sister was born just as they were hitting their thirties. Two years later, I came along.

When I was two years old, my parents took my then four-year-old sister and me to Okinawa, Japan, where my father had gotten a job teaching math and coaching basketball on the military base. The four of us spent two years in Okinawa. I have a few vague memories that I'm able to place in those early years only because of the unique location. I know there was a Japanese man who helped my parents with yard work and a croquet field across the street where locals would play, but most of the experiences I remember were with other English speakers.

Upbringings

My parents were friends with other Americans and I went to an English-language preschool. I played at the playground down the street and went swimming in the ocean. I was stuck in the hospital for a while after a piece of coral broke off in my knee while I was swimming. There was a tree I loved to climb in the front yard, but both my sister and I steered clear of the bushes because that was where the spiders lived. I don't remember much else of this time, but I do have a faint memory of having to roll up the windows on the car as we drove down the street because of tear gas at a political demonstration.

I don't remember having to worry about money all that much as a child. My parents always hated to buy on credit. When they wanted a new car, they would save up and pay for it in cash. We had plenty of money but it didn't manifest in a "keep up with the Jones's" fashion. My parents were frugal and deliberate with some frills but not show-offy. I never went hungry or worried about having clothing or books for school. I see this now as an example of how class privilege sticks with you your entire life, regardless of your access to capital. For better or for worse, this is exactly how I relate to money—saving and spending little to save for the future and rarely having debt or needing to buy on credit.

We returned to Mankato when I was four and lived in the house my parents had bought and were working to pay off. There was a small wooded area down the block. A lot of it was private or fenced off, but this didn't mean anything to us as kids. (We learned early how to hop fences.) We built tree forts by hoisting skinny logs and settling them into the crooks of branches. Then we could climb up one tree and run between several or perch lookout over a small trail. Sometimes, the neighbor kids would all work together on one fort and, other times, we would build forts opposing one another and play at warring with bows and arrows made of twigs or running twine across popular trails. In the winter, the snow would cling to the trees. After a fresh snowfall, I wouldn't want to walk past the first climbable trees so that I could stare across the untouched blanket. But eventually the snow would be full of tracks. Snow walls and forts would be built for snowball fights.

Conspiracy to Riot

When I was five, I started school at Jefferson Elementary, the neighborhood public school. My parents were both teaching at rival Mankato high schools. I spent the morning in day care and walked to school in the afternoon for kindergarten. In first grade, I walked with my sister in the morning. This only lasted until I was old enough that our parents no longer made her walk with me. Usually, I was left walking half a block behind. I knew she cared about me; she just couldn't let her friends see. I really wanted to be as cool as she and her friends were.

One day, I was invited to go with the older kids to climb on the roof of our school. This was big-time trouble as far as I was concerned. I knew that getting caught on the roof of the school could get you a "blue slip," the most severe punishment our school handed out short of suspension. But I had been invited, and that excitement was enough for me to overcome my fear. We walked to the school and snuck behind it, an area that was also off-limits. The school ran along a small cliff. We snuck behind the school, between it and the cliff, to where the roof came closest to the ground. I stood back and watched while the other kids started boosting each other up. Suddenly, someone inside flung open a curtain and started yelling at us. I don't think I even heard the first sentence finish. I turned and sprinted as fast as I could all the way home.

Having parents who were teachers created an interesting relationship to the institutional hierarchy of the schools. I worked hard to make my parents proud of me, which, in my mind, meant excelling in my school work and being "well behaved." I had to respect the teachers because they were mirrors of my parents. I knew how hard they worked both inside and outside the classroom.

I remember getting through my homework while watching television after school: MacGyver and The Highlander series. I wasn't a tough kid or socially popular, so academics were the way I could achieve status among my peers. I had plenty of support from my parents, who would check my homework if needed but didn't smother me. My father taught various levels of high school mathematics, including advanced placement calculus. He was the head of his school's math department. I took after him academically and excelled in mathematics. Early on, I was placed on an "accelerated" mathematics track.

My mother had an English minor and would read through papers and other writing that I did. It came in handy to have a parent who excelled in English. I imagine that, to this day, my spelling and grammar usage fall somewhere around a seventh-grade level. In elementary school, we would have a spelling test on Monday with ten or so words. We would take the same test with the same words on Friday. One year I won a "most improved" spelling award for averaging the greatest progress between the Monday and Friday tests. I was able to learn it and hold on to it for the week, but it didn't share the systems and constant rules of mathematics and so it rarely stuck.

Our family went to church and I understood that this was another way that I could demonstrate how "good" I was. Being a "good Christian" was another way society doled out status. My father was brought up Catholic and my mother Protestant. They decided a good middle ground was to raise the children Lutheran.

I went to Sunday school and confirmation classes. They had all the worst things about school–social awkwardness and sitting in desks for hours. We were probably taught things about the Bible, but I don't really remember anything about it at this point. What I like to remember about going to church was how typically Minnesotan the experience was—potlucks in the church basement with a dozen different types of "hot dish" and jello salad. There was also the self-sacrifice and the constant, nagging guilt with its companion, resentment.

My mother also practiced a more contemplative and meditative informal spirituality. I have memories of meditating with my mother as a youngster. I chose a whale as a spirit animal for the wisdom I perceived it to hold and worked to develop some sort of practice. With my limited knowledge and resources at the time, it was more like playing at meditation. This doesn't mean it wasn't useful, as play is for kids. I do think there was something important as these are some of my first acts of intentionally driven thoughtfulness and empathy. On the other hand, I would later remember the "Eastern" influence on our home and be critically aware of the cultural exotification these experiences fed.

My mother once told me that a difference between my sister and myself was that I was more interested in growing up. I think that it was because, in my young world, the older you were, the more power and authority you held. I didn't have an analysis to understand it, but I felt how it worked. I also wasn't hoping to unite the powerless, or get authority so I could undermine it. I just wanted to get out from under. I remember getting angry because my elementary school was K-6 until the year I was to be in sixth grade, at which time the school switched to K-5 and I felt robbed of my year at the top of the pecking order. It seems like a trifle now, but I think that a general sense of powerlessness permeated my childhood.

I was part of an experiment that my school district tried in which all the sixth graders were sent to one of two schools that were only for sixth graders. That year, there was a meningitis outbreak. I think three kids in town died from it. Every kid in the district had to take medication for it and it turned everyone's urine bright orange, staining all the urinals. In sixth grade, this was pretty interesting. I started having to ride the bus to school. This marked a change socially. Up to this point, I had mostly hung out with the kids in the neighborhood. The closer they lived, the more time we spent together. Now, cliques began to form and we were socially stratified. I was accosted as a "fag" a half-dozen times a day. I started getting in more scuffles with other kids after school. There was a dweeby Mormon who used the same bus stop as me and he became my best friend at that time. As I didn't get much validation from other peers, our friendship did a lot to shape my direction at that time. We talked a lot about religion and spirituality, mostly within the bounds of Christianity. I began getting deeper into religion (which mostly just meant talking about it and reading the Bible).

My friend and I also started learning magic tricks together. Within a few months, we were putting on shows together and performing. This became a primary hobby for me until the middle of high school. I had also played a bit of basketball growing up and started playing on the school team. It was my sport of choice in part because my father was a basketball coach at his high school and I had grown up watching many of his games. But I lacked confidence and didn't get along with the other kids on the team, so I never really became that strong of a player.

In seventh grade, all the kids were put into a brand new middle school. It was more of the same, although the new school was more sterile and prison-like. I am conscious of my world view beginning to expand during this time. I remember watching a video on clear-cutting and slash-and-burn in the rain forest and thinking to myself, "It's a good thing we are getting information about all of these destructive things so that when we are adults, things can be different." This also fed into my feeling of haste to be an adult so that I would be able to change the problems that seemed so obvious in the world. I presumed that, since we all could clearly see these problems, they would solve themselves. Or, at least, we could all agree to work together to solve them.

Seventh grade classes were easy enough, but the social antagonism got worse. I still remember instances that seemed particularly harsh, including being named in some homophobic graffiti. Looking back now, while the individual instances of abuse seem petty, the context of the inescapable social groupings and the formative phase of life still stirs resentment. In large part to get away from the harassment, I went to eighth grade at a private Catholic school. I escaped much of it, but Mankato was a small city, and I couldn't escape my own social awkwardness.

Coincidentally, going to Catholic school occurred right around the peak of my Christian spiritual exploration. I had gone to Catholic Mass with my grandma for Easter many times, so it wasn't totally new, although there is a lot of ritual that I didn't wield with proficiency. I don't think Catholicism is responsible for turning me off to organized Christian religions, but it was one more instance of coming up spiritually "empty handed."

It was right around this age when I got my first job. I had shoveled snow and mowed lawns, but this was much more official, a paper route delivering the weekly shopper, "The

HOME Magazine." It was only two or three hours a week, but it was awful, especially in the winter. I would carry two heavy bags full of papers and my fingers would freeze quickly since they were exposed to the cold as I fumbled to get rubber bands around the papers. I was proud to have a job even if I wasn't making much money or having much fun. I was good at saving money. It always seemed to me like there is probably going to be something off in the distance that I would wish I had saved for. Maybe that makes me predisposed to resist material excess.

I went back to public school for high school. I continued to be tracked into advanced classes, most of which continued to come fairly easily with the exception of anything that involved spelling words correctly. I also explicitly chose classes and extracurricular activities based on what would look the best on a college application. My experience performing magic brought me to audition for the school's theater productions. I was involved in most of the school's productions in the four years I was there. I had given up on basketball and early on in high school and had a falling out with my Mormon friend, which left a bit of a social vacuum. Through some acquaintances in classes, I started going to punk shows and got into the local punk scene.

In many ways, the punk kids were just another social grouping—a prepackaged identity to try out for a while. We all hung out in the same areas of school before classes or at lunch. Then, within the larger group, there were people who were closer friends. We would look for each other in the sea of faces, huddle in circles in the halls, and share a table at lunch. I like to think that there were things that made this group special.

While the punks could be harsh critics of what they saw as the normal way of being or doing things and often were quite judgmental, they were more open to people honestly expressing themselves and searching for new ideas. It was a social grouping consisting almost entirely of misfits, kids whose social awkwardness or eccentricity put a halt to being granted a lot of social status amongst the general high school populace. I think there is something useful, if not beautiful, in people saying, "You don't like me for whatever reason, well, fuck you. We outcasts will hang out with each other and grant status based on how uncomfortable we can make you feel." Punk Rock.

While we all felt pretty outrageous and different at the time, it was only the case within the context of our school and our small city. The differences were mostly aesthetic. For example, the punk scene was just as male-dominated as any other mainstream analogue. Often we could see it, believed it to be bad, but didn't have the tools to fight it in any real way. Most of the bands and projects were led by male-assigned folks. I remember noticing one night that all the women that I was hanging around with had gotten into the scene through a boyfriend. Usually, when that relationship ended, they left the scene. If not, they were quickly approached by those hoping to be the next in line (myself included).

It wasn't too long before I was invited to play in a band. I had played percussion in band class since sixth grade and some kids wanted a drummer. The standards were relatively low and I accepted their invitation. Now when I wasn't in school or in theater, I spent most of my time with the band or with others in the scene. We would practice a few nights a week and on weekends we would go to shows or hang out downtown (which is about four blocks long and half a mile from where I grew up). Most of the time, the shows would be somewhere like an American Legion or an Eagles Club Hall. If it was early in the day or there wasn't a show going on, I would go down to my favorite corner in downtown Mankato.

There was a new coffee shop that quickly became a high school hang out for the "alternative" crowd. It was called The Fillin' Station and had some retro fuel pump memorabilia. Across the street was the local punk/alternative record store, Ernie November's. Later on in high school, a venue/social space opened next door to Ernie's called Slacker's. On a Saturday night, I would walk downtown after dinner and have coffee at The Fillin' Station, hoping to run into some friends. We would go poke around the records at Ernie's and play some pinball at Slacker's. If there was a show, we might go. Then we would fight the boredom, go get a jug of "lemon-lime flavored drink" and sit on the curb chatting, then walk back and forth across downtown or the train tracks, exploring our town in one way or another.

Our band started playing more shows. We mostly played around town and every so often would go to an even smaller town in southern Minnesota. As we became better and more experienced, we played as far and wide as Minneapolis and Winona, Minnesota. I didn't know much about Minneapolis at the time, but I remember we played at a venue called The Inferno and visited the collective punk record store, Extreme Noise. I stopped seriously performing as a magician mostly because I didn't have the time and I no longer had a friend counting on me to practice.

Monica Bicking

My parents' political and personal prospective revolves around a class analysis so strongly that my family history has only been told to me as it relates to class. My father's mother grew up poor during the Great Depression. She tells the stories common to the Great Depression of mixing dye into butter and not always having enough to eat. Her family was Pennsylvania Dutch, a poor immigrant group from Germany with their own accent and culture.

My grandmother excelled in school. After high school she wanted to go to college. She applied, got in and went, but at the expense of her relationship with her father who disowned her for attending college. While my great-grandfather was separating himself from his daughter, his daughter was separating herself from the Pennsylvania Dutch. My grandmother changed her accent to a more upper-class proper English and continued to excel in school. She received her master's in Chemistry, a field unheard of for women, and married an upper-class man, John Bicking.

The Bickings were once wealthy; however, when my grandfather was growing up they were no longer wealthy, but solidly middle-class, owning their own gas station. Even so, my grandma had traveled a long way from her Pennsylvania Dutch upbringing. After my grandma's father died it was revealed that

43

he was secretly rich and was throughout the entire Depression. He had made some good investments, but never let anyone know, including his wife. There was no reason for my grandmother to have struggled at all during the Depression. While my grandmother left the Pennsylvania Dutch, she never abandoned her mother or brother, whom she took care of in their old ages. I admire that she never let her family hold her back from what she wanted, but also never abandoned them.

My father grew up in an upper-middle class suburb of Pennsylvania. I imagine his upbringing as a TV show. They were a white family of four, one boy, one girl, a dad, and a stay–at–home mom who made cherry pies. Like in a TV show, my grandmother would have preferred to continue her work in chemistry, but family came first. As my dad and aunt got older, to my grandparent's dismay, the family started to look less and less like a TV show. My aunt did not make it through college on her first shot and got married three times. My father did not attend an expensive liberal arts or Ivy League college, but rather Michigan State, where he met my mother, who was not the woman of my grandparents' dreams.

I know much less about my family history on my mother's side. My mother's mother moved out of her parents' house in her teens because her mother had died and finished high school at her landlady's encouragement. She was very smart and most likely this is why she was encouraged to finish. She met my grandfather in the factory and got married when she was eighteen. She had five kids, leaving the factory after her second. My grandfather continued to work at the factory until retirement. He was a part of the union and got a decent wage and pension. The family was working-class, but never struggled for basic necessities.

While my mother's childhood was very painful with abuse, alcoholism, and mental illnesses running rampant, my grandparents worked hard so that their children would have a better life. They sent all five children to college, something that they never had the privilege of attending. They engrained a strong work ethic and working-class pride in their children. My mother became a communist in college, a foreseeable political outcome of a daughter of a white union family in the late '60s. She was active in SDS, where she met my father and they began their journey together.

My parents married before the end of their college career and the two families did not mesh easily. My mother was not who my father's parents had imagined for him. My grandmother had worked hard to leave her working-class roots behind, and my father marrying into them was far from ideal. Not only was he marrying a working-class woman with working-class pride, he was also spouting communist rhetoric.

My mother did not want to fit in with an upper-class family any more than they wanted her. She had a healthy mistrust of the wealthy. Being judged and unaccepted by them only reinforced it. My grandparents did eventually accept my mother when she had my brother, but they would always be from two different worlds.

Upon graduation my father was drafted into the Vietnam War. Although a communist revolutionary, not a passivist, he grew up Quaker and was able to become a conscious objector (C.O.). I often think about how lucky my father and our whole family are because he grew up Quaker. Everyone's life would be drastically different had he gone to prison, war, or underground.

My parents moved from Michigan to Minneapolis because there was good anti-war work going on and some potential for paid work. As a C.O. my father could only get government- approved jobs that were aiding others. During this period my parents worked at a home for children with mental retardation. The stories about this home could make the most hard-shelled person cry. The children were under-stimulated, neglected, placed in burlap bags and tied to cribs. Directly before my parents got their job, the home was featured on the local news for being a wonderful place for children.

All of the abuse was extremely secretive. When a parent or other outsider came to the door, a special doorbell would ring so the staff knew to clean things up. The parents would be stalled in a very nice waiting room. My parents, appalled by the conditions, eventually cooked up a plan to get the home shut down. They contacted city inspections and arranged for a reporter to come to the back entrance so they could show them around. It worked, and the home was shut down, the children were placed in hopefully better facilities. Recently my father told me that an investigative report showed that some of the children were only borderline retarded upon arrival, but were under-stimulated and abused for so many years that they would never recover. Of all my father's stories of activism in their twenties, this story impacted me the most. It is a story of evil, direct action, and hope. I am very proud of my parents' roles in this story.

During the '70s and very early '80s my parents switched jobs and moved frequently. My brother was young during this time and stories from this period always fascinated me because it was so drastically different from my life. For my entire life my family had extremely stable work and financial situations. When I was born, my father stayed home with me and worked on cars as an auto-mechanic, the same work he does to this day. My mother finally had found a teaching job and would only change jobs once, when I was three, to her current school. We only moved once, and that was ten blocks away to upgrade to a nicer, bigger, house. I remember thinking as a kid how much our family was, like my father's, similar to the ones on TV. I had a mom, a dad, and a brother. We were a white, middle-class family of four. I clung tightly to the image of the TV family and every time my family failed to meet those standards I became emotionally shattered, taking months or years to recover.

While there are isolated instances of my parents being politically active in my youth, most of their activism was set aside for my childhood. I learned about political activism through stories and discussions, not through example. Like any good TV family, family dinners were the glue that kept our family together. However, we did not take turns talking politely about the neighborhood gossip. We talked about politics. My parents and brother argued frantically about recent events and the state of the world. My brother is eight years older than me, and I was not able to keep up with them. While I was given a chance to talk about myself, I did not participate much in the family discussions. I did learn a lot from observing them, however.

I think watching these family dinners were key in developing critical thinking and argument skills. By the time I was ready to participate fully in the discussions, my family was falling apart. My brother had moved away to college when I was ten, my mother and I moved to Mexico away from my father for a year when I was twelve, and my parents separated when I was fourteen. My family ceased to be a family, but rather individuals who loved each other but did not know or understand each other. We all became secluded into our own worlds. Only recently have we rediscovered what family means. My brother, after fourteen years, has finally moved back, and our family has begun to grow astronomically. With partners, partner's family, and children, we have had to redefine family.

When I was born my grandmother bought me $10,000 worth of Merck stock. Merck is a large pharmaceuticals company. My grandfather worked as a chemist at Merck for decades and had become very wealthy as a result. It was a small company when my grandfather started and the employees received stocks. The company did extremely well and the stocks became worth a lot --so much, that my grandmother could easily afford to buy $10,000 worth of stocks for each grandchild, assuming it would go toward college. These stocks did better than anyone expected, and I came out with well over $100,000, and some of my cousins got even more money. This money has had a huge impact on my life story. While my parents were middle-class, making $30,000-$50,000 combined, we enjoyed luxuries others with that income would not have. Neither of my parents' jobs had retirement benefits, but they knew they would get inheritance and did not have to save for retirement. They also did not have to save for their children's college.

A few times growing up my parents dipped into my trust fund in order to provide me with educational experiences they could not have otherwise, mainly foreign travel. While my parents were not rich, their children and mother/mother-in-law were. This provided an invisible safety net that allowed them to spend more of their money and save less. They never borrowed money from my grandmother and I'm not sure that that would have ever been an option, but they still benefited from the economic privilege of the people around them. I likewise benefited from the money long before I had access to it.

With my money I was able to take a year off between high school and college without earning enough to live off, go to any college I wanted, and buy a house. Economic privilege extends well beyond the things one can buy. My grandmother has ensured that I will never have to be poor. Unlike all of the other grandchildren, I have made decisions with my money that make it highly unlikely that I could ever dig myself an economic hole I could not buy myself out of.

I have only had access to my money for the past two years. Up until that point it was up to my parents how the money was spent and they only gave it to me for educational (with a loose definition) costs. I was aware that I would have the money afterward and chose to minimize my educational costs so that I could spend it on other things. I also felt an obligation to finish college, since that was what the money was intended for, and only spend the leftover money on other things. From age 22 to 23 I carried a heavy weight around with me: rich-person guilt. I had over $100,000 invested in a pharmaceuticals company. It can't get much worse than that.

When I was growing up my parents were communists, and I was taught to hate rich people even though my family benefited from the rich people in our family. Now I was rich. My parents had divorced when they were in their early fifties and my mother was left without a retirement plan and without the expected inheritance. She clearly and fairly resented me for having so much money. I gave away a few thousand dollars to anarchist projects, but it did not put a dent in the money I owned. I did not want my money in Merck, but like all rich people I remained selfish. I did not want to give it all away.

One of the reasons rich people are so entirely selfish, especially ones from rich families, is that they cannot imagine life without that safety net. It is a scary prospect to give away that net, and I would assume for people without that net there are scary periods. Money is such an important part of our world, and without it, it can be hard to survive. Even though morally I felt obligated to give all my money away, I was too scared and selfish. Instead I bought a house. I bought a house a few blocks from parents' houses for $105,000 cash. I spent all but a few thousand dollars, which I would save in case the house needed something major. With economic privilege you can easily get more economic privilege, and that is what I have done. I will never have to pay rent again, meaning I can either work less or save more. If things ever get rough I can sell the house and get my money back. I can probably even make money.

I live with five housemates and my partner. I do not charge rent. It never occurred to me. I have made a selfish choice, but I would never want to make money off my friends. We split utilities evenly. We live collectively, but of course there is a unique dynamic because I own the house and my partner and I plan to live in the house for decades, if not forever.

We have more interest in improving it and ultimately many house improvement decisions come down to us. It works well enough, but it is definitely not a collectively owned house. I feel good about my decision and no longer carry the same guilt. I recognize that I have economic privilege that I have not chosen to give away. I recognize that is 100% selfish, but I am happy that the money is no longer in Merck stock and that my friends can benefit a little bit from it as well.

When my daycare was shut down by the state because of false rumors of abuse from a disgruntled employee, the parents were forced to get to know each other to find a solution. The daycare went underground, shifting from house to house. The children and parents became close and most of the children went to the same private Quaker elementary school that my mother taught at. Even the kids that did not go there stayed in touch, reconvening in the summers. It was an extremely unique group of parents and kids. What group of kids goes to daycare in Philips, one of the poorest neighborhoods in Minneapolis, and ends up going to private school? When we all went off to school, the daycare provider followed us and became our kindergarten teacher. School was not scary or even new. It became an extension of my community. My mother taught there, my daycare provider and my friends came with; it was a natural transition.

The school was not full of rich kids like most private schools. Although only a few kids were on scholarships and most kids came from solidly middle-class backgrounds, parents sent their kids there at a sacrifice. They sent them there because education was the number one priority. The school had a strong conflict resolution program and hands-on learning approach.

The parents were generally on the same page about academics, morals, and values. Most parents could be described as ex-hippies. It was more than a school, but rather a community. While there are clear benefits to this, it came at a price. There was very little racial, economic, sexuality or thought diversity.

Attending that daycare and school has provided me with a community and conflict resolution skills rarely found in my peers. While some of us grew up to be friends, and other relationships are more like distant cousins, I know that we will have each others' backs and so will our parents. When I was arrested and being called a terrorist I knew they would all be there to support me, and they were. This community is why I have chosen to live in Minneapolis. Not only am I privileged to have such a strong support network, but it has also provided me with a sense of belonging to a larger collective.

The only hiccup in my elementary school education was that I had a lot of trouble learning to read. While my other peers were reading chapter books, I would just flip through each page and count to thirty to make it look like I was reading. It was extremely frustrating. I remember sitting with a teacher and sounding out words. She would cover the part of the word that I wasn't reading I would read the sounds. I remember the word "together." I could read to-ge-ther and she would tell me to say it quickly, which I did. Then she exclaimed, "There -- you read it!" But in my mind I only heard "to-ge-ther," never "together." She would think I was reading, when I knew that I wasn't.

Given the right parents and teachers, these days, I would probably be diagnosed with mild dyslexia. To this day, I cannot sound out words. I have learned to read by memorizing whole words. I cannot connect sounds with symbols in a way that allows me to sound out new or made-up words. I am also a slow reader, feel uncomfortable reading out loud, cannot rhyme well, mispronounce words more than others, and don't really hear a difference between many sounds such as the g and j sounds. While these things are mildly annoying, they do not come up very often. I learned to read, and by fourth grade caught up with my peers. In many academic areas I even excelled. While I didn't have a diagnosis, I had parents that never thought I was stupid and teachers that didn't give up. I was extremely fortunate to go to a private school where they could give me the extra attention I needed so that I could overcome my difficulties. Many people never get that attention and never become fully literate. Despite my good fortune, the long process of learning to read was a huge blow to my self-esteem, a blow that I am still recovering from.

Even though I was well above grade-level in many other academic areas, my inability to read well got in the way. I was very good with numbers, but teachers constantly thought that it was more holistic teaching to use word problems to teach math. Even after I learned to read, I could not do word problems well because they often use language to trick you. I learned to cope well and am smart enough in other areas that it was possible. Throughout high school and college I did very little of the reading because it took so long, but was able to excel because of my ability to think critically and write solid essays. My private-school education and biological intelligence gave me the privilege to get by smoothly where others with the same learning issues have been held up.

In my family, intelligence was the most important trait in a person. My mother's family was poor but smart, which gave them the privilege to attend college. My grandmother was able to leave her poor Pennsylvania Dutch roots because she was extremely intelligent. My father looked up to his father because of how smart he was and would comment that the only person smarter than his father was my brother. Anyone that knows my father would call him extremely smart. I once asked my mom if I was smart like my brother. She stated, "You are smart, but Ian [my brother] is special."

Recently my aunt pointed out something to my mother I have always known, but was a revelation to her. She said, "Being smart is just like being beautiful," meaning, it is not something you choose; it is something you are born with. A privilege. The fact that this was a revelation to her helped me understand why it was so hard for me not to be as smart as many of my peers and my family. Instead of appreciating and recognizing the privilege of my above-average intelligence I have always wanted more. In my family, intelligence was treated as one's worth, not just a trait. My mother was right; I am smart, just not a genius. I am still coming to terms with that.

While I would not trade my daycare and elementary school education and community for anything, it was a bubble— so that when I left that bubble for Junior High, my mind was blown. I was shocked by the outside world. Instead of going to public school for seventh grade like most of my peers, I went to Mexico.

My mother had always had a dream of taking me to Latin America and teaching English. We left my dad with the house and mortgage and went to Mexico. My brother had already gone had off to college. It was a remarkable experience, but I'm sure it was nothing like what my mother imagined. It was extremely hard for both of us. While we had both traveled in Latin America, we were not prepared for the cultural differences.

My mother taught at and I attended the John F Kennedy International School in Queretaro, Mexico. The people at this school were extremely wealthy. Although we had both encountered rich people before, they were at least rich and a little ashamed. These people were proud of it. They had the largest houses that I had ever seen and several live-in maids. While it takes much less money to have large houses and live-in maids in Mexico than the United States, it was still a display of wealth I had never seen before. As I stated before, my mother has many strengths, but getting along with rich people is not one of them. She has never been able to fit in with them and found it impossible to appease the parents.

I, on the other hand, was completely clueless. I went into this school telling people that I was a communist, which did not go over well. Coming from my bubble, I didn't know anyone thought that communists were bad. I dressed wrong, had glasses, and didn't have braces. We also had the least material possessions in my life. We lived in a two-bedroom apartment with no car, and while U.S. dollars go far in Mexico, money was tighter than normal. My school was extremely expensive and we were paying an American mortgage and rent. Coming from a middle-class family, it was weird to have fewer material possessions. It did not cause me stress, however, until my peers started to make fun of me.

For eighth grade I went to a wealthy private school in South Minneapolis. I didn't fit in there any better than Mexico, although the kids were nicer to me. I had to learn about a whole new culture about wealthy Americans. I was anything but cool, but I wasn't teased or mocked. I had a few friends and was distracted by the rigorous school work. I worked harder on academics that year than I ever did in high school or college. It was not a good junior-high experience, but it was easier than my previous year and I was happy to be home.

For high school I went to a large public school a few blocks from my home. I fit in better there than either of my junior highs. It was a diverse crowd, and I found where I fit. Freshman year I did not make friends as quickly as I wanted, but it was new and exciting. It was an academic break from my previous school and I was able to focus on having a social life. High school was looking like it would be a fun experience during the beginning of my freshman year, but came to a crashing end during spring break.

That spring break, my parents announced their divorce. I was affected by the divorce more than anyone had anticipated. Puberty was hard, but I held it together. When peers made fun of me for being smelly and hairy I held it together. When academics proved to be too much, I held it together. While my self-esteem was slowly disintegrating, I held it together and clung onto what I had.

When my family fell apart, I fell apart, completely and utterly. I could no longer hold it together and handle the other aspects of my life. It became clear that what made me able to cope with the challenges of adolescence was the stability and support of my family. Without that, I was a mess. I fell into a deep and dark depression. For the next two years I lived under a dark cloud that I thought would never end.

I went early to school and stayed late so that I would not have to go home. At home my parents had stopped parenting. My mother was depressed and could barely manage to make dinner. My father had no idea how to relate to a teenage daughter who was depressed because of his actions. I stopped looking to my parents altogether.

While I spent many hours in the school building, I spent very little time in class. I would skip class and sit in the halls and talk with friends. Because I was white and charming, the hall monitors never bothered me. I found a group of depressed girlfriends and we would spend the days in the hallways talking about how horrible life was and the destructive methods we used to cope. I would walk out of class in the middle if I found it boring.

There were two teachers who my group of friends was able to relate to. We would eat lunch in their rooms and sometimes hang out in their rooms during their prep times. They spouted their advice about every aspect of our lives. I'm not sure that their advice was ever all that valuable, but our relationship with them was. They were adult attention that we craved. They were a needed outside voice. They were the only people that I opened up to that weren't depressed teenagers.

While I chose to spend excessive hours in the building it only fed the depression. My school was built without windows so that it would be riot proof. As a result, many days I would never see the sun. I would get to school when it was still dark and leave after dark. I found classes unbearable. They were boring and irrelevant. I would shudder every time a classmate spoke because I thought their comments were so meaningless. I thought about dropping out, but the inertia was two strong.

Despite missing the majority of my classes, I got good grades and graduated with highest honors. I never turned in an assignment late. I would write the essays and do the homework and do it well. While I liked having something other than depression to focus on, I could not handle the classroom. My teachers were understanding and did not penalize me for my attendance and I'm sure that their forgiveness directly correlated to my racial and intellectual privilege. I think my teachers could also see the state I was in and knew that failing me would not help. It would just hinder my ability to fulfill my presumed future of college and a good career. Although I have not taken the path they assumed, I am grateful for the understanding of my teachers and those who reached out to me. I'm not sure that I could have handled failing out of school.

While I was deeply depressed I always maintained some sense of normalcy. I didn't want people, mainly my parents, to know the extent of it. I wanted to keep it for myself. I didn't let my grades drop because that would have been an alarm for them. While I wanted to appear normal for adults, depression was normal for my peer group. Compared to my friends I was often better off. One of my best friends, who did not attend my school, struggled with depression and anorexia. She was in and out of hospitals and from time to time she would call on me for help. She called me when she overdosed on caffeine pills in a suicide attempt. I drove her to the hospital. She was fine. I never attempted suicide and can't imagine doing so, although I did contemplate it at the time. I believe that seeing the darkest of depression that my friends went through allowed me to skip over it. While I had given up on being happy, I knew I never wanted to be that bad off. I fought to stay afloat in whatever way I could, constructively or destructively.

Not all of my friends were depressed. I had a group of male friends that I would kick it with. While these young men were good people and I still care deeply about them, it was often a disempowering experience for me. I was figuring out what it meant to be a woman in a group of men. I dated most of them and was usually playing a passive role of the girlfriend. I would watch them watch TV. I would watch them play basketball and watch them have fun. Individually, usually with my current boyfriend, I would have meaningful interactions that helped me grow, but in the group setting I resigned myself to passivity.

My brother and his partner were also small lights in my time of depression. They are eight years older than me and consistently reached out to me. I felt safe telling them about what

I was going through. I looked up to them and they gave me some small hope that adulthood would be better than my life at the time. While I felt I could open up to them, they lived in Chicago and I did not feel like they understood me. I appreciate their efforts and now realize that the many stories I told them about my depression must have been very scary to hear. The times people reached out to me gave me something to hold onto, but were not enough to get me out of the depression.

At some point in this mess my parents found me a therapist. I enjoyed the attention and a sane voice, but I wasn't getting any better. About eight months into therapy I admitted to cutting myself. I had been cutting myself for months but kept it well hidden. I cut in places where I would never have to let the scars show. It helped. It was better than what I saw as the alternative: illicit drugs and suicide. It brought me a sense of peace. I knew that if I told my therapist she would tell my parents. I broke my cover and told her anyway. I was sick and tired of being depressed and realized I couldn't get out of it alone. I couldn't get out of it unless other people started to take it seriously. I never cut after that.

That day was the beginning of the end of my depression. My therapist sent me to a psychologist who put me on Zoloft. It worked. I still hated life, but occasionally I felt a sense of joy, something I had not felt in years. I started to have interests outside of depression and started to become the person I am today. I started getting into the anti-war movement and finding a point to life. Despite my family and therapist's protests I took myself off Zoloft after only a few months. I knew that with new interests and meaning I did not need the drug to stay out of depression. I was free.

By falling into a depression and coming out of it I learned some of the most important life lessons. I learned agency. I had felt so out of control of my own life. I felt stuck in school and stuck with my messed-up family. I didn't think there was anything I could do to better my situation. I have always been very concerned with what other people thought of me and wanted to meet their expectations. I learned that sometimes I needed to put myself first and that sometimes other people did not know what was best for me. I have made many key decisions in my life that I'm not sure I would have made without this lesson.

Eryn Trimmer

My grandparents on my mother's side lived in California. My grandmother came from old money and was sent to pilot school to avoid "gold diggers" looking to marry her. It was there, in Hancock Pilot School in Santa Maria, CA, that she met my grandfather. He was in the Navy Air Corps, slightly too young to serve in World War II. They moved back to Santa Barbara, where my grandfather was from. His parents owned a liquor store in Santa Barbara and my grandparents worked there on and off. My grandparents rode motorcycles, flew airplanes and partied a lot. They were written up in the newspaper for flying cross-country. My grandmother owned a series of cocktail lounges and lived a carousing lifestyle.

My mother was born in 1950. When she was four, my grandfather died in a motorcycle crash during a race. My grandmother re-married an "evil step father," a raging alcoholic and abuser. My mother's childhood was riddled with neglect. When my mom was fourteen, her mother died, and she moved in with her father's mother, affectionately known as Mimi. Mimi is the only parental figure that my mother really talks about, and even then sparingly.

Coming of age in the late '60s and early '70s in California, my mom was exposed to the free speech movement and Vietnam War resistance. She was more involved in counter culture than political organizing. She and her friends had a DIY ethos, especially around health food. My mom went to college, where she began dancing. She moved with some friends to New York to continue studying modern dance. It was there that she came across what she would study for the rest of her life: the Alexander Technique, a method of body awareness that re-educates one to move with ease and efficiency.

My grandfather on my father's side grew up in Nanking, China. His father was a white missionary doctor at a hospital there. In the lead up to the Japanese invasion of Nanking in 1937, most foreigners left the city. My great-grandfather stayed behind and helped establish the Nanking Safety Zone. The Nanking Safeety Zone was an area where Chinese civilians could go to avoid the pillage of the city. It is credited with saving thousands of lives, although hundreds of thousands of civilians were still killed in the massacre.

My grandfather, 15 at the time, and the rest of the family, were vacationing in the hills above Nanking when the Japanese came. They slipped around the troops and made it on a train to Hong Kong. My Grandfather went to school in Shanghai during the war until they were allowed back into Nanking. He would tell us stories of being a teenager and dogging the Japanese troops, throwing things at them and otherwise causing a ruckus.

My grandfather went back to the States while my great-grandfather was interned by the Japanese, where he treated both the prisoners as well as the Japanese guards. After the war, my great-grandfather worked in a hospital in Lahore, Pakistan, switching religions when he realized which would be most useful to his humanitarian goals. Growing up I didn't hear much about my great-grandfather as a person, but he was revered as a heroic member of our family, a larger-than-life man who put his own safety second to helping others.

My grandmother's father (on my father's side) was a pacifist. He worked for the state department during World War II and subsequently worked on the establishment of the United Nations.

My grandparents on my father's side met at Swarthmore College. They were both pre-med but neither of them ended up going to medical school. My grandfather joined the Navy and went to Japan after the dropping of the atomic bombs. He returned home and worked in construction. My grandmother went back to school and became a biology professor. My father was the second of four children.

My grandparents divorced while my dad was in college. He majored in theater, which led him to go to an Alexander

Technique workshop. After college, he tried to join the circus but wasn't accepted. He was also interested in writing, aspiring to write the next Great American Novel. He moved back to Florida and built houses with my grandfather, continuing his study of the Alexander technique. He also began studying Aikido, a Japanese martial art. My dad wasn't particularly career-oriented, preferring to indulge his creative side in a myriad of ways.

My parents met at a four-week Alexander Technique workshop in Nebraska. My dad was teaching a little class on Aikido. My mom said that if he was serious about her, he needed to move to where she was living. She was in San Francisco at the time, finishing her Alexander Technique teacher training. My dad moved in with her, but they didn't stay too long before moving to Florida. There they both focused on Aikido. They stayed there for a couple of years before moving to D.C. in 1981 because of the world-renowned Aikido sensei (teacher) there.

My parents moved into a small apartment in Northwest Washington, D.C., 11 blocks from the house I would grow up in across the border in Maryland. They bought the house four months before I was born. My dad had taken a computer training class, wanting a change from carpentry and a steady and better paycheck. My mom got her master's degree in education and began teaching English as a second language. When I was born in 1985, my mom stopped teaching and stayed at home with me.

I was a happy kid. I remember one of the first times that I learned of some of the turmoil of my mother's childhood, stuff I was too young to really understand. She told me that her goal was to give her kids a completely different experience than she had growing up. In this she succeeded.

Both of my parents continued practicing Aikido and the Alexander Technique throughout my childhood. Although never exactly my community, since most of them fell in the category of my parent's colleagues or students more than friends, these are the people who watched me grow up. As a little kid, I remember hanging out with groups of adults after class, feeling special as one of the few kids around and (often) the child of the teacher. I went to a local preschool with a teacher I was completely enamored with. There I met my best friend as a little kid, a boy named Trevor. We hung out all the time. Though I loved playing with friends, I was a somewhat shy kid and usually let them take the lead. One of the games I remember best, because it was an exception to this, was sliding down the banister at my house. I was the instructor and would (kindly) critique Trevor's technique. I would give him awards as he advanced to more difficult maneuvers. This game made me feel extremely empowered, and gave him just as much joy.

At four years old I started going to preschool at Lowell School, a private school in Northwest D.C., which I continued attending through third grade. It was a progressive school with a focus on encouraging creativity, problem solving and healthy social interaction. I had a huge crush on a girl named Tessa in second grade. We were friends enough that she invited me to her birthday party. After I accepted the invitation, it was discovered that I was planning on going to a football game with my dad that same day. I really wanted to go to the party, and could have decided to do that. Instead, however, to not let my dad down, I chose the game. The worst part was that she gave me the ice skating trophy from her birthday party after I hadn't gone, I was crushed that I had let her down. This is a pattern I would repeat throughout my life, trying to make the "right" choice, but not prioritizing my own needs and desires.

In second grade, my parents adopted my sister Tanya from Bolivia. I remember sitting in my dad's lap and him asking me if I wanted a sister. I really did and I told him so. After a failed attempt to adopt a child in Bulgaria, I got to go to Bolivia when they picked up Tanya. She was two years old. We stayed in a hotel overlooking the zócalo in La Paz.

Apparently, after a few days I threw myself on the bed and lamented, "When are these people going to learn English!" My culture shock must have worn off, however (if not my elitism…). We took a boat to an island on Lake Titicaca where reed boats were made. There I met a group of boys about my age. We gallivanted about, exchanging tricks and skills. It made me feel special to connect with boys from a different place with whom I couldn't speak and who had different games. Despite these differences, we could relate on the level of children having fun.

I was proud and excited to have a new sister. Many of my friends had siblings, and I wanted one too. My friends, however, would complain about their younger sisters. I had some slight feelings of jealousy as she took the spotlight after her arrival, but for the most part I didn't feel competitive. Tanya and I hardly ever fought. I didn't really like fighting and she wasn't overly annoying. I do remember teasing her. Not as ruthlessly as many siblings, but enough to feel bad about.

I started going to public school in the fourth grade. Starting public school where academics were graded, I quickly switched to "gifted and talented" classes and easily got As. I enjoyed being a computer helper in a time when most fourth graders didn't know how to use one.

The best part about public school was the opportunity to make friends with the kids in my neighborhood. I remember the anxiety of making new friends. Luckily, we were young enough that it was barely about coolness or social standing, but rather compatibility. I recall sitting by the phone, being afraid to call them. However, I quickly had a gaggle of neighborhood buddies, with frequent sleepovers, riding bikes to school together and fun adventures. It was very different from friendships at my old school, where play dates had to be arranged ahead of time and needed rides. Now there were ample friends practically just outside my door. Not only did this allow me to satisfy my desire for play, but it gave me a sense of belonging to have a stable, more accessible friend base.

I've always been a quiet and shy person, coupled with being easygoing and generally happy. However, positively interacting with other people gives me huge pleasure. I don't think of my shyness as coming from a particular aspect of my upbringing or formative experiences, although I'm sure that had an impact. Insecurity plays into it, but not a gaping lack of self-esteem. I do have a general anxiety about putting my opinions out there, which in extreme circumstances leads to difficulty in my even being aware of what my thoughts and feelings on a subject are. From a young age, this has led me to want to please others—teachers, parents, friends–and to have a general fear of conflict. Perhaps this is one reason anarchism appealed to me on a personal and not just a political level—it has given me a reason to know what I believe in and stand up for it, consistently pushing me in the aspects I have difficulty with. It also validates in an intellectual way the good feeling I have when working cooperatively with others, as opposed to competitively or through hierarchy.

My family went to Quaker meetings on and off during my childhood. My dad grew up Quaker but is now an atheist. I think my parents were looking for community as much as religion since my mom, although spiritual, isn't very interested in religion either. It was a local meeting that rented out a couple of rooms in a house converted to commercial space just a few blocks away. It was unprogrammed [1] and quite liberal. The child care was fairly boring until my friend Jack from a block away joined, a fourth grader looking for some sort of spirituality.

Although I can't recall much specific religious or moral teaching I got from going to meetings, it added to my general upbringing of "peace" and "non-violence" during my childhood. My parents didn't allow toy guns or other military toys, although there was an exception with a potato gun I had because my dad thought it was neat. I was raised with a strong foundation in somewhat vague liberalism and non-violence. The non-violence was grounded in hippie influences and Quakerism, but was also connected with the Aikido my parents did. The goal in Aikido is to pacify the threat of your opponent without hurting them unnecessarily. It is more about the peaceful resolution of conflict than a way to destroy your opponent. Although against wars and such, my parents' interest in non-violence didn't extend much into the political realm.

My parents separated when I was 12 years old. I remember them telling my sister and me around the kitchen table and all of us crying. Initially, I didn't feel too bad about it. I rationalized that if it didn't work for them to be together, then they shouldn't be.

My dad moved into the basement at a friend's house a few miles away. My sister and I would go over there on Wednesday nights. At the time, I thought seeing my dad so infrequently was a temporary situation, and it was surprisingly easy for it to normalize. It wasn't until a few years later that I realized my dad was no longer a parental figure in the same way he used to be. He was withdrawn, both physically and emotionally. We still understood each other well and got along well, but he wasn't involved in my day-to-day happenings and, as was his style anyway, he wasn't there to criticize me or give me advice. For the most part I coped by trying to accept it, but I definitely felt rejected.

Middle school was a time of negotiating ever-present social hierarchy. My group of friends had coalesced, giving me some social standing. Even within my not-too-cool-but not-too-uncool group, there was jockeying for position. A new person attempted to join while one of the "alpha males" teased him for almost a year non-stop with others joining in or quietly being friendly. I was friendly to the newcomer but wouldn't dare defend him in front of the group. Speaking out in opposition to a whole group of people is something that has always been hard for me and something that I continue to struggle with. Luckily, he was eventually accepted and we remain friends to this day.

My mom soon had a new partner, a man named C.T. He was a co-founder of the first Food Not Bombs group, an anarchist and author on consensus decision-making. My sister Tanya was fiercely defensive of my mom, blaming C.T. for my parent's breakup. I was somewhat ambivalent toward him at first, it being in my nature to see the good in people. C.T. had a very strong personality that clashed with my desires for a low-conflict environment. He came off as very judgmental and big headed. At the same time, I had been getting into radical politics and that aspect of him interested me.

C.T. moved in when I was entering high school. He tried to bring order to our house both physically and mentally— creating systems to run the household better, instituting family meetings, and attempting to instill values in me and my sister around self-discipline. I remember many a fear-filled talk with C.T. about why I hadn't done something that I said I would do, and even said that I had wanted to do. Of course I "wanted" to help out around the house more and "valued" pulling my own weight—I had a forceful man whom I feared and looked up to asking me if I did. But fear was never a good long-term motivator.

My dad also had a new partner, a fellow Aikido enthusiast named Jane. They bought a house together in Silver Spring, Maryland, about a five-minute drive from my mom's house. My sister and I were still going over there only once a week after school.

The parenting styles of C.T and my Dad could not have been more different. My dad was completely hands off, trusting me to make good decisions (or not caring; the line was rather blurred). C.T. could find a crucifiable sin with my most sincere attempts to do right—but he was there, guiding me. Both of them influenced me a great deal, and as I became an adult I tried to take the best parts from both—interacting with others in an active way guided by values, while being relaxed enough not to shame those around me if I don't agree with them.

Luce Guillén-Givins

My maternal grandfather was a child of Croatian immigrants, and was raised a practicing Catholic. In his twenties, he found politics and joined the Abraham Lincoln Brigade[2] fighting on the anti-fascist side of the Spanish Civil War. During the war he became disillusioned with communism, largely a result of the role played by Soviet officers and, in particular, the execution of hundreds of fellow anti-fascist soldiers. When he returned to the States, his brief dealings with the Communist Party in New York left him feeling disgusted at their dishonesty in describing Soviet involvement in the war, and he left the party for good.[3] Wandering the city without political cause, he ended up at a Catholic Worker house.[4] There, he befriended Dorothy Day, with whom he corresponded until her death in 1986, and my understanding is that she was responsible for his full return to the Church.

My maternal grandmother was born into a non-churchgoing Presbyterian family who sent her to a Catholic high school for the good education it provided. She converted to Catholicism in her twenties. The faith it takes to set aside your upbringing and embrace a new faith necessarily runs deeper than what most people who inherit their religion understand. Following tradition, and intensified by the fact that my grandpa's work as a member of the Merchant Marine kept him away from home and family for months at a time, my grandma did the work of raising their four children as educated, practicing Catholics.

My mom and her siblings were lucky to be raised in an upper middle-class neighborhood of Seattle, though by income alone they were certainly working-class. My grandpa had dropped out of school and first gone to sea at 16, and years later found steady employment with Standard Oil. He was forced into compulsory retirement at 65, just months short of hitting the 15-year mark that would have qualified him for a pension. Instead, he returned to seafaring and longshoring through the union and received a union pension when he eventually retired. My grandma, who had gone to college and for a time worked as a statistical chartist, had been out of the workforce since the '50s. She began substitute teaching in the late '60s and became a full-time teacher in late 1977.

In the late '70s, my mom went to Reed College in Portland. She was there for two years before dropping out. She joined VISTA[5] and spent the next year living in Kentucky and Ohio and doing social work. When she returned to Seattle in the early '80s, she became active in the Catholic Worker movement, moving into "Peter Maurin House." She was also involved in the beginnings of a Sanctuary[6] movement in Seattle, though the group she was involved in was eventually shut out of the work due to internal divisions. In the year prior, a Catholic priest and cousin of hers had been involved in declaring the first Sanctuary church in the country.[7] In 1982, she moved to Yakima, where she did tenant and life-skills support for developmentally disabled adults, and then social work advocating for migrant families throughout the area.

As my grandma says when describing her kids, my mom is "the compassionate one." As a child, I observed my mom as being ever ready to aid those in need, friends and strangers alike. I remember things like driving home with her and stopping to give a ride to a mom and kids she had noticed walking home under the Arizona sun with bags of groceries, and her assisting friends and acquaintances with limited or no English proficiency in filling out paperwork for jobs and assistance.

Amongst activists, I've noticed a tendency to intellectualize politics of solidarity to the point that individual acts of kindness and good will are replaced entirely by impersonal work that reaches for high-minded political goals but fails to engage on a human level. By contrast, I've always admired my mom for the example she sets, one of profound compassion and empathy for people across ideological and social boundaries and that manifests in concrete ways. Through a series of career changes (now she's a public librarian), my mom has continued to make her living working with underprivileged communities, especially immigrants and refugees, and has never stopped living this work after hours as well. She succeeds in forging genuine personal relationships with the people she encounters, refusing to deal with them as statistics; these relationships reach into every aspect of her life and define the ways she sets priorities and divides her time. As I become further and further entrenched in an activist subculture, it's often my phone conversations with her that keep me grounded in the realities of American society for those struggling to survive in it.

My dad is from Mexico's borderlands, a tiny town called Ejido Michoacán de Ocampo, outside of Mexicali, Baja California. The Ejido[8] was comprised of land seized from the Colorado River Land Company, an American corporation, by my great-grandfather and his compatriots. The Mexicali Valley then and now boasts the largest concentrated Chinese community in Mexico; many Chinese immigrants were drawn to work in Mexicali as they were being viciously repressed and run out of the U.S., only to face similar attacks there over the next decades. In the 1920s and '30s, there was a concerted effort by the Mexican government to stir up violent anti-Chinese sentiment, and this should be understood as the subtext of the 1937 land grab, known as "El Asalto a las Tierras,"[9] that won my family their place in Northern Mexico.

Though in Southern Mexico the Ejido system was about legally restoring land to the indigenous people who had always lived on and worked it, in this instance it was used as an effective diversionary method at a time when poverty and destitution riddled the nation. People from Central and Southern Mexico were enticed by the potential of the Northern frontier, worked up into an anti-immigrant frenzy to deflect attention from the government that didn't serve them, and eagerly manipulated into "settling" problem areas (problematic only insofar as a national minority were a local majority) in the North. In the end, they only got dry, alkaline land whose yields were never much and would only be increasingly dependent on unsustainable irrigation schemes and dangerous pesticides, but the Mexican government got a highly patriotic outpost of small landowners on its Northern edge.

My dad was the third of 12 kids born to my abuelita, from the Mexican state of Jalisco, and my abuelito, from the Mexican state of Michoacán. They were farmers and lived in what are best described to an American audience as third-world conditions. The farm land my abuelito held, some privately and some in common with the Ejido, would go to the eldest. My dad spent his early years as a goatherd and avoided school as much as possible. Recognizing the lack of opportunity in store for him in the Ejido, he made his first crossing into the U.S. to do migrant work at 14 years of age. Sneaking across the border in the '70s and '80s wasn't like crossing today, at least not for people from the border region. Still, amongst my dad's stories are several about dangerous crossing experiences and one in particular about traversing the vast Yuma desert on foot. Eventually, he worked his way up to Washington State. Since he was the only person from Mexicali amongst many migrants from Central Mexico, he soon earned the nickname "Chicali." Several of his brothers and cousins followed a few years later. I spent my first eight years largely in this community of Mexican immigrants and their families.

Not unlike my mom, my dad's example to me was always one of hospitality, always looking for ways to assist people in need, whether they were cousins from home, new coworkers, or new acquaintances. He never approached this way of being from a place of political analysis, but rather as a practice in keeping with the culture that sustains migrants and immigrants in foreign lands, and which sustained him for years. Observing this throughout the years, in concert with my mom's work, instilled in me an understanding of the ways that communities dispersed over huge geographical expanses manage to live and grow while resisting the oppressive forces of globalization. This understanding has helped me to maintain faith in the potential for transnational resistance movements as a whole.

My parents met in Yakima, WA in 1983. They lived in the same apartment building, and I think they shared a sense of being out of place; they were shy and away from their families and childhood communities. They moved in together and were married shortly thereafter. Their honeymoon took them to Canada, where my dad was able to get a green card and re-enter the country legally. I was born in September of 1984, a couple hours from my mom's family in Seattle and a couple days from my dad's in the Ejido. After a few months, we moved to the Imperial Valley, looking for work opportunities for my dad and to be closer to his family. My mom uprooted herself and transplanted to a foreign country, whose language she didn't yet speak fluently. For the first three months, we lived at his family's house in the Ejido, and then we moved to a tiny rented guest house across the border in Calexico, CA.

My dad's days started as early as 2 or 3 a.m., waking before dawn to be bussed hours away to wherever there was some crop to harvest. While he was at work, my mom was left to her own devices, navigating unfamiliar towns amongst people she barely knew and with whom she had little in common. The recollections I've heard are that as she was integrated into my dad's family, she demonstrated the openness and warmth that have always characterized her. But I imagine that the experience was lonely, difficult, and often boring. In many ways, she and I only had each other at that point. After six months, we returned to Yakima, in search of work for my parents and better opportunities for me.

Pablo was born in 1989, when I was four. I remember being fascinated and thrilled, though it also meant losing my place at the center of the universe. We played together and loved each other's company. We fought as much as any pair of siblings, but were also each other's fiercest advocates in the face of any parental injustice. Even when I was too young to babysit, I felt quite responsible for Pablo, which was reinforced outside the home, where eldest siblings are often expected to keep the younger ones in line.

At this point, my dad had begun working as a landscape gardener, which he has continued ever since. The work was steadier and paid better than seasonal farm labor, but he was laid off in the winters and would spend much of that time back in Mexico, so there are long periods in my early memories of being a three-person family.

I went to kindergarten at our parish school, where I could attend free of cost because my mom worked there at the time. I started shortly before my fifth birthday, and I have only positive memories of the place. Nonetheless, my parents decided to move me to public school largely in reaction to the disturbingly classist and racist tendencies of St. Joe's. Although the parish itself was comprised largely of Mexican immigrants and their kids, the school catered to the children of rich, white people. While most of the parish children attended public school, many of the students weren't from the parish or even, necessarily, the city. At school, these kids were treated with deference and held to a much lower standard of behavior than the others. My mom quit and I started first grade at the neighborhood public school, which I attended for the next three years.

My parents had been discussing a move for some time, for myriad reasons. Yakima offered little in the way of opportunities and we lived in a community riddled with crime, drugs and gang activity. My mom wanted to get us out of that environment while we were still young, and my dad wanted steady year-round employment and to be closer to his family. Further, my mom had finally completed her bachelor's degree and was seeking better teaching positions than those available in Yakima. We had a cousin living in Tucson, so we had visited the year prior while on a trip to the Ejido.

We moved there after the school-year ended in 1993, leaving my dad behind to keep the house and his job in case it didn't work out in Arizona. My mom applied and was accepted to a master's program at the University of Arizona, and so we were able to move into the school's student-family housing. The following September, my dad packed up the rest of our things and drove down to join us.

The student-family housing was on the edge of the city, great for exploring both the wilderness and an adjacent illegal dumping ground, which were equally fascinating to me. I absolutely loved it, and never tired of roaming the complex and surrounding area with the other kids that lived there. Their families were from all over the world, and I quickly found a new best friend from Nepal. Her mother babysat us during the school year, and they became an extension of our family for the next couple of years. The school I attended that year drew largely from our housing complex, so the student body was incredibly diverse. Despite the many positive aspects of this student-family community, the buildings were dilapidated and infested with giant sewer cockroaches and toxic mold.[10] And, our housing was already cramped (Pablo and I slept on a pull-out bed in the living room) and my mom was pregnant, so we were in serious need of more space. The following spring, my parents bought a small house. Andy was born several months later, in July of 1994. The move from Washington had been really hard for me because it involved a bit of culture shock, shifting from a bilingual environment to an English-dominant one, and adjusting to a totally different climate and local culture. But by the time Andy was born, I had adjusted to the changes.

I started at yet another school in the fall, and liked it as much as every other school I'd been at. In these years, I remember wanting to help more than I could. My mom was working full-time and going to school, and my dad was often working seven days a week. I would read to my brothers and put them to bed, and eventually I started babysitting quite a bit. In middle school and high school, I spent most summers watching them while my parents worked, an arrangement I was generally happy with.

School was always really easy for me. I loved going, loved my teachers, and never had serious disciplinary problems. For most of my time in school, I was at the top of the class and was consistently viewed as a student with great potential— someone who would make real achievements and who required little academic support to excel. I was particularly skilled in reading and writing, and I had been articulate (and talkative) from a young age.

When we lived in Yakima, I attended a bilingual elementary school. The student population was quite underprivileged, with a sizable number of immigrants and children of immigrants. A combination of related factors— parents with limited education, general lack of resources, systemic racism and classism—meant that the school had a disproportionate number of under-performing students. In addition to a natural aptitude for academics and a certain level of self-confidence, I had the benefit of an educated mother, two parents who felt it important that I focus on school, and the consequent support that many young children lack. The gap between my abilities and those of most of classmates was pretty significant, and eventually I was put into a program for "gifted" students that pulled us out of the regular classroom once a week, though I have virtually no memory of whatever it was that we actually did at these times.

In the third grade, I was in a bilingual class where the assignments were so easy for me that I always finished early. The teacher started having me tutor a small group of my classmates who were far behind the rest, several because they barely spoke English, while he conducted class. He killed two birds with one stone in that way, keeping me busy when I otherwise would have gotten bored and providing extra support to some of his needier pupils. When I remember this, I hear echoes of the criticism that smart kids are often asked to assist others rather than being offered enrichment opportunities for themselves. Though this was definitely an example of the way that I was socialized to be responsible for other people, I think it was actually good for me. I can't look at where I am today and say honestly that I

was robbed of any educational opportunity, and I'm grateful for
the fact that—unlike many of my "gifted" classmates of later
years—I wasn't allowed to develop a sense of entitlement over
my peers because of my intellectual privilege.

At a new school in Tucson in the fourth grade, I refused
to take the test to get into the "gifted" program there. I would
definitely have passed, but for some reason unknown to me, I
wasn't interested. Halfway through fifth grade, and in yet another
school, it was recommended to my parents that I take a similar
test. I did, passed, and began a program similar to the one in
Yakima, where I was taken out of my regular class once a week
for some set of special projects with other "gifted" kids that I
mostly don't remember. When I started middle school, however,
I tested into a self-contained program for "gifted" kids. The
classes I took for the next three years offered me much more in
terms of scope and depth of education than I would have gotten
in regular classes.

Arizona's educational system is pretty abysmal and,
although I didn't understand this at the time, at the point that
many of my peers were starting to flounder in a broken school
system, I was protected and enriched in the bubble of "gifted
and talented education." This continued into high school, when
I tested into the public college-prep school and was tracked
straight into the private liberal arts sector.

For most of my childhood, I didn't feel strongly about
my racial identification. I felt that I was half-Mexican and half-
American, half-white and half-brown, half my mom and half
my dad. It was this strong feeling of containing two half-selves
that I think was the subconscious motivator behind my decision
at 5 years old to demand that my mom's last name be legally
added to mine, so that everything but my birth certificate reads
"Guillén-Givins." Outside of my immediate family, though,
these half-selves inhabited different worlds with little overlap.

I love and value time spent with all of my relatives, but
my dad's family lives a different life than I do. Despite a mixed
heritage, I am definitely American. It's where I'm comfortable.
But they, even those who also moved to the U.S. and whose
children were born and raised here, exist in a world between

countries, with ties holding them much closer to Mexico than I can pretend to be. As a kid, I loved going to the Ejido, where I could run free with my cousins, exploring the mix of farm-town features and junkyard aesthetic that characterizes the area. But as we all grew up, differences in our life experiences and opportunities (education-wise, most of all) only magnified the gulf between us. With childhood play no longer present to bond us, my trajectory kept me going in another direction.

On the other hand, I have always been at ease with my mom's family, who speak English, which is my dominant language, and with whom I share more in terms of interests, style and education. Because of my closer identification with them, and the relative ease with which I navigate white society, it never occurred to me that I might be considered an outsider by white people; this was compounded by my sense of alienation from my dad's relatives. I felt very comfortable identifying as mixed race—this is accurate, after all—and leaving it at that. My comfort must have been nurtured and maintained within our family unit, because even our choice of which "race" box to check on school forms (many didn't offer "mixed" and wouldn't allow you to check "white" and "Hispanic") was often a cause for contention with school bureaucrats, who seemed to prefer that you pick whichever would offer you the fewest benefits in the given circumstance.

I didn't realize 'til much later that I evaded acquiring some of the psychological factors often associated with growing up in an underprivileged ring of society. The way I generally remember my childhood, I didn't really encounter even minor instances of overt racism. Yet, when I mention this to my mom, she's quick to point out incidents that I have totally forgotten. In her telling, it wasn't that I didn't encounter racism and classism but that it didn't really phase me.

One of the biggest barriers for children of color is the internalized racism that they develop growing up in a white supremacist society, and there's certainly a parallel for children who grow up poor and working class. This means that even when "actual" barriers are not present, their low sense of self-worth and the ease with which they resign themselves to the bottom rungs prevent them from developing fully and positively. Fortunately for me, the combination of the support that I received from my family and some of my inherent personality traits protected me from the psychological ravages of racism and classism, allowing me to excel in areas where my peers often did not.

However, being privileged in this way also meant that I didn't fully grasp my status as "other" in the U.S., or the wide-reaching effects of systemic racism and classism on contemporary society. I was able to see the ways that these forces had affected my dad—the blatant racism he dealt with from law enforcement, the difference in treatment he received because of his accent, the limited opportunities open to him—and likewise the effects on his entire family. I never thought so explicitly about this, but as an American-born child of mixed heritage with a relatively easy time of it in the area where I spent most of my time (school), I suspect that I felt like the problems he faced were rapidly overcome through generational changes. He, like most immigrants, labored and suffered so his children would have it better, and the outcome was successful.

It wasn't until I started to observe the social and academic difficulties that both of my brothers experienced and, simultaneously, left the comfort of my parent's house that I began to really understand and take seriously the depths of racism and classism, as well as their effects on whole communities, and to question my own status and the privileges I enjoyed. Whether because of personality or circumstance or both, I was able to mature without having to battle racism very personally. But as I watched my brothers grow up and witnessed the ways that racism restricted their avenues for growth, I became quickly and acutely aware of how real it was for all of us. Youth of color, particularly boys, are criminalized from an early age. They are treated with suspicion and impatience, and are quickly abandoned when they most need academic, emotional and psychological support. I developed a much stronger sense of my own place in a racialized society, and a lot of accompanying rage, only as their experiences left me realizing that everyone picks a side in this country.

Conspiracy to Riot

When I went away to Macalester College in the fall of '02, I was suddenly stripped of the shelter provided by my family, who had no need to label me since I was one of them. Now I too was subject to the ideas of people who didn't know me or anything about my background, and I found out quickly that people perceived me as a person of color. I have very light brown skin and brown hair, but my features are distinctly mestiza.[11] As my two years at Macalester wore on, I only grew more and more aware of the differences between my life experiences and those of my mostly white peers, and had to ascribe much of that to our racial and cultural differences. Though I'm of mixed race and have white family, I identify as a person of color because I understand that nobody develops separate from race in the U.S., and because it is what best positions me to deal with the racist attitudes that pervade our society.

I was raised Catholic and what I learned and saw in the Church and in the people of faith that I've known has profoundly influenced, and probably irreversibly affected, the course of my political development.

Though stereotypes hold that Mexicans are devoutly Catholic, I saw very little of this amongst my dad's relatives. Except for my abuelita (my dad's mom), I don't think they attended Church regularly, and aside from baptism and funeral rites, whatever faith they may have held was rarely evidenced. My primary religious influence comes, instead, from my mom's family. My mom and her siblings attended Catholic school for at least some portion of their schooling, and they were raised in a parish community. They grew up around the time of the infamous Second Vatican Council ("Vatican II") that dictated profound changes in Church practice, including the shift from Latin to local-language masses and the rearrangement of ceremony so that priests faced the congregation rather than the altar.

My mom was the only one of her siblings who continued to practice after leaving home, though her older brother returned to the Church decades later. I think their parents provided a wonderful example of owning your spirituality, rather than being owned by it. They were (and my grandma continues to be) sincere and devout, without being dogmatic. They demonstrated an ability to take the good that the Church provided without the bad or the crazy. And they were always able to make decisions independent of the Church when reason or conscience demanded it.

I was aware from a young age of the faith-based radical work that my mom had been involved in, as well as my grandpa's connections to the Catholic Worker movement. Though I went to Sunday school throughout my youth, I learned more about Catholicism from my mom than I did there. Her portrayal of the Catholic Church was of the new, more egalitarian one envisioned by Vatican II, and the tenets of Liberation Theology[12] that she imparted to me imprinted on my developing sense of morality. When we moved to Tucson and I met our cousin, a radical Catholic priest, I was even further impressed with the ideas of Left Catholicism. His life of direct service to the oppressed, particularly migrants and refugees passing through or settling in the border region, was yet another example to me of the ways that faith moves people to be agents of radical change.

A lot of people think of the Catholic Church as a conservative and severe church that focuses on guilt and the threat of eternal damnation as a means of control over its people. Though this may speak accurately to many people's experiences in the Church, it couldn't be farther from my own. I don't remember ever hearing about Hell or being bothered with archaic concepts of cardinal sin or proper respect for authority. Maybe this is because I didn't, or maybe I was just impervious to that sort of thing, but what I learned through Catholicism was that our obligation to justice and peace—in that order—supersedes any obligation to "the laws of Man," and that we could rely only on our own moral compasses to navigate a society fraught with hatred, greed and violence. The heroes I held as a child were people who, compelled by their faith, committed acts of protest, solidarity and direct aid in clear violation of U.S. law, such as members of the Sanctuary movement, war resisters throughout the 20th Century, and religious folk who joined forces with revolutionary movements fighting U.S.-backed dictatorships throughout Latin America.

But, I don't think I've ever actually believed in God. I was at ease with the idea that others did and felt the same motivation to good works that many ascribe to their faith in a higher power, but I've always been unconcerned with the question of whether or not a god exists. I suppose I've never thought that knowing one way or another would change anything for me, and so I never dwelt on it.

Despite my early and current feeling of affinity for the Church, at the age when most Catholic teenagers receive confirmation, becoming full adult members of the Church, I was becoming disinterested in spirituality and fed up with what I perceived to be repressive teachings of the Church hierarchy. At one point, I stated to my mother that I was unwilling to attend mass anymore because I was so offended by the homophobia and sexism of official Catholic doctrine. She insisted that I had to attend as an example for my brothers and, probably after much argument, I acquiesced on the condition that I would not be confirmed. Though I'm sure I was furious at the time, in retrospect I appreciate that my mom wasn't willing to cave to every political whim of mine. I don't mean that there wasn't some legitimacy to my grievances with the Church—in fact, I know these are grievances my mother held before I was even born. But her stance forced me to consider my choices in a context in which "getting my way" at every turn wasn't an option. This was preparation for adult life, where you pick your battles because you don't have the energy to win every one, and so you have to learn to prioritize. The incident also undermined individualist tendencies that, to the extent that they inform my political path, are counterproductive. I had to learn to assess my personal desires and think more deeply about which choices I should prioritize based not only on their effects on me, but on the people around me. Not attending church at that point might have been personally satisfying, in the way that revenge often is, but there was more to my attendance than my own feelings about it. In many ways, I went to church as an act of communion with my family, and my mom knew that each piece that fell away would destabilize the rest. Ultimately, my attendance wasn't about personal beliefs or faith—it was about my commitment to my family, and to supporting my mother's efforts to hold us together.

Max Specktor

My maternal grandmother and grandfather grew up in Denmark and Norway respectively. My grandfather joined the army as a young man, fortunately only after World War II. My grandmother's family had front-row seats to the war, however, as they were forced to house German invaders during the occupation of Denmark. They both moved to Sweden after the war, where they married and raised a family.

My mother was the third out of four children. Growing up in Sweden, she attended some schooling in Stockholm and was active in radical art groups and to a lesser extent in various pro-squatter and anti-war demonstrations. She moved to the United States while in her 20s to train as a clown and perform.

A couple of my mom's closest friends from Sweden moved to the Twin Cities with her, which made the move a lot easier for her. She was involved in the beginnings of the Heart of the Beast Puppet and Mask Theater, which is a radical theater troupe that started in south Minneapolis, and continues today as a vibrant progressive theater that puts on the Mayday parade and festival every year. She continued to perform in theater, and eventually began a career in special education in schools and in art centers, as well as being a personal care attendant.

My dad's parents grew up in the Twin Cities, born to Polish/Ukrainian immigrants. Both Jews, they were raised at a time when there was a lot of anti-Semitism in Minneapolis. It got to be so bad that my grandma's family had to move out to the country while she was a kid. My grandpa fought in World War II as a member of the Army. It definitely had a huge impact on him and remains the subject of almost all of his stories to this day.

My dad grew up in St. Paul during the '50s and '60s as the oldest child of four. It is easier to write about his family because I saw them much more growing up. My grandfather ran a small construction company where my father and his brothers worked. My father was old enough to witness and participate in the '60s counter-culture and the radical movements that existed around the same time. He attended Macalaster College in St. Paul, but ended up dropping out after about a year and a half, but not before he and his friends had formally hijacked the editorial of the school's newspaper and printed their far-out political diatribes. He continued to write for various leftist newspapers, doing friendly reporting for the anti-nuclear movement and the American Indian Movement. He continues to write for The Circle, a newspaper of the local American Indian community, and owns and edits the American Jewish World, the local Jewish community newspaper.

I was born March 3, 1989, during an intense blizzard. I was the middle child of three boys. Growing up, our family traveled to Sweden about every other year, which ended up dominating my fond memories of early childhood. Other than that, and my religious identity, I had a fairly unexceptional childhood and adolescence. I went to public schools for all my education, spent most of my free time hanging out with the other kids my age on the block and singing along to MTV. Of course, my parents had politics that were significantly left of center and had friends with unconventional lifestyles, but that was pretty much the norm in the neighborhood where I grew up. I played a lot of organized sports, but by the time I was in middle school, I was more interested in skateboarding and getting into mischief with the neighborhood kids.

As part of my Jewish tradition, I attended Synagogue at the Temple of Aaron in St. Paul, meaning I went to religious classes every week, studying the Bible and Jewish culture. It always felt a little forced going to these classes every week, especially when my close friends didn't have to do the same thing. But at the same time it felt a little cool to be slightly different, of course only as long as everyone was respectful of those differences. I definitely believed in God for the majority of my youth, but it was mostly just about performing the rituals. I guess I am still spiritual in a sense now, but growing up I imagined I could talk to God and be heard, and would do it regularly. I actually was fortunate to have my religious teachers complicate the idea of God for me and even tell me many times that it was okay if I didn't believe in God, and of course I was never threatened with going to hell if I didn't.

The traditional aspect of Judaism is something that I still hold onto very enthusiastically. My family always had Friday dinner together for Shabbat (Sabbath), and ate the ritual meal. This is something we continue to this day, giving my life at least one point of balance every week. I also studied and learned the history of Jews as a people, which generally consisted of persecution and serial nomadism, but fostered an understanding of systemic oppression in me, and showed me the importance of standing up for the underdog.

Chapter 2
DEVELOPING POLITICS

Eryn Trimmer

Early in high school I had begun going to punk shows with my friends, mostly at St. Andrews Church in College Park, Maryland. The music there was primarily hardcore, mostly apolitical, but with enough connection to anarcho-punk that that radical politics and projects were mentioned from time to time.

My friends and I had been jamming for a while and eventually started our own band. We played a few shows before breaking up. I enjoyed it a lot, but it wasn't a true passion of mine. The better musicians in my group of friends would continue making some great music for many years. The punk scene was where I first heard about anarchism, although I definitely didn't understand what it was. I recall a punk show I went to in D.C. in which the band casually mentioned "Hey, we're all anarchists here anyway, right?" That got my heart beating a little bit faster; I wanted to learn more about anarchism but it was definitely a bit scary at first.

My peer group very much discouraged political thought out of the norm. One of my friends allegedly said he was an anarchist over an instant message to another friend and got teased terribly for it. For my friends, it was much better to simply be uncool as opposed to trying too hard to be cool; being a "poser" was the worst of sins. No one thought that anarchism was any sort of political (or anti-political) philosophy, but rather something that someone trying too hard to be a punk would label themselves as. Maybe if we were in a band, were good at skateboarding, weren't so good at school, etc., then we could wear punky clothes and have mohawks. Being a punk was an untouchable holy grail, something that we dared inch toward but could never embrace.

In the run up to the 2000 election, I was excited about Ralph Nader. I went to a Nader campaign rally with C.T. I liked Nader's dismissal of two-party politics. The notion that both the Democrats and Republicans were funded by corporations and had those interests at heart rang true for me. From there, it was only a short leap to the inefficacy and inherent injustice of all political party organizing.

I wanted to start putting some of these new political ideas into action. I went with the one actual punk in high school, whom I didn't know very well, to a group called Positive Force DC, a long-time youth activist group that used punk shows to raise money for progressive and radical causes. There I met people for whom punk wasn't about style but rather a cultural counterpart to organizing for radical social change. I began to realize that what I really wanted was not to be punk aesthetically, but to be involved in organizing for social change. I had always been an idealist—and I was more and more realizing all the problems with the world. I never became highly involved with Positive Force D.C, but it introduced me to the radical activist scene in D.C.

I hadn't heard much about the protest in Seattle in 1999 at the time, but as I was becoming politically aware, the anti-globalization movement was in full swing. I learned about the IMF and World Bank as global institutions whose programs prioritize corporate profits over human and environmental welfare. I began going to some organizing meetings for the convergence against the IMF and World Bank meetings being held in DC in 2002. They were largely organized by the Anti Capitalist Convergence (ACC), a coalition that formed around protesting the IMF and World Bank meetings in 2001. The IMF and World Bank canceled their meetings that year because of 9/11 and many protest groups besides the ACC also called off their plans, but the ACC had gone ahead and marched on the World Bank headquarters.

By 2002, resistance had grown again, although it was still mainly anarchists doing the organizing. This was my first opportunity to see what anarchist organizing for a large-scale convergence was like. The ACC had points of unity against capitalism, imperialism, and patriarchy and for a diversity of tactics, non-hierarchical organizing and a respect for security culture, among others. I went to a non-violent direct action training as well as witnessed my first spokescouncil meeting. The plan was to shut down the city the day before the IMF and World Bank meetings. Dubbed "The People's Strike," the shutdown wasn't too successful, but it was quite a sight to see. Six hundred and forty nine people were arrested that day, most in mass preemptive roundups that would later be deemed illegal and lead to a complete reversal of policing protest in the District of Columbia. I witnessed people locking down in the streets with lock boxes, a broken bank window and excessive force used by the police.

Shortly after arriving, however, I was arrested for obeying police orders as to where to go. I was outraged by the fact that the police had the power to, at their whim, take away basically all of my freedom (i.e., put me in a cage). It was a feeling of powerlessness and anger. Due in a large part to my growing up with the privileges of a middle-class, white, male-assigned person, this was something that I hadn't felt very often before. Feeling injustice so personally made me more invested in taking on other injustices that weren't directly about me. If this is what it feels like to spend a few hours of my privileged life behind bars, imagine what other people are going through every day.

The next major event that helped shape my political development was the Iraq War, which began while I was a senior in high school. Seeing the lead up and follow through of the invasion of Iraq through my new political lens really blew my mind. That so many people seemed oblivious to the blatant ways that the Bush administration beat the drums of war, whipped up nationalism, and used twisted logic to justify the invasion was frustrating. That the administration then completely ignored the biggest protests in history was no huge surprise, but the fact that people then didn't step up the dissent in more ways was.

That almost all the Democrats in Congress voted to fund the war was a perfect example of the impotence of the system of representation. I felt that people were not outraged enough at the injustice of the war and our lack of a say in it, and of those who were, few were willing to do any more than hold signs and march. I took part in many of the large marches against the Iraq War, but they had begun to leave a bad taste in my mouth—does anybody care that we're walking around out here?

There was a call to disrupt business as usual on the day

the war started. I took part in a march that attempted to block the Key Bridge connecting Virginia and Washington, D.C. There I saw the police tackle a well-known anarchist for no apparent reason. (I suspected that they were trying to take out the "leaders.") Although this action was somewhat successful, it was a far cry from a true disruption of business as usual. I also helped organize a walkout at school that was quite successful in numbers, if not effective in action. Hundreds of students walked out of class. Some people wanted to take to the streets in front of our school, which was a very large intersection, but the purveyors of "civil" and "orderly" dissent won out and instead the crowd did a lap around the building and then fizzled out. Although the disruption on the day the war started was minimal, I at least felt like I was involved in something more than purely symbolic protest, which was beginning to be a significant distinction.

During my year between high school and college I got more involved in the D.C. chapter of Food Not Bombs. From C.T., I had learned a lot about the theory behind the project and felt really good about the goals and tactics of the group, although in practice our chapter probably wasn't that effective. There is a large and quite visible homeless population in D.C. and a lot of charities giving food and shelter. Food Not Bombs groups try not to just be another charity. Rather, the idea is to highlight how inhumane and shameful a system is that wastes so much food when there are so many people hungry. Servings are not supposed to be just a charitable act but also street theater, an opportunity to point out the skewed priorities of our society.

Our chapter served once a week at McPherson Square and ended up just being the vegetarian option in the range of other charities serving nearby on the same day. People liked the food and ate it all, but the political aspect was lacking. Still, it was empowering for me to gather so much food that would have otherwise gone to waste. I remember literally filling my mom's minivan with soy milk one day. It was invigorating to be able to gather so much from the scraps of capitalism and get it to those who could use it. Dumpster diving particularly was fun—it felt like the trappings of society were lifted. The fundamental life story we had been told—that one must do well in school so you could get a good job so you could afford to feed your family—was clearly not true; you could just go to the grocery store dumpster and get tons of good food! Couple that with squatting for a roof over your head and who needs an "education" or a job? I was realizing that the possibilities for how to live weren't as narrow as I had been taught.

Sophomore year of high school, I began dating Maxine (though I'm not sure if we ever went on a date...). When we met, we were both getting into more radical politics. We shared a passion for wanting to make the world a better place and we would spend hours analyzing, discussing, reading to each other and otherwise figuring out what we thought about the world and how best to change it. We pushed each other to try to live in ways that would bring about the world we wanted. On the one-year anniversary of 9/11, we made t-shirts that said, "Capitalism Kills Remember 9/11" and wore them to school, getting more than a couple of stern looks from our teachers.

During senior year, we experimented with having an open relationship. Although challenging, it was also uplifting to put our values into practice. It was a way to incorporate the principles of autonomy and freedom, as well as accountability, into the most intimate aspects of our lives. The institution of marriage (and by extension, monogamy), with its ties to the church and the state seemed not only outdated and repressive; it quite frankly didn't work out for a large part of our generation's parents.

At the same time, the current models of "free love" (if you can call it that) forefronted a profound lack of commitment and the patriarchal commodification of sex (i.e., you're more of a man the more sex you get with as many different women as possible). Polyamory seemed like a good model in that it incorporated commitment as well as freedom. The challenge was putting it into practice when we had been raised to think of our romantic partners as "ours" and equated them loving someone else as rejection. In our case, it worked out all right, each of us ending up with other partners and remaining good friends.

At this age, anarchism was a concrete framework that

rejected at a fundamental level all the injustices we saw and experienced. The mind-numbing experience of forced schooling, the debasement of parental authority and lack of understanding, the promise of becoming corporate slaves as long as we did well in school, the racial and social class segregation of our classes, and on and on. All of these problems could be ascribed to the fact that our society is based on hierarchy and domination. If people just took control of their own lives and we created a society in which everyone affected by each decision got a chance to weigh in on it, we would be in a much better place.

Senior year, Maxine and I joined a youth theater group called City at Peace. Every year, the group writes their own musical based on their lives. It is comprised of a racially and economically diverse group of teenagers from the D.C. metro area, most without significant theatrical experience. The first half of the year we spent getting to know each other and telling our stories, as well as receiving acting, dancing and vocal training. This was the first time I got to know people living hugely different lives from mine so close to me geographically. The time was structured under different categories such as race, gender, sexual orientation, etc. As we looked at our lives from these different points of view, we gained an understanding of how power plays out in our day-to-day interactions. People shared very intimate parts of their lives. From there, we used those stories and the journey the cast went on together to write the musical.

I played a teacher who was the primary support person for a teen who was suffering from depression. My character was also suffering from depression and committed suicide toward the end of the show. This was a challenging role to play, as much because I was a gregarious and popular teacher as the fact that I was depressed. The show was quite stressful and overwhelming, but also rewarding.

In City at Peace, I got to hear firsthand the effects of sexism, racism, poverty and abuse in various forms, with an analysis of the systematic way that these interactions are perpetuated. Although I wished we had also examined things such as capitalism, it was definitely an expanding experience.

I began a serious examination of my own privileges and arrogance. Getting to know the other cast members was not only enjoyable (as well as challenging in many cases), but it led me to think about my idealistic views in the more real context of the environments many people are in every day. I learned that not only was it problematic for me to think I had insight into how others should deal with problems they were encountering (racism, for example), but also that it simply wasn't true that I did.

My parents' divorce was conflict-ridden and their anger seemed to grow with time as opposed to dissipate. C.T. led a campaign to try and get me to stand up for my mother in the face of what he saw as my father's disparagement of her. I didn't see it as so black-and-white. Although my dad could barely mention my mom's name for all the scorn it engendered, he mostly just wanted to have nothing to do with her. Things finally came to a head when I or my sister let it slip that my dad was adopting a son, something he had asked us to keep private. I thought it was weird that he would want to keep it a secret but didn't think too much of it. When my mom found out, however, she was really hurt. With C.T. sharing his analysis with her, she thought my keeping the secret meant that I thought (consciously or not) that she was unworthy of the information or that she would use it in a harmful way. Why else would you keep a secret from someone? At the time, I bought into this logic. It was hard for me to see my mom so upset and I wanted to make her feel better by validating her feelings and apologizing. This is what I did, and I told her that I would work to rebuild the trust in our relationship.

At this point, I really had no tools to analyze and understand what I should think about the conflicts between my parents—nor should I have been placed in a position in which I had to pick sides. C.T. was trying to get me to grow up, analyze patriarchy, and stand up for my mom. He had good motivations, but both the manner in which he went about it and the situation that he used didn't work for me. My parents' conflicts were way too emotional for me to be able to think rationally about. I just wanted to do whatever I could to get the pressure off me. The situation was too emotional of a training ground, so much so that, if anything, it has hindered my future ability to deal with conflict.

The specific incident about keeping Tolya's adoption secret especially created a rupture between my mom and me. She suggested that I take a year off before college to work on our relationship and be in therapy. This sounded good to me; I wanted to have a good relationship with my mom and wasn't excited to go to college. However, this was really just another way for me to delay the decision of going to college or not. I was pretty sure that I didn't want to go but felt a lot of pressure from my parents and grandparents to attend. My mom's analysis of our relationship didn't sit well with me, although I wasn't self-aware enough to know this at the time. I didn't work on our relationship particularly or go to therapy since the motivation for those things wasn't really coming from me.

My sister Tanya's relationship with C.T. was much more challenged then mine at this time, and it only got worse. C.T.'s forceful parenting style, which certainly rubbed me the wrong way and shut me down, was even worse for Tanya. She was a constant disappointment to him, but rather than fight him outwardly, she tried to please him, which was pretty much impossible, and she ended up taking the stress of that internally. After I left my mom's house, C.T. ended up moving out primarily because he sucked all the air out of the house for Tanya.

At some point, my sister and I began going over to my dad's house every other weekend. This was too little too late, in terms of creating a parental relationship between my dad and me. My dad and Jane got married and adopted Tolya, a seven-year-old boy from Kazakhstan. He was almost deaf, and therefore learned American Sign Language. Jane knew ASL from her work as an educator, but my dad had to learn it. I didn't know ASL, but in the time I spent with Tolya, we had a great time playing together. Because of the limited time we spent together, however, I wouldn't say we've developed a deep brotherly connection. By this time I wasn't particularly upset that my dad was moving on with his new family. I was old enough to feel as though I was moving on myself anyway.

As a kid, I liked being outside a lot. I likened our backyard, which was completely overgrown with weeds and vines, to a jungle that, in my smallness, I could literally explore. However, aside from a few "car camping" and hiking trips, I didn't spend much time in nature growing up.

The last two years of high school, I spent time in the hills of New Mexico with a program called The Tracking Project. It was a group of twenty or so young men and six teachers, a minority of both being American Indian, the majority white. The heart of the program was learning traditional skills such as animal tracking, fire making, medicinal plants and shelter building. We also did martial arts and other physical activity, made music, and told stories. This time spent away from the city, as well as learning skills that deepened my awareness and appreciation of nature, allowed me to coalesce my innate appreciation of the natural world. I learned the obvious fact that everyone's ancestors were indigenous to somewhere, something that led me to the realization that my place as a white urban dweller didn't have to be one of complete alienation from nature.

I now have serious critiques of the program. Although I think the teachers had a good understanding of the problems with cultural appropriation, it wasn't discussed openly. Also, while many of the effects of colonization were discussed (such as alienation from the land base), the fact that we were on American Indian land—and what that meant--wasn't talked about. Despite these highly problematic shortcomings, the program helped forge a lifelong priority of mine. Although I don't spend as much time out of the city as I would like, my desire to see the natural world flourish greatly informs my work.

I took some classes at the University of Maryland the year after high school while I was still living at home. The two that interested me most were a GLBT studies class and a women's studies class. This was the first time I had tried to read political theory that was written without trying to be accessible. While frustrating, it was also invigorating to find a morsel of information in a difficult article that was comprehensible and apply it to real life. I learned that identity politics can be exceedingly complicated, but the goal of trying to counter oppression by understanding where it comes from spoke deeply to me.

After that year, I attended Earlham College in Richmond, Indiana. My father had also gone there, as well as a few other family members. It is a liberal Quaker school. I thought that it would be a good environment to push things in a more radical direction. Soon after arriving, I met John,[1] an anarchist who was both very intelligent and yet spoke of theory accessibly. Missing a few of our first classes, we helped organize a school-funded trip to attend the 2004 RNC in New York. I hadn't been planning on attending the protests and wasn't really aware what the more radical plans were for the convention, but it was fun nonetheless.

John exposed me to books like The Revolution of Everyday Life by Rauel Vaneigem as well as hundreds of 'zines. I was ready to take my analysis to the next level and he was the perfect companion to do it with. Besides learning new theory about how radical societal change happens and what types of changes would be desirable, I was also exposed to materials about radical history. I hadn't previously been aware of very many different radicals throughout history, and the application of anarchist ideas to very different social circumstances was interesting. We started a little distro and tabled at the student center, made posters denouncing electoral politics (this was the run up to the Bush-Kerry election), and brought speakers and trainers to the college about various issues and skills. I hitchhiked for the first time to go to events in Indianapolis and Bloomington, Indiana.

I was having a wonderful (and even educational) time, but none of that was coming from my classes. I didn't have a major but was thinking about either economics or environmental science (or a combination). I thought that if I understood economics, the all-powerful force behind so much of the logic of our society, I could better denounce and confront it. It didn't take a lot of looking at the world through the lens of "incentives" to realize that the only reason to know the details of economics would be to reform it, not transform it completely. As for environmental science, I respected my teachers because the health of the environment really was a priority for them.

However, they were depressed because they knew how bad it really was and they didn't see anything changing anytime soon. We talked to the farmers whose pesticides and fertilizers were polluting the local ponds, and of course they were just trying to make a living as best they could. Creating "incentives" for organic farming could help—but it seemed to me that true sustainability could only come from living closer to the land, a complete change from the logic of industrial civilization. The class wasn't talking about the kind of fundamental shift in which staying alive and the destruction of the environment would not be pitted against one another.

Social science classes, which I enjoyed more, were also frustrating. It was safe to critique the past, but the present was out of bounds. A teacher I had for two different classes about "the West" and American Indians seemed quite radical, able to craft a very insightful critique of Indians in pop culture during westward expansion, for example. However, after William Kristol, a neoconservative intellectual and co-creator of the specific plan that justified the Iraq war, was pied while speaking at Earlham, she turned stiff with anger and discomfort when it was mentioned in class and asked that we didn't bring it up. Conveniently, she could not see contemporary colonization and resistance to it if it was right in front of her. I soon knew that it was a waste of money and time for me to be in college. Not that I didn't think there was use in intellectual pursuits, but I was learning much more out of class and knew I could research things fine on my own. I was eager to see more of the world and engage with it.

After I went away to college my Dad and Jane adopted another child from the same orphanage in Kazakhstan, Olivia. She was eleven and deaf. After a while it became apparent that there were issues with her integration into the family. She was disturbingly manipulative and was not relating to my Dad and Jane as parents. After a huge amount of conflict she was taken to a psychologist and diagnosed with attachment disorder.[2] She began therapy, part of which included my Dad and Jane essentially treating her like a little kid, in an attempt to have her learn new ways of relating to adults.

Olivia's behavior enraged my Dad and Jane to such an extent that I felt as though they were relating to her mostly from a place of anger. They would make jokes about giving her away or wishing that they had never gotten her, yell at her, and ignore her. It was awful to see my dad that way; it really brought out the worst in him. Olivia spent some time with the family of a long-term friend of my dad's and seemed more functional with them. Eventually they said that they would take her indefinitely, and my Dad and Jane accepted the offer. Hearing this made me angry and sad, that my Dad would essentially give up on her and the responsibility he took on when adopting her. However, I think it was the best thing for her, and that's what's most important. The summer after my first year of college, I decided to join a project out of Bloomington, Indiana that was resisting the construction of a NAFTA superhighway, Interstate 69. This was an attractive undertaking for me because it combined resistance to the multitude of damage done by "free trade" and a tangible construction project that wasn't wanted by the locals.

Despite the overwhelming local resistance for over a decade, the Indiana department of transportation was intent on going forward with the road. It was part of a broader plan to create more efficient trade routes in North America and attaching to highways constructed under Plan Puebla Panama (PPP), a transportation infrastructure plan in Central America and Mexico. In this manner, we saw our resistance as an attempt to be in solidarity with those resisting the PPP and other free trade projects in Latin America.

Our organizing was lacking for a variety of reasons, not the least of which was a deficit of numbers and experience. The organizing was heavy on informal networks, which was great for a lot of reasons but also created challenges. There were no explicit goals stated and plans for reaching them, so at times it was hard to know what to do. Despite this, there were a lot of people who brought a lot of good ideas and energy to the project. I learned new skills and made new friends.

I learned a lot about how anarchist organizing works that summer. It was the first time that I took responsibility for making concrete organizing work happen. One of the biggest lessons was just how difficult it is to try to stop the state when they want something. I got to see up close and personal the extent that they were willing to lie to the public and create the false appearance of democratic processes. Anarchism was becoming less of an idealistic notion about some future society and more about how to structure our resistance to the goals of capitalism and the state. The campaign against I-69 continued long after I left, with some of the main organizers facing outrageously fabricated felony charges. As of this writing, the road is under construction, with less resistance now that the struggle seems lost.

A large part of that summer for me was falling in love with Monica Bicking, my current partner and co-defendant. We had been at Earlham together but had been more acquaintances than friends. Soon into the summer, I was head over heels for her. I had never felt this way before; I understood that cheesy love songs were really attempts at trying to explain these feelings that sounded so cliché when put into words. I could not get close enough to her, physically and emotionally. I was planning on traveling in Latin America and she was going to be studying in Mexico for the fall semester, so we made plans to meet there. I thought it was silly that she had any doubts at all that I would actually follow through.

I wanted to see more of the world. I really enjoyed living in Indiana for a year after having lived in the same place my entire life. At the same time, I didn't want to travel just for the sake of traveling alone. I wanted to connect with others in struggle. With the Mexican and Central American connections to I-69, I thought it would be neat to meet others resisting free trade infrastructure there. After staying with my mom for a couple of months and saving up some money, I hitchhiked to Texas and then took a bus to Mexico City. I had been studying Spanish the past year or so in anticipation of the trip, but had very little real-world practice with the language. I ended up meeting someone on the bus who let me stay with him for a few days while I got my bearings.

Before leaving, I had emailed a few different groups I had found online that seemed promising in terms of the work they were doing and asking if they would give me a floor to sleep on. I had a bit of time before Monica and I were going to meet, so I went to the squatted social center at UNAM, the public university in Mexico City. The person I hung out with most, "El Gato," took me under his wing and showed me around, as long as I bought him a beer or two or three every day. It was a mutually beneficial arrangement, but one that left me feeling uncomfortable as he got more insistent that I buy him beer. Maybe I should have accepted the "gringo tax" as a more honest way of relating than if we had ignored the fact that I had more money and privilege than he did and yet was in a position of wanting to connect with him. Although the folks at UNAM were interested in hearing about the projects I was involved in, most seemed more interested in drinking and making art than social struggle.

I met Monica there and we headed south. One of the most unique times in our travels was the time we spent in Oaxaca. We connected with a group called Consejo Indígena Popular de Oaxaca "Ricardo Flores Magón" (CIPO-RFM), which translates to the Popular Indigenous Council of Oaxaca "Ricardo Flores Magón."[3] It is essentially a network of indigenous communities in struggle. While we were there ostensibly as international human rights observers, this wasn't a particularly active time of military or paramilitary repression. Therefore, we went to a few different communities to try and find one that could use us for something. We ended up doing a variety of activities, from picking coffee to teaching English. This was the first time I experienced a situation in which the link between social struggle and survival was so intimate. New projects such as green houses and bee keeping helped them sustain themselves economically and therefore extend their autonomy. In many ways, "organizing" was simply interwoven into day-to-day life.

While staying in a coastal town in El Salvador, I was scouting the beach for surfing waves. A local pointed over to a spot farther down the beach, saying that the waves were better over there. I went to check it out, down a tree lined path. On my way back, the same man met me in the path; he had a broken bottle and told me to give him my money. I stalled a bit, telling him to chill out, and two other men came out of the trees. I didn't see any other way out of the situation so I gave him my money and watch. I had about $30 dollars and a cheap sports watch. A woman came out of her house because she had heard them yelling. I told her what happened and she scolded them. I went back to my hotel room and cried. I felt completely powerless. It was a feeling that was so awful I didn't think anyone should have to feel it. I called my mom and she suggested that I go to the police, she thought it would be good for me to contact some agency in the situation. I thought that at least going to the police could help stop this from happening to anyone else—and in that moment how I was feeling was the most important thing. Despite Monica's objections I went to the police station and told them what happened; they didn't seem to care much but told me they would tell me if they found the money.

Once I recovered emotionally, I began feeling immensely guilty about going to the cops; how could I have justified calling the police on a petty criminal when I ostensibly was in solidarity with the poor, against the state and its violent arm—the police? I was most likely dreadfully rich compared to my mugger, not to mention my American citizenship and white skin; wasn't this simply class war in action? And I had gone to the state, that protector of hierarchy, asking them to defend my money and privilege.

I also began to question notions I had had about whether violence in the name of justice was warranted. I could think of no cause that would justify how I had felt under the threat of imminent physical violence. I supposed that it would be worth it if it was stopping worse feelings or actual violence against another, but if there were other ways, those would be much preferable.

This experience taught me that ideology does nothing in the face of strong emotion—that if I truly want to be an ally to the poor, for example, that must come from as much of an emotional place as an analytical one. To this day, this experience reminds me how difficult it is to truly work against the forces that give you privilege, whatever those may be.

We got as far as Costa Rica and then headed back. While

the legendary PPP resisters remained elusive, we had a great time camping, staying in the red light districts of different cities, meeting some very interesting and kind people and just enjoying each other's company. We traveled in the U.S. a bit before realizing that we had had enough travel for a while and were ready to stay in one place for a bit. Monica wanted to go back to Minneapolis. My criterion was simply somewhere new, so we both went back to Minneapolis, where we remain to this day.

Garrett Fitzgerald

I developed the most politically based on the ideas that came out of my coffee shop discussions with friends. Mostly we talked about how repressive the environment felt around us, about being herded through the educational system, not feeling challenged intellectually but still forced in the institution's rigid bounds. On top of that, students, who should be allies, displaced their frustrations on each other. It was a stressful and intense time—feeling like everything was awful, but not having anything outside of the context of youth to compare it to or any tools to change it. I also felt the desire to make something tolerably better that brought some of us to start our own anti-racist group. We called it United For Equality Mankato (UFE).

My experience growing up in Mankato was very white. People of color were well-hidden from my reality. At the time I entered high school, I could count the people of color who I was acquainted with on my fingers. It was a little different across town, where there was an influx of Somali immigrants, but for the most part, the culture of Mankato that I knew was white to the bone. My experience was so white and normative that I had no idea where to begin in being an anti-racist ally.

I remember we had a lot of early conversations in which we talked about ourselves and the work we wanted to do. During one conversation in particular, I remember us talking about the Minneapolis Anti-Racist Action (ARA). I didn't know anything about ARA at this time but the analysis that was imparted to me was something like: "The ARA is an activist organization because they are actively, aggressively confronting racism using physical force when necessary, and we can be either an activist organization or a pacifist organization." I now see this analysis as glib, but at the time I trusted it and it caused me a bit of heartache and confusion.

My mother had always considered herself a pacifist and so, in these matters, what she taught me was my default. Through this overly simplistic analysis, I couldn't both be a pacifist and be active in confronting racism as I understood it. Ultimately, I didn't feel prepared for fighting Nazis in the street and so decided I wanted the group to be a pacifist organization. In the context of how it was presented, the choice was disempowering, but it was honest about where I was at.

I later dismissed the overly simplified ideas that I was fed and my analysis became more thoughtful, open, and sophisticated.

Those of us who were involved grew collectively in our understanding of the world around us and our part in it. UFE was less of a springboard for action and more of an agent for our scholarly growth and what would become great practice for working in small non-hierarchical groups in the future. Ultimately, UFE ended up being more for the kids who were involved than it was for our community or communities of color.

Right around this time, there was also an effort by some folks at my high school to form a "Gay Straight Alliance" (GSA). Some of the members of the GLBT (their self-identification) community around the university were helping out. I went to a few meetings and helped pass out rainbow ribbons to show solidarity for "National Coming Out Day." Homophobia was more overt in Mankato and it probably would have been easier for me to find productive work to do through GSA. However, working as part of a student group was less accepted from my peers in the punk scene and this made it challenging for me. The group was short-lived and didn't continue into the next semester.

When I turned sixteen, I got a job at a local grocery and general store. After school (when my schedule permitted) and on weekends, I would go stock shelves and the like. It was boring and mind-numbing at times, but I kept at it. I worked off and on at this store until the winter of my senior year when the roof caved in under the weight of a wet winter snow. The store was going to have to throw away all its stock. That knowledge, combined with bored teenagers and the fact that a building without a roof is pretty easy to get into, meant that kids started coming to class with backpacks full of candy and other salvaged goodies.

Also in my junior year, I talked to the principal, the drama advisers, and the faculty who normally directed the school's theater productions and received permission to add a third play to the schedule that another student and I would organize, direct, and produce. This was the first time in years (as far as I knew) that students had directed a full-length production. We had six weeks. During the last week and a half, we spent eight to ten hours a day after school putting things together. We had no budget, but we had a space and could use the props and scenery that the school had for stock. Because we had no budget and were providing our own labor, we had to get creative. We used old prom decorations and dug through old sets so dusty and deep in storage that I'm sure they hadn't been used in a decade. We couldn't find a faculty member who was able to give enough time for us to get space at school for our rehearsals, so we found space around town or would secretly prop open doors at school so we could sneak in at night or over the weekend to get more work done.

Considering where I was in my artistic development and the tools at my disposal, the play was a success. It taught me a lot about organizing from the ground up with nothing. I learned how to beg, borrow, and bend the systems to scrape together the bare minimum to accomplish something meaningful. Also, I learned about how, where, and when to compromise or do without.

In my junior year, I fell in love with a girl who lived on the other side of town. We hung out in the same circles, knew each other from around, and eventually became closer friends. She, a mutual friend, and I would spend a lot of time together walking around parks or train tracks, or driving out into the country, or climbing up on rooftops to look at the stars. I think we all felt helpless in our lives and so would dream of other ways of living that involved breaking away from our current situations. We wanted to disappear and ride freight trains to cities where no one would know who we were and we could start over and be whoever we wanted.

It became a complicated, unrequited love triangle. The ins and outs are not of particular significance, but there are a lot of ways that the time we spent together was formative. Some things that happened at the time helped later in life to reveal patterns of patriarchal socialization that shaped my self-reflection and larger analysis.

I didn't realize it at the time, but I was missed by my other friends during the few months that this went on. I was so absorbed in spending time interacting with this person that it became the whole of my social life. My pursuit of this person also played itself out in a very hetero-normative fashion. I had watched too many John Cusack films in which the boy pursues the uninterested girl until he convinces her how great he is, she finally gives in, and they fall in love. Men are traditionally the protagonists and active agents in these stories, which gives the impression that the world is there for us and that we will get whatever we want if we want it bad enough.

I made this same mistake a year later in the summer after my senior year. I fell for a woman, Pam, and obsessed over it for almost a year. Pam would become a really important part of my life in the future. I spent most of my free time with her and, when we were apart, most of my thoughts were of her. While these were difficult times for me and left me with a lot of baggage around rejection and self-worth, it was mostly the fault of myself and my socialization. My actions didn't just hurt me. My behavior became persistent and, while genuine, manifested in very manipulative ways. I know that, while I am still friends with these past loves, I hurt them and reinforced the negative socialization that views and values women primarily in their utility toward men as objects of love/lust without regard for what they independently accomplish or who they are. This was a hard lesson to learn.

During my senior year of high school, I was expected to begin working at and making choices about my future. I was taking a few advanced classes, namely advanced placement calculus and physics. These classes were more challenging, but most of the difficulty came from lack of time or academic exhaustion. I was taking a full load of mostly upper level and AP classes, I was working on the theater productions, playing in the punk band, applying for colleges and scholarships, and prepping for the ACT test.

As I had always been good at math and related sciences, I thought a lot about going to school for some sort of engineering degree. I even went to an engineering camp my senior year to see what kinds of engineering degrees there were and what the various fields were like. My other option was going into theater and studying acting or a related field. I was okay at theater without much training. Since sixth grade when I was performing as a magician, I had been interested in storytelling, entertaining, and being the center of attention. I knew that it would be a lot of work and that I would probably never make much money at it, but I decided I was up to it–that I would rather try to do what I love than play it safe and always be wondering "what if?"

I hadn't totally made up my mind as to which direction I would pursue as I was applying for different colleges and universities. I shot big with the NYU Tish School, Julliard, and University of Southern California. My backup was UW-Madison. It was cheap (relative to other universities) because of the tuition reciprocity agreement between Minnesota and Wisconsin.

I had spent the bulk of my academic life up to this point making myself look good on paper so I could get into the school I wanted. That got me through the first round with all the schools. For Julliard and NYU's Tish, I passed the written application and was invited to come to an audition. The auditioning faculty for both schools were touring to a few major cities. I got my parents to drive me down to Chicago from Mankato for the auditions. This is the first time I remember being in Chicago.

There were maybe twenty people at each of the auditions

I went to. All of the other kids were from arts high schools and theater magnet schools. I had prepared the required two monologues from other projects I had done in high school drama club, and had gone twice after school to get feedback from a drama teacher. The only training I had was the experience in my small-city, after-school theater productions. The kids I was auditioning against had full-on acting curriculum and year-long classes in which all they did was prepare their monologues for these auditions. I was totally out of my league. Still, these auditions were so competitive that, in both auditions, only two of the forty people got called back for a second audition. Just to be there was worth something. Looking back, however, I'm pretty disgusted by the culture of it. I wish I had known better at the time so that, even if I had made the same choices about continuing with theater, I wouldn't have judged myself by their standards. That closed the door on those schools.

I was accepted into USC after writing an entrance essay on how watching the X-Men cartoon on Saturday mornings as a child taught me about tolerance for diversity. (I later learned that some fans of the X-Men comic theorize that the dialogue between two characters, Magneto and Professor Xavier, was based on the rhetoric of Martin Luther King, Jr. and Malcolm X.) I was also given an $8,000 scholarship, but unfortunately the tuition for one semester was $35,000. There was no way I could afford the difference. So I fell back and got excited about going off to Madison in the fall.

At some point in this last year of high school, I first started thinking about anarchism as a serious theory for building a more humane and compassionate world. On one hand, I had my most politically and socially minded friends who, if not explicit anarchists, fronted anarchistic ideas (as sophomoric as they may have been in their development at the time). On the other hand, I had my mother, whom I respected as wise and intelligent and who had a lot of criticisms of anarchism (as normative as they may have been in their development). I would debate at the coffee shop and at home, both with fervor. I would play both sides of the conversation:
"If we didn't have a government, someone horrible but dynamic

like Hitler would just swoop in and take power."

"But Hitler was democratically elected, and, either way, people who want to dominate others gravitate toward positions of power and with the state in place they have an easy path and means with the whole military (and paramilitary) apparatus and judicial system in place to maintain their order. At least without a state apparatus, we would have a fighting chance."

"A fighting chance! You mean you want violence in the streets? You want death all around you? Look at all these turbulent parts of the world. Would you rather be there? At least here and now you're safe."

"Maybe I'm 'safe' the way the trustee in the prison yard is 'safe' from the other inmates. The constant threat of force is violence, and besides, we might not see it in our white-washed hamlet, but less-privileged people in this country and folks in countries all over the world are faced with very direct, real, and deadly violence on a regular basis to help keep us 'safe' and over-privileged."

"But people are going to fight. War is inevitable. Wouldn't you rather have an army and a government to help protect you? Otherwise people are just going to take everything from you and kill you."

At this point, I mostly still understood anarchism through state-friendly propaganda: the barely present and always sensational high school text book paragraphs and corporate media. I thought to be an anarchist you had to be into property destruction (which at this point I wasn't) and that you couldn't be a pacifist (which at this point I considered myself).

While I now believe that you can be an anarchist-pacifist who isn't interested in property destruction, I probably wouldn't have realized that if I hadn't first decided that I was going to make anarchism a more present theory in my life. And, I wouldn't have decided to make anarchism a more present theory in my life if I hadn't gotten over my hang-ups concerning the title of pacifism and tactical sabotage.

While most of my theory came slowly over time, I clung with such fundamentalism to the issue of property damage that I can still remember the moment where I was convinced that, yes, it is possible to imagine an instance when property damage could be justified.

I was with some friends in my parents' basement and one of them had just gotten a VHS tape in the mail. It had two documentaries on it, "Pick Axe" and "Breaking the Spell." There was footage of, among many other things, folks breaking windows and wheeling around dumpsters. I was a bit uncomfortable and really felt like the most conservative person in the room. There was a woman being interviewed on the street. Asked about the property destruction, she exhibited displeasure. Then the interviewer asked her what she thought of the Boston Tea Party. "It was great," she replied. I lived that moment with her from my parents' basement. The Boston Tea Party was a non-state-sanctioned act of property destruction (felony level, I might add) that, in my upbringing, even the most normative folk saw as an amazing and justified demonstration of citizens' dissent to their "rulers." To this day, I cite the Boston Tea Party to anyone who holds maintaining property rights as fundamental.

I graduated from high school in the top ten percent of my class and as a member of the National Honor Society (NHS)—all part of my "looking good on paper so I can have a good future" outlook. While I was still playing the game of being a good student, I had enough friends who were smart but underachievers by their own apathy. I interpreted any status that I was given for my academic positioning as bullshit. I remember being disgusted with myself for wearing the gold chord that all the honor students were given to recognize their "achievement."

Having been to jail and to court, I can say that the public educational system is still right up there as one of the most oppressive systems I have had to negotiate in my life. I took a lot of shit from peers in my youth, I believe more than most. However, that doesn't mean I was nothing but a victim. I both often took sides with the institution over my peers and, when I felt attacked, used my privilege to gain status and even dominate in unhealthy and unproductive ways. It's not the worst of what went on within those walls, but it's one of the roles, one of the parts I played.

A lot of things were forced to an end over that summer.

I helped friends pack their things to move out of town. My band played its final shows. I prepared to move to Madison. I decided that when I moved to Madison, I would begin a vegan diet and had a final chicken sandwich at a fast-food restaurant with my parents.

Academics were not a noteworthy part of my first year of college. It was formative in a typical way, being away from home and dealing with new people in a new place. I remember the first day after I moved in, I was exploring the area on skateboard. I was skateboarding down a big hill when the board started to wobble and I fell off. I stood up a little shaken, my shirt and pants torn and a baseball-sized bloody sore on my leg. I hobbled back to the dorm, rinsed it out with soap and water and duct-taped a wad of tissue to the sore. My mother would not have approved.

First-year students were expected to live in the dorms and I was roommates with a friend and former band mate from Mankato. I have found that I am often most critical and judgmental of people in whom I see the things I don't like about myself. My first year of college in the dorms, I was surrounded by privileged youth. I obviously shared many of the privileges and resented them for that reflection. I had a hard time making friends and for a long time mostly just hung out with my roommate. Just as I had been in a hurry to get through high school, I was in a hurry to get through college. I took overloaded course loads every semester while working in the dining hall and being involved in the theater.

For the first few months, I was still completely preoccupied emotionally with my friend, Pam, whom I had spent the summer with and who had moved to Minneapolis to go to school at the U of M. I really didn't want to be in college and spent a good chunk of my free time riding my skateboard as far away from the college as I could, or riding a city bus to its last stop and trying to walk and skate my way home. Getting away from the campus let me pretend that I wasn't a student, that I wasn't one of those privileged youths.

Sometimes, I would skate with my roommate to a sandwich shop called Radical Rye that was owned by a person who accidentally killed someone in a bombing of a military science building on the university to "bring home" the Vietnam War. They had a poster of Che Guevara and pretty good vegan chili.

A few weeks into that first season away, my roommate woke me up to tell me that planes had flown into the World Trade Center buildings in New York City. I didn't believe him until I saw it for myself. It's a complicated event and I didn't feel one way or another about it right away, although I felt like the news coverage was outrageous. I immediately criticized the reactionary way grief was harnessed and turned to nationalism. I think this should be an important lesson to every anarchist. In times of general crisis, people without experience at self-governing will flock to fascism rather than to autonomy or liberation.

I did start making a few friends, but it was a slow process for me. Most notable was the "girl with the biggest smile." I could feel the free spirit inside her and she loved my impression of a baby being born. She had been turned on to old-school hip hop by her boyfriend and shared her new love with me. We would listen to Diggable Planets, study together, and walk up and down State Street. She was also a great support with my social and emotional struggles, and I like to think I provided her with the same.

I made a 'zine a few years later in which I recalled a time we climbed up on the roof of a campus building to watch a meteor shower. We accidentally set off a silent alarm and security showed up. Narrowly, we talked our way out of an expensive ticket.

The girl with the biggest smile introduced me to her friends and neighbors in her dorm, and I would listen as she played me songs on the guitar. As of this writing, I haven't seen her in about six years, and I heard she just had her first baby. I wonder if the birth was anything like my impression.

Pam had given me a copy of a 'zine titled "Evasion" that I read in those first weeks at college. The 'zine chronicles the various adventures of a young man who, committed to being homeless and jobless, travels around the country on freight trains and by hitchhiking, getting his food out of dumpsters. This mirrored to me a lot of the dreams I had in the years before my high school graduation, staring at the stars and fantasizing about the life I could lead. The format of the 'zine made it feel like it had been made by a peer–someone like me, reaching out. It made all the things written of inside attainable to me.

I started "dumpster diving" for my food and experimented with seeing how little I could spend on food each day in order to contribute as little as possible to capitalism as I understood it. Before the winter hit, I planned my first hitchhiking trip from Madison to Minneapolis to visit Pam and other friends who had moved there from Mankato. It was my effort to have the best of both worlds, on track for a college education and normative success, while also trying to feel the freedom of a drop-out. I liked the feeling of challenging myself to see how far I could go without falling back on my privilege. What if I got sick, or hurt, or arrested? Could I get through it on my own? I was hoping to prove that I could reach those limits alone and make it through.

That's really what a lot of it came down to–proving myself, mostly to myself. I like to think I have moved past the need to prove myself in that way. It is important for me now that I face and always consider my privilege instead of trying to hide from it. This is the only way I have found to achieve an integrated sense of self. Still, riding trains and living on the edge of the road strikes a romantic chord in my heart. The responsible thing is not to mistake the romance and challenge for socio-political struggle.

So one Friday after class, I grabbed a map, packed a bag, and took the city bus to the furthest east-west on the interstate. I wasn't quite sure how long it would take. The way I figured it, if I turned around halfway through the weekend, I would make it back in time. The first few rides took less time to get than I would have imagined, but it wasn't always that way. I ended up getting dropped off in Eau Claire, Wisconsin as the sun was setting. I stood on the on ramp until the sky was dark. I gave up and went to explore Eau Claire. I didn't want to wander too far from the interstate, so I stayed in a sort of "every town," strip mall area. It was still early in the evening, so I went to a book store and read in a big chair until the store closed. I ended up skateboarding around until I couldn't stay awake anymore. I hid my bag and went to a hotel. I walked in like I belonged there and went straight up the stairs to the top floor. There was a big chair in the hallway where I sat and slept.

When I woke up, the sun was just coming up. I went back out to the on ramp and got picked up within an hour by a person who was headed straight to the neighborhood in Minneapolis where my friends were living. He told me how he had been out working the apple harvest and was traveling to the Seward Café in Minneapolis because they had the best vegan biscuits and gravy anywhere. He talked about his trips hitchhiking and other ways he had found to travel for free.

I got to the café, made phone calls, and got a cup of coffee. It was still early and I hadn't gotten enough sleep, so I napped in one of the booths. Pam showed up and brought some of the people she had met in Minneapolis with her. Being so socially inept myself, I was impressed with all the friends she had already made at college. While I was spending my time feeling socially isolated and distancing myself from the people around me, she had built a ring of friendships with folks she had gleaned from the campus population. I don't know if I intellectualized it that way at the time, but I do remember feeling happy for her and wishing I had relationships like that back in Madison.

I only stayed a few hours; Saturday afternoon was the midpoint of my weekend, so I turned around and headed back. After my overnight stay on the way out, I assumed I would be crashing out somewhere along the way back. I got lucky, however, and got back that night. My first ride took me to just outside of Minneapolis. It was with a crazy-talking, late-middle-aged man who couldn't drive and so went thirty down the interstate with his hazards on. He was smoking a cigar the whole time we were in the car and told me he would take me to Madison for twenty bucks. I politely declined.

After that, I was picked up by a trucker going all the way through Madison. He played Christian rock tapes and spoke some of the lines to make sure I heard them. I ate some Jolly Ranchers that I had brought along to suck on when I was worried I might fall asleep. I made it back to Madison and was back at my dorm by three o'clock on Sunday morning. I spent the rest of my Sunday sleeping and walking around Madison wishing for another adventure.

When I first moved into the dorm, I got a job at the campus food service. Student jobs and work-study jobs are a bit of a joke. It seems that inefficiencies exist in the institution for the sake of creating employment. I cooked, closed, cleaned, served, worked the register, and was a barista at a little café in the basement of the food service complex. With the work always changing, I rarely had the same supervisor and didn't really get to know any of my co-workers. This made it easier to care even less about the institution and, therefore, easier to take advantage of it. I would sneak bagels or fruit home in my pockets and snack while I was working. This helped with my efforts to eat for as little money as possible.

As I was getting over my awkward attempted romantic episode with Pam, the girl with the biggest smile had just broken up with her boyfriend. We talked on the phone one night about all the things we both were feeling and wishing we had a way to forget them. Just like that, I departed from a major socialized Christian hang-up and began exploring alternatives to traditional monogamous relationships. We were helping each other feel better by fulfilling compatible needs. It was smelly and clumsy and awkward. It was also fantastic and beautiful.

Throughout the year, I was taking a few introductory theater classes and was in a student production of The Rocky Horror Show. I helped build the set for a production of The Tempest and worked back stage for another production or two. During one of the work sessions, the topic turned to September Eleventh. One of the women working with me said something to the effect of, "I don't fucking care about those people. I'm an anarchist." While my relationship to anarchism was not yet fully established, this was the first time I felt personally taken aback by a blanket assertion that I didn't agree with being made about anarchism. I believed then, and I still do, that you can both be an anarchist and care about people. In fact, I think most anarchists I know, who are worth their salt and who really stick to their guns (so to speak), do so out of a deep feeling of care for others. This moment is important because I was deciding what I thought anarchism was about.

My feet became more and more itchy for travel, and the more I scratched, the itchier they became. I went on a few more hitchhiking adventures that year, one of which was down to Chicago to see one of my favorite bands at the time, The Faint. I had spent my last dollar at a show on a Friday night but I had a paycheck in my pocket. I hoped to hitch down to Chicago, get it cashed, and make it to the show. I had twelve hours to make it, which should have been enough time, but just as I got out to the on ramp, it started raining. I hoped that seeing me standing out in the rain would encourage people to stop and pick me up. Not so. No one wants a wet stranger dripping a stinky puddle on their upholstery. I didn't get to Chicago until past seven o'clock, all of the check-cashing places were closed, and I was dropped off on the other side of the city from where I needed to be.

All I had was my skateboard and determination. I asked some folks for directions and they told me it was too far for me to skateboard. They plugged the fare for me to get on a bus headed the right direction. I asked the bus driver to let me know when I should get off, and rode the bus for a while. When it was just me and one other person, the bus driver told me that this was my stop. I asked him for directions to the venue but the other person behind me interrupted. He was the head of booking at the venue and would walk there with me if I hurried. We briskly walked and made small talk. I told him how I had planned to cash my paycheck to get a ticket but missed closing time and asked if he had any ideas for me. He told me that he had some extra passes into the VIP section and would give me one. He also told me to find him after the show because he might know a good place for me to stay the night.

The VIP section was in the balcony and was full of reporters and people wearing ties. Not only was I the only one soaked through from being in the rain all day, I was the only one rocking out. I was able to get over my inhibitions and really enjoy the show as part of this amazing journey I was on. After the show, I met up with the man who had helped me and he introduced me to some friends of his who owned a large space in Chicago where I could crash for the night. First, however, they were going to a party at a friend's apartment. I tagged along, still damp and way under-dressed for their crowd. I was still committed to living sober and wasn't drinking or using drugs but was happy to be out of the rain and have a place to crash lined up. At the party, I was able to mingle, playing a novelty role as the token dirt ball. People asked me about my trip and I tried to make the stories entertaining enough to warrant my presence.

I had gotten up early for the trip and was getting pretty exhausted. When folks were ready to leave the party, I was glad to. They took me back to their place. I just lay down on the floor and fell asleep, unable to be uncomfortable because I was so tired. One of the housemates woke me up in the morning and told me that when I was ready, he had decided that he would take me back to Madison. He hadn't been there in a while and had some friends he would like to visit. I was grateful to have the ride. It was easy and comfortable. I bought him lunch when we got to Madison. He left to go see his friend and I hurried to finish up my schoolwork for Monday. I saw some of that group of friends a few months later when I went to Milwaukee to see the same band. I'm grateful for their generosity.

I was auditioning for a lot of the university's theater projects, but with little success. At some point, I was talking to a graduate student about being from Mankato and what I wanted to do and he asked me why I hadn't gone to the University of Minnesota. He said that their theater department was much better and had more opportunity. I thought about my reasons for coming to Madison instead of the U of M and they all seemed silly when so many people seemed to think the U of M theater program was so much better. By this time, I had probably made as much progress socially in that year as most people make in a week. I had a few friends, my roommate and I had started a band with some kids in our dorm, and I had been invited to move into one of the nearby housing co-ops the next fall. But, my transfer was accepted and I decided to go to the U of M the next year.

I had spent a lot of my time at the university reading about riding trains and was looking forward to trying it out over the summer. I was planning on catching one out of Minneapolis and heading west to Seattle. My aunt lived there at the time, so it seemed like a good destination. This year was also the year of the G8 in Calgary, Canada, and I was hoping to find a way to get there for the protests that were sure to take place.

I didn't have a personal relationship with anyone who had ridden trains, so I headed up to Minneapolis planning to figure it out on my own. I stayed a few nights with some friends in Minneapolis, sharing my plans. Upon hearing that I was planning on going by myself and that I was headed west, a friend of mine informed me that there were some kids in town who were going to ride to Portland, Oregon in the next few days and offered to introduce me.

We went to a birthday party that night and I met the three folks who were headed west. One of them had ridden one train before and the other two had not. Not a lot of collective experience, but the idea of being with a few other people made me feel safer, and maybe the little knowledge we had could take us further together. It came in handy right away, picking a good place to catch from, being able to spot a good place to ride quickly, and being able to get there fast and discreetly.

There's a feeling of a lack of security when riding trains. The trains and the machinery, while able to cause great harm, aren't the reason for this feeling. I felt insecure because no one is looking out for you, but people are looking for you. Rail security is hunting for you and, if they find you, it's just you and you have little recourse. I have done more risky and stupid things on trains to avoid security than I would ever imagine doing otherwise. It makes my guts twist.

It's amazing how quickly you can get to know someone when you are stuck together in a space the size of a walk-in closet. We talked about all sorts of things and ate lots of fun snacks and treats. Two of my fellow travelers were also trans folk. This was my first time really getting to spend time with people who were strongly and actively empowering themselves in their position outside the assigned gender binary. All of my new friends were kind and generous.

In this world, where you are almost always surrounded by civilization and its institutions working to maintain their particular order, riding freight trains is one sort of moment when you get as close to freedom as I imagine possible. There is freedom in being in motion–when each moment you are in a new place, leaving behind the old and able to be whomever. More so, you are hidden away from civilization and, from the perspective of a stow-away, signs of civilization are enemies to your will. I imagine it may be a similar feeling to living off the grid in the desert or Arctic. I have never been in a black bloc, but I've heard people describe it similarly. The chains around our wrists become so visible and so heavy that all our energy must go into breaking them or slipping out.

In a particularly beautiful moment, we were rolling near Glacier National Park at about ten miles per hour. There was snow on the ground, our breath was steamy in the frosty air, but the sun was warm. Right next to the track was a brown bear, close enough for us to touch (had we dared). We looked each other in the eyes, not with hostility or deference but simple acknowledgment as two beings crossing paths.

We spent three nights and two days without getting off that train and wound up in Seattle early in the morning. The sky was just getting light as we hopped off. In Seattle, we went to the Pike Place Market, got some coffee, and used the bathroom sink to clean ourselves up. We said our goodbyes and went our separate ways; they down to Portland and I to my aunt's.

Exploring a new city for me always involved a lot of walking with an eye out for interesting places to sit for free or cheap. Seattle's waterfront, especially the Pike Place Market, with its park benches with a view and its ample produce dumpsters, made a great place to people watch for an afternoon. I fixed up an old bike at my aunt's and used that to get around. I rode downtown and around my aunt's neighborhood. I tried to help run errands and get groceries for dinner for when she got home.

We also borrowed a car one weekend for a drive through the mountains. It was a great way to spend some time together.

I stayed for about a week and a half before my feet started to itch for the road. My next destination was Calgary, but I still had a while to get there. I decided to give myself a few days. I would hitchhike heading as far south as I could until I felt I should stop, hang out for a while, turn around, and head back north.

It took half a day to get out of Seattle. I finally got picked up by a woman who said she had a son just my age. The way she figured, he did some of these same things, so she better pick me up hoping that someone would pick up her son too. As the sun went down, I was stuck in a Portland suburb. I hadn't gone as many centimeters on my map as I would have hoped. The next day, I took a morning bus, backtracking into Portland, hoping the change of scenery would lend me better luck. I went to the highway and got a ride, which ended up dropping me off at the exact same on-ramp where I had spent the night! I had to believe in some sort of fate to keep from going crazy. I finally got picked up and kept on my way.

The last ride of the day was a man in a large conversion van. It was like an apartment inside, including a kitchen and a shower. We drove for a bit and he asked if we could stop in on some friends of his just off the highway. I always get frustrated when folks want to veer of course, but I'm from Minnesota so I'm not good at disagreeing, especially when I'm getting a free ride.

We pulled off into a run-down residential area. We went to his friend's house and hung out for a few hours talking about nothing in particular. The driver's friend offered him a beer. The driver turned to me and asked me if I minded driving. Again, being Minnesotan, I lied and told him I didn't mind at all. So he downed a few beers and I got the keys. I appreciate his knowing his own limits.

I had been looking at maps all trip and decided that, with how long it had taken me to get this far, I had better stop soon. I decided to make Eugene my final destination.

I had heard of Eugene from the Seattle WTO aftermath. I also knew that these reports overstated the role of the "Eugene Anarchists" (likely to make the protesters in Seattle look more like outsiders). It reminded me of Madison–people said it was a liberal town but my experience was less that people had leftist politics and more that they smoked a lot of dope. Likewise, in Eugene, I didn't see any rallies or wheat-pasted propaganda, but I did get offered acid about ten times in the first half hour.

On one of the main roads in Eugene, there was an old home-bum flying a sign for spare change. I went up and started chatting with him. I was hoping he could turn me on to a good place to hang out or spend the night, as well as things I should make sure I saw while I was in Eugene. While we were chatting, another person about my age approached and joined our conversation. He introduced himself as 'Bama on account of his being from Alabama.

'Bama was a bit of an adventurer. Unlike most of our contemporaries, when he got to a new town, he would get a hotel room and look for work, keeping some of the money and sending the bulk of it back to his mother. He wasn't working in Eugene and wasn't sure where he was going to go next. I told him about my trip out to Seattle and my plans to go to Calgary for the G8. He was interested both in checking out the G8 and in trying out riding trains. He had been watching the tracks in Eugene, but didn't really know how to start. We made a deal. He would let me crash on the floor of his hotel room; then I would use my limited train knowledge to get us on something headed back north. We would try to make it to the G8 together.

So that was what we did. I stashed my stuff in his room and we rolled around Eugene together getting food, sneaking around, and exploring. We got up early the next morning and headed to the tracks. Some locals advised us that we had a few hours to wait before anything headed north, but that's not all that long in train time.

We rode through a beautiful sunny Oregon day on our slow-moving train. It was great to be on a train again and 'Bama loved it. We hid inside when we went through highly populated areas, but mostly we chilled out in the sun, chatting and patching holes in our bags. Just around dusk, we started to roll into a yard. The train stopped and we waited and waited. We spent a few hours waiting for the train to go again before we finally got sick of it and jumped off. First we got out of the yard, but then we walked down the road to the "front" of our train. Sure enough, the unit had been removed. It was a lot of fun taking the train, but we were only as far north as Portland. After walking a bit, we found a good place to crash for the night.

In the morning, we got on the bus and headed to a place we had heard was good for catching northbound trains. It's always slow going traveling this way and so time passes much slower. Each day feels long and jammed packed full of activity even though you hardly do anything. We talked a lot about where we were going and formulated plans knowing that they would change at the next fork in the road.

There is a lot of waiting involved in catching a train. It's hard to remember if it took ten hours or two. I'm always anxious, but exercising patience. Eventually, we hopped on a ride that was clearly heading north across the river. Our well-laid plans and best guesses missed the target, however, because the train crossed the river and then made a hard right to head east along the river.

It was a hot and sunny summer afternoon and we ceded control over our situation for the time being to the tons of metal we sat upon. We passed quickly into the rain shadow of the Cascade Mountain Range, which combs the coastal moisture from the clouds and leaves the other side dusty and dry. We took off our shirts, put on sun screen, sat on the floor of an empty forty-eight (the name often used to denote a forty-eight-foot car designed for holding shipping crates stacked two high), and alternated talking, reading, writing, and always drinking as much water as we could get down.

The first time the train stopped for a crew change was in the small town of Wishram, Washington, in the foothills of the Cascade Range. We hopped off the train just outside of town and walked down the tracks with the train and the river to our right and high, steep cliffs to our left. Everything was dusty and dry. Near town, there were water trucks spraying the ground to keep the dust down. You could watch the dark wetness recede as it evaporated, leaving the dirt pale once again.

The moment we reached what seemed to be the town

proper—a bar, a church, some small homes and trailers, and a small train yard—we found a water spout and refilled our supply. We changed out of our long underwear and put on slightly cleaner shirts.

On this day in Wishram, there was an annual community event held in a field between the bar and the train yard. There were folding tables around the perimeter with folks selling hot dogs and popcorn. We joined the crowd to chat with some of the folks, including a woman we had seen working on the train we had just left. She said the train was headed a little further east and then cut south down into California and back around and up to Portland in a big loop. The event was just finishing up, and to avoid having to take their things home, people offered us as much popcorn and watermelon as we wanted, which was as much as we could carry.

After mingling and chatting with the strangers, we decided that we would head back out of town to the west and find a place to camp out for the night. Just out of sight of the town, we set our bags in an open area between the tracks and the cliffs. The last few moments of sunlight were taken full advantage of by diving into the Columbia River. It was toe-numbingly cold and felt even colder compared to the hot, dry air. Climbing out, I dried quickly and rolled my sleeping bag out on the dirt to lie and watch the light fade from the sky.

The night brought its own spectacular moments. Without the lights of the city or even a hint of cloud cover, the stars were about as bright as they get. Between us and the stars were huge numbers of bats that came out with the moon. We lay on our backs with watermelon juice dripping down from the corners of our mouths. Each time I ate a hand full of popcorn, I would throw a few kernels into the air. The bats, mistaking the popcorn for bugs, would dive low over our heads. I hated to close my eyes but eventually fell asleep, waking only when trains slowly rolled past.

In the morning, we decided to hitchhike back to Seattle. Toward the end of the day, we got picked up by a man driving with his two young sons. We sat in front with him, and his sons squeezed into the little seats in the back of the cab. He mixed himself a screwdriver in a large gas station fountain drink cup. I generally think that picking up hitchhikers is safer than popular culture wants us to believe, but picking up a pair of men while drinking and driving with your kids in the back seems like a lot of high-risk variables. I was grateful for the ride and glad to make it back to Seattle before sun down.

With a brief "Hello, I'm fine" to my aunt, we spent the night. The next morning, we hitched to a small city north of Seattle where we thought it would be easier to catch a train to the border. We were busted by yard security within the first hour of reaching the yard and again hit the highway.

The next day I learned that Canadian border patrol is not big into letting dirty, crusty, poor-looking travelers into their country. They also don't like when you walk up to their little building instead of being in a car. Because allowing non-Canadian citizens into Canada is largely at the discretion of the border patrol, they gave us a hard time, searched our things, and asked a lot of questions before turning us around and giving us all sorts of things we had to prove before they would let us across.

We spent the night in the border town of Blaine, WA making arrangements. We bought bus tickets and printed out ATM receipts that showed our account balances. We couldn't afford a hotel room reservation, but we found a hotel in Vancouver, BC to "plan" to stay at while there. The next day, we were back at the border station and the border patrol wasn't any happier to see us this time. The whole bus had to wait while we got our "special" treatment. We were searched and taken through all the questions again. They finally let us through, but our stay was conditional. They gave us a piece of paper saying that we had to return to the border patrol on our way out in a week or less. If we failed to do so, a warrant would be issued for our arrest. The G8, the reason we were going to Canada, was in two weeks. This presented a problem for us, but we would deal with that later. For now, we were in Canada and that was what mattered.

We got off the bus in Vancouver, picked a direction, and started walking around to see the city. While the folks working the border were mean-spirited, rude, and authoritarian, the demeanor of everyone else we met in Canada seemed generous and kind. We found a park full of people and approached some folks who looked equally road weary. It turned out they were from the U.S. Northwest and were also planning on heading to Calgary for the G8. We decided that the four of us would head to a yard that night and try to catch east together.

It's nice to have a second person to travel with for company. With four people, as long as you are getting along, you are rolling with a crew and you feel safer even if it sometimes means moving slower. We got lucky and got out of Vancouver that night. The mountains were cold. Everything was colder than when I had first come west. It took one day and two nights, and we hopped off the train in Calgary at around five in the morning.

The next few days were spent exploring Calgary. We found a park that, although it was closed at night, had good hiding places to sleep in. We woke up in the mornings and built big fires to cook on and make coffee.

One day while walking around town, I ran into two friends of friends from Minneapolis who had also come out early for the G8. They joined us at the park along with some locals we had met. Now, every night was a mini-party as we drank coffee and munched on dumpstered bananas.

After a few days, 'Bama and I knew that we had to figure out what we were going to do about the travel restrictions hanging over our heads from the border. We hitchhiked down to the border hoping to get it figured out and then hitch back. At the border, the Canadian patrol told us that we had to cross back into the U.S. and then we could try to re-enter. It didn't play out this way, however. This time, both sides of the border gave us grief. They lied to us, saying that we had been fingerprinted in other states. They brought in dogs and searched through all our things. They were generally gruff and rude until they caught us exchanging the legal number for the protests. They asked what the number was for and I told them it was for our lawyer. This quickly made them a lot more polite.

We tried crossing several times. On the Montana side of the border, there was a little village that was basically for truckers who crossed there and for the people who worked on the border. There was a cute, old-time-looking hotel/bar/diner in one building. It was the highlight of the day.

At the border, we were again given a list of things we had to prove before they would let us across. There was a friend in Calgary who said she would "house" us officially so we could get across. When our friend's father answered the phone call from the border patrol, he said there was no way he was "sponsoring protesters." That sealed the deal. There was no way they were letting us back into Canada, at least not this trip.

Feeling dejected, we gave up our hopes of making it to the G8. I invited 'Bama to come to Minneapolis with me and see the Midwest. As we started walking the thirteen miles to the next town, planning to hitch south, we were constantly approached by border patrol and warned that we better not try to cross illegally or we'd get in lots of trouble.

It was slow going through Montana. Even on the interstate, the cars were sparse. I learned later that, in the previous census, Montana was the only state whose population declined. There was a rest stop near some train tracks and we figured we could try to hitch from there and, if we didn't catch a ride, we could spend the night by the train tracks and cross our fingers that something might come by. We were stuck there over night and most of the next day.

Eventually, we were picked up by a man in a large van. The van had two large French poodles in kennels in the back. They were all on their way home from a dog show; according to this man, it was just like the movie "Best in Show." A few minutes into the drive, the man began crossing the yellow line. I looked over at him and his head was down and he was asleep. I woke him up and offered to take over driving. So, there I was, with 'Bama, two poodles, and this sleepy man, rolling down the Montana interstate.

We had a few more rides, including a long shot with a trucker all the way through North Dakota that was a great way to end the trip, bringing me home to friends in Minneapolis and then down to Mankato, where I was relieved and 'Bama was planning his next move.

Conspiracy to Riot

'Bama wanted to head to the East Coast, but I was a
little too road weary for that journey. I agreed that I would go
with him down to Chicago and see him off on his trip east and
then return home. My heart was in the right place, but I think
this was a bad choice. 'Bama and I had already spent quite a bit
of time together and traveling can be pretty stressful, especially
when so much is out of your control. Our relationship was
also problematic because I introduced him to train hopping
but did not have all that much experience myself. Making the
selfish choice of not wanting to be responsible for misleading
him, I stepped away from helping plan our trip to Chicago
and from helping him plan his trip to the East Coast. I made
sure he had the tools at his disposal, but I imagine he still felt
a little abandoned through the process. We made it to Chicago
fine, being that it is a fairly easy ride from Minneapolis. Our
friendship was stressed as we walked several miles around
Chicago exploring different catch-out spots. After all of our time
together, we parted fairly suddenly as 'Bama decided to jump
on a city train and go alone to look for his ride. I headed to the
interstate to hitchhike back to Minnesota.

Things got steadily worse for me on this trip. I was
pulled off the interstate by a cop who said he would take me to
a truck stop (where I hoped to get a ride) but where he actually
took me was a truck loading dock and warehouse (which is an
extremely unlikely place to catch a ride because no trucker wants
to get caught picking up a hitchhiker in front of the boss). As I
was walking away from the warehouse, it was getting dark. I saw
a train going by on an overpass and decided just to get on it and
go. Anywhere seemed better than being stuck where I was. I ran
up to the overpass and, in my desperation, demonstrated some of
the riskiest behavior I ever have on a train.

First of all, the train was going way faster than I could
run alongside it (I would say around seventeen miles per hour).
I grabbed on, it pulled me along as I pulled myself up. However,
there wasn't a floor in the car I was on, which meant there was
no place to hide. Coming up on the other side of the train was
a security SUV shining a light on the train. If I stayed put, they
would certainly find me. I was on a forty-eight container car

that had two shipping crates in it. I climbed up on the edge of the container car, about a four-inch-wide lip, held onto a crate, and scaled along the outside edge of the car, keeping the cargo between myself and the SUV and hoping not to get whacked by a pole or tree branch that could easily knock me and my heavy pack off the side of the train. Fortunately, I made it, and was lucky that the next car down the line had a floor. I jumped in and tried to relax and see where this car was taking me.

Most of the trains in Chicago don't really go anywhere; they just move cargo to other parts of Chicago. I woke up on the train in the morning and had only gone a few miles. On the bright side, I had made it through the night and I had a new day ahead of me to figure out a plan. I picked a new spot to catch that, while it seemed less likely to bring me back to Minneapolis, would be an easy way to get out of Chicago. I spent the bulk of the day in a well-hidden, wooded area near the tracks, waiting for a train to creep by.

At the catch-out spot, I met a couple on vacation who were headed to Texas. It was nice to have some other people around and especially some new folks to get to know. We chatted and they said it would be okay for me to share a car with them. It was later in the evening when our train finally came and I was once again happy to climb on and fall asleep, even more hopeful this time of getting out of Chicago.

My new friends nudged me awake in the morning. We had arrived in Kansas City, which was likely the best place for me to get off if I wanted to get closer to Minnesota and not further away. I hopped off and, after studying the information I had on Kansas City trains, decided to first try hitchhiking north. After waiting for an hour or so, I was picked up by a man who told me he would take me north, but had to make a few stops first. In the past, folks had done the same sorts of things and it often ended in some of the greatest hospitality I had ever received.

We drove around in his junky red car. He was Latino, and I guessed from his English that he was first generation. We did our best to make conversation amongst vast awkward silences. The silence and the car ride back and forth across town made me more and more uncomfortable, and I debated in my head whether this discomfort was anything apart from my normal uneasiness amplified by the difficult communication, or something else.

I went along with it until he brought me back to his house and told me to come with him, that he just had to grab a few things. The house was in what appeared to be a mid to low-income development a block or two from the interstate. I remember it being a single level duplex or quad-plex.

Inside he offered me a soda. I said I was okay but he insisted and told me to come over to the fridge to pick one out. I walked over and pointed to a bottle. As I did, he put his hand in my crotch and said, "Can I touch your dick?" I said no and pushed him away. I swore a lot and backed out of the doorway. I was first full of adrenaline and wanted to break something or go back and confront him, but that passed and I was just glad to be away from the situation. I was speed walking down the shoulder of the interstate just trying to make distance.

I think about this moment now, not as something that scarred me but as an experience that refined my ideas of social privileges and their interplay. I certainly would call what happened to me a sexual assault, but to leave it at that lacks nuance and is a disservice to those most affected by sexual assault. We live in a rape culture and, as a person socialized male, I benefit from privileges ascertained through the systematic domination and violence toward those socialized female. This makes the way I experienced sexual assault markedly different.

This situation was further complicated by issues of race and class. Had I been assaulted by a rich, white man, I imagine I would have felt much more powerless, angry, and afraid. However, in the actual situation, I don't have to make too many assumptions beyond what I saw to realize that I carry with me much greater privilege than the man who assaulted me. I am clearly white and he was clearly not. I was raised with class privileges that as far as I could tell in the time we spent together, the man who assaulted me did not share.

Socialized classism, sexism, and racism are a part of every interaction we have with others, and when an overt act of physical violence coincides with a history of subtle and not-so-subtle social violence throughout a lifetime, the experience of physical violence is shaped by that history. That is not to say that it is okay to assault people who have more social privilege, but is simply a recognition that the way we experience violation is shaped in part by the social privileges that we do or don't carry. For me, realizations like this have increased the sophistication of my socio-political analysis. My experience of this sexual violence is contextually much different from the more common sexual violence against women who are underprivileged by hetero-patriarchy, the experience of which I will never really be able to understand.

This event was the low point in an already pretty rough few days, but I stuck with it and continued hitchhiking. I was able to make it back to my parents' house in Mankato in less than twenty-four hours.

In spite of all the ups and downs, hard times and failures, that summer was a new benchmark for me. I had experienced a sense of freedom that I had never achieved before. I had thrown myself out into the world and at its mercy, and I had made it through. It really made me feel like I could do anything, or at least survive anything. When I started classes at the University of Minnesota, my main goal had become getting through college as quickly as possible so I could get back to living.

I moved into an apartment, which was way better than being stuck in the dorms as a freshman. I was living with two other students. One was in his senior year of undergrad and the other halfway through law school. They were both a bit older but didn't treat me like the baby, which I appreciated. I like to think we all learned from each other mutually.

I registered for classes with overloaded semesters. The average class load for a student planning to graduate in four years was fifteen credits. I took at least eighteen and a few semesters I took twenty-one. At the time, I felt like I was giving up a lot of the "college experience" in order to get through it quickly. I didn't party or spend a lot of time socializing. But maybe I just socialized differently. I was still friends with Pam and other people from Mankato who had migrated up to the Twin

Cities, and they introduced me to friends of theirs who let me into their circles.

Most of my evenings during the week were spent working on various theater projects. It seemed like I was always working on a show of one sort or another and coming home well after dark to get to work on other homework. I also had a work-study job at the University of Minnesota as a janitor, mostly nights and some weekends.

Much of the little time that I spent relaxing was with my roommates. We would cook together or talk about our classes or politics or whatever. We all enjoyed working on bikes and our living room often turned into a workshop. In the winter, we would track the black slush into our living room to put our bikes up on a stand to adjust the brakes while we argued with (or just mocked) the CNN pundits. One of my roommates also worked shifts at Arise!, the local radical bookstore. He would talk about it and the work, problems, ideas, and hopes. I knew Arise! and, like many radical projects at that time, saw it as something I might like to become involved with after I was done blitzing my way through college.

While riding trains had given me a degree of empowerment and a knowledge that I was prepared to overcome at least some sorts of obstacles, college still served a purpose as both a springboard to independence and a leash prohibiting full actualization: not without use, but for me the process was too slow. I felt ready to face the world. There was obviously relative freedom compared to being in high school, but life was still greatly guided by this institution outside my control or influence. In these conflicting ways, it was formative, as I get the impression it likely is for many.

Beyond what seem to be normal (or normative) university experiences, there were a few things that stand out from my two years at the University of Minnesota. First, I began to identify socially with an alternative culture in Minneapolis. Some might call it a "punk scene" or "radical scene" while others might call it a "community." It was a social grouping that I entered in large part because of the friends I had from Mankato and other people I met through these friends. This grouping intersected with the folks I met through my housemates and others who I ran into hanging around the places we all went. I was around other people to whom my experiences riding trains and hitchhiking were normal, not crazy. I began to feel more and more a part of this particular in-group, which also gave me a relationship to, and an investment in, Minneapolis as a location.

There was a lot of politically charged talk on campus, but more important for my development, there were a few campaigns that I felt compelled to be a part of. Most notable was in the fall of 2003, when the U of M clerical workers' contract expired and they went on strike.

The university was having budget problems and, as seems to be common, the lowest-paid workers were losing their livelihood while the administration was graciously giving up their parking spaces. I wrote a brief statement for a 'zine that was compiled in the aftermath. I was asked why I thought, as a student, I should care about the clerical workers.

As a student of this university, I automatically come from a privileged position. As a seeker of higher education, it is my responsibility to be sure that it is brought to me in an ethical way. Because of the hierarchical employment structure of the university, the higher level administrators can cast aside the concerns of the majority without any discussion or thought. I believe that this arrogance led to unwillingness to work with employees. Hopefully, the strength and solidarity generated during this strike will make the higher level administrators think twice before they try to push us down again.

This effort was the first time I really took a role in a "campaign" in which we strategized how our actions would build on one another to an eventual outcome. I joined up with this campaign after attending a rally.

Most of the work of organizing is boring and thankless. It involves making fliers and hanging them up in effective places, going to lots of meetings to brainstorm ideas, networking with others who you can help and/or who can help you, writing letters to the editor, and talking to people to build energy for an issue.

I talked about the strike in most of my classes and some teachers were supportive enough that they started having classes off campus so that students who wanted to go to class, but wouldn't cross picket lines, could go. Other faculty signed a mass letter in support of the strikers. Local businesses donated space, goods, and services to help support the striking workers.

As the efforts reached their peak, we organized a student sit-in in the university president's office. We were demanding that the university call the strikers back to the table and make some concessions to the strikers' demands. We went in to the office and demanded to see the president. His receptionist said that he was out, and we said we would wait for him and all sat down in the office. To avoid arrest, we negotiated to fill the halls and only leave a few people in the reception area. They also let people come and go from the building, which allowed other students to join us and let people who wanted to rotate out to go to work leave and come back. We received secret support, in the form of donuts and sandwiches, from the clerical workers who hadn't gone on strike and were stuck at work. There was also a memorable solidarity statement from Perth Students of Murdoch University in Western Australia, who had a pirate-themed occupation of an administration building on their campus.

Eventually, the president agreed to have a meeting with a group of the concerned students. In an effort to rotate leadership, a few of the original sit-inners and I gave up our places at the table to help bring in other students who were starting to arrive. After the meeting, with the president having given nothing but lip service, the students who had been in the meeting again sat-in inside the building. Those of us who weren't inside spent the day outside in an all-day rally. I spent most of the day outside the president's window, banging on a wok with a metal spatula, and had the claim of being the only person at the rally threatened with disciplinary action (for violating campus noise restrictions).

Some of those students whom I felt closest to in this struggle and I met together in an apartment one night and started putting a plan together to block a major road through the campus. We decided that we would use locks to join us together and make it harder to remove us. We talked into the night about what we needed to make this happen, what might occur, and if it was worth it. The plans were made and prepared, but at the zero hour the university and the union reached an agreement. Our action became moot and was aborted, but we watched closely to see how the union members voted. I cried, so full of joy like a weight was lifted. For these strikers and their families, my work had made a difference and now this particular struggle was complete.

Other groups in other struggles used similar tactics to achieve their ends. Students sat in at the president's office to protest the war in Iraq and to fight the closing of the university's General College. Neither of them was quite as successful, I think in large part because folks tend to focus on the more dramatic actions when they plan a campaign. However, what made the sit-in so successful in the clerical workers' strike was that the groundwork was laid and the political context was such that the university was forced into a no-win situation. In this particular situation, the university was trying to portray itself as compassionate, fair, and even-handed. The students were trying to expose the disparities between the big-wigs and the workers to show that the administration didn't really care about the "little guy."

The students were also viewed as acting outside of their own self-interest to do the right thing by sitting-in. That meant that the administration either had to arrest a bunch of well-intentioned, self-sacrificing students and continue to have their offices disrupted, or meet our demands. Either way, they lose. We had spent a great deal of time and thought laying the ground work with an awareness of the context. That is why it worked. When I first felt the "gotcha" moment, I knew that from that day forward I wanted to be a part of actions that were well-thought-out and strategic, that would succeed not just because of sheer will, but by making smart decisions.

I had another moment of epiphany working on the strike that has stuck in my mind since then. It's a story I sometimes tell in discussions of action and privilege: I was at a meeting on campus in a building that was otherwise closed for the night, although there may have been a few other people wandering about. We were in the middle of the meeting and one of the female-assigned comrades had to use the restroom. She asked where it was and was told that the woman's room was down the hall at the other side of the building while the men's was the next room over. She made a joke and went into the men's room instead of walking all the way down the hall. I remember thinking, "Wow, what a great way to undermine gender norms. I should start using the woman's room to fight gender polarization." Quickly I realized that there is a distinct difference between a man invading one of the few spaces our society reserves for female-bodied folks and the actions of a woman refusing to acknowledge the absurd boundaries of traditionally male-held space–especially in lieu of having to walk across a building. I had been aware of these ideas before, but this moment sticks out as one where I finally knew it. From then on, I worked to be chronically aware of the contexts in which actions occur and the power and privilege dynamics that surround them, from which they can never be divorced.

Throughout the rest of college, I was peripherally involved in anti-war demonstrations and a transit workers' strike that took place in the Twin Cities metro area. I had a hard time connecting to them, however. The anti-war movement was broad but lacked any cohesive strategy or way to escalate. Everyone was told that if we got enough people to show up for a march that the President would have to listen to us. This obviously wasn't true, and even if folks didn't know that beforehand, most people learned quickly. Without a meaningful way to continue struggling with increased militancy, people began dropping out.

I had similar feelings about the transit workers strike. The union's leadership discouraged any community action beyond joining pickets and rallies, but didn't discourage the organizing of complex ride service tantamount to scabbing. Without a way to be involved that I found meaningful, it was hard to feel good about putting lots of energy into the campaign.

Between my second and third year at the U of M, I asked myself whether I would rather spend my summer taking classes so that I could finish up and graduate at the end of my third year, or if I would rather travel. Turning over the question for a while, I realized I could do both and decided to take part in a summer study-abroad program. I considered going to Germany and every

Anglophone country, but ultimately I decided to study abroad in Japan. I found a program that included language classes, but had no language requirement. Most of the other students who were a part of this program were studying computer science, economics, business, or some other field in which their experience in Japan would lead to greater enjoyability. One other student was in the arts. He was from Los Angeles and went to Cal-Arts. We became good friends and spent most of our free time hanging out and trying to spread some artistic temperament amongst all the economists.

I spent six weeks in Japan. I learned a lot of Japanese, which I have forgotten almost entirely. My friend and I kept in touch after our return to the States and sent mail art and letters back and forth in an old shoe box. We would later visit each other on occasion when we were in proximity.

Being in Japan taught me a lot about cultural normativity, international cultural exchange, and exotification. For example, pornography seemed much more prolific in Japan. You could buy it almost anywhere, but it was against the law to show pubic hair. American hip-hop (or as they called it, "black music") was also really popular at the university I attended, but when I told the students what the words were, they were surprised. They had little knowledge of American hip-hop culture, it being enough that the music was fun to dance to. Having grown up in a punk scene, I was also surprised that all of their punk clothing boutiques had shirts covered in swastikas. Experiences like these reminded me of the miniature Zen rock garden we kept on our front porch back in Mankato, or my t-shirt with the kanji symbol on it that I couldn't read.

The U of M the theater department was more supportive of experimentation than the University of Wisconsin. There was also a lot more work being created and put on. Every semester, I was working on at least one theater piece and sometimes more. One of my introductory classes was with a professor who had trained in the "Margolis Method." It was created by Kari Margolis, who was also faculty at the U of M. Up to this point, most of my experience was with folks trained in what is known as the "American Method" (or "The Method"), which encourages actors to delve deeply into the psychology of the character. Compared to the American Method, the Margolis Method was more physically based. In my past training, practitioners of The Method had looked down on physical theater, but I gave it an honest shake and was surprised at how much I took to it. So much so that I sought more training in the Margolis Method and made it central to my studies. I took a few more classes at the U of M with Kari Margolis, worked on pieces that she helped facilitate, and took classes that she or her more advanced students held off campus.

I put a lot of thought into how I might blend my desire to pursue theater with my desire to actualize social change. I studied theater history, especially the theories and history of the avant-garde. The theorists of the avant-garde movements were intentional about how they were changing their arts in an effort to explore something new and radically alter audience perception and, hopefully, societal perception.

Bertolt Brecht was one theorist whom I paid close attention to. He was a Marxist and believed that while the principal need was for theater to entertain, it was also important for theater to educate. He believed that theater was a place to exchange ideas. In other theater, the action unraveled as if fated, but Brecht was a materialist and desired a theater where the outcomes clearly stemmed from the behaviors and choices of the characters. The lesson was that we all have agency in our lives and our choices will affect the world we create around us. There is no fate to blame. Brecht is also often looked at as a main contributor to the rise of agitprop theater, a highly politicized theater meant to spur the audience to action.

While I took a lot from Brecht's intentions, I found some of his work oversimplified. He worked to keep the audience at a distance so they could maintain a critical eye. This often stopped me from really being able to enjoy his work—I loved being swept away by the world the theater created. I believed that it was possible both to let the audience get swept up in a story while also maintaining a critical eye. Imagine watching a horror movie in which the victim is about to open the door that the monster hides behind. You are frightened for them and absorbed in the story but you can still shout out, "No! Don't go in there!"

I also put energy into studying the avant-garde movement Futurism. While the most prominent Futurists were Italian and were fascist and nationalistic, it wasn't their politics that attracted me. The Futurists believed that they were creating cultural property for a whole new society. Along with making theater and all sorts of other art, they put out cookbooks that designed extravagant yet absurd meals in which every element was crafted to fit a purpose.

While I was not interested in nationalism, I grabbed onto the idea of actively creating cultural material that shaped a society from within. More specifically, instead of creating work designed to enlighten the normative American to the need for change, I wanted to create cultural property for those who already dreamed and worked towards a better world—art that was created by and for revolutionaries and belonged to them.

This sort of cultural property is more present in the field of music, in which radically minded songwriters write songs for their own in-group instead of writing as an outreach tool. They play their music in basements and underground spaces across the country. This is what I wanted to do with theater.

For my final graduation project, I created a folk-punk musical called "Fortunes from Gleaning." The musical was about two young traveling punks who crossed paths on their independent journeys riding trains and eating out of dumpsters all across the country. I wrote it to take a minimal amount of equipment and space. It was also about thirty minutes in length, the same time as the average punk show music set. The idea was that it could be performed sandwiched between bands in a stuffy basement anywhere in the country.

I graduated from college in 2004 and was more than ready to get on with my life. The thing about college, and schools in general, was that I spent most of my formative years within them. I believe this really made being in classrooms somehow feel right and normal, or like something I'm supposed to be doing. This is why I never dropped out of college, but the recognition of which is what made me decide not to even consider any graduate level work until I had a reason better than it "feeling right."

I had been doing so much theater in college that I wasn't yet interested in going out and auditioning professionally. I decided that I would spend my summer traveling and that the object of my travels would be to attend the 2004 DNC and RNC, both of which were taking place on the East Coast. I hunted around for some folks to travel with, but ended up doing the trip solo. I concluded that being stuck on a train for days is a great way to know those you're with, even if it's just yourself.

I gave myself plenty of time and traced the path that I had taken with 'Bama a few years back down to Chicago. Having been turned off of catching trains out of Chicago, I took the commuter rail out of Chicago and hitchhiked to Elkheart, Indiana, which is the crew change freight train's first stop east after Chicago. In Elkheart, I dumpstered sandwich crackers and some of those health shakes for seniors. When the train came, I hid between the wheels of the trailer and rolled out my sleeping bag right away, knowing it would get cold. The wheels and the trailer created a wind tunnel and I buried myself in my sleeping bag with my crackers and my shakes.

The sun came up and, a few hours later, the train got off the main line and pulled into a yard of some sort. I ducked off with a wink and a nod to a worker and sneaked into Harrisburg, Pennsylvania. Hitchhiking through the rain, I made slow progress and spent nights in hotel stairwells, under overpasses, and, once, inside an abandoned school bus. I finally made it to Boston, still several days before the DNC, and looked up a friend from college in Madison. He was not too keen on my dropping in and didn't really care much about the protests in general, but saw that I had nowhere else to go and obliged me.

I spent a few days getting to know Boston and the surrounding area. I walked to where the convention was going to be held and everyday saw the fence get taller and thicker. Boston became known for its "free speech cage," complete with a mesh netting so thick that you could hardly make out the other side and National Guard members with assault rifles perched on the surrounding buildings. While none of the lawsuits filed to alter the "free speech zone" were won, one U.S. district court judge said, "One cannot conceive of what other design elements could be put into a space to create a more symbolic affront to the role of free expression."

It was clear then, and is even clearer post-RNC, the way courts are used (and abused if you believe there is actually a proper place for modern courts) in the lead up to these events. Protest organizers had to spend a great deal of energy fighting the "cage." The court bureaucracy is slow and the event has a set date. Even if the court had ruled the cage illegal, the decision probably would have been appealed by DNC organizers. A favorable ruling wouldn't mean the cage would be taken down; it would simply mean grounds for future lawsuits if folks wanted to spend the next five years fighting in the courts. Four years later, around the RNC in St. Paul, the police and Host Committee would use the courts and other bureaucratic stall tactics to change and delay the March Coalition's route permits.

I went to a few open meetings of The Bl(A)ck Tea Society, the anarchist collective organizing against the Boston DNC. I picked up some of the resource materials they were giving out. The Bl(A)ck Tea Society had coordinated housing and transportation (including both free bikes and a guide to public transit) as well as securing a convergence space for groups to meet in. They had also planned a non-permitted march and a "really, really democratic bazaar" where folks could give away or trade skills or crafts or whatever they had to share. Finally, a call had been put out for a "day of decentralized direct action." This basically meant that on this day folks would engage in actions that they decided upon autonomously with small groups with the hope being that the broad range of actions that took place would reveal the diversity of the demonstrators who chose different targets with different meaning, but would still be acting in concert as a way of unifying all of their reasons for resisting the DNC.

I went to help out with the bike space and then secured a bike for myself to use to get around town. I was also able to find some fresh housing so I could give my college buddy a break. At the new house, I met several other folks, mostly punks and anarchists, who were in town for the protests. Now I had some friends to roll around town with checking things out. Each day was full of adventures as we helped prepare for the protests, go dumpstering, and tried to navigate the Boston area.

The days of protest came. I went to virtually everything. I marched in several marches and went to even more meetings about marches. There were a few times when the marches got tense. Once, the police ran into the crowd and grabbed a kid. They pulled him out of the march and searched him without cause. The whole march stopped and chanted at the police until, finding nothing illegal, they let the kid go. On another march, there was a two-faced effigy of the presidential candidates, John Kerry and George W. Bush that was marched into or near the "free speech" pen and lit ablaze. It quickly crumpled to the ground and other folks gathered around and added their fuel to the fire. American flags, copies of George W. Bush's biography, and pictures were among the things thrown in. In my mind, this symbolic moment—a demonstration of collective anger and joy— was the high-water mark for the DNC protests.

But the fire was soon out, and a phalanx of riot police pinned in the already tight crowd. A few police snatch-squads moved in and arrested folks inside the crowd. They only arrested a handful, but they mostly happened to be members of the Bl(A)ck Tea Society. One organizer in particular was held for "possession of a hoax device" for having a papier-mâché pirate hook as a prop in the "pirate bloc" section of the march. Police said the hook was actually made to look like a Molotov cocktail. I stayed in town a few days after the DNC until things died down a bit and then, in my usual way, headed out of town.

There were a few weeks between the DNC in Boston and the RNC in New York, but not enough time that I wanted to get too far from the East Coast. Before leaving Minnesota, I had talked to my former teacher, Kari Margolis, who was taking a leave of absence in the next year to open a training center in rural New York. She was planning on spending the summer in New York getting things together and they had just closed on a property when I left the state. We had agreed that she would let me stay at their new place for a few weeks, and in return I would spend some of that time helping to fix the place up. If we had time to train and maybe make some theatrical work, all the better.

When I arrived at the old rural house, no one was there. It turned out that no one had yet arrived from Minnesota. I spent the next few days camping out on the old wrap-around porch, pulling weeds from the driveway, exploring the surrounding parks, rivers, and hamlets, and hitchhiking to the closest city to buy some oatmeal and peanut butter. I tried to avoid drawing attention to myself, but one day while working in the front yard, the realtor drove past and spotted me. She pulled into the driveway and gave me the third-degree. Having just came from the street protests in Boston, I put on my best face and was polite but evasive. Later, she called Margolis and got the story straight, returned, and was quite friendly. She even opened the house so I could prepare my oatmeal on the stove instead of over a small fire out back.

After a few days, Margolis, some family, and some other students arrived in a big Ryder van and we were ready to get started. We spent the next few weeks fixing up the old house. It was an old inn keeper's house and was on about an acre and a half. Margolis had also closed a deal on the old inn down the street. It was in rougher shape, but had a lot of promise, and we spent a lot of our down time dreaming about what was to come of our labors.

There was a lot of cleaning, scraping, and painting to do. I learned how to install my first toilet. When we had done enough work in a day, I would go for a swim or a walk in the woods, climb some trees, or have a big bonfire. I was into it. It was great to be working on a project with such a small, tight group of folks, and it was amazing to be in this beautiful place with unlimited potential and things to explore.

When my few weeks there were up, I talked with Margolis and her husband. They invited me to come back after my time at the RNC. They had liked the work that I had put in and were willing to pay me to stay and continue to help. Besides, there was a lot of work to get done on the inn building and they needed the help. I had no plans for after the RNC and it seemed like a great opportunity, so I accepted.

I had been to New York City before on a trip with my family, but this time I didn't have the time or desire for any sightseeing. I drove into town with some friends from Mankato. We were in town just a day or two before the convention and accompanying protests were to begin. As I think is common for many at these events, we showed up unprepared. The first thing we began frantically searching for was housing. There were online housing boards, and we finally found a place to go. It was a squat in the Bronx called Casa Del Sol. I was really excited and inspired when we arrived.

The building was like a hive, buzzing with activity. It was laid out in a way that reflected the values and resources of those involved. We had to enter the main common space through a basement window. The stove was propane powered with the tank out in the backyard that you had to run out and turn on before you began cooking and then turn off immediately after. There was a toilet, but instead of busting up the concrete floor and framing out a new bathroom, they just put the toilet where there must have once simply been a drain in the floor. It had a shower curtain hanging around it for privacy. I also saw a handful of folks that I recognized from the Boston DNC, which was exciting for me. However, at a big meeting for the space that night, there was a lot of talk of the possibility of the space being raided and everyone arrested. Folks who had been around seemed to think that this could happen any time and we needed to have a plan and people needed to know the risks of being in the space.

We spent that night there, but one of the kids from Mankato that I was there with was "unarrestable," that is, she wasn't in a position where she could handle the consequences of arrest as they would have been harsher for her than for many others. Because staying at the space seemed too risky, we decided to try to find another place. Our quest for a decent place to crash is probably the most memorable part of my RNC experience. We spent the next night in the car in Brooklyn and then the next few nights we drove out into New Jersey and slept in a park, then drove on to Staten Island and took the ferry into Manhattan, spent the day in the city, then back to Staten Island

and then to our little park in New Jersey. This was mostly all because we couldn't find a comfortable place in the city and this route was the cheapest we could find in terms of tolls.

We knew the websites to go to for finding out information about what was going on, but we still had a really hard time plugging in. Before the protests began, we went to a know-your-rights training and that was about it. Then the days of protest began.

I remember marching in a few marches, thinking that something crazy just had to happen. The "anybody but Bush" fervor was rampant, and all the symbols of the war machine were packed into these few square miles. When I reached the end of the huge anti-war march, the parade "marshals" were there congratulating everyone on a job well done, telling them they really made a difference and to go home feeling proud. It made me sick.

And so, all that energy and outrage was squandered as folks patted themselves and each other on the back and went home knowing they did their best. The war, of course, kept on. But the people who were in the marches believed they did all they could to stop it. And, maybe they did in that context. What should they have done in that moment, penned in by police and dispersed by marshals without any infrastructure in place for the average demonstrator to plug in to that would amount to much more?

Like in Boston, there was a "day of decentralized direct action." In retrospect, I should have worked harder to come up with a plan for myself for this day, but like in Boston, I had no plan and neither did the friends I was with. Feeling disempowered and frustrated with all the marches and tired from our stressful sleeping arrangement, we left town early, the night before the day of decentralized direct action, hoping to at least have a fun road trip back to the house in up-state. I would later learn that my experience was not unique, that most other folks who came in from out of town were not prepared for the day of decentralized direct action, but may have been interested in being part of other actions if there had been an effective mechanism for plugging in.

I returned to the home I was making in rural New York. There was a lot to do, and a lot of things that I didn't have a lot of experience with but learned pretty quick. We started off doing a lot of demolition on the old inn building. We were unsure how deep we were going to have to go, so we took our time. The demolition helped me understand how all these things went together, demystified it, and helped me believe that fixing these things and putting them back together is something I could probably figure out. With due respect to the professional trades people I have met since then whose precision and speed put me to shame, I maintain that believing you are capable of fixing a problem is the biggest roadblock to a lot of this type of work, and probably many others. We ended up gutting the whole building. We were quite the sight, a bunch of actors in dust masks carrying buckets of busted-up plaster down the narrow old stairs.

I also spent a lot of time getting to know the area, the artists I was living with, and our neighbors. I would go on walks or jogs every night. The house and inn were right along the Delaware River; right across the river was Pennsylvania. It was really a beautiful place to walk at night with bright stars, fireflies, and the sound of the river rushing underneath. There was also a lot of history in the area. Most of the official contextualization of the history was at best Euro-centric and normally pretty culturally supremacist, but if you could see past that, it was beautiful and there was a lot to be experienced.

One of my favorite places to go was a park on a former Revolutionary War battle ground. It was thickly wooded and full of mysteries. One day, the park was filled with the sound of frogs calling out to find mates. Another time, we found a small hole in some rocks and inside were several old jars. We took a jar home and opened it. First, we poured out a bunch of cedar chips. Inside that was a paper towel that, when unrolled, revealed a dead rat that had been mummified. We put the jar back together and returned it to its place, hoping that we would avoid any sort of curse that might be surrounding its ritualistic burial.

On weekends, I would go over to neighbors' homes for dinner parties or they would come sit with us on our wrap-around porch and watch the fireflies. We would sometime talk politics, but it was hard and a little alienating being the only self-identified radical in the bunch. I had ideas about what I wanted to do, or how I wanted to live, or how I wanted to fit into the community that might have been obvious in anarchist circles but were a struggle while alone in these social groups. It's an interesting phenomenon. I believe an individual can have a proportionately large effect in situations like this. I encouraged reduction in water use, got us composting, and reduced our oil usage by making sure there was plenty of fire wood available.

However, I too had to compromise and was discouraged from dumpster diving, as folks were worried about how it might reflect on our group's presence in the community. Perhaps more importantly, I wasn't really given a lot of room to grow as a radical/revolutionary. I spent a lot of time reading and thinking alone, but for the most part had no one who shared enough of a radical analysis that we could converse in greater nuance about our world. In one conversation with the neighbors, after going back and forth with our political criticisms, someone said, "Well, at least we live in America where we can have these conversations." Statements like this almost make me laugh out loud now when I am on trial largely for allegedly going to meetings and having conversations.

At one point, someone in our house said I was the "social conscience" of the group. At first, I was proud of this statement, as it indicated that I was helping to push the group in a more positive direction. Upon reflection, however, I believe that the idea that I alone was in charge of making sure socially responsible decisions were made allowed others to continue to avoid thinking about those sorts of things themselves. I saw the venerating of socially responsible behavior as a tactic for not actually engaging with the problems oneself.

I was excited, then, when a student came who was more open and interested in a radical analysis. We quickly became close friends and spent a lot of time working and talking together. Due to a lack of space, we even ended up sharing a room, which seemed to work out well. We would fall asleep talking and wake up to the train across the river rolling by and echoing off our hillside.

Although I lacked the space for the political growth I would have liked, I still remember this time fondly. I learned a lot of new skills and was proud to be a part of the project. I also really deeply care for and love the people I met. I remember stopping at a small-town thrift store and one of the other students found an old VHS tape of Salt-N-Pepa music videos, interviews, and concert footage. We took it home and watched it so many times that we learned all the moves to "Push It." A few weeks later, we were at a small town bar and found it on the jukebox. The way we all danced together, it felt like we were in a musical. In this confined space, we took care of and entertained each other.

As we reached the end of the summer and were drifting into the fall, there started to be less work that we could do and it looked like the inn was going to need a more serious overhaul. The handful of students who had been working on the project went away for the winter to return in six months to pick up the project again when there was more work we could do. I drove with a few other students back to Minnesota and moved in with some friends in Minneapolis.

Even though I was only in Minneapolis for six months, I used the time to do the sorts of things I wanted to do while I was in college but didn't feel like I had energy for. I didn't have a bedroom in the house I lived in, so I lived out of the garage all winter. I built a tent out of plastic construction sheeting around an old bunk-bed frame and had it pushed up against an electric heater that was built into the wall of the garage. I insulated it with old blankets.

Some of the folks who I lived with worked on a local anarchist newspaper called Daybreak. It was an easy and obvious choice to start going to their collective meetings and try to get involved. I don't think I really contributed much, but I helped where I could. I wrote a few articles and op-eds, I did a little work with layout, and helped with distribution. Like many anarchist projects, it was always behind schedule. Deadlines were missed and the quarterly paper ended up coming out two or three times a year based on when it got pulled together. It was a great experience, less for learning how to run a paper and more for my continuing education in collective process.

In this time, I also got a job with the Spokes Pizza Collective. Spokes Pizza was a pizza parlor operating out of the Seward Café in South Minneapolis. The collective had been around for about a year and a half at that point and the whole time the operation was shaky. It was started with hardly any capital and was only open three nights a week. The plan from the beginning was to run out of the Seward Café until the business could get on its feet, and then it could be birthed out into an independent existence. Unfortunately, running a pizza parlor out of an already functioning restaurant created more problems than it solved, but there was nowhere else to go. So, we all worked to keep the businesses afloat. We worked for ten cents over minimum wage when we were on shift and we were paid for our management work in sweat equity; that is, our unpaid labor was recorded as an investment in the businesses and would get paid out as soon as the businesses turned a profit (i.e., likely never).

There was a lot of work to do at Spokes and mostly everyone did almost everything at one time or another. I delivered pizza on bicycle almost every weekend throughout that winter. My favorite and most memorable night was during a blizzard. It must have dropped eighteen inches of snow, but, as is sometimes the case with big snows like that, it was actually a bit warmer so it wasn't so bad being out delivering pizza. There were hardly any cars on the streets and teenagers were running around playing at midnight. I had to get off the bike and run with it half the time, but I got the pizza where it was going every time. It was a little behind schedule, but folks were understanding. I got bigger tips that night than ever.

Spokes achieved a mixed reputation that tended toward the extremes. A lot of people loved that the ingredients were organic and they could get a wheat-free crust. But it lacked consistency and using a café's oven instead of having a pizza oven meant it took longer than folks are used to. I left to return to New York before Spokes closed, but it burnt out before I returned. Spokes wasn't making progress in its business plan and running out of the café was proving to be unsustainable and creating a lot of tension and resentment between collectives.

I took the long road back to New York, the one that passes through Los Angeles. One of the other students lived out there and we wanted to ride trains together. My comrade from Japan also lived in L.A., and I planned to visit him.

I had planned on catching a train to L.A., but after missing it the first night out, I decided that I was too antsy to wait around town another day to try to catch again. The next morning, I hit an on-ramp to start hitching.

It was slow going at the start. I had been spoiled by the trucker who had taken me all the way home from Montana years before. I didn't realize how slow the going would be and how far apart the towns were. It took me two days to make it to Bismark, ND. As the sun was setting, I was starting to feel a little desperate. I hung out at a truck stop for a few hours asking around and eventually found a ride headed west. The ride was with a trucking team, two Korean immigrants operating out of Toronto who made the trip from Toronto to Seattle taking turns sleeping and driving, which kept them on the road almost constantly. They didn't speak that much English, so the conversation was light, but in right around 24 hours I was at a truck stop just outside Seattle hunting around for a place to spend the night.

I made it into Seattle the next morning and then worked south toward L.A. About six days after leaving Minneapolis, I got my last ride into L.A. It was with a woman who first brought me to her home near Bakersfield. She fed me and let me take a shower. I helped her fix a ceiling fan and complete some other odds and ends around her house. We talked a bit about working in communities and she flattered me by telling me that, whether I knew it or not, my influence on people whose paths I cross was remarkable and meaningful. At the time, those sorts of comments made me feel really good about the choices I was making and the life I was living. As I move away from that particular lifestyle, I wonder if there is any sort of lasting, meaningful effects of the ripples I caused or if it's all just a sentimental desire to rationalize my carefree lifestyle of the day.

My friend from Japan picked me up in downtown L.A. and the next few days were spent hiking in canyons and exploring the city. We met up with the friend I made out in New York and intended to travel with. We made the most of our time—skinny dipping, dumpstering, and eating at vegan cafés. I was really glad to know these folks and the time we spent in L.A. was memorable, but that was in spite of, not because of, the city of Los Angeles, whose over-dependence on cars and shallow aesthetics were a major turn off.

My friend from New York and I waited in L.A. for the right train for about five days and finally caught anything we could heading north. We hopped off in San Louis Obispo and hitched north towards Oakland. There should be a line drawn from west to east down San Louis Obispo to mark the change from southern California to northern California. It is where the dreamy north ecology of Big Sur and Santa Cruz butts up against the uber-capitalism of the L.A. area.

We spent the afternoon, evening, and night waiting for a train in Oakland. When it didn't come, we headed for the onramp. Come afternoon, we were kicked off by the police. While walking down the street feeling dejected and unsure, I looked over the top of a security fence and saw a train rolling behind the Ikea. We climbed the fence and, within the span of those two minutes, we went from dejection to butterflies of elation. We were back on the move.

The train was headed for Chicago and we were hunkering down for the ride, but we had eaten a lot of our food while waiting for trains and so were already running low. We had to start rationing our food, which made us both a little edgy. I made myself feel better, in true Minnesota fashion, by secretly giving my friend slightly more than I took for myself. Imagine my surprise when my friend confronted me three days into the ride, telling me that she had been feeling unconsidered. We talked about it and it seemed that, in my effort to support my friend's physical well-being, I had turned my frustrations toward our situation inward and become more emotionally distant. Meanwhile, I had been feeling unconsidered because of a perceived lack of mindfulness towards our physical well-being by her. We both agreed to try harder and the problem was solved for the time being.

Conspiracy to Riot

This part of the story is simple, but it sticks out in my memory and I have told it several times because I think of it as a lesson in my gender socialization. My friend being socialized female and myself being socialized male, I was trying to be a physical provider and my friend was trying to provide comfort and emotional well-being. We both de-emphasized the other's efforts in our minds and, in my case, I was acting out of ignorance. I have tried since then to be less hung up on some perceived responsibility to provide for the physical needs of everyone around me. Although it can be a hard cycle to break out of as we all often continually reinforce each other's socialized behavior.

Our train stopped short of Chicago, in Iowa, and we hitchhiked to a truck stop where we were able to get a ride to upstate New York and then make our way to the artists' center the next morning. All in all, from the time we finally got out of L.A., it only took us a week to cross the country (more if you include the five days of waiting in L.A.).

Back in New York, it started out much like it had been before. It was good to see the neighbors again. They had knocked down the whole inn building (including the roof we had put on the year before) and rebuilt it one wall at a time. So, now we were into doing new construction.

We started having class five hours a day, five days a week. This was great except it started to complicate things a bit. Whereas before I had been working for room, board, and a small stipend, I was now working for a wage and, in return, paying for rent and classes. I don't know that it worked out that much different financially in the end, but it put a lot more pressure on me to make sure I was working a certain number of hours.

Also, money began to mitigate my relationship with Margolis and her husband. I began to resent the role they filled in setting the terms of our micro-economy. She set the rent and price of training, but also set my hourly wage. This resentment was further fueled by what I perceived as an obvious disparity in our standards of living. It's not that she was particularly unfair, but I lost some empowerment and sense of ownership as I lost more and more agency.

But, the training was exciting, the wood stove was warm, and Margolis was the only one offering me this sort of experience. So while I kept with it and found a lot to be grateful for, I also began to feel less and less ownership and investment over the project, which in turn made me more selfish in how I related to the space. I was trying to work eight hours a day, train five hours a day, and pick up any extra work I could over the weekend to make sure I wasn't going into the hole on expenses. The core group of three students cohabitated with the students who came on retreats for a week or two, which meant meeting a lot of great folks who were bringing their unique perspectives to the space, but it also made the house feel always in flux with new personalities in the space.

I lived this way for a year, making more and more sophisticated theater work and learning all sorts of new construction skills. I framed, sheet-rocked, painted, hung siding, installed huge bay windows. You name it, we saved costs on the building by doing it ourselves.

It was hard for me to maintain perspective from within that community. The small, tight-knit theater community validated the choice to stick at the work and, in the context of the space, the theater we were making was treated like the most important thing we could be doing. I always felt a little uneasy about it, but I let myself believe that what I was doing was important because it was what I wanted to be doing. If it was important and had meaning, then it was okay for me to hole up in the woods with a bunch of actors making theater for each other. I left after a year, hoping to return but uncertain enough not to commit. I haven't been back since, although I really appreciate the time I had because I got the chance to experience what it's like to live with friends in the middle of nowhere. The training also gave this clumsy kid an awareness of his body and its physics like never before. There are days when I passionately hunger to return, but I can never reconcile spending another large chunk of time in retreat and disengaged from the work that I see as so socially imperative.

I was unsure what to do next with my life and so I returned to southern Minnesota. My parents had moved outside of Mankato and I stayed with them for most of the summer. I would bike the seven miles into town and visit friends or work roofing. I tried to get involved with some community projects, but they all lacked real inertia, which made them all pretty frustrating.

Toward the end of the summer, I ran into a friend from high school who was the only other person from Mankato who I had heard of going train hopping. He had spent some time in northern California and was looking for an adventure, maybe heading back that direction. While I was figuring out what I wanted to do, rolling around the west coast was as good a way to spend time as any. I had met a person out in New York who had some land in California where they panned for gold, so I made getting out there to meet up with them my goal. I also wanted to try riding some smaller trains around the Midwest and so proposed that we take our time getting out of the state exploring some of the side tracks.

We took days bumping around between midwestern towns: from Mankato to Sioux City, Iowa, to Lincoln and Omaha, Nebraska. We got off a train in Denver and went downtown to explore. Downtown, we ran into a few other travelers who were asking for spare change on the streets of Denver before either going on to the next town or going home to get ready for the next semester at college. I approached my traveling as more of a pilgrimage than a vacation and tried to limit what I asked of others to things that didn't cost them anything; a ride or a place to spend the night. I was frustrated with these kids because I felt like they were being irresponsible and disregarding their privilege. However, the responsibility was more a gradient than a binary, and so, just like being in college and resenting other students, their irresponsibility reflected my own.

We finally neared California but hopped off our train early since it was headed towards L.A. and I didn't want to get stuck there again. We hitched into familiar San Luis Obispo. Once there, we met some punks who had bought an RV and were cruising up and down the west coast. It was slow going. We probably only traveled sixty miles a day, but we were on track and we were comfortable.

From the time we left Mankato, it had taken us two weeks to make it out to my friend's land. The two weeks after that were spent camping by various streams, panning for gold, and helping with odd jobs for the neighbors. Panning for gold is probably the best summer job I could ever recommend. We camped out along the stream and woke up with the sun. The sky would get bright before the sun made it up over the mountain top and I would get out of my sleeping bag and go down to the creek to fill a pot with water for coffee. I would drink coffee and eat breakfast with my friends while we waited for the sun to come above the mountain and warm the stream. We would pan for a few hours, eat lunch, and pan for another few hours before the sun fell behind the other mountain and you could no longer see the gold flecks in your pan. We would make a big fire and a big dinner, then pass around a guitar and tell stories until it was dark enough to go to sleep again.

I woke up one morning and could smell fall coming. It was almost September. I had previously thought about trying to get work on a freight ship for passage to Japan, where I could stay with friends for the winter, but I had already achieved my goal for the trip. I had figured out what I wanted to do with the next phase of my life. My travel companion wanted to go spend some time alone by the ocean, so we all said goodbye and went our separate ways. I was in such a hurry to get back to Minneapolis that I hitchhiked to near Portland, Oregon in about twenty hours and showed up just as my train was coming by. I slept for the whole first day on the train, and two days after that rolled back into Minneapolis.

To further my plans upon returning to Minneapolis, I started writing up a platform/program based strongly on the Black Panthers' 10-point platform and program just to get a sense of where I was at and what I was working for. I felt the need for an organization that helped do the work that many radical collectives did (running spaces, feeding people, operating alternative businesses and so on) but also one that placed revolutionary politics in the foreground. This is part of why the Black Panther Party (BPP) was such an inspiration to me.

While I didn't agree with the whole of their predominantly Maoist philosophy, I appreciated that, by being a unified party with many independent projects, BPP was able to take their revolutionary philosophy to what might otherwise seem reformist actions (what they called survival programs). While the BPP is best known in the mainstream for their armed patrols and self-defense, they also worked as crossing guards at dangerous intersections near schools, organized a free breakfast for school children (which was arguably one of their most successful actions that was recreated by chapters all over the country; now free breakfasts for low-income families are the standard in public schools all over the country), and created a people's ambulance to aid community members during medical emergencies. The only thing that separated a lot of this work from that of a church group or a non-profit was that the BPP maintained their politics through all their work.

I saw the need for this because of a stigma around radical activists. There is a prolific false dichotomy that there are good activists helping people and bad activists being confrontational. The reality is, they are two edges of the same blade. Many of the people out putting their bodies and freedom on the line confronting the system are the same folks working in their neighborhoods to create alternatives and build communities.

In Minneapolis, I moved in with a handful of folks I didn't know all that well. I liked some of their ideas and fed off their excitement about the house they were putting together. After my experience over the summer, I was feeling pretty laid back. Maybe California had rubbed off on me, but also the pilgrimage itself had been refreshing. I felt comfortable with my place in the universe and I didn't think anything could disturb me.

I moved my things into this new house. The first night there, folks were having a party for a housemate's birthday. They were turning sixteen. I had been used to getting up with the sun traveling and roofing, so I went up to bed with the party going on the floor below. As I had been moving in, it was explained to me that there was a clog in the toilet so not to flush it, but a plumber was coming in the morning. I left well enough alone and steered clear if for no other reason than the smell, but the party-goers must not have been able to read the sign. While lying in bed, I heard the toilet flush and its contents begin to spill out and splash onto the floor. It was bad enough having this stomach-churning slurry stuck in the toilet bowl and now it was all over the bathroom floor.

But it didn't stop there. The toilet hadn't been caulked to the bathroom floor, so the slop seeped under the toilet and started to run down along the waste pipe. Now, part of the reason this toilet was so prone to clogs was that there was an almost ninety degree turn in the waste pipe just above the kitchen ceiling. That meant that as the shit and urine cascaded down the waste pipe, it formed a large pool on the kitchen ceiling. As the pressure became too great, the slop streamed down from the ceiling onto the kitchen floor in the middle of the party. Not to have their party end before its time, the attendees ran to a neighboring house that had a free box full of old t-shirts. They brought the shirts back over and used them to dam up the stream into a contained reservoir still on the kitchen floor.

There the reservoir was left for the remainder of the party, until around five o'clock when folks decided to go home or pass out. I woke up about an hour and a half later to go out job hunting. I realized that my feeling of being centered in the universe had not been as strong as I had thought, as the sight and smell that I woke to put a substantial dent in my esoteric armor.

Monica Bicking

While I had traveled to Ecuador and Mexico and had seen children selling gum and asking for money, and knew that their life experience was drastically different from mine, I didn't become passionate about the injustice of child labor until I read about it in Times Magazine for Kids. The article was about Iqbal Masi, a child activist who had recently been killed. He was sold to a factory in Pakistan as a young child and weaved rugs. He broke out of the factory and became an anti-child labor activist.

He got the media's attention and traveled around telling his story. At the time of the article, he had just been killed, most likely by people working for the factory. He was my age, and I was touched by his story.

This was 1995, and there was a wave of child labor awareness and activism. There were boycotts against Gap and Nike. Reporters were sneaking into factories and broadcasting the factory conditions. It became public knowledge that U.S. companies had factories abroad where there was slave-labor, child-laborers, and horrific conditions. I was young and outraged. I was living in a culture where kids stuck together and adults were the enemy. While I loved many adults, they were the rule makers and enforcers. There was a clear hierarchy where they were on top and I was on bottom. While the child laborers were across the world, they felt like my people. It was an adults' world that was enslaving, killing, and torturing them. While previously I had been mildly concerned about the world outside my own, child labor was the first time I really connected with a political issue. It seemed much more real than war or rainforest destruction.

Soon after learning about child labor I joined a theatre group called Solidarity Kids and would stay with them through high school. They were working on a performance about Iqbal Mashi and child labor. I played a young boy in a rug factory. It was a wonderful experience. It was fun. For the first time I faced deadlines and pressure. Most of all I was surrounded by other children who cared about child labor and were motivated to do something about it. The adults were supportive and followed the children's lead. The play was a hit and we performed it many times over many years. As we grew older we started to write our own plays. The first play I co-wrote was about child labor, but we quickly expanded our political thinking and started to address other issues.

Solidarity Kids was funded by the American Postal Workers Union. They flew us all around the country to perform at different conferences. As we began to write more and more of our own plays, more and more controversy grew between us and the union. Our interests diverged from the union's. We stopped writing plays with a worker theme, and as the Iraq war started we started writing about war and corporate interest. Slowly, Solidarity Kids started to fall apart and we stopped being kids.

I was in Solidarity Kids for eight years, almost its entire lifespan. It was an entirely empowering experience. It felt kids led, and we did in many ways. While it was kids led, there were important adults who made it happen and allowed us kids to take over. I give most credit to the director. He did all of the shit work and felt most of the pressure leading up to a performance, while we enjoyed the glory and did much of the creative work. Solidarity Kids was also the first activism I engaged in. While it was far from any sort of direct action, it did teach me the value of thinking about people's experiences outside of my own and acting for my political convictions. It was also extremely empowering to write our own plays about our own experiences and concerns and to have adults listen and encourage us.

As a child my family went on several foreign vacations, which greatly impacted how I saw the world. The first was to Ecuador when I was nine years old. I don't remember a whole lot from the trip, but am sure that seeing how different people live broadened my view of the world. At one hotel I became friends with the housekeeper's children. I had a fun time learning to communicate without a common language. I remember seeing their mother wash their clothing by hand on a scrub board. While I'm sure that was the first time I had seen a scrub board used for anything other than music, it did not symbolize a different way of living that it does for me today. From my perspective I was just a child playing with other children. I was more fascinated by tag than how much money they had. Despite that, I think seeing other lifestyles allowed me to have a broader understanding of the world outside my own at a younger age.

The next time my family left the country was two years later to Mexico. My family was part of the first wave of tourists to come through Chiapas after the Zapatista uprising. My parents, like many foreign activists, decided to come to Chiapas both to see what the Zapatistas were all about and to support them. These tourists changed the economy of Chiapas and the term "zapoturismo" was coined to describe them. While tourists were changing the economy, Zapatistas were changing the views of many foreigners like me.

Because I was ten years old I had very little understanding of what was going on. I have no recollection of anyone telling me what Zapatistas were. They probably did, but obviously it was not memorable. To get to Chiapas we flew into Cancun and took a bus over. As one can imagine, the difference between Americanized, touristy experiences, Cancun and the bus to Chiapas was dramatic. The bus was an old school bus and we were the only tourists on it. My parents and I did not speak Spanish yet and everything was a bit blurry. I don't remember exactly how long the bus ride took, but it was over twelve hours. It was during this bus ride that I first saw people using arms to stand up for their rights. Presumably these people were Zapatistas or closely related politically.

About halfway through the trip the bus was stopped by a large group of people in the road. Many had guns. We were stopped at a fork in the road. The people were only blocking one side of the fork, not the side that our bus was going. The bus driver stopped anyway, probably a good idea with hundreds of armed people in the road. The people were blocking the road to the nature reserve Agua Azul, where there were indigenous struggles against the government over the land. They weren't letting traffic through to the reserve. With a bribe, they did let our bus continue on to its destination, the capital of Chiapas, San Cristobal de las Casas.

At ten, I'm not sure what I got out the experience. I was a sponge, but did not have the means to truly process what was going on. I remember that I was not as scared as one might expect. When we arrived in San Cristobal everyone was extremely friendly. Paint had spilled all over our bags underneath the bus and people happily helped wash out the clothing and string them up between dead busses at the station. I did not perceive the armed people in the road as hostile. I was just fascinated and continued to follow the Zapatista struggle into adulthood and visit Chiapas again.

The first protest I remember attending was one against the Gulf War when I was not yet in kindergarten. The reason I remember this protest so clearly was that it was the first time I saw my parents truly frightened. The police had become violent and we were on the run. While I have been in similar situations since then, I can't imagine what it was like for my parents to be in that situation with a young child. Luckily, we ran past a house whose residents invited us in. The event impacted me greatly. I never saw police as good and have always been uneasy around them. When I entered kindergarten that year while most children researched animals, I decided to do my research project on war because I wanted to better understand why we were at the protest and what had happened.

While I attended several more protests growing up, they were not especially memorable until I started to attend the protests against Highway 55. Highway 55 was a highly contested road expansion only a few blocks from my house. It would be going through parkland that I had biked through during my childhood and felt connected to. People were outraged. Not only was it going through parkland, but it threatened a spring and would be destroying several oak trees that were sacred to the Dakota people. People lived in tree sits, locked down to houses, and camped out to protect the land. Police responded with a night-time raid and were extremely brutal. I was only a distant supporter of these actions, attending a few of the biggest protests, but I remember feeling awed by the tree sits and other actions.

At one of the last protests I remember a friend encouraging me to cross the police lines. He said something along the lines of, "You should cross because you're underage and nothing bad will come of it." While I did not chose to cross the police lines, his words of encouragement stuck with me and made me realize that risking arrest was a needed tactic in any cause.

My senior year in high school I started to find meaning in my life by speaking out and organizing against the wrongs I saw in the world. The first international conflict I became enraged by was the Israeli occupation of Palestine. I decided to participate in a civil disobedience action with the Anti-War Committee against the Israeli occupation and to bring awareness to a massacre that had recently happened. We sat in the middle of a downtown street at rush hour and linked arms until we were pulled away by the police and arrested. I had always thought of civil disobedience as a legitimate way to protest. The only reason not to commit civil disobedience was because you did not want to face the consequences of an arrest. As a minor with supportive parents it was very unlikely that there would be any consequences for me. The first time the opportunity for civil disobedience came up, I took it. As the only minor arrested I was separated from the group. They put me in a holding cell and within fifteen minutes my very proud father was there to pick me up. They released me without pressing charges and I went to the jail support rally for the adults.

While my first arrest was momentous the real learning experience came during the support rally. As the night went on the support rally turned into a small group of people that sat around and shared stories from Palestine. The people sharing the stories were both Palestinian and American. They were stories of harassment, inhumane conditions, and murder. After hearing the stories I became more outraged and realized that I wanted to learn more about the conflict. My Jewish friend, who had recently visited Israel, and I decided to embark on a project where we would interview and Palestinians, Rabbis, and activists to create a documentary and attempt to better understand the conflict. We were coming from two different places, but both knew that what was happening was wrong and had a desire to learn more. While the video was not amazing, education and knowledge about the conflict allowed me to have a deeper analysis and understanding. Even though we can know when something is wrong without knowing much about it, understanding more about the conflict empowered me to speak out, argue, and share a deeper analysis.

I committed civil disobedience again that year when the Iraq War started. I was part of a much larger effort to shut down the Federal Building by blocking the entrances and inside metal detectors. I found that being part of a much larger effort was an even more empowering experience. I also liked that the effort seemed more strategic than just blocking a road. It was a step closer to direct action. When we linked arms in the street with just enough people to get from one side to side, it was clearly just for the publicity. We were quickly and easily removed and the people stopped in the road were random.

When we blocked the federal building they had a harder time removing people purely for the sheer number of people committing civil disobedience and the huge supportive rally. The crowd was more unruly, which I found energizing. After that protest I became interested in hard blockades and making it actually difficult for the police to remove us. Hard blockades make it more difficult to remove people because the protesters attach themselves to materials such as barrels filled with cement with locks, chains, and other means. Unfortunately every plan to use hard blockades fell through. They are more effective at blockading, but also much harder to pull off.

The day after my high school graduation I got on a plane and went to Honduras. I was working with the program Amigos de las Americas (Amigos), a non-profit that is youth-led and sends teenagers into Latin America to help with community projects. While there are huge issues with privileged, mostly white, youth entering into communities they know little about in an attempt to fix complicated issues rooted in colonization and industrialization, I enjoyed my time there and feel okay about the projects I worked on.

I was placed in a small community with another young American woman for eight weeks. The community asked for volunteers to help them build a small kitchen off of the kindergarten, the only school in the community. We lived in a one of the nicest houses in the community with a family of five. The mother was a kindergarten teacher and the father worked in a nearby city where employment opportunities were greater. Amigos had been in the community several times working on different projects. My Spanish level was higher than that of anyone else who had volunteered there, so people were especially welcoming and excited to get to know me.

Each day we worked with men from the surrounding area to build the kitchen. Before we had arrived they had already made adobe bricks for the walls of the kitchen, all we had to do was flatten the terrain, build a foundation, walls, and roof. Amigos has virtually unlimited resources for a motivated volunteer. As a result, we decided to hold a community meeting where we asked attendees what else they would like to see in the community. They asked for a community garden next to the new kitchen. We received seeds and fruit trees from Amigos and planted them with the women who had requested them.

We had few other projects we worked on. We played educational games that Amigos had taught us and cleaned up trash with the children. We also taught in the kindergarten classes and made a girls' soccer team. It was fun to play with the children and they were eager to be around foreigners. In many ways I feel that both the volunteers and community members benefited from Amigos. As volunteers we learned an immense amount. To begin with, we learned Spanish, how to build an adobe building, and basic gardening skills. By calling a meeting, choosing which projects to work on, and requesting material assistance from Amigos, I learned many basic organizational skills. The community obviously got material assistance.

While I currently hold several critiques about Amigos and similar projects, what bothered me at the time was that in order for the community to get material assistance we had to be there. The community really didn't need our help at all to build a kitchen or plant a garden. They had far more skills than us and plenty of available manual labor. What they wanted were the supplies for the projects and the way they chose to get it was by hosting Amigos volunteers. While I enjoyed my time there, my presence was unnecessary, which made me feel consistently uneasy. The last thing I wanted to do was make their lives harder or be somewhere where I wasn't wanted. I don't know how community members felt about our presence, but I do know that the volunteers were unneeded.

It was assumed that after High School I would go to college. Both my parents had gone to college and two out of four of my grandparents had. College was a wonderful experience for my parents, especially my mother. My mother's home life was unpleasant and by getting away to college she had space to find and enjoy herself. She learned that she was smart and played

an active role in SDS. My father also greatly enjoyed his role
in SDS and found his classes both challenging and interesting.
I was not so sold on the idea of college. I spent my senior year
of high school attending classes at the University of Minnesota.
While this was a great improvement from high school classes, I
wasn't at all excited to go to college. I remember telling people
that I had to get good grades in high school so I could go to a
good college and get good grades in college so I could get a
good job so I could work until I died. I felt trapped by a life plan
I hadn't chosen for myself. As a result I did not go directly to
college after high school. I couldn't stand to be a disappointment
so I applied to college, chose a college, and deferred my
acceptance for a year.

Instead of going directly to college I went to Chicago
where my brother lived. I was fairly involved in the anti-war
movement of the time and wanted to continue in it. I got an
internship at the American Friends Service Committee (AFSC)
a Quaker non-profit. Quakers are pacifists and the organization
was a huge part of the non-profit activism in Chicago. I worked
in the anti-war department which consisted of a few interns
and our supervisor. After years of depression and high school I
lacked confidence and a voice.

The woman I worked for was the opposite. She served
as a powerful role model whom I spent at least forty hours a
week with. She was opinionated and passionate. She taught
me many organizational skills and had a lot of influence over
me. The two large projects I worked on that year were a silent
auction that brought in thousands of dollars and the large annual
anti-Iraq war march. While I learned a lot that year, by the end I
realized that I never wanted to work at a non-profit and get paid
for my political work. While AFSC does some good work, it was
inherently flawed. The internal dynamics and hierarchy got in the
way of good projects. I saw that by getting paid for activist work
it could be limiting to the point where one did not end up doing
the work they wanted. I left AFSC wanting to find a better and
more empowering way to organize.

A year after I graduated from high school I went to
Earlham College, a Quaker, private, small liberal arts school.

While I only stayed at the school for one year and disliked many of my experiences there, it was where I was introduced to anarchism and began to form the politics I have today.

Earlham is in Richmond, Indiana, a few miles from the Ohio Border. When I arrived on campus in August of 2004 there was already a buzz around the upcoming elections. It was George Bush against John Kerry and the majority of the campus felt that Kerry was the only hope to end the war and turn the country away from right-wing politics. Ohio was a swing state so many students felt obligated to canvas for Kerry and work on get-out the vote campaigns.

I was not so convinced that Kerry was going to be of much help. From everything I could tell, he wasn't against the Iraq or Afghan war. Despite my general skepticism, I succumbed to the pressure of my peers and mentor from AFSC and participated in the electoral madness. While I refused to campaign for Kerry I decided that I would join the get-out-the-vote campaigns in Ohio. The whole time I went I felt nauseous. After the first house, I knew what I was doing was wrong, but I kept going. I only went once and for a few hours, but it was life changing. I went door knocking; the leaders had chosen neighborhoods with poor voter turn-out, mostly poor neighborhoods made up of mostly people of color. I went from door to door telling people to vote and how to register to vote. Many people engaged me in conversation, asking me what difference would it make, whom I wanted them to vote for, where was I from. I answered honestly. I no longer cared what my peers and mentor thought; they weren't around. I answered that I didn't think their lives would be any different if they voted, I didn't think they would be any better off with a new president, and that I was from hundreds of miles away and had no clue where I was.

I took a lot away from that experience. Having people ask me direct questions and answering them uninhibitedly solidified my beliefs around electoral politics that I didn't even know I had. Voting wasn't going to change a thing for most people. People who don't vote, don't vote for a reason. They already know that it won't change a thing for them.

Developing Politics

The day of the election a good friend came into Ohio from out of town to get-out-the vote and poll watch. I went with her. I partially went because I was still unable to express my discomfort around such activities and partially because I was really excited to see this friend. I also voted for Kerry. While my political views were solidifying, my political actions were lagging behind by a few months. I was not yet solid enough in my political thought to accept the isolation that can come with being radically different from the people around you.

As the college year progressed my political analysis deepened as well as my isolation. While I had many wonderful friends, they could not relate to me politically. I found classes painful. I had entered Earlham as a sophomore and declared international relations for my major. In high school I first became empowered by political organizing against the war. International relations therefore seemed like a good major, but as I quickly tried to fill my required classes I found that most of the classes were in political science and very narrow in their analysis. They were making assumptions I was not willing to make. They were asking questions such as, how can we best spread U.S.-style democracy to other countries? While I was asking, is our government system a good system? My classes were not a place for me to grow intellectually or otherwise.

Halfway through my second semester, while unsatisfied, I still had no intention of dropping out of college. It was better than high school and I had wonderful friends. I had started to get to know the few anarchists on campus. Eryn Trimmer, my co-defendant and partner being one of them. I would not call myself an anarchist for quite a while still, but found that I had more in common with them politically than anyone else on campus. I became a go between for the liberal activist group and the four anarchists.

Near the end of the school year, Earlham invited Bill Kristol to speak on campus. Kristol is a neoconservative and the architect of the Iraq war. The school brought him to speak as part of a program to bring diverse voices to the campus. Because we were a liberal school it was considered diverse to bring a conservative to school. While many students agreed with this, a few of us felt that bringing a white male that often frequented Fox News and was the architect of the Iraq war was not actually bringing a new voice to the table. We did not think he should be at our school and did not want to hear what he had to say. We communicated through email about what to do. One student decided to throw a pie in his face. I was not sure what I thought about pieing Kristol. In my mind there was definitely nothing bad about throwing a pie in an awful man's face; I was just not yet convinced that it was a good tactic.

After the pieing, the school was in chaos. I quickly found myself defending it strongly. As one of a few (less than 10) students willing to defend the pieing, I had people knocking at my door in the middle of the night to yell at me. My closest friends had nothing to say to me. Professors were furious with me. There were people picketing the campus calling the pieing a hate crime. From my point of view the entire school lacked perspective. While I knew the other people who agreed with the pieing, they were just political allies, not friends. The isolation was hard for me to bear and I felt a deep sense of betrayal.

The school expelled the student who pied Kristol. They got ahold of the emails in the lead up to the pieing and questioned each of us about our knowledge. I said nothing and was placed on disciplinary probation. When visiting the school five years later someone asked if I was part of the Kristol 7. I laughed. I had never heard that term before as I left the school soon after the incident, but it seemed fitting as I had recently become part of the RNC 8.

After the pieing I began to truly question if Earlham was a good place for me. I had enrolled in a program in Mexico for the following semester which I was committed to; however, I told myself that if I found anything better to do during my summer vacation I would do my semester abroad, but never return to Earlham. I quickly found that there are many things better than college to do with my time and dropped out of Earlham.

I spent the summer after my first year at college in Bloomington, Indiana working on an anti I-69 campaign. I-69 is a highway that is being built from Canada through Mexico as infrastructure for NAFTA. NAFTA and CAFTA infrastructure projects not only destroy the environment, but also support systems that allow for workers in Latin America to be taken advantage of. This project was the perfect fit for me. It addressed many of the issues I had been concerned with in the past, such as child labor and NAFTA. It avoided some of the key problems I had with past projects. Unlike the war protests, presidential campaign work, and my internship at the American Friends Service Committee, there was nothing abstract about I-69 work.

At Earlham College, I had been exposed to ideas of direct action and it made a lot of sense to me. Instead of electing someone to do something for you, do it yourself. For instance, if you want the U.S. to stop sending troops to Iraq, lock down in front of the doors of a recruiting center instead of voting for the person who spouts the shorter time line for ending the war. I-69 work was direct action because it was attempting to stop NAFTA by not allowing the roads to be built that make NAFTA the best option for the U.S. I also liked that it addressed the problem where I lived, instead of making it purely a foreign-relations issue.

I did not yet consider myself an anarchist; however, I started to exclusively hang out with them as they were the people working on anti I-69 work. While I agreed completely with anarchist theory, it took me a long time to claim the name because of all the negative associations with it. In Bloomington I was first exposed to some common American anarchist sub-culture, such as getting all of our food from dumpsters and hitchhiking.

While I was thoroughly enjoying my life with the anarchists, I was a newbie and hung back on many of the organizing elements. The organizing was dramatically different from any previous organizing I had done, for better and for worse. We were a generally disorganized group. Our meetings didn't have agendas, note takers, or facilitators. As my first time working with anarchists I thought that it was normal and well-thought out strategy. It was not. I remember at one point I got fed up, and I asked if I could take notes or if that was somehow an anarchist taboo. People were fine with my taking notes.

We had rented out a convergence space which most of us also lived in. Mixing living and working quarters did not work that well, as the house quickly became more about living than working. Both inside and outside the house, the dynamic of the group was horrible, but in many ways I did not know any better. Because rejecting all forms of domination is a key aspect in anarchism, the organizing process of any anarchist group should try to reject forms of domination.

One way that many anarchist projects reject hierarchy is by working through consensus, a process that allows every person in the group to stop a decision if they disagree with it. Groups also often discuss the forms of domination existent in the group such as patriarchy and racism in order to take steps to overcome them. In every other group I had worked with we did not address these issues because it was not key to our political philosophy. While I-69 did work by consensus we spent little time addressing the horrible group dynamics, which hindered our ability to be effective organizers. It was not until I left I-69 work and worked with other anarchist that I realized how much internal work was missing.

While our organizing was inefficient, we all gained experience and would become better organizers. I also fell in love that summer, greatly hindering my interest in work. That summer is where I got to know Eryn Trimmer my co-defendant and partner. It was the beginning of a long journey together.

At the end of the summer we had not accomplished as much as we had hoped. We had thought that construction was going to start that summer which would have allowed for direct action tactics such as tree sits and lock downs. It did not start so most anti-I-69 energy went into building connections with other organizers and people who would be directly affected by the new road and into small demonstrations. There were several demonstrations at department of transportation offices, and a large demonstration in Indianapolis where the capital was vandalized and dozens of people were arrested, with only one person charged who was later acquitted. I left after that summer, but anti I-69 work continued and while always flawed, did a lot of good work.

Developing Politics

After I left Indiana I went to Mexico for a study abroad program. While I had already decided to drop out of college, I followed through with my commitment to the program because I was eager to improve my Spanish. Eryn had decided to meet me in Mexico once my program was finished so that we could travel throughout Mexico and Central America and connect with people who were working against NAFTA and CAFTA infrastructure. While we were unsuccessful in making many lasting connections, we learned a lot about each other and the world.

While in Mexico I visited Chiapas twice. The first time was with my entire study abroad program, a group of around twenty people. We visited the autonomous zone of Oventic. By this time I was an anarchist and very excited to visit a real autonomous zone. I was excited to see people living out what I could only dream of. When we arrived we were taken in small groups to see the comandantes of the zone. They wore the traditional Zapatista ski masks and explained the rules of the zone. Once inside we stayed for several days hanging out and taking classes. I could now speak Spanish well and had some context for what the Zapatistas were doing. I was an adult.

It was fascinating talking to people who were participating in something so revolutionary. There was one man whom I spent most of my time talking to. He spoke about many things, but one of the things he focused on was the participation of women, perhaps because I was one. He spoke about how women participated in the political aspect of the zone and took leadership roles; however, this is not what I observed.

There were not many women in Oventic. Among those there, few if any interacted with the internationals. I remember a few women with children. The only women I spoke with were at a small store. The store sold artesian goods that the women had made which consisted mostly of embroidered and woven clothing. I no longer remember what we talked about, but I do remember being impressed by the conversation. There were two women in the store and one did not speak Spanish, although she seemed to understand some of the time when I spoke. Because traditionally women have been discouraged from leaving the private domain, it is not uncommon for women, especially older women, to only speak their indigenous language. This could be one reason that so few women interacted with the Spanish-speaking internationals.

It is clear that the women in the store were better off in many ways than before the Zapatista uprising. They had a worker's collective where they organized with other women. They were getting a better price for their work (partly because of zapoturismo). It was also clear, however, that in many ways most women were still in the same traditional gender roles as before. It has become clear to me that no matter how dramatically and quickly gender roles change on paper, it is a more gradual process in everyday life.

After my semester was over, I returned to Chiapas without my classmates. Eryn and I were there for New Years. The Zapatistas were having a large gathering and starting a march that would go around Mexico for their "Other Campaign" where they were trying to outreach to other Mexicans. Thousands of indigenous people, men women and children, marched into the capital of Chiapas from their indigenous communities. It was an inspiring site. Many had balaclavas on; others had bandanas covering their faces. Everyone was very small—making it clear that the rumors that the Zapatistas were actually Europeans, not indigenous people, could not possibly be true.

Among the marchers was the spokesperson, often referred to as the leader, Subcomendante Marcos. I was very uncomfortable when I saw him in the march. He is mestizo and stood out in the march because he was a foot taller than everyone else. He was surrounded by women with linked arms. I understand why this was done. As the perceived leader, Marcos would be a likely target if someone were to kill a Zapatista. This was reduced with women surrounding him. I understand the practicality of it, but the symbolism of it made me uneasy. Indigenous Zapatistas women and children have already suffered the most from killings. In one instance Mexican soldiers raided a town and massacred many there. It was mostly women and children, since the men were in the mountains as guerillas or working in the fields.

Why should indigenous women put their bodies at risk for a mestizo man? It seems very contradictory to the values and written word of the Zapatistas. Why should the most oppressed in a society protect the most privileged? (Marcos is also highly educated.) I worry that it reflects that things have not actually changed regarding women in the Zapatista movement. I also worry that the indigenous Zapatistas who have organized themselves so well feel like they could not keep it up without Marcos. If this were not true, why would people be so willing to risk their life for him? Since Marcos was at least a foot taller than every woman surrounding him, it would not have been hard to shoot him without shooting any women. As a movement, why would the Zapatistas want to send the message that they will sacrifice indigenous women for a highly educated mestizo man? It doesn't make sense and makes me think that perhaps many of things the Zapatistas write are just words.

My encounters with Zapatistas have been both inspiring and discouraging. I'm glad that I have seen a small portion of what they do in person. If I had only read books about them and what they have written I would probably think that they are flawless and placed them on a pedestal. It is a good reminder that even in radical revolutionary movements some types of change are gradual and that no movement is perfect. We can change some things quickly and dramatically, but it is a much more gradual process that takes generations to change the way we interact with each other and the assumptions that we make about one another. I think that this is perhaps why identity politics often get lost in political discussions. It is not as simple as overthrowing a government. It involves a change in the way we think and interact with each other.

After Chiapas, Eryn and I traveled to Oaxaca, Mexico. We connected with an anarchist group that sends internationals into rural communities that were having issues with paramilitary violence. The Mexican government and paramilitary groups are much less likely to commit acts of violence with internationals present. We were there during an especially tame time and the group was unsure where to send us. No communities had been attacked recently, but the group also did not want to send us away, as an attack could happen at any time. They first sent us to a small mountainous community where we were to hang out and help with the coffee harvest. It rained the entire time, so no one worked on the coffee harvest and we were unsure what to do with ourselves. We had very little interaction with any villagers and played a lot of cards. It was hard to tell if we were wanted or not, so we chose to sit back and wait. The community decided that we were unneeded and we were sent to a different village.

The second village was much bigger and very excited about our presence; however, they seemed mostly excited because we were Americans, not because of any shared political ideas or because they felt safer with us there. They wanted us to teach the middle-schoolers English. Teaching English was against the Oaxacan group's mission. They wanted to support people in their indigenous languages and culture and felt that teaching English promoted the opposite. They saw that many people were leaving their communities for the United States which, while it brought money into the community, came at a great cost.

Eryn and I decided to teach English anyway. It was never a real question. We were in a much more privileged position and it was not our place to determine what was best for the community or to withhold knowledge that we possessed. When I first entered the classroom I asked how many kids had immediate family in the States. Everyone in the room raised their hand and I realized that English really might be a useful skill for many of them, whether or not it was the best for their community.

The third community we were sent to was closer to what we had originally expected. They wanted us to be there and seemed to be on the same page as the group in Oaxaca. They were working on being a sustainable community and were excited to show us their projects. They had a green house, beekeeping, coffee, and other means to support both their financial and food needs. They were also happy for the extra hands for the coffee harvest and improving the road into the town. We found the town inspirational and still talk about wanting to keep bees to this day.

After Mexico we hitchhiked down to Guatemala. Over my lifetime I have spent a lot of time in Mexico and was surprised how different Guatemala was. In both Guatemala and El Salvador, people were eager to share stories of brutality from the wars. Partially because these wars happened before my lifetime and in another place they seemed a part of history, and I really did not understand the lasting impact they had until I got there. In Guatemala we met with organizations who were still trying to get justice for people who disappeared in the '70s. While that was not entirely surprising, I was surprised to hear that government was continuing to use the same tactics. We talked to people who had friends who had been disappeared very recently. We did not connect with people working on anti-NAFTA infrastructure work, but I was inspired that people continued to resist the government even when the danger of death and disappearance was real. People were far from apathetic.

When I worked at the American Friends Service Committee, I connected well with an El Salvadorian man who worked the front desk. On several occasions he told me stories about his experience during the war. They were horrific stories of people being cut open and mutilated. Unlike in Guatemala where I was completely removed from the war, the second I stepped into El Salvador I thought about his stories. I would stare into the distance in the direction of the mountains and imagine what the survivors were doing now. The conversations we had with people reinforced his stories. I was genuinely surprised that people would want to share stories with us given that we were random Americans. We were hitchhiking so we met an assortment of people who did not all have the opportunity to talk to foreigners regularly. I feel that peoples' eagerness to share their stories with us was partially because in some ways it validated their experiences. I was impressed that they had not let all of the tragedy in their lives silence them, but pushed their stories to be heard.

Our next longer stop was Costa Rica. In Costa Rica we did not attempt to meet with organizers, but decided to take a

more traditional tourist route. We enjoyed nature. We mainly
stayed in a National Park that was far off the beaten path. It
took us all day to hitchhike in because no one went on the road
after which there was a small hike. We camped and enjoyed
the jungle, monkeys, and hot water springs. After some heavy
experiences it was very grounding to go camping. We decided
to head home after that. While our trip was very educational,
we were not connecting with the type of people we thought we
would. We were not meeting anarchists or people working on
anti-infrastructure projects. We knew that if we were starting to
get worn out we should head home then, because there was still a
long road home.

On the way home we got a ride that probably impacted
me more than any other aspect of the trip. The driver was an El
Salvadorian trucker who eventually shared that he had been to
the States when he trained at the School of the Americas. I was
speechless and almost broke down into tears. The School of the
Americas is where they taught Latin American armies torture
tactics that they later employed on their prospective countries
The people that went to the School of Americas were the people
who murdered, tortured, and mutilated their fellow countrymen.
They were who we were hearing the stories about. Aside from
the Americans, they were the bad guys. Not everyone was sent
to the School of the Americas; it was reserved for the leaders, the
worst of the worst.

A year before I had gotten this ride I had gone to Georgia
for a protest at the School of Americas. It is a moving vigil,
where the names of the murdered and disappeared were called
out. The protest was especially meaningful to me because on the
way to the protest I was in a horrible car crash where the van
flipped several times and I was sure that I was going to die. Life
and death were heavy on my mind during the protest. A year
later, I was meeting someone who went to that school and he
was very nice. He bought us cokes and chips and even waited
while we went through customs at borders. It blew my mind, but
it made me really understand that even people who commit evil
acts are victims of a larger problem.

We need to be held responsible for our actions, and

such acts cannot be tolerated, but I realized that it is important to understand that most people who do really horrible things do so because their basic human needs have not been met. Whether it is food, shelter, love, or the threat of those things being taken away, something was amiss for him and his fellow soldiers. Seeing this man's good side made me realize that we all have good and bad parts and we need to create and defend communities that allow for that inherent good in everyone to thrive.

Returning to the States after being away is always a hard adjustment for me. Eryn and I were in Chicago and planning on traveling in the states awhile before finding a place to settle down. Hitching out of Chicago is always horrible. We were getting short rides from one exit to another. We were stuck in South Chicago for a while, where almost everyone is black, when someone decided to shoot blanks at us. It was scary and I broke down. I understood why I was unwelcome in the neighborhood and that people did not appreciate two white, upper-middle-class kids asking for ride, but was still hurt. I was finally back in the States, but I was more of an intruder than ever. I was severely homesick and wanted to be somewhere I belonged. We decided to ditch our travel plans and go to Minneapolis, where quickly we settled down into a life not that different from our life today.

Only the most privileged of people can travel in the ways I have. Every time I travel, I enjoy it, but I also question the impact I have on the people and places that I travel. As a tourist, I am not always wanted. I negatively affect economies, cultures, lives, and the earth. I have also learned that sometimes people appreciate outsiders that will hear their stories, want the money that I bring, and desire to find common ground. I know that I have grown from my travels. I have gained a broader prospective and understanding of the world. I have brought that home with me, and it enriches the work that I do here. I do not think we can determine if overall it is good or bad for me to travel. I have found that it is impossible to live in this world with my morals and values and not be hypocritical at times. I believe that high values are important, but impossible to live up to. I learn a lot from traveling and try to do so conscionably, but recognize that I have not always been welcomed or appreciated and for very good reason.

Max Specktor

My parents were both fairly connected to the local radical activist and arts communities in Minneapolis, so I was exposed to a lot of stuff as a kid that was formative and still inspires me today. I remember one fall when I was a kid going to some event at the Minnehaha Falls near the Mississippi River in Minneapolis. This was during the time of the "Minnehaha free state," where a number of radical environmental activists, along with Dakota people and other American Indians, had occupied a section of land considered sacred to many people in order to protect it from a very unpopular highway rerouting that was in progress.

I mostly just remember seeing the people living in the trees and being slightly confused as to why they were pissing in buckets. But it also looked very fun, getting to live in a tree. I don't think it ever once crossed my mind that this was an illegal occupation, and these people were doing much more than just hanging out in trees. The eviction of the free state, which was the largest police action in Minnesota history at the time, hit sort of close to home, when a close family friend of ours was arrested just for reporting on the event and had his camera and equipment damaged in the process.

The summer before high school I was assigned work for the history class I was going to enter. I remembered being fairly pissed that we had homework over the summer, but it was just reading one book, which I was generally pumped about. We were assigned to read A People's History of the United States. Of course, I didn't pick it up until about a week before school was supposed to start, but I was really fascinated after opening the book. I remember that while reading, I grew continuously more surprised and angered when reading about the corruption and

171

atrocities that went on and continued to occur. At first my attitude was generally more forgiving toward older history, like learning of the genocide started by Columbus and the first European immigrants; I figured it was so long ago, and that crazy shit like that just happened back then. As the history "progress"-ed, I came to understand more clearly how these genocides continue to play out today, and that ideas like "manifest destiny" and the power structures that support such ideas are exponentially more dangerous today.

Now, I'm not trying to say that a book assigned by my public school was responsible for my entire political consciousness, but it definitely got the ball rolling, and spurred me to find more information that could help me deal with this new understanding of our world. During my first couple years of high school I read a ton, within and outside school, and fortunately, I was able to get credit for some of the material that I wanted to read anyway. Apart from this and one or two other classes, I mostly didn't care for high school at all, and I only survived thanks to a program that allowed me to take classes at the University of Minnesota during my junior and senior years of high school.

One of our big projects in freshman English class was to write a ten-page report of an "American Hero." So, while many people started researching the traditional heroes, I picked Abbie Hoffman, one of the founders of the radical, hippie-inspired, Yippie movement. I was definitely interested in the '60s and their resistance movements at this time because it was my parents' generation, and I always held some fascination for what was going on during their time. I had seen a movie on TV about Hoffman, and was inspired by his political theater.

The real value of learning about his life, however, was just reading about a turbulent time from a radical's perspective and seeing that these rebellious events aren't just something confined to history but are a part of continuing struggles and ideas. There are definitely a number of other personal histories of that time period that I wish I had read, but it still opened up my eyes to a lot of things— specifically, the ways that we can engage and fight this system, without working within it. This was

172

the point where I began to give up on the idea that flying straight and going to college (or further) as the most effective way for me to have any say in this world. I don't think I got a very good grade on the paper.

Another pretty important source of radical literature for me at this point was, in an ironic way, CrimethInc. My brother had ordered their anarchist primer, Days of War, Nights of Love, while in high school and suggested I read it. Their history and analysis made me even angrier than reading A People's History, yet it also suggested some alternatives that piqued my interest. At the time I held a lot of conflicting views from the book, some that I still hold today. The big one at the time was the book's aesthetic of dropping out and crime. I still have a similar conflict, but the reasons for my original views had more to do with the sense that these actions were morally wrong; at the time, I had imagined revolution as some sort of moral choice. I began to develop a sense of revolution as a strategy for collective survival and with this framework I started to think about these tactics more seriously.

So, with an open mind, I tried to critique their position from a strategic point of view instead of with a moralistic argument. In fact, it led to one of my first writing efforts outside of school, in which I tried to diagram what I believed resistance/changing of society should look like. I described society as a circle where we are marching in line, stuck going around and around forever. We may think that we are making progress, but that's only because our line is so huge we can't see that it just goes in circles.

To gain freedom, I imagined we needed to get everyone to break out of line. People who want to live off crime and society's excess would break out of this line but be stuck, enclosed by the circle, moving freely, but confined to the area within the circle. These people would naturally be looked down upon as weirdos for not doing what everyone else is doing. But if everyone could break out of line then there would be no human cage to hold any of these people, and that's what I wanted: a mass refusal, or at least enough of one to break the line permanently.

Developing Politics

During the spring of my 8th grade, the preemptive strikes began in Iraq. I hadn't been paying much attention to the political climate in the aftermath of 9/11, but finally people my age were talking about the current events, and speaking out about the real reasons behind the war. I walked out of middle school as one of a handful of students who were able to leave without any punishments.

In high school, I continued to participate in the walkouts, but at this point I was also involved in promoting the protests in advance. The group that generally called for these protests was Youth Against War and Racism (YAWR), and consisted of students from across the cities, but was in fact controlled by paid organizers from Socialist Alternative. I felt like I had a good amount of agency in helping plan the actions, but in reality all the actions fit the formulas taught us by the adults from the socialist group. This repetition and hierarchy made my involvement in the anti-war movement very uninspiring. I was committed to doing organizing work, but I wanted to be part of something that was more than a front group.

I began my first real job when I was 14, as a dishwasher at a Jamaican restaurant a few blocks from my house. Our next door neighbor was friends with the owner's daughter, and so my neighbor's son and I both got jobs there at the same time. The owners and most of the employees were part of the same family and spoke with heavy Jamaican slang, so I felt like an outsider at first, but enjoyed the work. I didn't make much money— getting paid under the table and less than minimum wage, but it wasn't very hard work, and I got to eat as much as I wanted, so I didn't complain. I quit after one of my friend's paychecks bounced and my paycheck was over a week late.

During the school year throughout high school, I would work as a Hebrew tutor at my synagogue on the weekends. This basically meant I goofed off with my friends, and taught the kids just enough to make their parents feel like their traditions were being passed down to some extent. I just thought it was silly that all these parents were paying a lot of money so that their kids could learn to repeat a bunch of words that they didn't even understand.

174

The summer after freshman year, I got a job with a local theater company called Heart of the Beast, which happened to be the theater group that my mom worked with when she first moved to Minnesota. I was part of a group of high school kids that worked full-time to create a puppet show that addressed issues of global justice, focusing specifically on water and water privatization, and we performed the show for free around the inner city.

Aside from the global issues we were talking about, the project also taught me about injustice more directly, because most my coworkers/artists were kids who got the job through a job program for low-income youth. I learned about the juvenile justice system from kids who were in an out of lock-up, and first generation immigrants who were struggling to keep up due to language barriers. Our theater pieces were all about greed and corruption, but didn't exactly leave any of us with a clear course for action. All in all, it was an inspiring few months.

Early on in high school some friends and I started a band. We played punk rock. I had received classical training on the piano, and wanted to pursue music further than just my school band. Throughout high school we played a good number of shows and spent a lot of time practicing and fucking around. One of our first shows was at an above-ground punk venue for youth called the Twin Cities Underground. It was a pretty sweet project, although I took it for granted at the time. It was run by volunteer staff (who were probably parents of kids in the neighborhood) and operated as a show space/hangout for teenagers. I wasn't really into the scene at the time, but now I really appreciate that places like that exist for youth, whether or not they are legitimately run.

My favorite shows of ours, however, were the ones in the basements. We would play at one of our houses or some other friend's house to a packed basement of good friends. It made a lot more sense to perform for our friends, instead of for complete strangers. The majority of the bands and entertainment that I experienced were in my friends' houses or underground show spaces. This was obviously partly because of the age limitations on public venues, but it also made it harder for this entertainment to be commodified and commercialized. And these parties weren't just underage kids getting drunk; there were folks of all ages and that's what made it exciting.

Music wasn't just important for me in an artistic, creative sense; in this case I was joining a community of sorts, one of my own choosing, outside of school and family. I played in the school jazz band and ensemble, and made many friends in high school, but I never felt like I belonged to any legitimate community within that system. Not that the community fostered around basement shows and punk music was completely ideal, but it definitely was more exciting and life-affirming.

I think that investing more time in these activities and friendships made me ever less-excited about attending school. It wasn't that I hated the arbitrary work and testing more so than before, but more that I completely divested from any serious social connections. Basically, I realized that it is possible to create our own circles and communities outside the sterile environments of school and work.

As I started gaining interest in the community that existed surrounding the punk scene, it became important to also embrace the do-it-yerself (DIY) ethic. The shows and parties that I was going to could probably be described as a subculture, and the DIY ethic gave it that cultural element. After shows, if we were hungry, we would go dumpster-diving, as there were no places open to eat. Gnarly bikes would pile up outside the house, so you could tell there was something interesting going on inside. And when the cops came to bust a party, the revelers would show off their anti-authoritarian tendencies. The bands would teach themselves their instruments and make their merchandise by themselves. I knew this wasn't the solution to all the problems I saw in the world, but it felt like a community that would support what I wanted to do.

The summer before my senior year in high school I attended a camp put on by a local Quaker organization. The experience was a week-long experiment in cooperative living and non-violent communication. The structure was such that everybody was expected to contribute a certain amount of time to cooking, cleaning, childcare, and organizational work. The whole week there were also workshops that anyone could attend on a wide range of political/interpersonal topics and skill-shares. Beyond being just a relaxing weekend I found this to be a very educational and transforming experience. Later, I would notice that a lot of the anarchist gatherings I would go on to attend shared a lot of the same characteristics as this camp, something I've continued to value within the anarchist community.

One important idea that crystallized for me as a result of this camp was that of alternative infrastructure. Since I had until this point been politically active primarily doing counter recruitment work in high schools, I began to consider what an alternative to the military might look like. Obviously the camp taught non-violent ways of dealing with problems, but more precisely, what I came away with was something doubly subversive. I began to realize that by learning alternative skills and imagining viable alternatives, we can create sustainable infrastructures, and that this process necessitates a certain level of confrontation to the established systems. My dream coming out of this week was to establish some sort of alternative defense force, one that was based on principles of anti-oppression and voluntary cooperation. I wished to be able to steer kids away from military involvement into something that was more honorable and productive.

It quickly dawned on me that this was a very ambitious goal, and that it would take some serious organizing that I definitely wasn't cut out for at the time. It felt good, nonetheless, to have a very idealistic plan, something I continue to maintain to this day. Fueling myself with perfect visions of society, I started taking smaller steps toward realizing those dreams. A few weeks after returning from the camp, I signed up for a weekend-long workshop designed to train people in non-violent communication with the specific goal of being able to lead workshops in prisons with so-called violent offenders. The workshop involved sharing stories and personal histories, as well as brainstorming and active listening exercises. Beyond being a very valuable communication skills class, the workshop taught me much more because of its systemic analysis of violence, and the deeply moving personal accounts from other participants. I remember an epic feeling of hope learning that so much interpersonal violence in our society can be traced back to underlying systems of oppression—meaning that if those systems can be dismantled, so much of the bullshit in our world should be much easier to clean up. At the same time, I began to understand what restorative justice would really look like, and realized that prisons are never going to solve anything, that we can deal with our problems many other ways.

Shortly after returning from camp, I got involved in Food Not Bombs, a group that cooked food that had been donated or salvaged from dumpsters and shared it publicly. The cool thing about it was that it was not designed to be a charity, as everyone served themselves, and the volunteers hung out and ate the meal with everyone else. It wasn't meant as a solution to hunger, and we didn't believe that we were going to adequately be able to feed everybody who needed it, but it served as a symbol of the waste that society creates, and how that excess might better be used. I learned rather quickly that dumpster-diving wasn't something that we discovered and could therefore "share" with the city's homeless people, but was a skill that dispossessed people everywhere already used. At times I remember feeling proud for spending less on food and rescuing wasted resources, but I began to recognize that I wasn't going to solve any of the root causes of waste and hunger by trying to throw away my privilege and dumpster a new life. I wanted to politicize these issues, not fetishize them.

After being active in Food Not Bombs for some time, as well as learning more and more about food industries and their effect on our planet, I started questioning my personal dietary choices. It seemed that the popularity of being vegan also pushed me toward reconsidering my diet, but I wondered how easy that would be. I think a very important factor in my decision-making was the idea that a solely moral decision not to eat certain foods was a pretty weak decision for me. Basically, I never believed that we all should just change certain aspects of our life in a moralistic way so that the world can be saved. For about a year, I considered myself some kind of a vegetarian, usually meaning that I would mostly shop vegan, but eat anything if I got it for free, thinking that the more important impact was my economic impact on the industry, not the power of my moral choice. I didn't call myself vegan or vegetarian, maybe sometimes jokingly referred to myself as "freegan," but I still identified as one of these categories to myself. I met older radicals who would talk about the silliness of many vegans' politics, especially the ones who will criticize the cruelty of the meat industry and then go on to consume tons of soy products that are grown in totally fucked-up ways. I did, however, like to use the veg-argument with friends or family members to confront them with a conversation about domination over animals and other related topics.

I don't want everyone in the world to stop eating meat, but I like having the conversation with people to get them to wonder why we do feel like it makes sense to systematically kill any being for our own consumption. But for me it was never just because we should think of animals as nice, cute friends of ours that can feel pain. More than that, I wanted to confront my friends and family with the fact that whether or not we actually see it day to day, we exist in an ecosystem, and we can't think of ourselves outside that ecosystem. If we do, we will surely continue to destroy every resource at an exponentially growing rate, including the animals that service our meat industry.

Eventually I decided to become strictly vegetarian and give up meat for good, but it actually wasn't solely for any of the reasons I listed thus far. I made the decision once and for all when I was in jail. I think it caused this very specific emotional response in me. I felt like I had no control over my life anymore, I wanted to establish some self control, even in what seemed like a totally restricting situation. When asked if I had any dietary needs by the guard I responded "vegetarian," even if it meant I might eat less, because it offered me a personal choice and gave me a little self control. I don't want to belittle the trying experiences that vegans undergo while incarcerated, or for that matter anybody who is denied access to their needs while incarcerated, but it felt like a small victory for me, and even after getting out, it made sense that as long as my freedom could be taken away like that, I should live my life with as much self control as possible. Now I see my dietary choices as just one discipline, among many, of living my radical lifestyle.

I want to be very cautious about what I mean when I talk about a radical lifestyle, however. When I first considered myself a radical, or anarchist, I began to think about it in terms of living an uncompromising life, living at odds with all of our social norms. I wanted to travel unconventionally, not work jobs, and create spaces as free from oppression as possible. Now, what I see as a radical lifestyle has more to do with transforming the social structures in which I already live. I don't want to drop out, but I would like to strategically and seriously change the way that my social circles and I exist in relation to our environment and to each other. I can be vegetarian and still hang out with any of my meat-eating friends, and we can still relate in many ways. I can continue to be a feminist while going to parties where patriarchy permeates the music and the relationships, because I have the privilege to put up with the personal discomfort, and in doing so, I can talk about those subjects with folks who may have not given them much thought.

I think it's kind of silly to change friends because you think that your political or lifestyle choices create too much of a chasm amidst your friendship. Obviously there are friendships that have very tangible obstacles, or oppressive dynamics, that force somebody to rethink the relationship, but my friendships have always been one of the most important things to me, and I work hard to maintain the affinities that I have spent my whole life building.

Luce Guillén-Givins

Halfway through high school, I started looking around for a real way to be involved in a political cause. Through our cousin the priest and our church bulletin, I had heard about a local group called Coalición de Derechos Humanos ("Derechos Humanos" for short), which did awareness and advocacy work around immigrant rights and the border.

Conspiracy to Riot

The 2000-mile U.S./Mexico border, a little over an hour south of Tucson, is the most crossed border in the world and, at the time, was being heavily militarized at strategic points. Starting under the Clinton administration, Joint Task Forces of military and civilian agencies across the border region started constructing high-tech barricades in major urban centers, pushing illegal crossing out to isolated and dangerous expanses of the desert. Border enforcement agents have increased drastically in number, and the federal government continues deploying national guardsmen to the region.

The process has been a calculated accompaniment to the development of neoliberal economic policies such as NAFTA (North American Free Trade Agreement), which are characterized by the privatization of public enterprises, deregulation in the interest of corporate profit, and the forced restructuring of third-world economies in order to create a global underclass entirely dependent on a small number of major multinational corporations and their affiliated state entities. Border militarization is a necessary component of neoliberalism or "free trade," restricting the free movement of people to further limit their options for resisting these forces.

Militarization began in California and Texas long before it hit Arizona, pushing crossers in from both sides and causing Arizona's vast Sonoran Desert to sustain the highest number of annual illegal crossings and, consequently, deaths. Since 1996, thousands of people searching for work and the simple ability to feed their families have died crossing the U.S./Mexico border, most from exposure to the elements.[4]

Feeling a personal connection to these issues, I began attending Derechos Humanos' weekly meetings. At the time, border issues were rarely discussed and little understood outside of the Southwest, even on the Left, and we were involved in pushing the issues onto the national consciousness. My close personal relationship to immigration made the many issues at play ones I couldn't ignore and, having grown up a witness to the conditions of the U.S./Mexico border, I wanted to be a part of bringing it down.

Though I was a regular presence in the group, my

participation was limited by age and the fact that most of my time went toward school. Nonetheless, it was the first political community I was a part of, and I learned a lot from my experiences with the group. Through Derechos Humanos, I participated for the first time in planning protests, helped with the nuts and bolts of organizing a conference of groups working on border and immigration issues, and spent time with journalists working on stories about the border. The group was mostly comprised of people much older than myself, who had been activists and organizers for years, and one of the most important things I got out of it was the opportunity to see how small political communities sustain themselves over the long term. Though a commitment to creating large-scale societal change was what centered the group, I quickly saw that an ethic of love and caring on an interpersonal level was just as important to making movements thrive.

My time with the group also jump-started my political development. When I got involved, I already had a personal understanding of why immigration policies and border enforcement were problematic, developed through watching my own relatives and other members of my community struggle to make it in a society structured to keep them at the bottom. The dehumanizing aspects of these policies were apparent all around me, hitting home hardest every time I watched the ways that my dad was disrespected by authorities merely because of his immigrant status. But working with Derechos Humanos helped me develop a systemic analysis of the situation, framing the things I witnessed and felt personally within the context of neoliberalism, and illuminating the reactionary xenophobia and racism rampant throughout the U.S. that made such atrocities possible.

My involvement with the group also exposed me to other political happenings in Tucson, and I started to attend a variety of protests and events that interested me. This led to my first experience with riot cops, at a protest of the proposed FTAA (Free Trade Area of the Americas) in spring of 2001. What started as a small but lively march through Tucson's downtown ended with a police riot on 4th Avenue, the city's small counter-cultural corridor. As we headed down the street, we were flanked by cops with more gear than I'd ever seen.

Suddenly, they started running toward us firing less-lethal projectiles and barking orders; my first reaction—fear—was quickly counterbalanced by incredulity as I watched an officer trip over his own gun, so big it had been dragging on the ground. Having no idea what else to do, I ducked into the nearest restaurant to wait the whole thing out. Unscathed as I was, I left the whole situation feeling excitement and starting to dream about getting more involved in what I was starting to know as the "anti-globalization movement." It would be several years still before I realized that the movement I wanted to join was actually on its last legs, and by then it had managed to shape my analysis of global capitalism and the multitude of possibilities for driving it into the ground.

September 11th (which happened a month into my senior year of high school) elucidated my own politics for me, offering little new content but demonstrating that my ideas were much further from the mainstream than I had known.

In particular, I was suddenly aware of my total lack of patriotic sentiment. I wasn't trying to be anti-American or reject anything in particular at that point, I had just never received whatever education or indoctrination it is that leaves most people with a feeling of love for their country. Lacking any sense of personal connectedness to the attacks that had occurred in a place so far away from me, I didn't feel that the fact of their having occurred on "American soil" meant I should care more than I would have had they happened elsewhere.

I pondered the legacy of American imperialism that was reflected back on the entire nation that day, acknowledging the horror of the attacks but unable to accept the collectively held delusion that we aren't all culpable for the atrocities committed daily in our name. I couldn't think of September 11th without also thinking about the country's origins in genocide and slavery, and the brutal exploitation of the world's people and resources that the World Trade Center symbolized.

I was also forced to consider the term "radical" at this point, as the liberal reaction to 9/11—primarily, to self-censor and go into hibernation or, even, to jump on the warmongering bandwagon—caught me by surprise. Not even aware that an option outside the liberal/conservative dichotomy existed, I thought I was a liberal and made assumptions about how people "like me" would respond. I figured they would naturally see the lies and hypocrisies flying all over the place, and would think critically about the attacks, what they really said about the United States' position in the world, and any necessary course of action or reaction. When this response didn't materialize, I was compelled to search for others ways to identify myself. For the first time, I recognized radicalism—that is, an attention to the roots of any given situation—as a valid concept, and decided that it was a much better description of my political leanings.

Most importantly, 9/11 taught me that I wasn't a pacifist. I was immediately opposed to the wars of aggression that the U.S. embarked on after the attacks, but it wasn't because of any steadfast commitment to non-violence. Instead, it was because of an opposition to imperialism, capitalism and racism, as well as a recognition of who would suffer and for what ends in these particular wars. At the same time, I knew intrinsically that I would feel a strong sense of solidarity with the invaded of Afghanistan and Iraq as they began to defend themselves and their homelands against attack.

And I began to think intensively about resistance movements and the times when non-violence isn't an option, realizing I already recalled many armed struggles in my litany of inspiration. I was surprised by this, realizing that I had really just assumed I was a pacifist without thinking. I guess this was mostly because of the influence of Catholicism and the concept of the "sanctity of life" on my world view, though in fact there is a strong tradition of solidarity between devout Catholics and armed struggles for liberation.[5] Recognizing this tradition helped me define my own convictions.

But it was also a simple result of the fact that "pacifism" and "non-violence" are terms wielded with little meaning or sincerity in common discourse in the U.S. Though I have profound respect for people who commit to active non-violence and live accordingly, most Leftist and liberal activists throw the terms around because they know they're supposed to and because they're confident they won't be challenged to demonstrate any conviction.

The post-9/11 atmosphere also demonstrated that many of the same Leftists and liberals who were so quick to qualify their activism as "non-violent," as if that made it legitimate, fell silent as the Bush regime rolled out its anti-terrorism measures, viciously targeting communities of color domestically and abroad. Their passive acceptance of such brutal and oppressive measures rendered their feigned commitment to non-violence transparent. Reading Ward Churchill's essay "Pacifism as Pathology" helped me sort out, in no uncertain terms, the issues that 9/11 brought to the forefront of my mind. [6] Specifically, his essay clearly laid out the difference between the desire for peace that most of us share and the ways that some movements exercise a pathological permutation of "pacifism" that undermines our attempts at building the sort of just society in which peace is actually possible.

Eventually, I decided to attend Macalester College in St. Paul. I was considering a number of similar schools, but was drawn to Macalester for its urban locale. My visit to Macalester during the fall of my senior year coincided with the U.S. invasion of Afghanistan, and student activists had organized a walk-out, disrupting "business as usual" as an expression of opposition to the war. I enthusiastically joined, walking out of the class I was visiting along with a handful of students. I had never been involved in anything like the walk-out, which had a huge turnout relative to the college's small size, and the feeling in the air seemed to be one of limitless potential. Indicative of the fact that I was losing interest in focused academics and gaining interest in political protest, I finally made my decision to attend Macalester over other schools because I wanted to be a part of things like this walk-out.

I moved to St. Paul in the fall of 2002 to begin school and quickly became involved in about as many different campus political causes as I could. I wasn't sure exactly what I wanted to be doing, so I attended a lot of meetings and events in search of the right place. Having seen the size of the previous year's anti-war walkout, I had expected to find a large, organized activist presence. Instead, it turned out that the mobilization against the invasion of Afghanistan had been a rather isolated event, and the spirit of it was fleeting. A year later, the activist population was back to its usual, much smaller size. Though this disappointed me at the time, it was liberating in many ways because it pushed to me to jump into the activist fold with more initiative and confidence, rather than looking for leadership from other students or existing organizations. I was quickly integrated into Mac's small activist community and started to develop more meaningful relationships with a few of the people I was working with.

Over the course of my first semester, the groups I was most involved with were the campus Green Party chapter, the "Student Labor Action Coalition," and "Macalester Peace and Justice Committee" (MPJC). I met some wonderful, radical individuals through the first two but I wasn't particularly inspired or motivated by the projects they focused on. When I returned for spring semester, I turned most of my energy to MPJC.

MPJC, which has existed for years at Mac, was rather amorphous, shifting in focus and structure based on whoever came to meetings and was willing to do the work. It was the first time I recognized an opportunity to have a hand in determining the direction and nature of a political project, and I had developed a positive rapport with the few other people who were part of the group. News reports suggested that a U.S. invasion of Iraq was imminent, and so in addition to attending city-wide demonstrations, we started to formulate campus-specific plans for the day the war started. After meeting with a wider group of interested students, we decided to call for another walk-out that would converge on the commons. The plan was to set up a "peace camp" there, which would serve as a sort of visible headquarters for what we hoped would be escalating resistance to the war. The students would then march off campus to join with the larger anti-war march planned for that same day.

The invasion came over spring break, when most students were away. I attended the emergency demo in downtown Minneapolis and then began to prepare for the next week, when we planned to stage the walk-out after students returned. Though in retrospect the walk-out and "peace camp" seem pretty tame and limited by their focus on such a small student body, I definitely felt excited to be a part of them at the time. The camp stayed up 'til the semester ended and was quite successful at keeping opposition to the war at the forefront of students' minds. It also served the same function for prospective students visiting that spring that the previous year's walkout had served for me, attracting a number of incoming freshman who would go on to become committed radical activists beyond Macalester later on.

At the same time that I was enthusiastically involved in this campus-focused anti-war work, I was becoming involved in what I thought of as riskier and more exciting activities as well. I felt passionately that the "war on terror" was an issue that I had a personal, moral obligation to address, and this made me open to a diversity of protest methods and tactics that, a year or two prior, weren't even on my radar. In the company of slightly more experienced friends, I participated in my first banner hang and started exploring the art of political stenciling and graffiti. Those activities, which from my vantage point now seem safe and easy, were exhilarating and romantic at the time. In my mind, every small act outside of state-sanctioned forms of protest was another step toward a lifetime of resistance.

I was also arrested for the first time that spring, an event that felt monumental as I prepared for it and yet rapidly faded to the mundane. The arrest came through my participation in an act of civil disobedience in protest of the invasion of Iraq, organized by the Anti-War Committee.[7] I wanted to escalate my opposition to the war at every opportunity and the AWC's planned action seemed like a natural next step. More than 60 of us blocked the entrances to the Federal Building in Minneapolis, demanding an end to the war. I had been nervous and enthused going into the action, and I felt resolute throughout.

Even after a police horse stepped on my hand and almost broke it, I refused to leave except in handcuffs. By the time of our court date, though, I had already processed the whole event and moved past it. Though I didn't regret my involvement, the experience itself felt more like something I needed to get out of the way than it did a powerful form of opposition to the war, and I felt disillusioned with symbolic acts of civil disobedience.

Spurred by 9/11 and the invasion of Afghanistan, I had gone through a period of dramatic political development in only a couple of years. As I left home and began the transition into adulthood, I felt a sense of urgency about world events. Maybe more importantly, I started to feel real agency in this time period. Where before I may have, without thinking, relegated myself to a participatory but non-influential role in resistance movements, in this period I started to assume that I could take a much more active role in determining the course of events ahead of me. I thought hard about my political identification, trying to sort out my thoughts.

I was increasingly interested in anarchism, a political ideology of which I had previously been totally ignorant but which now seemed a perfect fit for my new sense of individual agency. What I was finding was that the movements I felt most affinity with tended to be populated by "self-proclaimed anarchists" or at least to model anarchist organizing structures, and so I began to take the term quite seriously. It was clear to me that dismantling systems of coercion and hierarchy was not only a fundamental step but, rather, the very heart of the change I wanted to see.

This same year, my mom sent me a copy of Dorothy Day's autobiography, The Long Loneliness. Dorothy Day was an uncompromising anarchist and the book was transformative for me, putting the concept of anarchism in clear perspective as an ideology of liberation. Though I no longer thought of myself as a pacifist, I was especially impressed with Day's demonstrated commitment to social justice through active non-violence, and felt moved by all aspects of her life. Her story was a rich refutation of the stereotype that anarchists advocated for chaos and destruction, demonstrating instead a lifetime of putting anarchists' principles like mutual aid into practice.

Though the activities I was involved in at the time were perhaps insignificant in the grand scheme of things, they were essential elements of my journey into committed radicalism. They were also important in that they were instrumental in forging relationships with people whom I count amongst my closest friends and comrades today. By the end of the year, I was already feeling disillusioned with the anti-war movement, turned off by liberals who dominated demonstrations and organizing. Their message of patriotism and moderation didn't resonate with me, and seemed unforgivably weak in the face of the unspeakable violence perpetrated by the American government. My interest in substantive radical change left me frustrated at the reformism of the movement, and I started to feel like I was squandering my energy there. Nonetheless, when the semester ended, I felt energized and looked forward to returning in the fall and building on what I had already begun. I spent the summer, part in Tucson and part in Seattle, consuming radical literature voraciously.

The following fall, a few friends and I decided to put together a Mac contingent to go to the FTAA[8] protests in Miami, scheduled for mid-November. We called a meeting (the first of many), and were thrilled to have several dozen people show up. We started discussing what might happen there and agreed to divide the group into those who were willing to get arrested and those who weren't. We got money from the Environmental Studies department to cover the cost of gas and some food, and we drove down in three cars. The 18 of us who went were evenly divided between arrestable and "unarrestable." I was of the former, and the group was largely comprised of then and future close friends and political comrades. Comically, the only Mac kids who ended up getting arrested in Miami were among the "unarrestables."

Miami was a mind-blowing experience for me. I had been at a few protests with riot cops before, but I had never been to a mass mobilization and I had definitely never seen so many cops in so much riot gear. Security preparations for the FTAA meetings involved a then-shocking $8.5 million[9] in federal defense money, earmarked from an Iraq War spending bill, and the months leading up to the protests had been filled with buzz about all the new weapons, especially widespread Tasers and Taser shields, that the police would be using.

Developing Politics

After the painfully long drive from Minnesota to Miami, we were quickly caught up in the gears of the police state. On our first day in the city, before the protests got underway, we decided to wander through downtown to see the fence and then try and find our way to the beach. As we straggled down a sidewalk, lost and trying to balance the needs and preferences of a group far too large for its own good, my friend picked up a coconut that had fallen to the ground, thrilled because he'd never seen a coconut right off a tree before. Suddenly, we were surrounded by cops and forced up against a shuttered business, then one by one ID'ed and searched. The cops alleged that the coconut had been intended as a projectile and proceeded to argue amongst themselves about how dangerous we were. When one officer, upon finding a pen in someone's bag, freaked out and started talking about the possibility that it was a cleverly disguised gun, our chances of reasoning with them seemed shot.

We were miserable, certain that we were about to be carted off to jail before the action had even begun. But after about 45 minutes, we were fortuitously saved by a big group of United Steelworkers and other union folks spilling out of an anti-free trade film screening that had just ended across the street. Observing our predicament, they started shouting "Let them go!" and the cops, now surrounded by dozens of burly men, finally gave up. From that point forward, the trip was defined by one law enforcement-related predicament after another, ranging from false raid alarms at the convergence center to narrowly avoiding police teams patrolling public transportation in search of protesters to harass. We got so used to wandering the neighborhoods between downtown and the convergence center with helicopters following us above and squad cars waiting around every corner that, months later, the mere sound of helicopters in a documentary about the protests sent waves of dread coursing through my body.

By the time the big day of action rolled around, our anger and energy had built up to the point of bursting, overriding the fears we all felt at the prospect of coming into direct conflict with the police. The affinity group I was running with had every intention of joining in the collective goal of getting through the fence to the meetings happening on the other side, but we didn't have any plan for how to do that, and it turned out that no one else had a workable plan either. The most exciting thing we did was form human chains to temporarily hold lines of riot cops off the crowds staring despondently at the fence.

By the end of our week in Miami, we had been pepper sprayed, clubbed, detained, and almost arrested half a dozen times; I had never experienced such sustained and intense police intimidation and harassment, had never worried for my physical safety and freedom as often as in those few days, and had never witnessed so much police brutality. Our collective experience had been one of fear, uncertainty and tension, yet it was combined with a persistent belief that something truly amazing might happen and the accompanying adrenaline-fueled excitement. My own desire to take in as much as I could, as quickly as I could, meant that even bad experiences were good for me; with each new experience, I felt like I was developing my politics and deepening my commitment to anarchism. And going through all these things with other people meant that I was developing a radical community, which I couldn't but think of as a positive step in the right direction.

The turnout for the FTAA protests was quite small, barely outnumbering the police. We utterly failed in our attempts to affect the meeting, though they were derailed from the inside anyway.[10] "The Miami Model," as it was termed, demonstrated a full recovery on the part of the State. Seattle was a thing of the past, and they once again had the upper hand at mass mobilizations. Though many people were radicalized by seeing the police state in action in Miami, as many, or more, were demoralized or traumatized to the point of throwing in the towel. Anticipating the protests, I had been beside myself with excitement. I felt seized by the spirit of militant street demonstrations, having read a lot about the WTO protests in Seattle, which effectively shut down the World Trade Organization's summit. And I had absolutely no idea that anarchist summit actions in the U.S. had peaked there.

I thought—and still do—that in the anti-globalization movement I had found the perfect intersection of all the issues that moved me. Here was an analysis of global capitalism and economic imperialism that put my own life into context. It explained the destitution of Northern Mexico, which I felt and saw every time we visited my family. It gave reason to the geographic and cultural disparities contained within my immediate family. It encapsulated the anti-border work that had first gotten me into activism, and tied it to oppression and injustice everywhere. Miami was a beginning for me at the same time that it was an end of the movement I thought I was jumping into.

Less than two weeks after Miami, I decided to drop out of school. I had been dissatisfied for some time with the elitism of the private liberal arts world, and felt very keenly that my place at Macalester was that of a token. I could be "successful," but only at the expense of my personal integrity; that is, a Macalester degree would give me upward social mobility and show that even working-class women of color can succeed, but it wouldn't assist in dismantling the institutionalized oppressions that made such success stories so few and far between in the first place.

But it was the excitement and potential I felt coming out of Miami that pushed me over the edge. The education I had received until that point was invaluable, particularly in women's and gender studies and history classes. But it was clear to me that I had learned all I could through Macalester and hit a wall. With no interest in academics, I could barely bring myself to attend classes and complete assignments. I no longer prioritized school work over the political activities I was involved in, and was happy about that.

Despite such clarity as to my personal feelings, dropping out of school was one of the hardest decisions I've ever made. I have always felt a strong sense of obligation to family and a deep-seated desire to make them proud. I knew that many of my relatives, but most of all my parents, felt like my academic success was a fulfillment of their own hopes for me. My dad, who didn't finish middle school, had worked his whole life that I might have the opportunity to go to a place like Macalester. He thought I might become an immigration lawyer, putting my skills and privilege towards a common good that held personal significance for us.

My mom was less attached to any specific career path, but hoped that I would pursue personal education and enrichment beyond the point that she felt she had abandoned it. From the other side of that decision, she could speak to how much harder it had been to start a family without the benefit of a college degree, and to return to school with young children. It was especially significant that I would be dropping out of Mac at exactly the same point in life at which she had dropped out of Reed. Knowing and respecting these things, I tried to explain my reasoning to them and, though I doubt they felt positively about the choice, they were as supportive and understanding as they have always been, for which I am still grateful.

I decided to finish the academic year and then temporarily withdraw, thinking that if I later decided to go back this would give me a better position to return to.

I spent the rest of the year focusing as little energy as possible on academics, though I took some incredibly insightful classes. Instead, I put a lot of energy into organizing radical speaking events. One of the few irreplaceable things colleges like Mac offer is easy access to enormous funds. Through MPJC, we were able to get the money to bring out an array of experienced and thoughtful radicals. Beyond setting up worthwhile and well-attended events, this offered us the opportunity to meet amazing people, some of whom I count as friends today, and to broaden our own radical networks.

The major campus projects I worked on that year were the Coca-Cola boycott[11] and a new student publication. The "Coke Kills" campaign involved a lot of student education and lobbying of the college, whose exclusive contract with Coca-Cola we were trying to end. At the same time, anti-Coke vandalism had been occurring across the campus (vending machines were routinely decommissioned, among other things), and this spurred a campus-wide debate on tactics and political change. I was among the few people who vocally supported such actions, pointing out that economic sabotage was an age-old and effective way of speaking to corporations, whose language is money and sole motivation is profit. I was shocked and outraged at the pervasive attitude that such property damage was in any way comparable to the violent repression enacted by Coke and their ilk.

Several friends and I had enthusiastically participated in this debate, along with other political discussions flying around the school at that time, and we were increasingly frustrated with the censorship and inaccessibility of the school newspaper. Despite a lack of other substantive content, our submissions were often rejected or only printed after heavy editing that altered the content. In response, we decided to use MPJC and Mac Greens funds to start printing a biweekly 'zine, sarcastically entitled, The Hegemon. The 'zine was amateurish in layout (and sometimes content), but we were quite thoughtful about the collective production process we used and consistently utilized satire and parody to make radical political statements. It quickly became a lightning rod of controversy (which it remained for the next year) in a sea of students, professors and school administrators who took great pride in their liberal and "socially aware" self-image. Despite its limited relevance—it was geared toward a Macalester audience and almost exclusively addressed campus-specific issues—the project was a needed outlet for me at the time, and it provided and created experiences that have served me quite a bit since then.

As the end of the school year approached, my best friend Sarah (who was also dropping out of Macalester) and I hatched a plan to go to Argentina the following fall, and I decided to stay in the Twin Cities and work for the summer. That spring, she and I had taken on a volunteer shift at Arise! Bookstore, a long-standing, volunteer-run, radical bookstore and "infoshop," and I was starting to look off-campus for other ways to become politically involved. The last day of finals couldn't come fast enough, as I got more and more dissatisfied with the limited potential of student organizing.

Though I had learned a lot during my couple years of activism at Macalester, it was clear to me that student organizing was severely impeded by being confined to the academic calendar. Even the most worthwhile projects didn't continue during winter and summer breaks, and momentum was always diminished or lost entirely over that time.

Plus, students tended to take a narrow view of things, couched in the privilege afforded them by society and often unwilling to make hard political choices that might have poked holes in the bubble they lived in. For many of them, "activism" was a phase that they went through in college and abandoned at the first post-graduate, non-profit job opportunity. Though elements of this critique apply across the board, it was specific to the experience of organizing at a private liberal arts college, where economic and social privilege abound, and in many ways is not appropriately extended to the realm of public universities. I plowed through finals by the skin of my teeth and felt immense relief as I moved into my first post-college house.

That summer, I got to live and work with several of my closest friends and comrades, continuing those and other relationships that were the singular most important thing I got out of my time at Macalester. We decided to go to the Republican National Convention protests in New York City the following September, and prepared a little that summer as we continued to engage in a variety of local political activities.

We didn't know quite what to expect at the RNC. It was the height of the "Anybody but Bush" era and occurring at the epicenter of liberal anti-war organizing, so the crowds promised to be enormous. But there seemed to be little explicit anarchist or radical organizing going on, and more attention to rallying behind the Democratic candidate than anything else. We went without any idea of what we would do and just hoped to find ways to plug in when we arrived.

A good friend from Mac had been in Boston working on the DNC protests and then moved on to New York for the RNC; after arriving, we relied heavily on her for everything from simple navigating to identifying activities and opportunities of interest. As the week progressed, it was obvious that we hadn't known how to plug in because the avenues really weren't there, or at least not accessible to anybody who wasn't already socially connected to the small radical networks operating within the anti-RNC infrastructure.

We attended all the big marches, which were slow, boring, and dominated by liberal Democrats possessed by anti-Bush fervor. It was disheartening to see so many people in one place and to feel the impotence produced by a collective unwillingness to address root causes of oppression. The issue at the foreground of the mobilization was the war in Iraq, yet the crowds were full of people sporting shirts and signs supporting John Kerry, who didn't even oppose the war. Emblematic of the problems affecting the anti-war movement all along, people had allowed their energies to be funneled into opposition to a single, horrible person—George W. Bush—at the expense of meaningful resistance to the systemic issues (capitalism, imperialism) that had produced the wars in Iraq and Afghanistan.

Though by all accounts many anarchists and radicals were heavily involved in anti-RNC organizing, it seemed that their work had been subsumed into bigger authoritarian and liberal formations. They counted more as manpower than as a unified radical force, and so their politics had little effect on the direction and feeling of the mobilization.

There were a few high points during the week for us, but most of them were silly. In particular, we had a great time standing outside of a Reagan memorial lunch[12] heckling attendees and holding a tongue-in-cheek banner that read, "Free John Hinckley."[13] Overall, however, our collective experience was trying and demoralizing. The mobilization was disappointing in many respects—feeling like a step backward in terms of anarchist organizing—and the general lack of things to feel good about at the mobilization exacerbated internal problems that our group had been developing and ignoring for some time. We weren't getting along, and we weren't talking about problematic power dynamics that had emerged over the course of several months. Our shared inexperience with collective organizing meant we all dealt with these emerging problems in destructive ways, and by the end of our week in New York, it was clear that the little "golden era" our small group had enjoyed was coming to an end.

When I returned to the Twin Cities, I began working full-time at the Macalester College cafeteria, where I had previously worked as a student. Other than my deepening involvement in the Arise! Collective, where Sarah and I still worked a shift and had begun to do volunteer coordinating, I did very little political work. The RNC and our internal group problems had left me depressed, and I became pretty reclusive, isolating myself because I didn't know what else to do. But I was excitedly saving up and planning for the three months that Sarah and I planned to spend in Argentina, and hoping that the trip would give me some purpose and direction.

On December 20, 2001, Argentina suffered an economic collapse that reverberated around the world. The country had been a poster-child for neo-liberalism, taking out huge loans from the IMF/World Bank as it dismantled all its social welfare programs throughout the '90s. Argentina boasted the largest middle class in Latin America and pegged its currency one-to-one to the U.S. dollar, and its citizenry were allowed to travel freely to and from the U.S.

In 2001, the government defaulted on its loans, resulting in an economic collapse of cataclysmic proportions. Militant "Unemployed Workers' Movements" (MTD) had been building in power and numbers for several years, and worker occupations/recuperations of abandoned factories were springing up all over the country. With collapse imminent, the government froze all bank accounts and the region's largest middle class suddenly found themselves penniless. Joining forces with the MTD and workers enmeshed in factory takeovers, these middle-class people poured out into the streets by the millions. During the *cacerolazo*[(14)] people sang, "Que se vayan todos," or "They all must go."

"They" were the politicians, the individuals responsible for the collapse, and the Argentines made good on their battle cry, running out four presidents in two weeks. In Buenos Aires, the capital and the largest city in Argentina, the president and his family had to be airlifted out of the presidential palace because the crowds surrounding it were so thick and angry. Recognizing that their government had failed them and was bound to do so again, porteños (residents of Buenos Aires) formed horizontally-run neighborhood assemblies (asambleas barriales) to do the work of governance and day-to-day infrastructural administration.

Sarah and I had read a number of 'zines and articles about all of this and, like many foreign radicals, were awestruck by such an immense and horizontal popular insurgency. We decided to initiate our post-college lives by spending three months there, observing and learning from the movements we had heard so much about. We both spoke Spanish, but didn't know anyone or any groups in Argentina or have any idea how we would go about things when we got there. Though it didn't give us much pause at the time, it was really an enormous undertaking to embark on such an adventure without any contacts or plan. I think what we had read sounded so amazing that we figured the movement would be impossible to miss upon arrival. This was rather naive, but not entirely inaccurate.

After two days on a bus from Minneapolis to Miami, eight hours in the airport there, and 11 hours on a plane (it was a lot cheaper this way!), we landed in Buenos Aires in early November of 2004. We stayed at a youth hostel for the first few days until we found more permanent housing at a residential hotel, where the inhabitants were an interesting mixture of Bolivian immigrants and random eccentrics. We stumbled upon our first (massive, by American standards) demonstration while wandering around downtown. We quickly learned that downtown Buenos Aires, particularly the financial district, was still shut down by protests on a weekly basis, even three years after the collapse.

Argentine Indymedia and the existence of several dusty old anarchist libraries (kept up by dusty old anarchists from an era when anarcho-syndicalist federations had a significant power base in parts of the country) were our lifeline in the first few weeks. We were especially impressed by the old anarchists, since there is such a huge generational void in U.S. anarchist subcultures, lending one the false sense that anarchism is only for young people. Through these resources, we compiled a list of upcoming demonstrations, sites of interest, and people who might offer us some direction and insight.

We were especially lucky to be directed to "Peter from

Boston," a very hospitable long-time expatriate, though of where is hard to say since his British accent suggested Boston wasn't his place of origin. Peter, who must get calls from every random radical tourist from the U.S., invited us over for dinner. After a brief and friendly interrogation, he provided us with contact info for some friends of his in La Plata, an hour and half by train from Buenos Aires. The Marcioni family turned out to be a family of anarchists. The parents had been involved in resisting the brutal dictatorship of the '70s and had been forced into hiding, and the five teenage and grown children were all heavily involved in several MTD throughout the province of Buenos Aires.

We met them a week later, and their hospitality saved what otherwise might have been a directionless three months. We attended demonstrations in both Buenos Aires and La Plata with them and stayed at their house on occasional trips to La Plata. This was a perfect solution to one of the problems we had faced, which was that we had confined ourselves to Buenos Aires proper where we could easily be self-sufficient, rather than travel out to areas where there was more radical activity (the MTD and the worker-recuperated factories had their strongest presence in some remote areas) and be a burden on the impoverished and struggling people whose movements we wanted to learn from. The Marcioni parents, however, were professors and lived quite comfortably by Argentine standards, so we felt we could stay with them guilt-free. They were an invaluable resource to us politically, answering our myriad questions patiently and thoughtfully, and personally, as we spent Christmas with them, saving us from a lonely holiday in the city.

What we found in Argentina was considerably less than what we had read about; the asambleas had all but disappeared by that point, their thunder stolen by a newly elected moderate-left president, Néstor Kirchner. Lost savings were gradually returned to enough of the middle class to placate them, and those who remained enthusiastic about these new social structures came up against practical difficulties and infighting, the most radical elements drowned out by more middle-class, reformist voices. The brief moment of solidarity between the asambleas and the MTD was replaced with feelings of blame and suspicion, with many asambleas willing to sell out the MTD as "thugs" and dangerous radicals in order to secure a foothold in post-collapse society.

But what we learned from the MTD and, to a lesser extent (since our exposure was considerably less) the worker-recuperated factory movement, was inspiring and informative. The *piqueteros*[15] had long given up on waiting for elected officials to legislate change, and had taken matters into their own hands. They were clear about the fact that their demands for welfare packages, often met with success, were an intermediary and life-saving step on the road to more self-sustaining community models.

Different neighborhoods were engaged in all sorts of self-education and basic skills development, producing everything from jams to shoes to tools. Their self-organizing was done at considerable risk to themselves—many piqueteros had already been shot and killed by the State, during and after the collapse—but they were undeterred, the murders only hardening their resolve and commitment to their struggle. The workers who had recuperated their own factories were building real-world proof that worker-owned, worker-run systems of production not only work, but can provide better-paying work for more people, and with absolute accountability to the communities in which they exist.[16]

The Argentine cultural and political context is entirely different from ours here in the U.S., but it offered us a glimpse of what popular radical movements can look like. One of the fundamental differences is the lack of reverence for law enforcement that pervades Argentine society. This is in large part a result of the collective experiences of years lived under dictatorship, but I believe similar sentiment is more common than not throughout the rest of the world.

As a result, despite the fact that police repression of political activity is often considerably more violent than what we see these days in the U.S., people are not cowed by law enforcement and in fact are less phased by police action than people here. They actually believe that they have rights that supersede state authority, a belief which has been systematically diluted nearly to the point of obliteration in the American psyche. Over the course of three months in Argentina, we saw people winning through direct action. When we returned to the U.S. in February of 2005, I had been reinvigorated, feeling more certain than ever that radical change was possible.

After a month in Tucson with my family, I moved back to St. Paul in March of '05, unsure of what I would do next. I moved in with friends, found work, and resumed my shift at Arise! Bookstore. While Sarah and I had been in Argentina, an internal debate that we had inadvertently helped set off weeks before leaving had been raging.

The issues that a few of us raised at the beginning were merely concerns about the categorization of books in the store, and when we brought them to the collective we had anticipated a thoughtful discussion. What we found, instead, was reactionary aggression, a response which caused us to suddenly read much deeper into small things that we had previously assumed were the result of carelessness.

Over the months, the argument had become a highly intellectualized and venomous debate about identity politics and covert racism, issues that I think were real and present. At the time, I especially felt that I was being singled out and attacked because my presence and my willingness to name racist attitudes and behaviors made white people who wanted to identify as anti-racist uneasy. I was totally unprepared for the experience, because until then I had given people the benefit of the doubt when a healthy amount of skepticism would have been more appropriate.

But well after the fact, I started to see that much of the vitriol was actually stemming from a resistance on the part of older, more long-standing collective members to new people and new ideas about how to revitalize a floundering infoshop. Many of the interpersonal power dynamics fueling the fire went unnamed, making the underlying problems impossible to address. In spring of '05, the conflict had reached a point of irreconcilability and a full third of the collective, myself included, quit.

Coming out of the Arise! debacle was in many ways

empowering. I felt a considerable amount of camaraderie with the other people who had quit the collective, and I was excited about the chance to build a new project that fit more squarely into the vision of anti-oppression work that I had been developing.

Up until that point, I had never thought of a community center as something that I would want to make my primary political occupation. But, in thinking about the different things we all wanted to do, we identified the lack of appropriate space as a major barrier. Though at that time the Twin Cities boasted plenty of spaces for punk shows and art, there was a serious lack of spaces that were available, easily accessed by a wide variety of people, and actively prioritized anti-oppression politics in their structure and policies. Because a number of the "quitters" were young mothers, addressing the needs of mothers and families organically became a focus of our work.

Between the springs of '05 and '06, we met weekly and with an intense commitment to developing a collective structure with a foundation on thoughtful process and clarity of intention. We had decided that we would seek non-profit status and prioritized keeping our records on the up-and-up toward this end. Our mission statement said,

The Jack Pine Community Center is a collectively run, intergenerational free space committed to popular education, anti-oppression, and the fight for justice, liberation, and autonomy. We seek to foster self-expression, self-representation and radical activism by providing a family-friendly space for skill sharing, events, meetings and art.

We had a much lengthier political statement that detailed our politics and intentions. We spent the year meeting frequently, processing a lot, pursuing 501(c)(3) status, and fundraising. Once we had provisional non-profit status, a little bit of start-up money, and felt that our collective was ready to make the next step, we started looking for spaces suitable for our purpose. Once we found a place, the process of moving in, setting up and opening was pretty quick.

The Jack Pine Community Center opened with a well-attended, all-day party on May 13, 2006. The day felt especially significant to me because it coincided with my intended graduation day, had I stayed in school. I was still working at Macalester's cafeteria, and that morning I had to work the "graduation brunch" that my former classmates and their families attended prior to commencement. Though I didn't regret dropping out at all, it was still a little hard to work that event and be reminded of certain societal markers of "success" that I wasn't meeting. So the opening of the Jack Pine was especially gratifying because it felt like a celebration of the work I'd been doing instead of finishing my studies, and in many ways was a welcome closure to my "college years."

The Jack Pine's first few months were exciting, and I felt like we were making rapid progress in making the space available and useful for political events and general community use. Though the collective itself was small, we quickly recruited enough volunteers to keep the space open for the 40 hours per week we'd set as our goal. Early on, I took the role of "volunteer coordinator" and kept that position 'til late in the summer of 2007. I also took on many of the responsibilities associated with programming, and was as often as not the Jack Pine point-person for whatever meeting or events happened over the week. I was at the Jack Pine at least five days a week, often for hours at a time, and I worked at a bookstore only a block away so I was rarely inaccessible. My ready availability and eagerness to do as much as I could handle created a snowball effect. In addition to whatever I had consciously agreed to do, I was the person most likely to be around when a problem or new task came up, and I started to feel like I had no control over my own time.

One of my flaws has always been a willingness to take on as much as, or more than, I can handle, and as rapidly as possible. I tend to have more stamina than a lot of people when it comes to workload, and though I often feel overburdened and stressed out, the truth is that I rarely wish I had less to do. Instead of wanting to relinquish duties, I generally want other people to match my workload and have found a lot of motivation in situations where I feel like my energies are matched. Of course, most people don't want more to do, and it's a frequent source of resentment for me and people I work with.

While I was increasing my personal contribution to the Jack Pine, a number of people were drawing back because of interpersonal issues or other life happenings. The few of us who remained at the core were left with even more to do, and this made already difficult group dynamics even harder to deal with. Like most groups, we started with a lot of differences—in privilege, experience and personality. Perhaps because we were mostly strong-willed and opinionated women, we were more willing than most collectives to address conflicts as they arose rather than sidestepping them. This was important, but it created a generally turbulent atmosphere—one which could be quite intimidating to newcomers—and often impeded our ability to work together and take care of each other. It also meant that when people were dealing with problems in other areas of their lives, the Jack Pine became an expendable source of stress.

One of our clearest intentions as a collective was to integrate mothers and families into radical organizing, offering them support and naturalizing their presence among childless folks who tended to be insensitive to their needs. We made strides in this direction by offering dedicated childcare space and making childcare a condition of space usage, causing a lot of people who used the Jack Pine to consider the needs of parents, or the reasons for their absence, in their own groups. But we began to conflate foregrounding the individual desires and needs of a handful of mothers with being accessible to mothers as a whole. This came from a good place: we had mothers in our collective and volunteer base, and answering to their wishes seemed like a natural and necessary starting place.

But the limitations of this approach were quickly evidenced by the fact that often addressing the concerns of one mom involved putting the concerns of another on the back-burner. After all, not all moms want the same thing and, like everyone else, they can hold strong opinions about what people "like them" need that still directly contradict what other moms will say. Using the mothers who populated the collective and volunteer base as consultants and representatives for a demographic they were part of didn't work. I imagine that it was often infuriating for them individually and that they didn't always feel that their personal needs were met, and I know from observation that our efforts didn't do much to attract mothers outside of the small social circles already constituent to the space.

Especially frustrating to me was that while we constantly struggled with being allies to mothers and families, we gave considerably less attention to other issues of oppression and power. The Jack Pine was a common hang-out space for neighborhood youth, most of whom lived in urban poverty and dealt with all the issues that accompany it. Many volunteers and collective members were unable to find constructive ways to deal with the variety of difficult situations that arose out of this context, and attempts to find radical solutions through the collective were uncomfortable at best and highly problematic at worst. It was clear that the relative privilege of those active in the Jack Pine and widespread lack of experience with lived experiences of classism and racism left many people involved in the project ill-equipped to offer real services to the community in which we were located.

This all became a clear lesson for me in the dangers of tokenization and fetishization of oppressed people. Genuinely wanting to address the ways that a whole group of people are marginalized or mistreated, it can be overwhelming to try to consider the big picture and the harsh realities that accompany it. As a consequence, we tend to focus on individual dealings with "affected people." While directly supporting the people we know is important to creating healthy radical communities, it doesn't necessarily affect broader systemic issues or do anything beyond meeting specific individual needs. If our movement is to have any hope of successfully addressing varied forms of oppression in a meaningful way, it will only be through balancing these approaches.

After many months, I was sick of the increasingly unequal division of labor in the collective, had begun to dread collective meetings, and felt that the only way I could avoid abandoning the project entirely was to back away from the official collective. Though I relinquished decision-making power and stopped attending regular meetings, I only took a brief hiatus before resuming many of the duties I'd previously held. It would be several months still before I stopped general programming work. In the summer of '07, I was preparing to leave town and head back to Tucson for several months. At this point, I finally stepped back from volunteer coordinating. By the time I came back to town, the "new collective" was preparing to officially close the space.

The unfortunate truth is that many radical spaces run by anarchists (whether they're called "community centers," "social centers," or "infoshops") set the bar pretty low in terms of actual accomplishments. Between paying the rent (or even just the bills for collectives lucky enough to own a space), staffing the space, and hosting events and meetings, collectives have their work cut out for them. This would be true regardless, but I think the fetishization of street demos and illegal activity, coupled with the transience that characterizes anarchist circles in the U.S., fosters an atmosphere that is isn't conducive to the consistency and hard, sometimes boring, work required to keep a space going.

Raising rent on a continuing basis often seems to be the biggest hurdle, though I would argue that spaces that offer something truly meaningful will have a much easier time doing so because the communities they serve feel that they are worthwhile. The argument is often made that spaces flounder financially because the communities they serve or, at least, are located in, don't have the money to keep them open. But frankly, I don't buy this. Anarchist-run spaces in the U.S. generally pay no more than a couple thousand in monthly rent and, in fact, many if not most pay significantly less than that. Without a guaranteed regular source of income (e.g., book or food sales), that money will most likely have to come through individual donations.

Though most poor and working people can't afford to make large donations to anything, many can in fact throw down $5-10 per month to something that provides tangible benefits. When you factor in more privileged Leftist demographics— which may vary in size but are found in most urban centers in the country—and their donating capacity, you're likely to cut at least a few hundred dollars off the top. If the space is utilized by

a diversity of groups for a diversity of purposes, then even small usage fees add up to make another sizable dent in costs.
The real problem isn't a lack of money; it's a lack of energy or interest (or both) for maintaining a space that's worth supporting.

Really, this is a two-pronged problem. One issue is the need for individuals able to put time and care into programming that utilizes the space and makes it worthwhile. The other issue is simply the difficulty that people often have in asking for money. Even if the funds are out there, people have to be convinced that they're needed—after all, there's never a shortage of worthwhile projects in need of funding. It can be uncomfortable and even demoralizing to always have to ask for money, to the point that folks will just stop doing it, reasoning that the other work they do for the given project is enough.

The Jack Pine was no exception to all of this. For the few months when our calendar was filled with worthwhile programming, we couldn't or didn't find extra energy to constantly solicit funds. And when programming, which was much of what brought the space meaning, dropped off, fundraising became an empty and unattractive routine. Because we had non-profit status, our other potential funding was grant-based, and we had gotten a grant for start-up costs that had pretty much single-handedly made opening possible. But, with minimal grant-writing experience and little collective interest in actually gearing our structure and programming to the sorts of activities and appearances that most foundations want to fund, grants weren't a realistic option for us.

Another major hurdle to maintaining a community center is the question of manpower. Because radical spaces are often an entry point for folks new to the movement or the scene, their volunteer base tends heavily toward people who are young, inexperienced and still unsure of their own interests. They volunteer for a weekly shift because it seems easy, but often within a few weeks they've lost interest and moved on to another project. That sort of revolving door makes it incredibly difficult to maintain a sense of common purpose and trust, not to mention any collective history.

The problem is exacerbated by the fact that capitalism

trains people to be motivated by financial and material incentives, and devalues any work-product that doesn't fit easily into consumer-driven society. Though many people recognize the value of volunteer work on an intellectual level, even sincere radicals often find themselves unwilling to commit significant unpaid time to projects that don't produce immediate and tangible personal benefits. In the long term, I think this is simply something that needs to be overcome if people are serious about creating radical change. That notwithstanding, we have to find ways to capture whatever fleeting energy people do have in the present and to funnel it toward projects that make them feel like their time is well spent.

The Jack Pine certainly dealt with these problems in terms of finding committed individuals to carry on the core collective's work, but we were remarkably successful for our first year and a half at maintaining a volunteer force large enough to maintain our weekly open hours. My sense is that many people found a sense of positive community at the Jack Pine and it was enough to keep them coming back every week.

But while many of these individuals stuck around, they seemed to hold in common a desire to do more than simply keep a space open for their few hours a week and a certain frustration at feeling like they weren't maximizing their potential. As a founder, one-time collective member and volunteer coordinator, I was frustrated by this. On the one hand, I agreed that much more could and should have been done with the manpower and resources the Jack Pine laid claim to. On the other hand, I felt overworked to the point that I lost all enjoyment in the project myself, and I resented feeling that people wanted tasks to be handed to them with easy instructions rather than having to take initiative in identifying and completing tasks themselves.

Though there are a significant number of long-standing, anarchist-run or -oriented spaces in the country, it often seems that their success is heavily dependent on a few committed individuals rather than any dynamic collective. I feel torn about this, since it seems almost inevitable and yet falls so far short of my own ideas of what it means to have community-run and participatory projects. With the Jack Pine, it was easy to see how this sort of thing happens. A year and a half after opening the space, only half of the already-small founding collective was still actively involved in any way, and a rotating cast of new members seemed unreliable and disinterested in the perhaps obsessively intentional processes and structures we had put so much energy into building. It was already true that the project was only viable with certain individuals at the helm, and those individuals (myself included) were burned out and struggling with next steps.

Though relinquishing control over the direction of the project was painful for everyone involved, we did it one by one over the course of months, hoping that others would step in to fill the voids being created while being ever-aware of our dire financial situation. These "others" we hoped for didn't appear, and in a final moment of concern for the future of the space, we attempted to establish an open "transfer of power" to pretty much anyone who was willing to assert an interest in the space and make some commitment to a new governing structure. A lot of people answered the initial call by showing up to the meeting and taking on particular roles and responsibilities, most of them folks who had been volunteers or involved in some other way in the space in the months prior.

Unfortunately, the "new collective" never took full ownership of the project. Concrete things such as taking over the bookkeeping and bank account just didn't happen, and it appeared that many of the individuals who had initially stepped up to handle the responsibilities of running a community center weren't ready for, or maybe interested in, the difficult task of getting the Jack Pine back on track.

Just short of its two-year anniversary, the Jack Pine Community Center closed. Though its best days were short-lived, when I think about the project and what it offered communities in the Twin Cities, I definitely feel pride more than anything else. Whenever I'm in the neighborhood where the Jack Pine used to be, I'm still approached by neighbors wondering what happened and lamenting its closing. And I don't think it's an overstatement to say that the space was a central and motivating feature in the recent resurgence, imperfect though it may be, of anarchist projects and energy in the Twin Cities.

We accomplished part of what we sought by providing a space that was welcoming and accessible to people who were interested in radical political work but not a part of the clique-ish social scenes that often dominate that work. We forced the issue of childcare at meetings and events, which may be only one step toward making movements family-inclusive but is nonetheless an important one. We also hosted an amazing array of radical events over the course of two years and, since the closing, the difficulty in finding appropriate spaces for similar events has been a problem to the point of being prohibitive.

Ultimately and despite its failings, the Jack Pine was a collective that for me modeled many of the things I want in groups and rarely find. The collective was all or mostly women at all times, and it was refreshing to work in an environment where patriarchy wasn't the biggest problem in the room. I especially appreciate that we valued assertiveness and honesty— traits that women are generally vilified for possessing—as integral to our project. We were serious about our stated goals and about creating processes that would get us there, and we held ourselves to a high standard. While this made the times when we fell short of it especially difficult, I believe it made the space better and it definitely helped me develop personal measures of success for the work I do.

On December 7, 2005, the FBI's "Operation Backfire" came to light with a series of arrests and federal indictments across the country for actions committed by the Earth Liberation Front. These prosecutions were the result of an intensive, multi-agency investigation spanning years, and hinging on a series of former ELF members turning informant. Along with a much broader government crackdown on so-called eco-terrorism, these cases are referred to as the Green Scare, recalling the Red Scare of previous eras.

As my own politics developed, I had been awed and inspired by many ELF actions, believing wholeheartedly that strategic targeting of the agencies and corporations who were responsible for irreversible environmental devastation was a worthwhile and heroic sort of radical political work. So when a national call was put out for a day of solidarity with Green Scare defendants a year after the arrests, I was eager to organize a fundraiser at the Jack Pine. A number of other people were interested, and we quickly got to work planning the event.

When December 7, 2006, came around, we had put together a panel of former ELF spokesperson Leslie James Pickering, journalist and Green Scare expert Will Potter, and local NLG attorney Jordan Kushner. The event was well-attended and well-received, and those of us who had come together to pull it off decided to continue working together as a more formal group.

For three years, this group (eventually named EWOK! or, "Earth Warriors are OK!") was one of my main political projects. Over the course of that time, we put on dozens of events, ranging from panels like our original December 7th one, to movie nights, to "Dealing with a Grand Jury" workshops. We fundraised for prisoner commissaries, promoted other forms of prisoner support such as letter-writing, and engaged in constant education and consciousness-raising.

Attempting to break out of the exceptionalism that often characterizes contemporary anarchist responses to the prosecution and incarceration of their peers, we made a consistent effort to organize events and spread information that linked Green Scare cases to a much longer history of state repression of political movements, acknowledging the existence of dozens of long-standing political prisoners in the U,S,, and framing all of these cases with an abolitionist critique of the prison-industrial complex.

The Green Scare, an ongoing current of repression that grows to include new cases every year, is shamefully notable for the fact that nearly half of all the defendants it encompasses have caved to state pressure and ratted out former comrades. Yet the examples of those who refused to cooperate, and the shock of seeing the damage wrought by those who snitched, has inspired a lot of people to proactively engage in educating activists about the realities of state repression and preparing whole communities for dealing with similar circumstances.

No exception to this, EWOK! has played a role in

creating a culture of resistance and non-cooperation within the anarchist community in the Twin Cities. The information and arguments we circulated constantly about combating state repression weren't new to the movement, but we exposed a lot of people to those issues for the first time in a way that profoundly affected community responses to the repression surrounding the RNC.

As the Cities prepared for the 2008 RNC, law enforcement started trying to recruit informants from within alternative subcultures to infiltrate organizing and report back to them. Our visibility as a group made it possible for one of these people to find us and tell his story of turning down the FBI's invitation to turn informant, and we were perfectly positioned to go to the media with this information, helping to broaden awareness of these tactics and shed light on the fact that state repression is an ever-present reality rather than something that only happens to other people in other places.

Our visibility has also positioned us to be contacted by folks in disparate parts of the country as they deal with government harassment and political prosecution and find themselves in need of support resources. It's disheartening to me that a small, young group out of Minneapolis like ours would be the best resource available to somebody living hundreds of miles away, and yet every time this happens, I'm reminded of the real value of our work and the work of other groups like EWOK! The dialogue we've helped to keep going around these issues has strengthened our community resolve to recognize and actively resist the state's attempts to sabotage our movements, and it reaches across geographical expanses that often serve to isolate people of conscience. That sort of isolation is dangerous for the individuals whom it deprives of the room to grow through engagement with other politically minded people, and dangerous for radical movements in that it creates circumstances quite conducive to cooperation with the state.

Our work became especially meaningful to me as my own legal case unfolded: I was lucky to find that the work I had done to support other targets of state repression meant that the feeling of solidarity was returned as soon as I was the one being targeted.

But it wasn't until October of 2009 that I saw compelling evidence of the importance of work like EWOK!'s. At that point, a friend of mine and fellow member of the group, Carrie Feldman, was subpoenaed to a federal grand jury[17] in Davenport, Iowa. She was firm from the beginning in her refusal to testify—due in large part to the time she had put in with the rest of us, educating people about the dangers of cooperating with the state—and her stance was a source of inspiration for everyone around her, especially as fear spread that other subpoenas would follow.

Several weeks later, another friend and fellow member of EWOK!, Scott DeMuth, was also subpoenaed to the grand jury and, like Carrie, refused to testify. The subpoenas had come out of nowhere, related to an Animal Liberation Front action that occurred in another state while Carrie and Scott were in high school in Minnesota, and the only thing that was clear was that the Feds were targeting the two of them merely because of their associations with other radicals and not because they had any real suspicion that they were involved in the action in question.

In November, several cars' worth of people accompanied Scott and Carrie down to Southern Iowa, where they refused to testify before the grand jury and were immediately taken into custody for civil contempt of court. Within several days, Scott was indicted under the Animal Enterprise Terrorism Act,[18] a move obviously intended to punish him for his refusal to cooperate, but which meant that he was released from jail pending trial. Carrie was held in custody for four months before being released for reasons still unknown to us.

The entire winter—for many of us spent driving back and forth over icy, blizzard-plagued Midwestern roads to visit Carrie and attend court hearings—was a depressing and scary time. We already felt drained after a year of dealing with the legal cases from the RNC, and we were acutely aware of the fact that our handling of support for Scott and Carrie was being watched closely by the FBI. Watching more friends go to jail had the potential to paralyze us at that point, yet I also thought—and still do think—of their decision not to cooperate as a cause for celebration. Remembering that Carrie woke up in a cage every day for four months with the option of getting out by compromising her principles, and that every day she reaffirmed her commitment to resistance movements by refusing to cave, made it possible for us to plow ahead.

Discovery produced in their cases demonstrates that both Scott and Carrie entered the sights of the state through their work with EWOK! and other prisoner support efforts, as well as their association with those of us targeted for our work against the RNC. Their cases are a frustrating reminder that the work we all do makes us targets, and simultaneously endangers our friends and loved ones. Nonetheless, they're also a compelling example of how building cultures of resistance gives individuals the strength to stand up to the state when necessary.

For better or for worse, the past year has seen EWOK! as a group dissolve, as those of us who comprised it have been consumed by our own legal cases and those targeting our friends. It remains unclear whether or not we'll regroup with the same focus that we formed around. Regardless, we've established a level of trust and mutual appreciation that I find invaluable, and the work we've done continues to permeate the radical community in the Twin Cities in positive ways, helping us get through our own cases and growing a movement of people committed to non-cooperation with the state.

Chapter 3

THE RNC WELCOMING COMMITTEE

CONCRETE ORGANIZING
AGAINST THE 2008 RNC

PRENC 5 3 RNC
PRENC 5 3 SEPT 1-4 2008
NATIONAL ANTI-RNC SPOKES COUNCIL
MAY 3

MPLS.STP.MINN

WWW.NORNC.ORG

St. Paul Principles

- Our solidarity will be based on respect for a diversity of tactics and the plans of other groups.

- The actions and tactics used will be organized to maintain a separation of time or space.

- Any debates or criticisms will stay internal to the movement, avoiding any public or media denunciations of fellow activists and events.

- We oppose any state repression of dissent, including surveillance, infiltration, disruption and violence.

- We agree not to assist law enforcement actions against activists and others.

Luce Guillén-Givins

When the public bidding process for the 2008 RNC began, my friends and I started cautiously discussing the possibilities should the Twin Cities "win" the contest. We were at once unenthusiastic about the prospect of a Republican dog-and-pony show in our backyard and eager for the opportunity to test some of the ideas we'd been developing through our experiences at mass mobilizations elsewhere.

When it was announced that St. Paul would host the convention, it was immediately clear to us that we had to be involved in the protest organizing. We had spent several years fleshing out a critique of the place of convention and summit protests in radical movements, and we were intent on rising to the challenge. Anarchists are always debating "the Summit Question," more often than not by dichotomizing the issue as if organizing for mass mobilizations necessarily has to exclude local, community-focused work. We felt that mass mobilizations could play a significant and positive role if done right, as arenas of radicalization, sites for capacity-building, and points of inspiration and renewed energy. I would later expand on these ideas in the epilogue to a radical Minnesota history zine that the Welcoming Committee produced.

The first publicly announced meeting of folks interested in organizing around the RNC was held in late October of 2006, about a month after the location was announced. I only made it to the second half, but the meeting seemed contentious and unproductive. When the next one was held in November, the cast of characters had changed significantly but the productivity level stayed the same. It took a third meeting, in January of 2007, before I noticed a nascent sense of group direction. This is the point that I think of as the RNC Welcoming Committee's inception.

Winter and early spring were spent hashing out points of unity, an initial call to action, and group structure. This period, which we refer to as "pre-infiltration" because no known informants were present yet, was difficult because the group's composition changed constantly. The WC's first months were also difficult because we were so far from the object itself. While the exceptionally large amount of lead time gave us clear advantages in anti-RNC organizing, it was a double-edged sword. It almost seemed that we had started too early to know what we were dealing with, especially before other local groups started working towards the convention in public ways. And because other groups got a later start, we were already much further along in our formative process when they came on the scene, and the difference in positions sometimes made constructive engagement difficult. The early start also meant we had that much more time to develop internal baggage and drama, which our fairly low level of collective experience made us ill-equipped to deal with.

As always, I was excited by the opportunity to build a project from the ground up. I approached the group with proposals and visions that I had already put a lot of thought into and processed fairly extensively with folks living in other places who planned to attend the protests. It seemed to me that there were only a few individuals present at this stage who had put equal prep-work and thought into the possibilities for such a project, and I found responses to my work to be dispiriting. I had hoped that enthusiasm and thoughtfulness from others in the group would challenge me to work harder and make my initial efforts feel worthwhile, but instead it seemed like people were either reactionary in their negativity or so disengaged that any sense of collectivity was lost.

Maintaining non-hierarchical structures is always difficult, but ever more so when the playing field is so markedly uneven. I think that anarchist groups suffer for their reluctance to start by laying bare the different places people are coming from, the different experiences driving them and, importantly, the varying levels of commitment they are interested in making to the given project. While doing this alone doesn't alter power dynamics or dismantle hierarchy, it's a necessary step toward that end, and I believe that doing so would have helped us equalize power dynamics within the WC early on.

Despite my frustrations, when the group started seriously

discussing a proposed planning convergence, specifically geared towards anarchists and anti-authoritarians, slated for a year prior to the convention, I gained confidence that our work would amount to something. The intention of this first "pReNC" (we held another one in May of 2008) was to assemble a diverse representation of anarchists from around the country, in hopes that we could establish some sort of "national anarchist consensus" on what our plans for the RNC and our organizing until then should look like. The pReNC was open to non-anarchists as well, but we stressed the goal of developing an anarchist strategy because we felt we had to understand our own goals before we could work effectively with more authoritarian groups. We spent the summer building up hype for the pReNC and developing a structure that we hoped would be conducive to the development of an RNC strategy that all participants would feel a stake in.

The pReNC took place over Labor Day weekend of 2007, comprised of a series of workshops and presentations, bus tours of St. Paul, meals, and the main event: an all-day strategizing session. The road there was a little bumpy because we really had no idea how to put together the strategizing session we wanted and required a lot of help from out-of-town anarchists, but in my mind the conference was successful. Two or three hundred people attended at least some part of the pReNC and almost a hundred of them, many representing groups from other parts of the country, attended the strategizing session. There, we came up with two main goals for the RNC: one, to execute a blockading strategy to disrupt the convention (this was eventually articulated as "crash the convention") and two, to "build our capacity" as a movement. Folks left the pReNC enthused about the potential of the protests and impressed with on-the-ground organizing in the Twin Cities.

It wasn't all silver lining, though. Membership in the WC changed significantly from before the pReNC to the few months after. Some of this was due to exhaustion and burn-out after an intense summer, but I think more of it can be attributed to the transience and youth of a lot of WC members. A lot of kids had initially joined because it was what happened to be accessible just as they were getting interested in anarchist organizing, and not because they had a specific interest in or commitment to mobilizing against the RNC. As they gained experience, they also developed a better sense of their own interests and priorities and, as a result, some left the WC for other projects that better suited them. The fact that the group lost a number of its core members and had to integrate new ones at the same time was a drain on energy and a barrier to building on momentum from the pReNC.

The other major drawback to the pReNC was that it provided a convenient focal point for the State. We kicked the weekend off by participating in the monthly Critical Mass bike ride[1] and since Minneapolis Critical Mass is, more often than not, tolerated by the cops, we didn't anticipate real problems with it and didn't put together any sort of contingency plan for arrests or other police problems. That was a huge miscalculation on our part. "Critical Massacre" was a straight-up police riot. Cops came out ready to beat down and arrest people, giving us a glimpse of what they planned for the RNC and sending the clear message that our protests would be met with brute force. Almost 20 people, myself included, were arrested, and dozens more Tasered, pepper-sprayed, and beaten. Thanks to a few people who sprang into action at pReNC headquarters, I was out by morning and everyone else was out by the end of the weekend.

The Critical Mass fiasco was only the beginning of our police troubles, though. Ramsey County Sheriff's Department sent two people—a narcotics officer using the name "Norma Jean" and a corrections officer going by "Amanda"—to scope out the events. They attended several workshops and started the process of identifying WC organizers. The FBI introduced their main informant, Andrew "Panda" Darst, at the pReNC as well.

Prior to the pReNC, many of us in the group had started to seriously consider the dangers of police infiltration of the event and proposed that the WC adopt some sort of vouching system for the strategizing session. To my surprise, the proposal was highly controversial. A lot of people thought that it would make the event too exclusive and elitist, and seemed to think that the possibility of police infiltration wasn't nearly as dangerous as the possibility of inadvertently turning folks away who were genuinely interested in protesting the RNC. My surprise quickly turned into anger and dismay, as I couldn't really relate to the idea that we shouldn't try to provide security for ourselves and our movement because we might make mistakes along the way; it seemed reckless to me to organize an event like the pReNC without some attempt at protecting ourselves and the folks whose participation we sought. In the end, the group consensed on a rather loose vouching process, whereby the security team checked references for everyone wanting to attend the strategizing session, mainly to confirm that they were genuinely representing themselves and their interest in the protests.

We weren't naive enough to think we could prevent all infiltration through this process or that, even if we could, it would protect us from all surveillance, but we figured that having some security procedures in place would weed out at least some of the potential informants. We were right about that—Norma Jean and Amanda didn't even try to attend the strategizing session itself because Ramsey County's investigation into us at that point only authorized attendance at open, public events, and even our loose vouching guidelines would probably have kept them out if they'd tried.

Panda was a different story, though. Unlike the county informants, he had a little bit of a history with the anarchist movement, having attended a CrimethInc. convergence in 2006. He's an urban explorer[2] with an imposing physical frame and puts on a soft-spoken, "nice guy" act in an effort to inspire trust. None of us knew him but we knew people who had worked briefly with him after the 2006 convergence, and this seemed to satisfy the loose guidelines we had in place. But as we went through the attendance list, we noticed a group of people we didn't know and who seemed to have no connection whatsoever to radical movements and no real reason to be at the pReNC. We realized that their only connection was that they listed Panda as a reference. The fact that they were so clearly out of place, and that the only person anyone in the group could come up with as a reference was himself someone with, at best, a tenuous connection to what was going on, raised big flags for us.

We asked Panda who the people were and what his relationship with them was, and he explained that they were all involved in urban exploring together. He left it at that initially, but hours later he took one of us aside to say that he didn't know the group of people in question well and he wasn't comfortable being their reference. He also went on to tell us that one of them actually cooperated with the St. Paul Police Department to identify vandals and graffiti artists; we looked into this and found newspaper articles stating as much, and when the informant came in the following morning, we kicked him out without hesitation.

The whole situation only exacerbated my suspicions of Panda, though; he told us privately that he wouldn't vouch for his "friends," but he refused to tell them that and even asked us to keep the fact that he was the one who outed the snitch a secret in order to preserve his relationships in urban exploring circles. I was disgusted at even the suggestion that we should keep his confidence and felt that the fact that, behind their backs, he was turning against people he called his friends didn't mitigate the fact that he was the one who brought them in the first place. I was further sketched out by the fact that he wanted to preserve a relationship with someone he knew cooperated with the police. It all said to me that, at best, he was spineless and lacking in good judgment or, at worst, that he himself was an informant or provocateur.

Those of us handling the vouching process felt torn between deep-seated uneasiness with Panda's behavior and our feelings of accountability to the WC as a whole, who had been lukewarm on the idea of having security at all and who I didn't feel would support us in just flat out denying all the people in this group—Panda included—attendance. We decided that we would confront him with our concerns before letting him into the strategizing session, but we didn't have any plan for where to go from there. We let his sketch-ball companions know they couldn't attend without other references, and they were furious but of course couldn't come up with anything but Panda's withdrawn vouch. They let Panda know they knew what he'd done, and when we took him aside to hash out the situation, he lashed out at us for having betrayed his confidence; I felt this was totally out of line, since we didn't owe him anything and had never agreed to shelter him from his own mess. I also sensed a typically patriarchal rage seething under the surface, which only increased my feelings of uneasiness. Nonetheless, we didn't have any "smoking gun" with which to keep him out and, while I wanted to exclude him anyway based on a gut feeling, the group had been clear that we weren't empowered to go on instinct alone. After rifling through his wallet and finding nothing incriminating, we begrudgingly let him in.

Though it exposed us to law enforcement in a significant way, I feel strongly that the first pReNC was an essential step along the way to the RNC protests. I think it's safe to say that law enforcement would have targeted us and found ways to infiltrate the organizing regardless, and avoiding big public events like the pReNC would only have isolated us without actually making us safer. And the successes of the weekend were oftentimes, in the months that followed, the only thing that carried us through. At least for me, it provided assurance that we were organizing for something bigger than our group and ourselves, and the goals we set forth then gave me a reason to keep going at points when I might otherwise have called it quits.

I left town shortly after the pReNC, in keeping with plans I'd made before RNC organizing got under way, and spent almost five months in Tucson. I stayed involved in the WC from a distance because I had every intention of returning by summer, doing most of the website maintenance and spending a lot of time organizing our national tours in the meantime. Weeks after I had left town, the Ramsey County informants, Norma Jean, Amanda, and a paid snitch named Chris Dugger, started coming around to WC meetings, as did Panda. By the time I got back into town, they had already established themselves in the group (with the exception of Amanda, who stopped showing up altogether), though the drama around who did and didn't trust them raged on into the summer.

Many other people joined the group while I was away as well, and the fact that I had maintained such active involvement from a distance made many newer members, who hadn't met me in person, resentful of me from the get-go. I felt real ownership of and investment in the WC's achievements, and I think that to folks who came in after I had left town, this seemed inappropriate. The environment felt so hostile to me that I reacted by keeping concerns about Panda, Norma Jean, and Chris to myself for the most part, certain that they would only be more fodder for the criticisms I received.

In January of 2008, I flew to Philadelphia to meet Eryn and Garrett and begin the Northeast leg of the RNC Welcoming Committee's tour, after which I flew to Seattle and met Rob and another member of the WC for the West Coast leg of the tour. Combined with the Southern portion and various Midwestern stops, the WC did events in dozens of cities all across the country, building up hype for the convention protests and providing information about the RNC and protest organizing and infrastructure to hundreds of people who, in turn, shared information with their friends and comrades.

People generally want to feel like their efforts are matched, and putting the work into a national tour reassured the anarchist public that this would be the case at the RNC and their time and energy in preparing their own groups for the protests and getting out here wouldn't be wasted. I think the tours were one of our biggest accomplishments, showing people that we were serious about our organizing and establishing a level of human contact that added to the draw of the mobilization. They were also incredibly gratifying for me on a personal level; I met amazing radicals all over the U.S. and got to spend time with old friends and strengthen new relationships. The tour magnified my feelings of connectedness to a nationwide anarchist movement, and I had a genuine desire to carry through on the organizing that made this possible.

Since the RNC, law enforcement and prosecutors have laughably suggested that our tour served as a recruitment drive for the WC or as a means of enlisting people in some sort of "criminal anarchist enterprise." This is false, of course. Our tour stops were public events attended by hundreds of people, only a fraction of whom were, or became, any of our personal acquaintances. We went from city to city, often staying for less than 24 hours, doing the same presentation over and over again and then taking questions and comments from attendees. We were trying to get people excited about the mobilization and build the confidence that we believed would motivate people to make the trip to Minnesota that September. And more specifically, we were explaining the blockading strategy and trying to get people enthused about plugging into it in a productive way.

But we weren't "recruiting" people to the WC, which was a Twin Cities-based group comprised of Twin Cities residents with specific infrastructural goals and had no interest in national membership. That the State has focused on our tour activities, criminalizing them wherever possible, is indicative of the fact that they recognize a threat in the ability of anarchists to build and maintain national networks of resistance. The WC tours weren't illegal, but they did demonstrate that what we do in one part of the country is seen, heard, and felt elsewhere, and this makes our movement powerful.

In March, I moved to Minneapolis and jumped back into day-to-day anti-RNC organizing. With fewer than six months to go before the convention, the climate was much more intense than it had been when I left town the previous summer. The Twin Cities activist community had kicked it into gear, and a huge variety of planning activities were underway: the coalition planning the big march for the first day was fighting its way through the permitting process; legal and medic collectives had formed and were putting on trainings; folks from out of town were even starting to trickle in and help with things like building bikes and getting food infrastructure in place.

But the next months would prove to be very trying within the WC, as stress and paranoia increased and wore at preexisting internal problems. Some of these problems were, I think, inherent to open groups such as ours. Our loose points of unity were all that held us together, and the vast differences in politics, vision, and commitment within the group were naturally difficult to reconcile. I think we would have done better, however, to discuss these more honestly and more often—differences that are acknowledged are easier to balance and respect.

In May, we held a second pReNC (called "5.3"), which was more contentious from its inception than the first one and, largely as a result, less productive. Laying the groundwork for a frustrating outcome, the WC failed to establish a common vision of the convergence within our own group. This was partly due to conflicting goals within the group and partly due to poor internal processes. Though our decision prior to the first pReNC had been to adopt the goals of the body convened there, the reality was that not everyone in the WC fully embraced this in the aftermath. For some people, I think it was the result of never having really been enthused about the pReNC plans in the first place, and for others who joined after the plans were made, it may have been a response to having had no investment in the WC's work before their arrival. The latter was a recurring problem for the WC, and I think for most open groups with changing membership—how do you build consensus and maintain it if the body of decision makers changes?

As one of the few people who had been around since day one, it was frustrating to me that folks would join and demonstrate little interest in or respect for the work that had been done and the decisions that had been made. Though we were in desperate need of increased manpower, I often felt that it would have been better for folks to start complementary projects that they could tailor to their own interests than for them to join the WC in midstream and try to redirect our energies. Yet, I can definitely understand the frustration of joining a group and sensing a resistance to revisiting major decisions that may have been made by a formation of the group that no longer exists. It would have been totally impractical to revisit every decision the group had made every time someone new came on the scene, and with time escaping us, I think it would have been foolish to consider a total revision of our two major goals—blockading and capacity-building. But we should have put more time into finding common ground within the group.

Instead of fostering investment in both of our stated goals, we defaulted to an internal division of labor between those folks doing "capacity-building," or infrastructural work, and those focusing on the blockades. The culture of the WC included a reluctance to engage in discussion and problem-solving around contentious issues (something I actually attribute to the culture of avoiding conflict that prevails in Minnesota), and this made it nearly impossible to have productive group discussions about the overarching protest strategy, which needed to happen to contextualize all of our work in a way that made mutual respect and appreciation possible.

As 5.3 played out, I was overcome with anger, feeling like my own efforts had been squandered. I also felt that I had been denied the room for personal participation in the strategizing session because I had to fill a logistical capacity (arranging facilitation and then running childcare) that no one else was willing to take on. It's fair that we all take turns sidelining ourselves for logistical purposes, but I had found myself in a parallel situation at the first pReNC and I hoped that this time around someone else would do what I had done before so that I'd be able to contribute in a different manner. That this didn't happen reinforced my feeling of not being valued personally or cared for within the group; I felt that the experience echoed a pattern of behavior where some people were encouraged to foreground personal desires without consideration for the ripple effects, while others were expected to pick up the slack without complaint. This problem is hardly unique to the WC, but speaks to a pervasive trend within the anarchist scene. It may in part come from a reasonable place—the healthy desire to take care of ourselves, rather than "serving" the movement at the expense of personal mental health. Yet it often plays out in a manner that enforces hierarchies built on the differing extents to which people are valued and nurtured as individuals.

I believe that if we're serious about revolution, and if we're in this to win, we have to enact a level of self-discipline and consideration for others that will sometimes override personal desire. And especially in a movement whose members are so disproportionately privileged, I question the foregrounding of personal desire and happiness over the collective good as a matter of practice. One has to ask who this is liberation for, in actuality, and how that measures up against an understanding of privilege and oppression in our society.

Ultimately, some useful things did come out of 5.3, namely the decision to divide downtown St. Paul into sectors with the idea that, in so doing, we could decentralize coordination of the blockades by asking groups across the country to pick a sector and take responsibility for coordinating within it. Other developments were a decision that we would focus on Tier One of the blockades[3] because we didn't believe we could realistically fill all three; the concept of "Swarm, Seize, Stay" as a way of executing the blockading strategy within Tier One; and the formation of a group outside of the WC to handle communications infrastructure for the RNC.

5.3 was also, however, the site of a significant security breach that was reminiscent of issues at the first pReNC. We had decided that we needed a much stricter vouching plan for the strategizing session this time around, for two reasons: one, we acknowledged the likelihood of greatly increased surveillance and State attention now that the RNC was only months away; and two, we anticipated that the strategizing session itself would be so hard to keep on track and make productive that any disruptive behaviors or unfocused input could totally derail it, and we thought that making folks go through the vouching process just to be there would discourage folks from attending who merely wanted to spectate or weren't seriously involved in organizing for the blockading strategy.

As with just about everything else at this point, the security plan was contentious to hash out and I don't know that anyone was really happy with how it had turned out, though for varying reasons. Many in the group felt that the security team should be comprised of an entirely different set of people than had been involved in security the first time around, and this was compounded by the reality that some of the people who had previously done security were members of Action Faction, the blockade-focused subcommittee that would necessarily play a large role in the content of the strategizing session. I felt that it was important not to concentrate all of this work within such a small group, both to even out work load and to share skill-building. But I was also cognizant of a highly reactionary dynamic within the WC that played into the planning; feelings in the group that some of us held too much power resulted in a determination to keep us at a significant distance from security work, which didn't allow for the benefits of having people who had been through it once in a position to share and act on lessons learned the first time around.

Nonetheless, the prevailing sentiment was that the team shouldn't involve folks from the first pReNC's security team, and so it went. We decided that folks seeking to attend the strategizing session needed to be vouched for by two people, and that "vouching" meant that you had known someone for at least two years, felt that they had a working understanding of security culture, and that they were honestly representing themselves as radical activists. Our preference was that vouchers be people we knew and/or that they were well-established themselves in the radical community.

We discussed as a group the fact that our vouching policy meant that even some of our own members wouldn't be able to attend the strategizing session. Many of us felt that this was totally appropriate—the fact that we were a large, open group meant we didn't all know each other very well and it would have been irresponsible of us to suggest to other folks in attendance that membership in the WC (which was attained by mere attendance) meant an individual could be trusted. But there were definitely people who were embittered by this policy, including the county informants and some of the folks who were closer to them. Though it didn't make things easier for us in the short term as it bred internal resentment that the informants worked to exacerbate, in retrospect I feel relief that the strongest advocates of such strict security stuck to their guns. As a result, Norma Jean and Chris weren't allowed into the strategizing session and were relegated to helping cook for the event. Later, when Norma Jean took the stand at a pretrial hearing, she referenced this situation with obvious enmity in her voice. It offers us some small bit of gratification to know that this person who befriended and manipulated people for pay at least had to put in hours of hard work over a hot fire to feed them all.

Victories of the vouching system notwithstanding,

there were two FBI informants who managed to get in. One was Brandon Darby, an egomaniacal sociopath who made his entrance into the anarchist community doing relief work in New Orleans after Katrina. As of this writing, we still don't have a clear picture of when Darby turned informant or the extent of his damage to the movement, but his outing in winter of 2008-09 through the federal Molotov case[4] he created for the FBI sent shock waves through the national radical community. We had been warned of the fact that Darby was an aggressive and divisive person and that we should be prepared for the possibility that he might engage in disruptive behavior during 5.3, but at that time as far as we knew, nobody had processed their uneasiness with him to the point of thinking that he might be an informant. We didn't know him except by name, but he had solid vouches and no one suggested that we should keep him out, so he was let in.

Looking back over the situation, I can only reflect, as many have since then, that if within anarchist communities we were quicker to call out abusive and divisive behaviors such as those exhibited by Darby and to collectively unite around not tolerating them, a lot of people would have been spared the pain of Darby's bad acts and his involvement in the RNC might have been avoided altogether.

Panda, though, was the Welcoming Committee's problem. Since the RNC, we've found out that Panda didn't actually provide the vouches required for attendance and, according to the protocol, shouldn't have been on the attendance list for 5.3. Several years later, it's hard to identify exactly the missteps that let him slide in anyway, but I believe a major factor was a predominating sentiment within the WC that folks who were perceived to have too much power and influence in the group should be kept at a distance from the security procedures for 5.3 in order to equalize power dynamics. Unfortunately, these were also the people who would have been best positioned to keep Panda out. The WC had designated a couple members to receive and verify vouches and create the attendance list for 5.3, and problems that arose during the process were never shared with the group proper or even, necessarily, with individual members upon request.

I don't know if Panda was on the attendance list or just coasted in on the fact that Action Faction, the subcommittee he was a part of, was responsible for certain portions of the agenda, but when 5.3 arrived he was allowed in and, unbeknown to us, recorded the entire strategizing session. The lapse is directly attributable to a severe failure of communication whereby the folks processing vouches assumed Action Faction would have kicked him out (AF was the only closed committee in the WC, until it was dissolved shortly thereafter) if there were questions about his trustworthiness and everyone else assumed he must have gotten his vouches in order if he managed to get onto the attendance list. Whatever the explanation, this incident exemplifies the serious lack of communication on many sides that allowed Panda to end up in places where he shouldn't have been. Indeed, he capitalized on this lack of communication, inhabiting shady spaces between different groupings of people and banking on the fact that interpersonal issues would prevent people from paying enough attention to him and his questionable status to catch him sneaking around.

Summer of '08 flew by, and people were streaming into town. It was a relief to have outsiders with skills and energy show up and take up some of the work that we couldn't do on our own, and the infusion of new energy was motivating for me at a point when I would otherwise have been utterly demoralized. It also felt like affirmation of the work we had been doing so long, and it felt really good to be told through this that our work had value for the movement. When close friends started to show up, I felt revived and grateful. They provided personal support and gratification that wasn't available to me in the WC, and helped me focus on the RNC and barrel through the remaining weeks as problems within the WC kept surfacing.

In late May, a car full of WC folks went to Madison to do a presentation on our organizing and the RNC at an activist conference that was taking place. I wasn't one of them, but the drama that transpired there was brought to the WC to deal with and was so infuriating to me that it clouded my judgment in dealing with related issues later on.

Among the travelers was Chris Dugger, the paid Ramsey County informant who was rewarded for his work infiltrating our group with a full-time job as a Ramsey County Sheriff's Deputy. I had very few personal interactions with him, and my only observations were that he fell asleep a lot during meetings and never contributed when he was awake. He also had a physical build, seething aggression, and ignorance of social issues that made him seem quite out of place and triggered "cop" alarms for many of us. The group had attempted to confront him and deal with people's fears in many ways the winter prior, before I was back, with problematic results. But, at least when I was around, his utter lack of a presence most of the time meant that he was overlooked more than anything else.

Even now that I know he's a cop and played a role in the investigation that has gotten us here, it's hard for me to take him seriously as a threat. Watching him on the stand during pre-trial hearings, I was struck by his total lack of savvy in answering questions posed to him and how he didn't even seem capable of twisting information to make us look worse—which all the other informants have done—let alone intelligently articulating anything about the year that he spent among us.

While in Madison, organizers there took WC folks aside to say that Chris was making people uncomfortable and they were worried he was a cop; thus he was no longer welcome at the event. Some WC folks were irate, jumping to Chris' defense. But Rob, who shared the fears and discomfort, refused to defend Chris, saying that he hadn't known him long and couldn't vouch to anyone that he wasn't a cop. Rob's response was justified, but among folks who wanted to give Chris the benefit of the doubt and who for various reasons harbored ill feelings toward Rob already, his behavior was harshly criticized. Eventually, the situation was brought to the larger group's attention and discussed at one of our regular meetings. We did a go-around, where everyone in the circle speaks his or her piece on the given topic, one person after the next, without interruption. As I recall it, only myself and a person from the legal collective voiced clear support for Rob. I felt crushed in this moment, almost wholly defeated by the groupthink that was so clearly creating an environment where people were pressured into feigning trust and affinity with people they had good reason to suspect and fear. The reactionary nature of the group's admonishments of Rob frightened me and undermined the already low confidence I had in the WC's collective decision-making and abilities.

A few weeks later, I got an email from some of the same WC members who had attacked Rob over the Madison incident, saying that they believed Chris and Norma Jean were informants, and asking those of us in receipt to help them do something about it. The email contained the reasoning for their suspicions, but despite the fact that I had had my own suspicions of the two all along, the reasons listed struck me for the most part as examples of individual discomfort and lifestyle differences rather than compelling evidence that either of them were cops.

I couldn't overcome my own anger at the fact that I and people I cared about had all been vilified for our attention to security and our reluctance to immediately embrace every newcomer as a trusted friend; the pReNCs and the Madison incident were only peaks in a months-long pattern of this behavior. I was furious that people who had been so resistant to addressing these issues all along, invalidating our concerns at every opportunity, would suddenly shift gears without acknowledging the history behind the whole situation, and I didn't trust their motives at all.

I thought, and email responses confirmed, that one of the other people behind this move to purge Chris and Norma Jean was Panda, who had all but disappeared from WC activity by this point and now claimed that this was because he feared for his safety in the presence of those two. Starting with his shady arrival at the first pReNC, Panda had always left a bad taste in my mouth. He struck me as manipulative, playing dumb to make people like him, and my experience was that he treated most women as being totally invisible, rarely hearing what they said or acknowledging their contributions. I sensed a quick temper and lack of genuine interest in collective work, and I felt that he often fell through on commitments and put people on pedestals as a way of absolving himself of responsibility for the work we were all engaged in. At that point in time, I had heard him use all sorts of excuses for his absence from the WC, which made me reluctant to believe any of them.

I also knew that he had stepped into something of a leadership role on organizing within Sector 5, though I didn't really know what exactly was going on because the Sector 5 organizing was totally separate from the WC. Knowing what I did, though, of his own narrative of his past activist experience (which was that it was almost nonexistent), I thought he had no business being in any sort of leadership role. All of this, added to my own observations of his ignorance and poor judgment, made me equally wary of the people who had gotten close to him.

Responding in knee-jerk fashion to my feelings about Panda and the individuals who had joined forces with him in such a sudden change of opinion, I shut the entire conversation down, arguing that the process by which this had all come about was really messed up and that instead it needed to be addressed openly by the WC proper or not at all, adding that I would block any proposal that came out of what I'd been privy to thus far. Frankly, and as I look back over the course of the Welcoming Committee's existence, this is one of my only real regrets. Though kicking the informants out at this point may not have saved us from prosecution, it would likely have changed the nature of the case significantly, leaving us an easier road ahead.

Over the summer, I felt overwhelmed by the conflicts and negativity plaguing the Welcoming Committee, which was nearly my entire life by then. But I didn't realize until afterwards how nerve-wracking and deeply frightening those months actually were. Many of us noticed being followed by squad cars, and cops would drive by our houses, shining searchlights into our yards and front windows and creeping along at a snail's pace. We also started to hear stories about random stops and searches where police questioned people about the RNC, often just because they looked like punks and anarchists.

The moments when I felt most vulnerable were on nighttime bike rides. I would often head home alone well after midnight, and though I'm sure that sometimes the squad cars were there to watch me and sometimes were there on unrelated business, I couldn't seem to bike fast enough and tried not to think about the fact that at those moments there was no one to see whatever happened to me. These were overt acts of harassment by the State, intended to induce fear, and we knew that they also meant that there was more serious surveillance activity underway that we couldn't see. It took the feeling of the next summer, absent the intense pre-convention law enforcement activity, for me to be able to compare and suddenly recognize all the moments of tension and terror that I hadn't really seen as such at the time.

Monica Bicking

About eight months after we had moved to Minneapolis, they announced that the RNC would be held in St Paul. Eryn and I had been looking for a project to get involved in, but were having a hard time making connections. I knew many people in Minneapolis, but few anarchists and no one who was working on projects I was interested in. Because of my connections with the Anti-War Committee in the late winter of 2007 I heard that they were getting together with other groups to discuss protests around the RNC. At the meeting I realized the large responsibility put on the people of Minneapolis to come up with protest ideas, food, housing, and other logistics. I also realized that this was not the group I wanted to do the majority of my work in. While it contained many excellent organizers whom I respected, a discussion developed where a few people started to talk about "good" vs. "bad" protesters and "what to do about the anarchists". Even though I had roots with these organizers and respected them and knew that they respected me as well, I knew that I would be better off working with the anarchists.

Eryn did some research and found that a group called the Welcoming Committee had recently started meeting. They would be working on logistics around RNC protests and had points of unity that we agreed with. They were an anarchist and anti-authoritarian group who would definitely not demonize anarchists. Within the Welcoming Committee, however, it was not unusual for discussions to erupt about "what to do about the liberals". While there were some fundamental differences between the Welcoming Committee and other groups working on RNC protests, and we may have spoken about each other in disrespectful tones behind closed doors, there was a level of respect for each other that had not been demonstrated at past protests.

All groups wanted to avoid the conflicts that have come up between protest groups in past demonstrations. The groups came up with and signed onto the St. Paul Principles, which stated that (not exact wording) we would not speak negatively about each other to the media, we would keep infighting to ourselves, we would not cooperate with law enforcements, and that we would keep a separation of space or time between our protests.

I believe these principles have had a lasting impact on the people and groups involved in making them. I think if the RNC were to come again, we would not be asking what to do about each other, but rather how best collaborate. Things still come up, and there are still tensions, but I believe, especially for the people involved in making the St. Paul Principles, they are still effective guidelines for working with and around each other by showing a basic level of respect.

In the late winter and spring of 2007, we were just dipping our toes into the Welcoming Committee. Both Eryn and I tend to observe before we are ready to participate. I like to know whom I'm dealing with before I share my own ideas. In these first few months we did little work, but attended meetings and got a feel for the group. At this period of time, the group worked well together. Many people were friends and enjoyed each others' company. As far as we know there were no infiltrators in the group yet. Even though the group dynamics would later take a turn for the worst, it was in this fun-loving time that the Welcoming Committee set its public tone: a tone of satire and humor. The W.C.'s sense of humor was one of my personal favorite parts of the group. It got its message across without taking itself, opposition, or media too seriously.

That summer, the summer of 2007, the G8 was going

to be held in Germany. Eryn and I had a close friend who was planning on attending the protests and suggested that we come along. By the time we were going to buy tickets, we realized it was unlikely that our friend would really be going. We decided to go anyway, because by this time we had gotten involved in the Welcoming Committee. We thought that attending the G8 protests would add to our organizing capacity. I had never been to any summit protest or an RNC protest so it seemed like a critical experience to have before organizing the support for a similar protest in our town.

We decided to go to Berlin early to get a better idea of the organizing and see the city. We were especially interested in seeing the squats, which are fairly well known in anarchist circles across the globe. The squats were inspiring. They were long-term projects that the city was forced to accept as legitimate. In certain neighborhoods, we couldn't walk more than a few blocks without seeing a squat. At this point in my life, being an anarchist had always made me feel isolated, but now it seemed as though anarchists were everywhere. And as people started to fill the country for the protests, they really were everywhere.

After about a week in Berlin we met up with some acquaintances of a friend who really took us under their wing. They came with goals and a group of friends to accomplish their goals. They were older than us and more solid in their politics and selves. I learned a lot from my trip to Germany, but most of what I learned was from these American anarchists, not from Europeans. In Germany I got caught up in a general sense of invincibility. We did not pay for the train because there were too many of us for them to enforce it. There was a true power in numbers that extended beyond the protests. It was so strikingly different from the States that part of me felt that our struggle was not worth it: there just weren't enough of us. It was invaluable during this period that I was with American anarchists who did not think our fight was impossible, who were active in their communities, and who actively strategized for American protests.

One point that hit me was how very different Germany

was from the United States at a protest in Rostock. This was the major protest at the G8 and it had a mix of mainstream liberals and radicals. At the end of the march there was a river and park with a family-friendly concert. Across the street radicals and police fought. While a few of the mainstream liberals tried to stop the fighting, generally people just hung out in the park and listened to the concert. When people wanted a break from fighting the cops they would retreat into the park. The police never entered the park. They probably could not have gotten past the radicals safely, but they also had no interest in attacking the concert. It was a scenario that I could not have imagined before seeing it.

There are many reasons a family-friendly concert back-to-back with fighting the police is a highly unlikely scenario in the United States. For one, I believe that the police would be more likely to attack the concert in the States. Even if they are not more likely to, people would generally believe they are more likely to and not stick around to find out. Another, arguably more important, reason is that most of the people in the United States who attend liberal protest concerts would find it unacceptable for other protesters to fight cops. It would be especially offensive to do so in their sight line.

There is a belief in the media, which carries over to the protesters, that there are good and bad protesters. In this narrative, the good protesters follow the permits and rules and get their message heard. The bad protesters break windows, fight cops, and make everyone look bad, diverging from the message. This dichotomy makes it very hard for radical and mainstream protesters to work together. They see each other as getting in each other's way. Mainstream protesters have turned radical protesters into the police, and radical protesters have disregarded the safety of mainstream protesters. Seeing that this dichotomy and how the bad feelings between protesters were minimized in Germany made me want to strive for better protester relations home. When the Welcoming Committee worked with other, more mainstream groups to make the St. Paul Principles, it seemed like the first step in this direction.

I was surprised to find that in Germany, Nazis still

have a large presence. I was advised not to go into certain neighborhoods alone because of the Nazis. At one point I was riding the train late at night with some friends when two Nazis started harassing us. It quickly became clear to them that there were many more of us than them so they backed down, but I saw that the threat was real. There is even a white-supremacists soccer team. There is also an anti-fascists team and when the two play each other there are massive fights and often riots among the fans. Eryn and I happened to be in Hamburg for one of these games. While we decided to stay in that night, people were still in the rioting mood the following day during a G8 protest march. At the end of the march, people dispersed only to start rioting throughout Hamburg.

In the chaos I got separated from the rest of the group. Riot cops were approaching from two directions and I seemed to be moving in slow motion. There only seemed to be one way out: jumping the large fence in front of me. I jumped it, relived to have gotten away, but a little preoccupied about all the friends I gotten separated from. My face was covered and I had several layers of clothes on that I started to take off to cool down. I looked around and I was in a large soccer field. It looked like soccer practice had just ended, and a player was walking up to me. He introduced himself as a player for the St Pauli's, the anti-fascists soccer team. They offered me food and beer and welcomed me to stay until things calmed down outside. I sure picked a good fence to hop. Seconds earlier I was running from riot police, alone, in a town I didn't know, and now I was surrounded by attractive shirtless men, food, and beer. The soccer players didn't seem fazed by me or the riot happening on the other side of the fence. They joked around about how they hoped their cars didn't get burned. They might be anti-fascists, but they were also professional soccer players with very nice cars. Not long after, I walked to our meeting point, amused at my good fortune.

While Germany was packed with fun, it was also a great time to network. Every American we ran into was eager to hear about what was being planned for the RNC protests. It was a little bit awkward because Eryn and I had really just started to work with the Welcoming Committee and didn't have answers to many of their questions, but it was cheering. It encouraged us to think critically and we returned to Minneapolis with new ideas and energy.

Off and on from the beginning of 2007 until mid-2009 I went to Goddard College. It is a small college near Montpelier, VT. It's an alternative school where students are on campus for only a week and a half out of the semester. In that week and a half they work with their advisors to create a curriculum. The students then go home and fulfill the curriculum they created.

I decided to go to Goddard for a number of reasons. For one, I felt an obligation to my family, especially my grandmother, to finish college. When I dropped out of Earlham I had decided to ignore any family pressure. I had decided that the misery that I felt there was not worth pleasing family. When I heard about Goddard I realized that it would be a way of finishing school that would not make me miserable. I could still do all of the other things I wanted to do in life and I would have the freedom study what I wanted to. Goddard's low residency program solved the major issues I had with Earlham. I could ask the questions I wanted to ask and I would not be stuck in a liberal arts college bubble.

When I left Earlham I had planned to study on my own: to read non-fiction and broaden my knowledge base. In particular, I wanted to learn more about anarchism and its history. Unfortunately, I had not done this. I got bored reading books and didn't retain much. I learned that to truly learn something, I needed to write about it. If I read something without writing about it, I never truly formed my own opinions about it or retained the information. I could not bring myself to write without an audience. There was no teacher reading it, so what was the point? By going to Goddard I had a point in writing and could learn from all those books I had sitting around. I hoped that after Goddard I would have the skills needed to study academics without a school setting.

Finally I hoped to improve my writing skills. I have very little confidence in my writing, which gets in the way of my organizing. I never volunteer to write anything. I had hoped that a college degree and more writing experience would change that. It didn't. In fact, this autobiography is the only writing I have ever contributed to the Welcoming Committee or the RNC 8 defense. I have also failed to continue academic studies on my own. Despite not meeting the goals I had upon entering Goddard, it was an invaluable experience. Goddard broadened and deepened my politics analysis greatly. After Earlham, I did not think college was a setting that would ever positively affect my political thinking, but I was very wrong.

The week and a half that the students are on campus together is unique. The first time I went to Goddard I was not prepared for the amount of learning that would happen. Everywhere you go people are sharing ideas about their study plans and lives. The students take the opportunity to learn from each other. The advisors do not presume that they know more about a subject than the students or even that they have something to teach the students, but rather they help the students reach both their academic and personal goals. Goddard students come from a range of backgrounds and are a variety of ages. They have jobs, families and other projects at home. The week at Goddard is a break from that where they can focus their energy solely on school. I became so immersed in the school during those weeks that Goddard would feel like a community where I would get wrapped up in the politics of it and greatly concerned with the administration's often poor choices.

Even though I had heard about the experience that Goddard provided I had spent so long feeling isolated by my politics, especially while at college, I did not expect to get much out of the week. When I arrived I was surprised to find that a relatively large percentage of Goddard students in my program were anarchists/radicals. Many of these students were further along in their political thinking than me and I found myself growing immensely in those short periods at Goddard.

While I already had firm handle on insurrectionary aspects of anarchism and my own politics, I had not been exposed much to identity politics. It was not an important part of my parents' political understanding and I had not yet come to it on my own. The Goddard radicals mostly identified as Queer or GLBT and were very aware of the importance of identity politics.

At my first residency at Goddard I made my first transgender friend. Back home I was working as a nanny. One of the children I worked with is probably transgender. He is male-bodied, but talked a lot about how he wanted to be a girl. He wanted to change his name, grow his hair out and live as most girls do. His parents were conservative and would not let him (he was four at this time). I was in a difficult position. The parents told me not to let him play dress-up or pretend that he was a girl. While I would never restrict a child in this way, I didn't feel good about letting him behave how he wished and then telling him to quickly change because his mother was coming home. I felt that would be extremely confusing to him, so I was always trying to delicately redirect activities before parents returned. Because of this job I came to Goddard with identity politics already heavy on mind. I found once I arrived that people were eager to engage me in conversation about it.

I only had three semesters left when I started the school so my senior project comprised the majority of my work there. After my first semester at Goddard I started to realize the importance of identity politics. I started to notice how I was treated and how I lived in the world was greatly affected by the fact that I am a woman and by my many privileges. (I am white, heterosexual, upper-middle class, and educated.)

Like many young women of my generation, I had thought that sexism was something of the past. As I became more and more aware of it, I realized how differently men treated me and had always treated me compared to other men. I became especially aware of this dynamic in the Welcoming Committee ,whose active members were largely men. I found that I was often interrupted and talked over and that men would forget that I had spoken at all. While I mostly saw sexism evident in group settings, some men were consistently condescending and patronizing toward me on an individual basis. (They mostly turned out to be informants.)

At the same time I was learning more and more about anarchism and finding that I increasingly liked it. One of the things that I liked most about it, that made it so different from the revolutionary ideas I grew up with, was that identity politics are in the forefront. Anarchism promotes the importance of means being consistent with ends. It isn't about prioritizing which form of oppression are most important, but rather doing your best to counter them all right now. This means that many meetings held by anarchists practice some form of consensus decision-making and trying to confront or acknowledge the forms of oppression present in the group. Despite this concept, in my life sexism was most prevalent at anarchist meetings.

Understanding that in anarchist theory, feminism was not inherently secondary made me curious about when women had successfully advocated for their needs during times of revolution, when sexism was not the issue on the forefront, but people were fighting for some sort of change. I decided to focus on this for my senior project. I looked for examples of when women have pushed for their needs, broken gender roles, and worked for sustainable change during revolutions where sexism was not the main issue. While theoretically sexism or any form of oppression does not need to be secondary in anarchism, identity politics have been secondary in many anarchist or anarchist-like revolutions.

I looked for groups of women that did not make their needs secondary, but rather both joined the general revolution and fought for their gender specific needs. I focused my study on the Paris Commune, Spanish Civil War, and Zapatista Rebellion. I found that in each of these revolutions, women's needs were not automatically assumed relevant to the revolution, but women had to fight to be included and in many regards were successful. My senior project brought together what I had brought to Goddard: revolutionary anarchism, and also what I had gained at Goddard: identity politics. By bringing them together, I was able to bring my political understanding to the next level.

Eryn and I returned to Minneapolis just in time for the first pRe-NC. People had worked all summer to put this on and were visibly stressed. Because we had been gone so long we acted mainly as participants. The pRe-NC was a year before the RNC and was the first time people were coming from across the country to meet in the Twin Cities to discuss what the plan for the protests would be. One group in particular came with a well-thought-out plan and presentation about a blockading strategy. While the Welcoming Committee was started as a clearing house of information, rather than a group to make strategic decisions, I was surprised that the blockading strategy was decided on during the pRe-NC, even though most Welcoming Committee members were not fans and stood aside during the consensus process.

After the pRe-NC, we worked to give people the tools they needed for their strategy whether this was food, housing, people or maps. While in many ways the logistics of the protests were simple and we had a year to work them out, the Welcoming Committee's capacity was minimal. There was a high turnover rate and many people had not worked together in the past. Those that had often did not get along. Generally we came from different social circles and had limited if any experience organizing anything of this size. Looking back, we probably had the tools that we needed, but we got in our own way.

There were at least two factions of the Welcoming Committee. The people that did things and those that people that did nothing. I feel that I started in the group that was not empowered to do even the simplest things, and moved to the "let's get shit done" group. In the group that did work, there were a few individuals that did exceptionally more work than the rest.

I found it very difficult to become empowered for a number of reasons. I felt that nobody cared about who I was and only saw me as a machine to get things done, not as a person. I often felt invisible. The drama among the people that already knew each other took over meetings. It felt like the people that got shit done, did so on their own time and were not interested in including other people. They came to meetings presenting ideas that were new to me, but that they had already thought out thoroughly. Effectively the important decisions were made outside of meetings. I felt completely disrespected by the people that got things done.

At some point I switched groups. I somehow became included in a closed working group with people that got shit done. On this side of the fence things looked different. It was frustrating at meetings when people would not step up for the simplest tasks. I started to live and breathe the Welcoming Committee. I became caught up in the drama and it overtook most of my thoughts and conversation. It seemed like the people who were in the Welcoming Committee, but didn't live and breathe it, couldn't understand where I was coming from. Most of all, it was frustrating that they thought we took all the power, when it felt like they were giving it to us by not participating. They asked for our opinions for the simple tasks but then complained about how everything went through us.

In the months leading up to the convention we were under a tremendous amount of stress. We were being surveilled , we were scared of infiltrators, and there was a lot of work to get done in a very short period of time by a not-very-functional group. I think that it was partly due to this stress that we were emotionally incapable of dealing with the group dynamics and our personal issues.

The Welcoming Committee never worked through its issues. It became dysfunctional beyond repair. It was a nightmare for everyone on every side. While I think we did a horrible job working together and being a group, despite all odds, we did an okay job doing the tasks assigned to us. We got a convergence center, traveled around the country, encouraged people to come, and connected with groups doing food, medical, and legal work.

We held consultations so that people could plan and strategize for the protests long before they began; we publicized the protests, put out a good guide, and made space for people to do as they pleased. One of our more precedent-setting accomplishments was the St. Paul Principles. They are a list of principles that anarchist, socialists, and liberals signed onto that stating that they would not involve police or media in any of their disagreements, that we supported a diversity of tactics, and would not get in the way of each others' protests. Even though the work load was not spread evenly in the group, there were plenty of people who knew what they were doing so that when eight of us were preemptively arrested the show was able to go on.

There were many sources of our issues, but I believe

that one of the biggest issues was a lack of respect for each other. In the future, I plan to prioritize working with people I respect. Obviously this is not always an option. The Welcoming Committee was an open group and we did not choose whom we worked with. I also plan not be so quick to judge people and lose respect for them. The seven of us (I had not worked with Erik Oseland extensively before the charges) whohad worked closely together in the Welcoming Committee did not always get along and did not always show each other any respect whatsoever.

When we first got out of jail and our support committee was made up of mostly old Welcoming Committee members, they shared that one of their fears was the personal relations of the eight. This made a lot of sense based on our behavior before the RNC, but was not an issue after. We might not all agree and still scoff at each other from time to time, but we have found a mutual respect for each other. With the pressure of the RNC behind us and the knowledge that we are all facing the same thing, there is a unity that was never there before. We have also all grown and matured immensely through the entire process. It has taught me that it's not just about only working with people you already like and respect, but it also about building those relationships. I have found that is possible and very rewarding to build those relationships with unlikely people.

Max Specktor

After graduating from high school, I began looking for something to occupy my time more productively. I had heard of a group of anarchists meeting to plan for the protests against the upcoming Republican National Convention (RNC), an event that I had been very pissed about since hearing the news of its location: St. Paul, Minnesota. The anarchist/anti-authoritarian group was called the RNC Welcoming Committee. It was a little difficult getting involved in the group despite the friendliness of most of the members; learning the jargon and getting caught up with where the group was at swallowed up most of my focus for the first few meetings.

It was, however, easy to get involved in the fundraising work at the beginning, which turns out, was also some of the work that the undercovers found themselves doing, as it is something that is universal to any kind of organizing and doesn't take much political analysis. I tried to hit the ground running, soaking up as much knowledge about consensus procedure, anarchist theory and history, and also just basic skills like taking notes and setting up events. I wasn't very active for my first few months in the group, but I continued attending meetings because it was a really intriguing process, and the people involved interested me a lot.

During that summer, I participated in a critical mass bike ride that was called in solidarity with the resistance to the G8 in Germany. There were only about 25 of us participating, but it was my first critical mass, so it was fun nevertheless. Eventually, after biking into St. Paul, we were all pulled over by a couple cop cars, and they attempted to ticket all of us, a very ambitious attempt. Unfortunately, I was one of those corralled and received my first-ever citation. It was only a small ticket, but in the process I bonded with a lot of the other participants and it was worth the small price. This seems to always be the positive side of repression: the communities under attack necessarily have to come together to protect themselves. After the RNC, many relationships were built to this effect and continue to be strengthened.

That fall, I attended my first large anti-capitalist protest. It was one of those meetings of the neo-liberal bureaucratic agencies: the IMF/World Bank. I was pumped—not because I knew too much about what I was protesting, or because I had a strategic understanding of how we were going to affect change, but mostly because I was gonna be around a lot of people who were at least as pissed as I was, and I wanted to see what we were capable of.

I also thought that, given the anti-RNC organizing that I had just begun involvement with, I should attend at least one anti-capitalist demonstration so that I could have even just a little experience in the field. The big lesson I came away with from this summit, was that the security forces aren't a joke. Crying "police state" isn't an exaggeration when you're dealing with blocks and blocks of riot-gear-wearing cops, surrounding a group of about 200 protesters, like we were the most dangerous collection of individuals in the world. It was definitely invigorating and inspiring marching next to people I saw as comrades, especially in the face of this juggernaut of a police force. The weekend was pretty stressful overall and despite there being only a handful of arrests, a lot of people seemed drained and a little bummed out after the events.

At the IMF/World Bank demonstrations, I heard some people talking about the upcoming "No Borders Camp" on the border of the U.S. and Mexico. Fortunately, after returning home I found some people who had converted a school bus to run on vegetable oil and were planning to travel to the camp in California. The trip there was half the adventure. I learned a lot from the older folks I traveled with, including how to spare change for gas money when the filtration system for the veggie oil broke down. After struggling to pay for the diesel across a few states, the bus finally broke down completely in New Mexico. Most of the passengers, including myself, took turns hitchhiking in twos and threes, after failing to ride a freight train.

We arrived about nightfall to a bustling camp full of excited people and surrounded by border guards with huge floodlights and automatic weapons. The camp was set up on both sides of the border with a huge wall in between the two camps. The wall dead-ended into a cattle fence with a river cutting it off beyond that. It was a very peculiar sight: murals spray-painted on the wall, tall ladders so that people could climb to the top and hang out with people from the other side, and people of all ages busy at work on some project or another. The border guards made it clear that they would raid the camp if anybody from the Mexican side attempted to climb over or walk through the cattle fence to the U.S. side, but they allowed people to pass through to the Mexican side from the U.S. side.

"No Borders Camps" are tactics or events typically held in European countries to bring awareness to, and directly confront, increasingly militarized borders and the global business interests that they protect. This specific camp was in Calexico, Ca. and Mexicali, Mexico. The way setting up the camp worked was that everyone met in the center of both towns at the wall and began marching together along the wall until they came to an open area where everyone quickly set up tents, while other people distracted the police by "negotiating" with them. It was so inspiring to see people taking back space that is generally one of the most protected and stigmatized public spaces in our countries.

The first morning after I arrived at the camp, we were planning on eating breakfast at the cattle fence so that we could share a meal with our comrades on the other side of the imaginary border. The border guards were very intent on controlling the cattle fence because it was an easy place for people to cross into the U.S., so as we approached the area, police in full riot gear marched in behind us to stop us from enjoying our breakfast, which is apparently a serious threat to national security. We responded by linking arms and facing off with the cops, and collectively negotiated with them to allow us to eat in relative peace. It was very important that we didn't back down due to threats of violence from the State, because of this we were able to win our demands. The camp wasn't perfect however, especially due to resources being unfairly divided between the two sides of the camp, and meetings being conducted in one language without adequate translation available for Spanish-speakers.

As part of the week-long camp, we visited a maquiladora where people worked in a textile factory and lived in shacks on property owned by the factory. We had the privilege of meeting some of the people who lived and worked there, and shared our intentions with them, a very powerful experience that re-instilled a strong sense of personal privilege. We also visited a detention facility where immigrants were held while awaiting deportation. We made as much noise as possible to let the detainees feel our support, as small a gesture of support that it was.

On the last day of the camp, a march was planned to walk back along the wall into the center of town. I was on the Mexican side of the border at this point, where protest activities were considerably more rambunctious. Many people were spray-painting anti-border and anti-capitalist slogans along the wall all the way into the center of town, while on the U.S. side the police were threatening protesters with everything in their arsenal. It brought to my attention that people who are more exploited economically acted with an increased urgency in their protests, while on the other side the more economically privileged people were threatened to remain passive or else their freedom could be stripped completely; it's not a coincidence that the U.S. imprisons the most people, otherwise those challenging this inequality would have no excuse for remaining passive. This is the sinister nature of borders: if anyone decides to cross over to better their position in life, they are also prevented from speaking out by the privileges that they can be stripped of at any time.

When the protests reached the center of town, everyone tried to rally at the fence, in part as a powerful symbol of international solidarity, but at the same time some people very literally began attacking this behemoth of separation with everything they could. At this point, the U.S. border guards began shooting automatic pepper-spray projectiles at everyone and started arresting people at random. After the crowd was dispersed, my fellow travelers and I met up and decided to stick around town and do legal support for the arrestees, especially one person whose immigration status made his release difficult.

Throughout this process, I learned how to write press releases and call media outlets to organize a press conference, and we widely fliered to the local population about the situation. It was interesting hearing responses from the locals on the U.S. side who were not generally familiar with police repression of this kind—beating and arresting young, white activists that is—even though they lived in an atmosphere of anti-immigrant repression everyday. I remember one conversation with an older Latino man on the street about the arrests, and he pretty much broke down about how great it was to see people taking a stand against these global systems of oppression, and railed against la migra (border guards) for their violent presence in his everyday life.

After leaving town, I went to San Diego with some of

the folks from the veggie oil bus to relax and unwind a little bit after the intense experiences of our short stay on the border. Unfortunately, many people are never able to relax due to their immigration status, but we were able to feel relatively safe just miles from the border. I hitchhiked up to Palm Springs, Ca. to spend Thanksgiving with my uncle and shared with him my stories from the camp. It was definitely the first time I really opened up to any of my extended family about my political convictions and lifestyle choices. I think he was fairly receptive to the ideas and goals of the camp, but probably thought us a little idealistic. He helped us get on our way, driving us back out to the highway to continue hitchhiking.

After returning home from the no borders camp, I decided that all I wanted to do for the time being was travel a lot more. And this time I wanted to do it without time constraints or much direction. A few weeks later a friend of mine, Nick, asked if I wanted to travel out west with him, and so we decided that we would hitchhike to San Francisco. I began by going to Chicago where we met up and prepared to cross the country mid-winter. This was early January, so we knew that it might be tough to accomplish, especially without any places to stay lined up. We began by getting a ride, from a high-school friend of mine who was visiting Chicago at the time, all the way to Omaha, Neb.

What happened that night in Omaha was to be a constant theme of our travels: relying on the generosity of strangers. We were going to have to sleep outside or in the cramped car, if we didn't scrounge up a place to stay, but I remember clearly feeling confident that something would work out. We asked random people if there was a neighborhood where younger people or "artists" hung out. From there we were directed to a street lined with hip-looking businesses, but they were all deserted as it was after 9 on a weekday night.

Luckily, we noticed somebody cleaning up inside a pizza shop, and on the window of the shop I noticed a flier for an event set up by an artists' collective. ("Collective" is a good word to look for if you want to find people willing to help out complete strangers; usually you have to be of a similar socio-economic background though.) We knocked on the window to the shop, and mustered up all the charm we could. We barely had to explain ourselves before the young woman was already on the phone, talking to her friend who agreed to host us for the night. Success!

After spending the night having great conversations, we hit the road the next morning with an extra bag of food, generously donated by our host. The hitch through the rest of Nebraska made me rethink the kindness of strangers. We only made it about 200 miles that day, and ended up sleeping outside in 5-degree weather. Total bummer, but the price was right.

The next day, we barely managed to make it into Denver just as night fell. We were in another position where we really had no clue where we were going to sleep that night, but a couple phone calls and an hour later we were being shown into a bedroom in the most rad collective house I had seen in my life. This is what I really gained from traveling, I was able to spend time experiencing other people lives and lifestyles, and seeing many different examples and degrees of intentional living.

I decided that this was what I was looking for when I chose to go traveling and take off from school. I wanted to decide for myself what my long-term goals were, and because I wasn't given many different options by those who sought to educate me, I went off to find out first-hand some alternative ways to define success. I thought that if I could go home and find people interested in living together collectively and supporting each other, it would most definitely be a success, something that I had previously taken for granted.

From Denver, Nick and I started hitching west through the mountains. The views were stunning; the snow was piling up and the temperature was dropping, but it felt like the wildest thing I had ever done, so I was ecstatic. By the end of our first day in the mountains, we climbed into a car driven by a man who was heading all the way to Los Angeles. So, the next morning we took a bus to the ocean and went for a swim (after taking off layers and layers of clothes, of course). Snow-covered mountains to sunny ocean beaches in one night!

From there, we headed up the coast to San Francisco. One of the craziest rides we got was from this guy from Malibu.

He had been a security contractor for Blackwater in Iraq and spoke openly about the experience. He didn't actually get into the details, but made enough implications to make me feel like I didn't want to share a car with this guy. Here we were sitting in the back of a giant pickup truck outside the home of a real-life mercenary, while he went inside to get sodas for us to drink on the ride. The craziest part about him wasn't the fact that he most likely killed people for money, but that he really tried to buddy-up to us despite our obvious differences. It's unfortunate, but true, that it's easy at times to find stuff in common with people you might despise.

We spent about two weeks in the Bay, trying to sample all that its many diverse communities and radical spaces had to offer. Just to name a few, volunteering at the Slingshot newspaper, squatting a house on Haight Street, cooking Food not Bombs in the Mission, and seeing punk shows at a radical cultural center in Oakland. I remember it being slightly difficult to find worthwhile places and people to hang out with in the Bay Area, but we eventually were plugged into a large scene by making a few connections. Ironically, this was a strategy similar to that of the undercover cops in infiltrating the Minneapolis anarchist community: they would show up at the public spaces like collective bike shops and social centers and chat up anybody they met. It worked for me in a new city as well. I don't think police have necessarily outsmarted all the anarchist subcultures, but I do think that this goes to show that no matter how "underground" we think our communities are, anybody is just a few introductions away from being a new face in the scene.

After procrastinating about going home, I eventually ended up going straight to Chicago via Greyhound, so that I could meet up with another person from the RNC Welcoming Committee and begin the southern portion of the RNC-WC national tour. We traveled around the southern half of the United States for about a month promoting the strategy for opposing the RNC that anarchists/anti-authoritarians had come up with in Minneapolis at the first pReNC in September of 2008.

These were mostly cities and communities that I had never visited, so it was very exciting meeting new people, but at the same time, it made it that much harder to get events and presentations set up with very limited contacts for local anarchists. This is something that I didn't put too much thought into at the time and seriously regret. Sometimes the traveling culture of many anarchists makes it very easy to connect with communities across great distances, but the other edge of that blade is that you can sometimes end up getting contacts for people who travel frequently and are therefore not the most plugged into their local radical communities.

Either way, I think that the way the RNC Welcoming Committee set up separate tours and covered a lot of ground gave the impression that we were connecting with lots of people, whether or not lots and lots of people were actually attending our presentations. Hopefully, we were generating more confidence among the people planning to come help us resist the convention.

Of course, we never had all the answers to people's questions, something that made me feel unorganized. I constantly felt uncomfortable telling older and more experienced anarchists why I believed that the blockading strategy was a good idea, or that it might actually work out. The only experience I had with any large anti-capitalist protest was at the IMF/World Bank where the police easily outnumbered us 3 to 1 and were able to control the streets as they pleased. Many people warned us that the era of the large anti-globalization mobilization was over, and these tactics were obsolete.

One big criticism was that we were being too ambitious and setting ourselves up to fail. We acknowledged this by framing the call as one of "Crashing the Convention," so that it left some room for ambiguity. Fortunately, there seemed to be a critical mass of people coming to protest the war, and the growing hatred of the Republican administration seemed to be shifting lots of people in a more militant and radical direction.

I was, however, most happy to talk about our number-one goal at the convention, which was to build capacity. This was especially relevant to me and some of my peers because we were the younger ones, who would most likely be benefiting and learning the most from all this organizing. I gained much of this knowledge through long conversations with more experienced organizers from around the country. These talks covered a wide range of topics: recent anarchist history, strategies for confronting global capitalism, economic globalization, the justice system and political prisoners, gender issues, and much more. It turns out that I got more than I bargained for, and am continuing to build this capacity as the dust refuses to settle.

There were many, many other things I was forced to learn along the way as well. On the tour, we stopped in Florida for the Earth First! Organizers Conference, a week-long retreat in a nature reserve in the Everglades that focused on radical environmentalism. I attended workshops, skillshares, and conference sessions, where organizers offered their visions for building a serious radical environmental movement that would challenge not just the ways that we are destroying the planet, but the infrastructure and systems that allow that destruction to occur.

In college classes, I had studied environmental justice and radical theories on wilderness and nature, but that week in the Everglades brought all that knowledge together in a cohesive critique and plan of action. Well, maybe the plan for action wasn't completely cohesive, but I decided that I had enough courage in my convictions to participate in the lockdown at the end of the gathering. We practiced with lockboxes (large PVC piping covered in padding and other protection, designed to chain protesters together) and picked our target: the construction site of what was going to be the second-largest power plant in the country. And it was being built across the street from an Everglades wildlife refuge, a very important ecosystem for a large part of Florida.

To me, the action seemed like a real success. We blocked trucks from entering the site for more than half the day, and according to the county attorney, we cost the sheriff's department $100,000 in their efforts to remove us. The greatest part of this civil disobedience action, for me, was after our arrests. Traditionally, civil disobedience means that you do your action, get arrested, and then it's over. But this time we decided as a group that we would continue our disobedience well after the initial arrest.

Conspiracy to Riot

The first act of rebellion, while in custody, was that a few people peed on the bus that they used to transport us to be processed. When they began questioning us for our identities, we refused to cooperate on any level. We didn't give any information, so we were just handcuffed in the holding cells with several people of our same perceived gender. We would make demands for food or to be un-handcuffed, and when those demands weren't met we would escalate our tactics. The people who had wet their pants intentionally, or because they couldn't hold it any longer, weren't given any new clothes, so most of the male-bodied arrestees got naked to protest. At one point, while three of us were being questioned completely naked in a room full of deputies, one of them lost his composure and cracked up, saying it was the craziest thing he had ever seen.

Not all of it was fun. At a certain point, the deputies, growing weary of our antics, hit a couple of the arrestees while they were handcuffed. This was very shocking for someone coming from my place of privilege with such a mediated relationship to violence, especially State violence. But it turned out to be strengthening when the victims of the assaults convinced other people to keep up the resistance.

I don't mean to speak on their behalf, but I'm fairly sure this whole experience was somewhat different for the female-bodied arrestees, as there were far fewer of them (indicative of the fact that police and the jail system perpetuates violence against women and sexual violence, making voluntary arrests that much less appealing) and most of the guards were large men. But we tried, and for the most part failed, to remain in solidarity with them and the State's attempts to divide us.

We eventually gave in and gave our real names, allowing them to process and release us--rather quickly, I will add, as I'm sure they were sick of our presence: a small victory. I ended up going back to Florida that summer to stand trial with some of my co-defendants and argue the necessity defense. We were saying that we felt it was necessary to break the law to fight for the greater good, but we learned the hard way that the law is anything but compatible with a radical worldview and actions taken in furtherance of those views. We were convicted of all three misdemeanors and sentenced to one year of probation and community service.

After returning from these 3 months of traveling and touring, I jumped back into the RNC organizing. At this point we were organizing the second big national strategy session, the pReNC 5.3. At the first strategy session, we had consensed on a strategy of blockading the streets of St. Paul, in an effort to "Crash the Convention." At the 5.3 strategy session, it was further developed that downtown St. Paul would be divided up into seven different sectors, so that groups who felt they had the capacity could claim a sector and be responsible for organizing the actions within that sector. We had effectively outsourced a good amount of the organizing that somebody was going to have to do, if we really wanted to blockade the entire convention. Outsourcing works for the imperialists; why shouldn't it work for us?

The plan was that everyone would go all-out on the first day of the convention, dividing into their respective sectors and blockading delegates from the convention center using a diversity of tactics. When we talked about tactical diversity, we meant that we didn't want to police the protesters, as there were thousands of police already planning on doing that work, and we refused to take a stance on which protesters were the good ones or the bad ones.

If we lived in a world based on restorative justice, instead of this one made up of prison factories, we could discuss tactical blunders and confront overly aggressive protestors in a public way. But instead we are forced to trust people to make strategic decisions on their own. Thanks to our mammoth prison industry, turning in a "violent" protester, would be a considerably violent act in itself. Snitches who say they are protecting lives are also ruining the lives of the people and families that they tear apart.

Most large protest organizations in the United States commit to a pledge of non-violence for their actions. Many of these groups probably do it because they are committed to lifelong pacifism, but I believe that for the most part these groups choose non-violence because they fear the State's backlash. By refusing to take a stance on this issue, we are putting ourselves out on a limb where our movements need to go. The State tells its citizens that they can speak out, but only non-violently, because the State has a monopoly on the legitimate use of force and they want to protect that monopoly at all costs. The State doesn't believe anybody should be prepared to defend themselves because it is the State's job to defend all the people.

We came out and said that the cops are never there to defend us; they're always going to be defending property and the civil order that allows a few individuals to hoard everything. And why would we promise anybody that the protests were going to be non-violent if we already knew well in advance that they were going to have the National Guard on reserve? It would be like planning a protest in a swimming pool and telling everyone that there's no chance of getting wet.

Another important meeting that took place during this period leading up to the convention was a facilitated discussion with other local organizing groups on the topic of violence and non-violence. Earlier, at a large meeting of the Coalition to March on the RNC and Stop the War, the St. Paul Principles (SPP) were agreed upon. This meant that, in theory, no group was going to condemn other groups publicly or work with police against other protest groups. It also stated that every group signing on would support a diversity of tactics. So, this discussion was organized with the groups that signed on to the SPP, so that everyone involved could actually have a better sense of what a diversity of tactics might look like and make it clearer what we were all agreeing to.

We began the meeting with an exercise where we imagined a spectrum with violence at one end, and non-violence at the other end. Then the participants were given a complicated situation and asked to respond where it might fit on the spectrum. The situations were ones in which the use of violence or non-violence is not a simple question of right or wrong. The very different tendencies at the meeting sparked heated debate, but the fact of the matter was that everyone was forced to gain a better understanding of where we, as anarchists and anti-authoritarians, were coming from. It definitely made me more excited about working with some of the other organizing groups in our city for future projects.

The next 6 months were a whirlwind of anarchist convergences, dozens of planning meetings, and lots of work getting ready for the RNC. I went to the National Conference on Organized Resistance to promote our organizing work, as well as attended the Bash Back! and CrimethInc. Convergences. The Bash Back! Convergence, a meeting of radical queers from around the country, was held to network and plan an action at the RNC. The CrimethInc. Convergence was a similar gathering, geared toward all anarchists, but generally appealed to those coming from a higher place of privilege. All of these events were overwhelming for me and made it seem as though we would be able to bring tens of thousands of anti-authoritarians to the Twin Cities for the demonstrations.

I think during this period of time I was experiencing a very manic optimism that made it seem like our movement was going to come together immediately and we were going to accomplish whatever we wanted. The reality of the situation was, however, that all of those meetings, convergences, and plans were building something, but that something wasn't just going to reach its peak at the RNC in 2008. It's something we are continuing to build as we continue to organize and maintain the relationships and skills we gained in those manic months.

In the few months immediately before the convention, stress and tension was building among the people involved in the Welcoming Committee. There were arguments over who might be a cop, what work we should prioritize, and the meetings continued to drag on. One issue was the amount of work that loomed ahead of us and the stress it caused; at this point we had committed to house, feed and transport everybody who would be come to be a part of the blockade strategy. We were anxiously waiting to hear from groups from out of town who would be able to assist with these logistics, but in the meantime we were making little headway.

Another issue was that many people were committing lots of time to this project, which created some sense of resentment and tension between them and people who were newer to the group or less active. It is always difficult to navigate personal relationships while working on some sort of project, but I think that difficulty was amplified by the intensity and frequency of the work and the meetings. I am proud of the work that our group was able to accomplish in light of all this. Fortunately, we received a lot of help from a lot of people who came into town shortly before the convention and threw all their energy into the organizing as well.

One of the biggest accomplishments we made as a group was in preserving our anarchist principles, while building solidarity with other groups planning protests at the RNC. We had no paid organizers or staff people, and we continued to reach every big decision by group consensus. We opened up a convergence center in a large theater two weeks before the convention began, built hundreds of bikes for out-of-towners, and printed thousands of resource guides, all while remaining an open and public group. We built a large network of radicals from across the country and strengthened our networks in our own communities. The St. Paul Principles weren't just a tool used by liberals and radicals to avoid butting heads in the streets, but served as the precedent for local activists of many stripes to continue making space for each other in common struggles and supporting each other through repression.

The mainstream news media was also forced to talk about anarchist principles that weekend before the convention. The images of anarchists' houses being raided and ambitious investigators showing off the tools of the so-called terrorists were broadcast all over.

Meanwhile, we were communicating through our networks, that we indeed were anarchists, that we were not organizing against the RNC to endorse our own candidate or to cooperate with the police and corporate media. We were standing up for the masses who didn't have a seat at the Republican National Convention, or the Democratic National Convention for that matter. And we were saying that these assholes in suits didn't have a permit to meet on stolen native land, and they definitely weren't going to be able to do it without the $50 million in security funding. We weren't asking them to leave, we were telling them to get the fuck out. The militant protests and blockades that Labor Day showed the world that people can only sit clenching their teeth for so long before their anger takes them to the streets.

Garrett Fitzgerald

There was news that both the RNC and DNC were looking at the Twin Cites for their 2008 conventions. I was looking for a good project to be a part of and so watched the situation closely. When it was decided that the RNC would be in St. Paul, I asked around and heard that some folks had already put out a call to get together and discuss a radical/anarchist community response. I went to the community meeting. I didn't really know anyone involved, but I took on some work and decided to put energy into this project that became known as the RNC Welcoming Committee (WC).

While working with the WC, I continued to work on other projects. It didn't take too long for me to get a job at North Country Co-op. I had friends there and experience in the co-op and collective movement. It was a good fit for me. I got to see a lot of my friends on a regular basis as they came in to work, volunteer, or pick up some groceries. As someone who wasn't super outgoing, interested in going to parties, or putting myself in other large-group social situations, NCC helped make sure I maintained social contact with people I might not otherwise run into. I was trying not to make the job that I did for money be the way I expressed my politics. By this point, I had learned that often even the most ethical jobs can come into contradiction with my conscience. However, NCC was a fairly socially responsible institution.

North Country Co-op had been struggling since before I was hired and it continued to have hard times. As the store was floundering, it was clear that those most affected by the difficulties were the workers. NCC was the oldest of the "new wave" co-ops in the area. It started out being run by volunteers who were also the primary shoppers. As there became paid staff, the co-op was run by a worker collective with oversight from a board of directors who were elected by members and volunteers.

The co-op movement's strength came, in part, from the fact that the co-op valued providing a community-focused way to get quality foods for cheap that otherwise couldn't be accessed through the grocery stores of their day. When they first started, people who shopped at the co-ops did so out of necessity. However, corporate groceries commodified some of the co-ops' more easily marketable values such as organically grown produce, free-range meat and dairy, and fair trade coffee. This occurred simultaneously with a general shift from purchasing whole foods and more toward convenience foods. The co-op moved from providing a necessity for people with limited means to being a nostalgic charity that many shopped at to quell their consumer guilt or as an attempt to keep sacred what was once a meaningful part of the movement decades ago.

As NCC struggled, the workers sacrificed to keep the store on life support, hoping for a recovery, and members made large loans to pull the store out of debt. The workers voluntarily gave up the collective model, hoping that a more streamlined decision-making process might help. They also accepted wage and benefit cuts and pay freezes. As NCC was in its final nose dive, some workers organized a union in a last-ditch effort to be a part of the management process and at least get recognition for their sacrifices. However, even after a membership vote to recognize the union, the board of directors stonewalled the process, negated the vote, and the store closed before the state bureaucracy for forcing recognition could be navigated. It surprised me and many of the other workers that an organization so committed to progressive values would engage in such union busting measures, especially after lending support and lip service to other union struggles in the community.

With the work that I put into NCC and the union effort in the time that I worked there, it became a clearer example of how capitalism, even soft-capitalism, corrupts and promotes selfishness and power grabbing. That doesn't mean that these institutions aren't worth having around, but it is evidence that alternative institutions alone cannot change the systems that they are designed to co-exist with. Whatever the internal hierarchy, these institutions still exist within capitalism and come to depend on capitalism and property law.

During this time, as I was settling into my life in Minneapolis, I was trying to find a way to integrate my past work in theater into my life. I was hesitant, however, to take just any work that came my way. One of the first projects I worked on was a work-in-progress that a playwright was developing about a video blogger who unwittingly positions herself as the figurehead of a revolutionary movement after her internet video goes viral. While the piece wasn't outstanding or otherwise worthy of note, I think of it now because of my current legal situation. The RNC Welcoming Committee first started to get attention, both from the radical community as well as from law enforcement, from a video posted on the internet.

My proudest theatrical effort was working on a rock opera entitled "Idigaragua" featuring the band Fort Wilson Riot. The politics of the piece were something I could get behind. It depicted effects of colonization, globalization, and industrialization through the epic experience of an arrogant American journalist who sees the effects of his culturally normative responses to the problems he encounters. Also, being a rock opera, the piece allowed for more potential to use the training I had gained while in New York. "Idigaragua" achieved local acclaim and was voted "Best Rock Opera" of 2007 by Minneapolis-St. Paul Magazine.

When I went to the first few RNC-WC, meetings there was a surprisingly large number of people. While the numbers were encouraging, most of the time was spent with everyone staring at their shoes, unwilling or uninterested in speaking to an issue or putting out ideas. This opened up space for others to go off on unproductive rants. It was slow going, but we decided to form some working groups to put together some "points of unity" and an initial call to action. I was proud to find a use for the platform/program that I had put together months before, and brought that to the table to be incorporated into the "points of unity" along with ideas from several other sources.

Once the points of unity were established and the call to action completed, the RNC Welcoming Committee went public. A web site was set up and the RNC-WC started promoting itself. A lot of the beginning work was about getting to know each other and formulate a sense of group identity. From that point, we communicated ourselves to the world in an effort to attract both locals to help with the work and folks nationally to begin getting them excited about starting to plan for the RNC themselves.

I think of these first few months as the golden days of the WC. There were still lots of problems and conflict, but it was fun getting to know new people and there wasn't yet a great deal of pressure. Internally, we were still figuring out how to work together. I think there was an early effort at group transparency (e.g., the bringing of decisions from sub-committees back to the group for consensus), which led to collective micromanaging that the group never really got over. It made every decision take longer than it needed to and led to epically long meetings (up to 5 hours), often with little concrete results to show for it.

This was balanced against another concern. While the RNC-WC was accused by some of being too sectarian, we still had a lot of differing ideas and philosophies within the group. This sometimes led to a lack of trust between members to make decisions with the whole of the group in mind instead of foregrounding their own ideas or agenda. It's hard to build this trust in an open group where membership is always in flux.

I subconsciously started to shape the work that I chose to do around working with the folks who I felt were working the hardest and were most committed to the work. It felt good to be working together with strong, committed radicals. We put so much positive effort into our work that the otherwise boring work we were doing was looked at as "sexy" by other WCers. This was an early lesson for me in how excitement and energy feed off each other.

The downside to this, however, was that there was less excitement around the other work that was just as important. It's another hard balance to find. To what degree should those with more energy have worked to spread out their efforts into other areas to make sure everything was kept up on, and to what degree is it legitimate for these same people to do what is exciting and rewarding for them? The abstract of this grew to be an ongoing tension throughout the span of the RNC-WC. Those who put the most work and time into the RNC-WC were also expected to be the most supportive and accommodating to others. I often felt that, while holding my own nose to the grindstone and sacrificing other things that I may have gotten pleasure from, I was also expected to make everyone else's work more fun for them.

Aside from getting our name and purpose out to the world and having some events to build hype and funds, the first major project the RNC-WC undertook was the "pReNC." The pReNC was a national gathering of folks interested in putting together some sort of loose strategy for the RNC. We wanted to get people thinking early about what they wanted to see happen so there would be time to actualize it. I remember postulating at the time that the more investment and ownership folks felt over the strategy, the more energy they were likely to put into it. Also, the more energy folks see being put into something, the more likely they are to invest energy themselves. The more people invest, the more likely they are to follow through. So, getting people thinking early about the RNC and putting a little work into it could really bring out a lot of folks.

Along with announcing the pReNC over the usual channels, the WC decided to make a video to promote the event and try to help build buzz. The WC was always trying not to take itself too seriously and decided to make a comical video spoofing the corporate media and State conceptions of anarchism while demonstrating our strong sense of community. If we really were just "black clad troublemakers," what would our day-to-day lives look like? How would the stereotypical "anarchist" depicted in media and government reports get ready for their day? How would they help their neighbors with yard work? How would we interact in a community full of the same sort of "knuckleheads"?

This video became known as the "'We're Getting Ready' video," and it created a lot of excitement for the pReNC. But, like most exciting things, there were folks who held the opposite view. We have learned that the Ramsey County Sheriff's Office (RCSO) used the video as the pretext for beginning their investigation into the RNC-WC, although I firmly believe that they would have found some other reason to investigate the RNC-WC even had there not been a video. Almost more comical than the video itself is how seriously the RCSO seemed to take it.

At this time, one of the other roles I had taken on was visiting other established collectives to let them know what we were up to and get a feel for their interests and concerns. While I felt well equipped for this role with my experience in several collectives around town, it made me the conduit for a lot of criticism. There was miscommunication with some folks whose groups or organizations were depicted in the video. Some believed this miscommunication to be deliberate and malicious on the part of the RNC-WC and were quite angry about being depicted in the video. On one occasion, I was pulled away from my breakfast at a neighborhood restaurant by an angry collective member who proceeded to give me a piece of their mind. I tried to listen, but stated that I was not empowered to make any decisions on my own and that I could either bring their concerns to the group or I could put them on the agenda and they could come speak to their concerns themselves. They stated that they would do so and I returned to my breakfast.

I left with the impression that there may be some sort of confrontation at the next meeting and heard rumors to the same. I took it upon myself to line up an outside facilitator for the meeting to try to keep everything as smooth and as fair as possible so we could have a legitimate discussion.

At the meeting, over a dozen folks showed up to support the frustrated collective member. The posture of many of our guests was angry and threatening. Facing this sort of posture is challenging for me. How does one move angry confrontation into constructive dialogue? I felt willing to compromise but also didn't want to give the impression that I was backing down due to threats. I wanted to listen and model what I believed to be constructive and positive listening and communication, but I felt like the concerns and work of the RNC-WC were silenced and minimized.

Ultimately, the RNC-WC decided to take down the video where we still had control over it (at this point it was all over the internet), and the conflict, though not resolved, was subdued. Unfortunately, this conflict played into a greater tension existing in the Twin Cities between people who thought (generally) that the RNC should be ignored as to not bring down repression and those who believed (generally) that the RNC had to be confronted because dodging State repression won't make it go away.

Next came the event itself, the pReNC. While it had its problems, I would agree with others who have stated that the pReNC was probably one of the greatest successes of the RNC-WC. A lot of people turned out and participated. It was productive and fun, and it helped build momentum, trust, and credibility for the RNC-WC. Folks who may have thought of the Twin Cities as "fly-over country" saw that we could put on a solid event.

Law enforcement has a lot of mythology built up around what the pReNC was and the RNC-WC's role in it. First, the RNC-WC was fairly hands off in terms of content. We basically handled logistics and got space together so folks could talk and work things out. In fact, for many of us, our filling of logistical roles meant that we were sidelined from involvement in many workshops and discussions. I spent most of the weekend cleaning up spaces after they had been used, trying to track folks who had been arrested at the "Critical Massacre" (a clever name we gave to a police riot during a monthly Critical Mass bike ride that occurred the Friday before the pReNC), helping administrate the use of the Belfry Center for workshops (as a member of the Belfry collective, I had committed to stay there and keep an eye on the place), and helping with security and registration.

The main hiccup of the weekend was the Critical Mass crackdown. The police presence was much larger than we had imagined and the only obvious reason was the pReNC being in town. For me, the Critical Massacre is emblematic of the police response to anarchist activity. At best, they bought into their own mythology and brutally arrested a bunch of bike riders because of their misconceptions of their intentions. At worst, they maintain an us-against-them attitude and have no problem behaving brutally toward those they see as undesirable, whether or not they are any real threat in the moment.

The ride wouldn't have been any different than any other if it hadn't been for the several plainclothes surveillance teams in unmarked cars, the state patrol helicopter overhead, the dozen or so extra marked cars, and a full stock of pepper spray and Tasers. The police made any excuse to attack and then beat, pepper sprayed, and Tasered dozens of riders and bystanders.

I had such little experience in knowing what to do (or understanding what I couldn't do) at this point that I mostly just paced, cleaned, and let myself be overwhelmed with survivor's guilt while staying up waiting for people to get released. Later that weekend, the number one goal out of the pReNC was discussed and became to "build capacity (a belief that the new skills that we teach, learn, and put into practice here will allow us to return to our communities stronger, smarter, and more empowered)."

One person arrested was charged with "assault on an officer." Months later, this case resulted in an acquittal after mountains of video evidence contradicted police testimony. Two and a half years after the incident (and a year and a half after the RNC), the acquitted defendant received a financial settlement for a lawsuit in response to the malicious arrest and prosecution. Looking back, I feel so much better prepared to handle these sorts of situations, which is what we meant by building capacity. My peers, mycontemporaries, and I have become so accustomed to unforeseen arrests that we have pioneered a new form of vigil we call "jailgating"—a tailgate party held outside the jail while waiting for folks to be released.

I didn't really go to any workshops, but they seemed to go well. Reading reports, I find it interesting how the informants never seemed to want to go to the workshops on non-violent conflict resolution or any sort of anti-oppression work. They flocked to the most controversial-sounding workshops and reported as if that is all that was going on and that such a workshop represents a hegemonic outlook of all present.

The RNC Welcoming Committee

I also wasn't around for a good chunk of the strategizing session, but I know that out of it came two main goals for the RNC demonstrations. The first was the capacity building previously mentioned. The second was the blockading strategy. Most folks wanted to steer clear of using "shut it down" type rhetoric, because actually stopping the convention was less the point. It would be unfair to act like there was any consensus on what the "point" was, but most people agreed that success could look like many things and we should nurture that without committing to a binary view that it is only worth blockading the convention if it is stopped completely. The ideas that came out of these events are often attributed to the Welcoming Committee. However, I maintain that this perception is inaccurate; it not only inflates the role of the WC, but it downplays the work that went in to intentionally including a nation of radicals in the process.

The pReNC is a major marker for me in the history of the RNC-WC, both because of what it accomplished and the phase it represented in the organizing, and also because of how drastically and immediately the reality changed. Even while the pReNC was going on, there were several WC folks who spent the bulk of the weekend packing or moving (not all out of the Cities, but some). The pReNC was exhausting, but afterward I felt like it was rarely so clear what work needed to be done. I wanted to immediately process all the information that had come out of the pReNC so we could start spreading the word to those who weren't able to attend so they would know what had happened and could find a way to plug in if they wished.

Not everyone shared my sense of urgency, but probably the bigger deal was how drastically and quickly the faces in attendance at WC meetings changed. Labor Day weekend marked the end of the summer, and many of the folks who had been involved in the pReNC planning either left town for school or were back in school in the Twin Cities and no longer wanted to spend their free time in four-hour meetings. Others left town or just left the project. On the other hand, several new folks started coming to meetings right before and right after the pReNC. This facilitated the absorption into the group of the informants, but they were just a part of a major flux.

One of my earliest memories of being in a meeting with FBI informant Andrew Darst was at a meeting shortly after the pReNC with a subcommittee called Action Faction. Darst had put together a proposal he was investigating. It involved using his purported urban exploring skills to open several secret squatting locations around the metro. He then proposed creating our own shuttle service to help move people from the squats to downtown St. Paul. He spent several weeks working on fine tuning this proposal until he finally got discouraged and was encouraged by the group to let it go. This was emblematic of his usually poorly thought out ideas.

The culture of the RNC-WC at the time tended to suggest that if someone had a desire to work on something and the energy to put into it, why not encourage them? If it's not what others want to work on, they don't have to, but no one should interfere with others working on what they want. In hindsight, while I think that this sentiment comes from a good place (I agree that we should all have space to follow our passions), it doesn't acknowledge that in collective work you share a responsibility to work toward some sort of collective vision. That can mean restricting the types of work you do in order to advance the collective vision.

To say the RNC-WC was never really great at getting new folks up-to-speed would be an understatement. We knew it was a problem and tried lots of things, but nothing really took. That winter brought forward a lot of complex feelings for me. I lacked experience in this sort of organizing, but most folks who wanted to take part in this project fell short in that area. Being ever accommodating, I went out of my way to personally speak with folks in town that I knew had experience and I thought might be interested in sharing it. This mostly led to my having to listen to a list of criticisms and excuses. Whenever an actual idea was put forward, it was with the caveat that it's "what you should do, but I don't have time/energy/desire to take part in it." Because I was one of the few people around who had been there since the beginning (and likely also due to my relative privilege and my becoming more comfortable expressing myself in groups), most folks treated me like I had more experience and knowledge than I did.

Something I pay a lot more attention to now is how willing people are to cede their agency when they don't know exactly what to do. As an anarchist, I want to believe that this is mostly socialized and not innate. There are hard choices to make in life. Sometimes, you just have to make them and face the outcome the best you can. The RNC-WC was wrong about a lot of things. I was wrong about a lot, but the only way to never make a mistake is to never actually do anything. Making mistakes is a part of making decisions and making decisions is what having true agency in your life means. Eliminating hierarchy, both formal and informal, requires those with power and privilege to go without it, but it also requires everyone to stop venerating folks and putting them on an unreachable pedestal. We should all strive to join those we respect as comrades in struggle. Since the RNC, this is one of my new mantras: "Work most to be what you most admire."

After the pReNC, having just a few of us left who had been at it from the beginning meant that each time someone stopped being involved or was indisposed, there was more responsibility piled on those who remained. Like finding a better way to get new folks up to speed, it would have behooved us to create a better structure for passing on our collective history. We never quite figured it out. As it was, a few folks became the keepers of the experience of how the WC had gotten to where it was. Unlike more permanent collectives, the RNC-WC was on a limited trajectory to end after the convention. That made it easier not to concern ourselves with keeping our infrastructure indefinitely sustainable, but we also tended not to learn from earlier mistakes. If a critical mass of more long-term folks weren't around, it was hard to make decisions and many ideas had to be revisited and mistakes remade.

During the months after the pReNC, the RNC-WC moved forward trying to synthesize the ideas from the pReNC. The group committed to sifting through all the information surrounding the RNC, culling out anything worthwhile, and putting it back out in a more easily digestible way. The intention was to provide people with the information they needed to do whatever they were planning, without forcing everyone who was coming to geek out on the RNC the way some of us were. Mostly this involved watching out for news stories or information on the RNC website. Most of the information we put out was readily available to the public; we just figured out where to look and made it more accessible. One thing that created a bit of a stir was when the WC published a copy of an official delegate transportation plan. It was characterized by mainstream media as a leaked document, but it was actually available to anyone who knew where to look. By the time the RNC was over, the WC's website was packed with all sorts of information about all sorts of planned protest activity, police press statements, and other goings on.

Being a hub for information created a similar social relationship with various protest groups in which the WC ended up acting as a sort of mediator between anarchists/anti-authoritarians and other groups and communities. While supporting general anarchist organizing, the WC was also part of the March Coalition with several groups that were not anarchist-identified. The WC endorsed the large anti-war march on the first day of the convention. Even if I didn't believe that the large anti-war march would stop the war, I also think events like that are important for movement building. There were a lot of folks who had never been to a protest before in their lives who protested at the RNC. Several of these folks marched in the anti-war march. I also believed that we were building movements meant for greater things than simply protesting the RNC. The more we support each other's work, the stronger we all will be. Further, the RNC-WC foresaw the police and media spin that creates a "good protester/bad protester" dichotomy and often suggests that anarchists crash otherwise "peaceful" or "law-abiding" protests and ruin them for everyone (often used to justify a brutal police crackdown on everyone).

The RNC-WC wanted to lay a groundwork of trust that would allow us to withstand those attempts to drive wedges between various groups organizing RNC resistance. To that end, we also helped create the "St. Paul Principles," a series of points that several of the major groups organizing resistance to the

RNC could agree were important and guided how we interacted with each other, understood each other's goals, and depicted each other. Ultimately, police and media attempted to drive these wedges, but the people who organized the march and other events knew better, and the St. Paul Principles hung together.

Early efforts of the State to divide us came when St. Paul Assistant Police Chief Matt Bostrom spoke at an event put on by a local "peace and justice" group. RNC-WC associates passed out literature in protest. An on-line news site, MinnPost, reported,

There will be no police officers infiltrating protest organizations, Bostrom promised. Police will be in uniform, not war-like tactical gear, he said. There will be no contract cops, similar to the Blackwater security forces. St. Paul police, not the Secret Service, will be in charge of policing outside the convention site at Xcel Energy Center.

Bostrom further went on to say that he would resign if the Secret Service took over.

More importantly, MinnPost reported that "he even hopes that peaceful protesters will help police weed out 'the knuckleheads' who show up in St. Paul with mayhem on their minds. He's gone so far as to suggest that maybe peaceful protesters can develop some subtle signals that will point police to those who are violating the law."

These divisive efforts were called out in a statement, "The Wedge is Older than the Wheel," where the RNC-WC retorted,

We will continue to stand in solidarity with our allies preparing all forms of RNC resistance. We further encourage our radically identified brothers, sisters, and others to join us in our extension of solidarity. We know the state lies. We know the media lies. Let us not allow them to drive wedges between us. We are the people and we will not be intimidated.

The St. Paul Principles were a bit contagious. Even

groups that didn't initially sign on to the St. Paul Principles before the RNC began standing by them in the aftermath. Some of the allies that the St. Paul Principles brought together continue to be some of the RNC 8's best supporters in the aftermath. For me, I was originally interested in the St. Paul Principles for the mutual political gain, but have found through them greater respect and mutual understanding for other organizers around the area.

Along the same lines, the WC made an effort to engage with the most affected members of the Twin Cities communities, such as those who lived in or around downtown, including the homeless population that used downtown shelters. We tried to make sure the needs of these communities were given serious consideration. To that end, we held a series of town-hall events and a never fully realized door-knocking campaign, and we attended a handful of neighborhood group meetings. This seemed most successful and useful around our own neighborhoods and around the convergence space, where neighborhood support was shown during and immediately after the raids before the RNC. But, regardless of the return, working with affected communities is an important value and is worth doing for its own sake.

Another major category of work done by the WC was logistical. This mostly meant providing or finding folks who could provide food, housing, transportation, and other logistical support during the convention. Some of the work the WC did was fairly abstract in terms of what we needed to do, what would help make the protests stronger, and to what degree it was important. Some things, however, were pretty straightforward. People needed to eat and they needed to have a place to stay. If they didn't have these things, it would greatly affect what they could and couldn't do upon their arrival in St. Paul.

If you live in Minnesota, the middle of the winter is a great time to travel. The idea came up of dong a tour to spread the word about the RNC. After a long, hard, few months, I was ready for a change of pace and agreed to help put together and go on the Northeast leg of the tour. Mostly each event included a PowerPoint presentation with public information we had gleaned about the RNC as well as information on the strategy from the pReNC. We would take questions and then back off and let folks talk with each other about what they might be interested in doing as a community.

The stops were at a variety of places. We did events for student groups that had us on campuses, events at group-houses, community centers, and bookstores. Each place had its own unique and silly stories, and most stops had a crew of folks who used the best of their means to show us a good time. I especially remember going to Indiana and meeting folks working on resistance to the NAFTA super highway I-69; Worcester, Massachusetts, where the community center had a full screen-printing studio and a child care center, and where the collective house we stayed at felt like living in the middle of the country; Vermont in the winter, where each new person we met seemed to move with extra deliberate intention; East Coast cities like New York and Philly, where folks had dug in for the long haul.

Syracuse, New York was one of my favorites. It reminded me a bit of both my home town of Mankato and my time in rural New York. Their community center had a great vibe, more friendly and supportive than most, and the folks who spent time there were a wider range of misfits coming together to make what they needed. In Maryland, we were stopped by the police for "changing lanes without signaling." Our IDs were checked, but we weren't ticketed. I figured the cops were on alert because of the event going on in this small Maryland town, but found out later that the traffic stop was requested by the RCSO in order to positively ID the occupants and make sure that the RNC-WC tours, talked about on the internet and in meetings filled with informants, were actually happening.

The tour was a great opportunity for me to get to know my now housemate and co-defendant Eryn. We drove for several long stretches, including a few overnights and through a frightening ice storm when I slid the car back and forth across several lanes, barely avoiding a crash and shaking myself up. Luce also joined us for the bulk of the tour, which she had helped actualize from the other side of the country.

One of the greatest moments of growth for me was on the tour when we made some time to visit political prisoners. It was my first time visiting anyone in prison. The first thing was how violating and powerless they make you feel as a visitor; knowing that the inmates face even greater abuse makes it really a slap in the face from the start. We had to fill out all sorts of paper work with personal information. We had to empty our pockets and be wanded with a metal detector. There were several locked doors to pass through and after each door we were interrogated with the same questions (had we brought anything in, etc.).

Hearing prisoners' thoughts, stories and willingness to share is powerful. If you have never visited a prisoner, I think everyone who is serious about being a revolutionary, or even just a good person, should make it a priority. I believe it was Huey Newton who said that the revolutionaries in prison are the closest to the front lines of struggle because they face the greatest repression, directly and every day, out of all oppressed people in the United States. I don't know that I agree with Newton one hundred percent, but I can appreciate the rhetorical point.

Since high school, I have geeked out on the "new left" of the '60s and '70s more than any other period of radical history. Because of that, it was also especially interesting to visit prisoners who were from those movements. It's inspiring, but not in a venerating and unattainable way. The folks we visited were real people who had struggled proudly and continue to do so. They are in the movement for life. Some might postulate that they must remain in struggle, in part because they can't turn away, move on, or ignore repression. It is happening to them and around them every day. Thinking of these folks reminds me how important it is to make a commitment to live a revolutionary life. They no longer have the choice. People in revolutionary movements often get sent to prison for extended periods of time, sometimes for the bulk of their lives. That is how high the stakes can rise. Further still.

The first prisoner I met was Seth Hayes. He is in prison in upstate New York, having served 40 years of a 25-to-life stretch. He has repeatedly come up for parole and been denied because of his past affiliation with the Black Panther Party and the Black Liberation Army, and because he maintains his ideals even though he is incarcerated. He also maintains his innocence, although that is less important to me. Seth was proud in spite of the degradation he faced and illness he developed while in prison. He was also interested in us, what we were working on, and how our tour was going. He didn't act as if he knew all the answers. He would nod and get excited, and a tight smile formed on his face. There is still a strong spirit inside him that I know the State can never crush, and it is that drive and truly deep-rooted love for people and willingness to struggle that inspires me. I have written to Seth a few times subsequently and am proud to continue keeping in touch. I also learned from him how excited people whom I might consider heroes or look up to are to get letters (especially if they are locked up). It is a perfect and beautiful example of mutual aid. I am honored to get to know, through the mail, many committed revolutionaries. I, likewise, hope that the thoughts I send along can bring a little joy, community, and strength into their lives.

We also took a day trip to visit a revolutionary I had admired for a long time, David Gilbert. He was also incarcerated in upstate New York. I first knew of David from watching a Weatherman Underground documentary. In the documentary, David is interviewed from prison and, while he acknowledges having made mistakes, he seems to still feel the effort the Weather Underground Organization (WUO) made was worthwhile. Others interviewed have gone on to be professors or business owners and have, in various ways (some larger than others) moved away from revolutionary struggle. David is in prison for life. He doesn't have the option to become a professor or own a business, but he could keep his head down and just watch TV all day. Instead, he chooses to struggle with the strength he has. He writes, thinks, critiques, and contributes to the revolutionary movement as best he can, which often amounts to more than the effort of many of his non-incarcerated contemporaries.

We did our best to plan the tour well ahead of time, but we still ended up having to deal with problems on the fly. Some events never came together; others had disappointing turnouts where we outnumbered the attendees. This kept us spontaneous and also kept our tail from the RCSO on their toes. We have since read reports of them wondering when we were going to leave to get to events that had been canceled. The most notable series of events that we missed, however, were a few days with a handful of stops in Canada.

We had done a few events in Northern New York along the southern edge of Lake Ontario and were doubling back through Buffalo to cross the border and make our next stop on the Canadian side. It was dark, late evening, when we made it to the border. The car we were driving was dubbed "The Sketch Mobile" in large part because it had been painted black and covered with spray-painted stencils, which made it stand out as driven by folks who were, as we say in Minnesota, "a little different."

On the Canadian side of the border, they asked us to pull over so as they could interview us and search our things. It was clear after the first five minutes that they weren't going to let us in, but they took the chance to press us for information. They separated us, took me aside, and said things like, "So, your friend said you are going to a protest?" When it was clear that they weren't going to get much information from us, they turned us around, saying that they "didn't think our intentions were genuine." It took about an hour and we were back in the good ol' U.S. of A. The U.S. side, however, didn't have the option of just turning us around and sending us back to Canada. They had to get to the bottom of it.

For the next six hours, we were questioned and our car was searched. Every piece of literature was copied. Computers were searched. The other folks were sat out on a bench and I was put back in a holding cell while they investigated. We started out playing dumb, trying to talk our way out of a search. Once the car doors got opened, our mouths were locked shut. They brought in a Joint Terrorism Task Force (JTTF) agent from the FBI, and he tried his hand at getting us to talk. The Border Patrol copied everything, but the FBI agent left with a folder only about an inch thick.

In hindsight, and especially considering what we have gone through since then and the level of surveillance we now know we are under, it wasn't that big of a deal. But, being detained at the border in the middle of night until the wee hours of the morning can be pretty intimidating. It's also a reminder that any "freedoms" we perceive ourselves to have stop when governments get uncomfortable.

Just before we pulled away from the border, we did a quick once-over of our car and noticed a computer missing. We went back to ask for it. They had "forgotten" to put it back in the car. They had ransacked the vehicle, opening sleeping bags and tugging at loose linings. I found our receipts in a much neater pile than we had left them, paper-clipped together on the dash. (I could almost feel the radiant heat left over from the copying machine.)

It's funny to me that I look back fairly fondly on the tour because at the time I felt more stressed and frustrated than at any other time during my work with the RNC-WC. The group lacked cohesion and a sense of common vision for what we were trying to do. There was also some hard personal drama both in the group and in my personal life. I spent most of the time outside the tours in my own head trying to think things through and make the best choices I could. I also watched a lot of Taser promotional videos off the Taser International website. Not the best way to lift your morale.

As the tours were winding up, planning was underway for the second pReNC to be on May 3. We called it the pReNC 5.3.

The pReNC came at a time of peak conflict between several people in the group. There were plenty of bad feelings to go around. This led to bad communication and a sloppy event. While generally folks left 5.3 more frustrated than they had felt after the first pReNC, I was still glad we had done it. The event confirmed for us, closer to the date of the RNC, what our capacity was looking like. We also used a vouching process which helped ensure that the people who came to 5.3 were folks who had already done work to get ready for the RNC and were generally up to speed on what had happened up to that point. The vouching process, however, didn't keep Darst from sneaking in and recording most of the event.

Brandon Darby, the FBI informant from Austin, Texas, was also at 5.3. He, like many, was frustrated by the event, although in his complaints about the event to the kids from Austin he was working to entrap, we were all a bunch of hippies unwilling to go far enough.

The frustration around 5.3 took a while to dissipate. There was a lot more conflict based on events up to and including the meeting. The little trust folks had built was whittled back and, when the group was restructured and refocused post-5.3, some of these hard feelings certainly played a part.

While energy still needed to go into hyping the demonstrations to those who hadn't decided to pay attention until right before, most of our work moved toward really nailing down final logistics. It seemed like there was always something that was way behind schedule. We didn't have enough bikes for transportation, we didn't have enough housing to put people up in, and we didn't have enough food or a place to store/cook/serve it.

Luckily, a few months before the RNC, we began getting serious help from larger national organizations more adept than ourselves at taking care of these concerns. Ultimately, the logistical aspects that were the most successful were the ones that we were able to almost completely "farm out" to other groups. Other groups took on the bulk of the leg work putting together childcare, food, medical care, legal support, and so on. The main logistical efforts that remained bottomlined by the RNC-WC were housing and the convergence space. In keeping with our clearinghouse role, we also helped compile the information being put out by all the other groups doing support work so that demonstrators wouldn't have to hunt down information on each support element independently.

Housing was nightmarish till the end. The city claimed it was going to welcome protesters (although we had known this to be a lie from the start), but there was no place for them to spend the night. In fact, police cracked down harder on folks being in parks after dark and the National Guard patrolled the river. The RNC-WC set up a housing board and most members of the WC opened their homes to as many people as they could fit. Couches, basements, attics, and even tents in back yards were all packed tight so folks could get a night's sleep without being harassed on the street by law enforcement.

Unfortunately, this still wasn't enough. We had talked to several churches and larger centers about housing people and some seemed receptive at first but, upon reflection (or talking to law enforcement), changed their minds. We tried to find cheap temporary houses and apartments, but there was no way we were going to get enough that way. We needed mass housing and we never really got it. I think that as the convention was underway and people were paying closer attention, more people opened their homes and other spaces were created where people could be safe. I'm not sure what we could have done differently (maybe pushed harder to convince the churches), but I'm sure there were folks left out to fend for themselves and that was a frustrating part of our reality.

As for the convergence space, the RNC-WC rented an old movie theater across the river from downtown St. Paul. It wasn't perfect and we often hear criticisms that are totally valid: people couldn't sleep there, the bridge was a choke point that could be used to keep protesters out of downtown or at least pick them up with surveillance. In the end, we looked at several places and spent way more money than we wanted to or planned on, but it was the best space. With the convergence space open and people beginning to trickle into town, the real work got started. We were now working full time at full speed. The RNC was the only thing in life for those weeks in August.

Eryn Trimmer

After a failed attempt at group living in a room off the kitchen in a dirty, overcrowded punk house, Monica and I got our own apartment. It was much nicer, but made it harder to meet new people, especially other anarchists. Not being very social, I was looking for a project that might be a good way to meet folks. After doing some solidarity work during the rebellion in Oaxaca,

I came across an announcement for a meeting of the RNC Welcoming Committee (WC) at the local radical community center, and Monica and I decided to check it out.

I wasn't too excited about the RNC as a project at first. I thought that summit hopping as a model of organizing wasn't very effective, since even at its best it's designed to have a short-lived, largely symbolic impact. However, I soon realized the importance that the summit model still holds in anarchist organizing and the valuable things that can only happen when a large number of people come together. After working with the Welcoming Committee for a short while, I became committed to doing RNC resistance in 2008 well. I was drawn by the sense of excitement and possibility of a radical group planning for something a year and a half in advance. Ten years after the Minnehaha Free State,[5] we were going to put the Twin Cities back on the anarchist map.

The Welcoming Committee had a lot of issues as a group, many of which I would bet are present in a lot of anti-authoritarian organizing like this. The composition of the group lent itself toward conflict. With something as large as the RNC, there were a lot of different people involved with a lot of different visions. The normal anti-authoritarian response to this issue would be to only work with those with whom you share a comparable vision. While this happened to some extent, as the WC was supposed to be limited to those who agreed with the points of unity, the reality was it wouldn't have been practical to create multiple public, anti-authoritarian, infrastructure coordinating groups such as the WC.

Another issue in relation to who was involved in the group was a lack of experience. Very few people had any experience doing organizing like this, I included, and a majority of the group hadn't even been to a mass mobilization before. This made it so that not only did we have to figure out how to do all the things we needed to, but also get on the same page about what it was we even needed to do.

My memories of the early days of the WC were carefree Outreach Subcommittee meetings at a coffee shop, brainstorming all the possibilities for the protests and getting to know new and exciting people. With the RNC being so far away, all things seemed possible.

After being in the Welcoming Committee "pre-infiltration" (as far as we know) for a few months, Monica and I went to the G8 protests in Germany. Having heard a lot about what mass mobilizations are like in Europe, it was inspiring to see firsthand. The three convergence centers were veritable complexes, including a squatted theater and complete former school. Three literal tent cities were set up near where the G8 was taking place, complete with circus tents, multiple "barrios," each with their own theme and kitchen, computer access, showers, and a bar (no alcohol served the night before the blockades). Anarchists (or autonomists) in Germany, although not respected by proper society, are no laughable fringe but rather a force to be reckoned with.

We started our travels in Berlin, where we were shown around by a short, cantankerous anarchist in his 40s who reminisced about the motorcycle-helmet-wearing black blocs of the '80s. There we got our first taste of the landscape of the German resistance scene, visiting different longstanding squats, getting fed by the daily meals of the Voku (people's kitchen, the German Food Not Bombs equivalent), and being warned which neighborhoods were known for their high rates of Nazi attacks. It took a while to get a handle on the different groups organizing against the G8. The German "liberals" all seemed to be anti-capitalist and some of the anti-fascists were also pro-Israel (and therefore pro-America and therefore pro Coca-Cola, of course).

From Berlin, we went to Hamburg, where there was to be a march against the Asian-European Meetings (ASEM). There we got a taste of German-style policing. The entire march was surrounded by police, who therefore controlled whether it went forward or not. If a protester did something that the police didn't like (or they just wanted to flex their muscles), the police would stop the march. The sound van would stop the awesome techno music long enough to say that the police had stopped the march and everyone would boo and shout. A police negotiator would then try to get them to let us keep going, which eventually worked. The sound van would then announce that we were going to be allowed to proceed and everyone would cheer.

Eventually, however, the police declared the march illegal and stopped it for good. The pent-up energy that had been contained for so long burst, and the march split into different groups running down the streets. It was then that I saw my first water cannon in action, a ubiquitous piece of German policing machinery. Looking like a heavily armored garbage truck with water-spraying antenna, the cannon rumbled down the road, spraying the fleeing crowd.

After the warm-up round in Hamburg, we proceeded to a camp closer to where the G8 was going to take place. The first big event was a pre-summit march in Rostock, the biggest town nearby. As the march formed, there were people dressed in black as far as the eye could see, lined up tight in rows. I realized then that the motley groups of marchers barely linking arms mostly wearing black that I had seen in the States could not be described as a black bloc.

The march proceeded through a mostly deserted town, many of the businesses having boarded up their windows. This march was too big for the police to surround completely, so they took a more hands-off approach. The one police car that parked a little too close to the march route got its windows smashed out before racing away. We ended at the harbor front area, where a stage had been set up for a concert. There, a back-and-forth exchange began between protesters and the police, with the police charging and being repelled by rocks and bottles and the protesters in turn gaining ground only to be repelled by water cannons and tear gas.

Though some of the acts on stage were a bit awkward about the situation, they continued playing to the enjoyment of those watching. It was exhilarating to watch, but I couldn't help questioning the efficacy of the street fighting. The prolonged and almost choreographed back-and-forth became almost funny. Back in camp, the question was swirling: Are the police in and of themselves a worthy enemy?

Now it was time to focus on the main event: the blockading of the summit, or if that didn't work, Plan B(erlin). The mass action was to be a few different groups walking through the fields to the security fence in order to block the gates. Monica and I decided to forgo the pre-packaged action and throw our lot in with a rag-tag group doing a blockade on a road instead. Of course, our action never got off the ground, but there were many successful blockades. We went to visit one of the gates that were being held by protesters, although it was the police who were really blocking the road.

Despite effective blockades, the summit went off without too much of a hitch, the important people being brought in by helicopter. It had to be decided whether to invoke Plan B. Were the blockades working enough to justify staying? In the end, it was decided that Plan B would happen, although the ambiguous success of the blockades probably meant it had lower numbers. We rushed to Berlin only to have the planned street party fizzle under intense police repression.

I came back to town feeling, if not exactly educated about how to make happen much of what I had seen in Germany, then at least incredibly inspired to try. Monica and I got back just in time for the pReNC, the national meeting that was held a year before the RNC. In the strategy segment of the meeting, there was a large thrust for blockading being the main action of the anarchists. After having witnessed the successes and failures of blockades in Germany, I, like much of the Welcoming Committee, was tepid about the idea. However, there really weren't any fully formed viable alternatives proposed, so blockades are what the meeting ended up with.

Large meetings are hard for a lot of reasons and this one was no exception. Within the "anarchist milieu," there are a lot of debates about what the goals of our so-called movement are and how to achieve them. Those attending the pReNC were self-selected, without any defined goals for the protest identified previously. Also, even a year out, there was incredible pressure to make a decision, since it took a lot of energy to organize this meeting and a lot of people traveled a long distance to attend. This pressure made it difficult for people to have patience for hearing ideas that they disagreed with.

As is the case with a lot of meetings, the most flushed-out proposal that was brought to the meeting was adopted. Other strategy options (a day of decentralized action? a march? theme days with a variety of different actions? attempted occupation of something?) seemed overdone, ineffective, or not appropriate for a public strategy. There was some resentment that the blockading being decided upon was a foregone conclusion. The Welcoming Committee had let the group bringing the blockading proposal present during breakfast, something that was probably inappropriate.

Although domination by the most prepared is still domination, you can hardly fault a group for coming to the meeting with a well-thought-out plan, and there really was space given for other ideas. About half of people at the meeting from the Welcoming Committee stood aside in the decision to make blockading the main event, which was a bit alarming. It probably would have been better if the strategy was something that the locals had been more excited about.

However, since the Welcoming Committee was simply a logistical body rather than one planning actions, and since we didn't see ourselves as any more important than non-locals in making this decision, no one seemed to think it was legitimate for us to bring that as a blocking concern. This gave us the challenge of having to promote a strategy that was never our darling, and even to keep re-educating the group about what the heck blockading meant. Having the strategy come from outside of the Twin Cities did, however, give us more credibility as a coordinating body of this national event, which allowed us to organize better around the country.

In addition to the blockading strategy, articulated as the goal of "crash the convention," we also had the goal of "building our capacity." This was to explicitly give value to all of the important activities besides what was to happen on the streets of September 1st. Not only did we not want to define our success on whether the convention was successfully blockaded, but we wanted to acknowledge that this alone would not create the change that we wanted to see. We needed to advance the abilities and strength of our networks, for new projects to emerge and new skills to be developed. We thought it was important to say that the networking, trainings, and support structures that happened for the RNC were worthy goals in and of themselves, not just to support action in the streets.

Besides outreach, the strategy that was adopted at the pReNC didn't affect most of the work of the Welcoming Committee. Most of our work was that of all mass mobilizations: coalition-building locally; making sure everyone coming into town would have housing, food, medical help, and basic information about the Twin Cities; and finding a place in which the various meetings, trainings, feedings, etc. could take place—a convergence center. Local outreach efforts were affected by a very different political landscape than that which I was used to in D.C. To my knowledge, I had never met communists or socialists (other than people trying to sell me their newspapers) before moving to the Twin Cities. Here, much of the local organizing is done by them, something that immediately began to expand the definition of who I considered political allies.

After the pReNC meeting, informants started attending Welcoming Committee meetings. We always thought this was a possibility, and indeed assumed it was a fact. There was a general understanding that, the Welcoming Committee being an open group, doing above-ground, legal, logistical organizing, it was okay if the cops knew what we were up to. Heck, the strategy of blockading the convention and the WC's role in the overall organizing was all laid out on our website.

There was one subcommittee, Action Faction, that was closed for a while, not because it was planning anything super sketchy, but because an important part of the strategy was the element of surprise and this committee was gathering information that could potentially aid in blockading. Ironically, the FBI informant, Andrew Darst (known as "Panda") was in Action Faction. Eventually, Action Faction ceased to exist due to infighting, poorly defined objectives, and the difficult power dynamics with the rest of the Welcoming Committee because of it being closed.

Andrew Darst first showed up at the pReNC and attended the strategizing session there. He had been at the CrimethInc. Convergence held in Winona, Minnesota, the summer before, which made people feel better about him since he wasn't a complete unknown. He had an imposing figure and played a good nice guy. He came from the urban exploring scene, which had tenuous ties at best to the anarchist scene, but at least gave him a verifiable history and maybe a few cool points. He also knew about computers. He used his experience with urban exploring and computers to entice friends, while feigning interest in things like anti-patriarchy to make himself palatable politically. The main method of information gathering that I saw him use, besides simple observation, was pretending (or not) complete ignorance about anarchist organizing to the point of annoyance. He would take on the role of mentee and make you feel like you were doing something good and important by teaching him. In this way he got closer to people and built trust with them.

Marilyn Hedstrom, a Ramsey County narcotics officer, posed as Norma Jean Johnson in the Welcoming Committee. She was a nice, middle-aged woman who claimed to have a new interest in radical politics. She used this supposed lack of experience to cover up her lack of understanding of what the group was trying to do, as well as her apparent inability to think for herself. Since she was older than most anarchist scenesters, she wasn't expected to fit in culturally. She used her gender, age, "desire" to fit in, and lack of experience to paint herself as completely non-threatening. Of course, all of these things can be real issues for people, which makes them all the more effective cover for infiltrators. She took on tasks like cooking food and driving things around in her van, things that wouldn't reveal that she had no real passion or understanding of what our work was about.

Chris Dugger was the most suspect in his behavior in the Welcoming Committee. He also used lack of experience as an excuse for his inexcusable behaviors. He used anger to show that he had legitimate feelings against the status quo and police. Initially this backfired, as people explained to him that the WC wasn't about fighting cops. He transitioned his story, saying that he wanted to learn how to effectively channel his anger. That basically became his accepted role, someone who didn't quite get it but that ostensibly wanted to learn from us. He said that he wanted to find a place where he fit in.

There were serious concerns about the trustworthiness of all the people whom we later found out were either undercover law enforcement or civilian informants. There are two generalizations that fit all of the informants: firstly, none of them ever cogently expressed why they were interested challenging the status quo through the RNC. Secondly, all of them used inexperience or the fact that they were just getting into things to excuse their tepidness about being fully committed, either ideologically or in terms of actually doing work for the group. The FBI informant was able to gain a lot more trust because he brought skills and at least fragments of a verifiable history to the table. I don't think applying these two criteria would do a very good job of sifting out all future informants. Many people have difficulty articulating their politics and lots of people are really just new to this sort of organizing. However, going through this experience gives me more confidence to listen to the voice in my head that says things aren't adding up.

Had we not thought that being an open group would actually make us safer (something, in hindsight, clearly born out of naivety), we very well might have asked at least Chris Dugger to leave. He repeatedly made statements that contained violent innuendo, made multiple women feel uncomfortable, and clearly did not care about the group (falling asleep during meetings, not taking on any tasks, etc.). When he was confronted about people having questions about his being a cop and his misogynistic behavior, he cried and made people feel better about him.

Probably not coincidentally, it was Andrew Darst who got up the guts to tell him that people thought he was a cop. Of course, I now wish we had asked him to leave because of his inappropriate behavior as much as the suspicions that he was a cop. But I also worry that this might have led to a false sense of security, something that could potentially have put us in more danger. I still think open organizing is valuable, but don't have illusions that it is necessarily safe.

Over the winter, the WC did tours throughout much of the country. I went on the Northeast tour with Garrett and

Luce. The tour stops primarily consisted of a PowerPoint presentation that the WC had put together about the strategy that had been decided on in the pReNC and information about the convention, the Twin Cities, and the protest infrastructure that the Welcoming Committee was working on. It was a lot of fun to visit many towns that I hadn't been to before and get a glimpse of the projects people were working on. Most of the people who organized our tour stops were fairly young and inexperienced when it came to mass mobilizations.

On the tour, we made an effort to be accessible to new people, stopping in small towns that might only have a handful of people interested. While it was inspiring to see the next "generation" of activists getting excited about the RNC, it saddened me that people even with my very limited amount of experience seemed sparse. This paralleled my observations about the Welcoming Committee itself.

We had a couple of tour stops planned for Ontario, Canada. The border police looked in our car and saw that we had a lot of literature. They said that they thought we were going to a protest of some sort and denied us entry, stating that we weren't permanently banned but that we probably wouldn't be able to get in for the next six months or so. The real trouble came when we turned around and then had to re-enter the United States. Despite it being unquestionable that we were U.S. citizens, and therefore couldn't be denied entry, they were curious as to why Canada had turned us around and decided to search our car. While doing so they tried to question us, unsuccessfully, and put Garrett in a holding cell. They proceeded to copy a great amount of the literature that we had, and called over someone from the FBI, who left with a large folder of material. It was a bit of a nerve-racking experience, mostly because none of us felt very well-versed in border law. After a few hours they let us go, our car a complete mess.

While in New York we took the chance to visit two political prisoners, David Gilbert and Seth Hayes. Both of them had been involved in political organizing and armed struggle in the '60s and '70s. Visiting them was sad—Seth has long past served his sentence but has been refused parole six times, even with exemplary behavior in prison. David Gilbert was sentenced to 75 years to life, and will therefore die behind bars unless something major changes. The most striking feature of both the prisoners, however, was how involved they both still are in political work, keeping abreast of current events and organizing in their prisons. We told them about why we were on tour and how RNC organizing was going. They were interested and supportive.

Talking with David and Seth shed light on my own organizing from a very different perspective, bringing up a lot of questions. How committed am I to liberation struggles? What does "being committed" mean? Would I still be organizing after being incarcerated for 35 years? Am I taking full advantage of what I am able to do with my freedom? How can I better support political prisoners? Although many of the questions that arose from the discomfort, sadness, anger and inspiration of these brief meetings don't have simple answers, being in that situation made them much less theoretical.

After returning from tour, work began in earnest for the next national gathering that we were hosting in the Twin Cities, dubbed the "pReNC 5.3," as it was to take place on May 3rd. It was a long and difficult meeting, but it came out with a few concrete decisions. It was decided that St. Paul would be divided into sectors to facilitate the sharing of space for blockades. No colored zones such as had been used in many past protests (red for high risk of arrest/willing to defend space, green for low risk of arrest/no confrontation, yellow in the middle) would be prescribed. An action model called Swarm, Seize, Stay (3S) was decided on, which was basically another way of describing how blockading would work through "swarms" of people. Most of the scenario details for how September 1st would go down, such as timing, was left to be decided in spokescouncils in the days leading up to the convention.

As the convention got closer, responsibility for the different aspects of the infrastructure began to separate, either taken on by separate groups locally or groups that were coming to town for the convention. Medics were going to be handled by the North Star Health Collective; food was mostly taken care of by Seeds of Peace; communications was being dealt with by the Tin Can Comms Collective. Although this had been how it was supposed to work from the beginning, this was a huge relief to us in the Welcoming Committee, which was getting increasingly stretched thin by all of the responsibilities. The first few out-of-towners, those sent as early liaisons from their communities, started arriving. They also happened to be great organizers, something that we desperately needed.

After months of searching, we finally located a convergence center that was large enough, not crazy expensive, would let us rent for only a month, and had a landlord who was okay with what it was going to be used for. The convergence center opened on August 15th, a little over 2 weeks before the start of the convention. We had an open house and invited the neighbors, a few of whom actually came, to try and show them that protesters/anarchists are generally a friendly bunch.

Once the convergence center opened, the whole thing began feeling real. Organizers from around the country first started trickling in and then flooding in. Trainings, workshops, meetings, and entertainment were happening daily. The first spokescouncil took place, and there was a sense of possibility—could we really do this?

Above: Left to right - Garrett Fitzgerald, Max Specktor, Nathanael Secor and Rob Czernik. Below: Rob Czernik and Luce Guillén-Givins on the RNC organizing tour.

4
Chapter
CONSPIRACY

Monica Bicking

The Saturday before the RNC, the convergence space was raided at night with about seventy people inside. I was not at the convergence space but got a phone call that it had been raided and there was going to be an emergency meeting in South Minneapolis. At the meeting we were getting frequent calls from those at the convergence space with updates. Around midnight the meeting ended with a working group meeting to put together a press release. At this point I was very disappointed because the convergence space had been boarded up and I thought we were never going to be able to use it again. While the convergence space had gotten some use, it was still days until the RNC, and it had yet to get most of its use. I had personally invested a lot of time into it and wanted to see it put to good use.

When we got home our house was packed with people who were staying there for RNC protests. We updated them and went to bed. I was sound asleep when I was awoken by a loud bang. A loud bang doesn't really describe the noise well. It was the loudest loud bang I had ever heard. It was so loud and unexpected that it haunts me to this day. After the raid I became frightened every time a door slammed. To this day, my heart races when I heard thunder.

The bang was the police kicking in our back door. They were screaming "Police! Police! Police!" I woke up and started screaming for Eryn to find my glasses. I can't see anything without my glasses and feel helpless without them. We found them and I thought of all of the "know your rights" trainings I had been to. I started to head downstairs with the plan of meeting the police at the door, stepping outside, and asking for the warrant. I didn't realize that they were already inside. In my half-asleep state I had thought that the loud bang was the police knocking on the door, not knocking down the door.

I made it halfway down the stairs when I was met by several police officers pointing guns at my head. I had never had a gun pointed at my head before and I remember the following moments clearly. I was trying to follow their orders precisely.

Put your hands on your head, kneel, lie down. In these moments I felt that I couldn't trust my body. Was I really putting my hands on my head? What if I was mistakenly putting them in my pocket? They're going to shoot me.

Apparently I followed the orders and was brought to my living room with several others. Because I was the homeowner they brought me outside to see the warrant. I read it out loud and said that I did not consent to the search. As I stood there I saw a well-dressed man rushing down the sidewalk. He introduced himself to the police as my lawyer. While I hadn't met him before, a wave of relief washed over me. I was also very impressed. It couldn't have been longer than twenty minutes after the police broke down our door, and I had someone claiming to be my lawyer.

The police brought me back inside the house and then led me back outside toward a vehicle. I finally realized I was probably being arrested and asked if I was being arrested. The officer said, "Well, what do you think?" I guess it was obvious that I was being arrested, but up to that point I hadn't assumed I would be. The night before, people who were even more active in the Welcoming Committee than me were just detained and released. If they were going to WC organizers, I thought that they would have started there. I also did not think we were necessarily going to be arrested because the warrant I was presented with was a search warrant, not an arrest warrant.

Garrett, Eryn, and I were all arrested during the raid. Everyone else was detained and released. After being arrested we were brought down to Hennepin County Jail to be booked in. I was terribly surprised that some WC people were arrested. I was aware that it is a common tactic of the state to arrest key organizers before protests in an effort to destroy the infrastructure so that the protests are less successful. I was somewhat surprised that they chose me to arrest because I was not involved in the organizing any more than many people that weren't arrested, but I was not surprised that they were choosing to arrest people. I assumed that they would keep us in jail until after the convention and then release us and not end up charging us. Jail was a new experience for me. They put me in the solitary ward. There were women who had been in there for weeks who screamed and moaned the entire time I was in there. There were seven cells lined up next to each other that faced a common room that only one woman was permitted in at a time. Most of the women were in there as punishment for kissing other women. I really started to understand how good jails are at stripping people of so many forms of joy.

Not long after arriving at Hennepin County Jail, the police transferred all of us to Ramsey County Jail. During this transfer I found out that both Luce and Erik had also been arrested. It was great to see Luce. I had been separated from the men right away and had not been able to talk to anyone. Luce and I were grouped together and she caught me up with everything that had happened since the raids. It had only been a few hours, but I had spent that whole time wondering what was going on. Luce informed me that we had many supporters and that people had gathered at my house and prevented it from being boarded up by the city inspectors. She had been arrested directly after a large emergency meeting held because of the raids. I was also finally able to get a hold of Coldsnap and get an update from them. I was starting to feel at ease.

Luce and I were originally placed in a cell together, only to be separated after a few hours. Once I got updates and had settled into a block, jail was fine. Boring, but fine. The other women in the block were nice and I got to catch up on some much needed sleep. The morning after my first night in jail Sheriff Fletcher visited me. He came to my cell and took me out to the middle of the block so that everyone could see us sitting across from each other. He said that he knew I would not answer any questions, but that he was going to tell me a few things. He showed me surveillance pictures of my friends. Told me facts about my family and generally proceeded to intimidate me. He also told me that he was going to release me with a mission. The mission was for me to deescalate the protests. He planned to release me whether I agreed to the mission or not and he would re-arrest me if any police officer was injured during the protests. I was released the night before the first day of protests.

Someone was waiting to drive me home from the jail.

I was able to tell Luce through the cell door that I was being released and she was able to make a phone call. While it was nice to have a ride, I was disappointed that no friends or family were there waiting for me. When I got home my close friends and family were there excitedly waiting for me. While they were loving and supportive, I felt isolated. The people that had been there during the raid had cleared out. In fact, there weren't any anarchists there to greet me. This was the night before the protests. I understand that people were busy preparing for the next day and did not want to be around someone who was definitely being watched, but I was disappointed in the radical community. I felt alone and was worried that people had thought I had snitched.

I did not think it was a good idea for me to attend the protests the next day. I felt like I would put everyone around me in danger. Instead, I spent the day at the wellness center. I finally started to see and reconnect with WC organizers. I was still processing all that had happened to me in the last few days. I had experienced my first raid, was booked for the first time, spent my first night in jail, and had a partner in jail for the first time. I was not in a place to help anyone with anything on the first night. I mostly just sat and watched. I watched as dozens of people came in covered in pepper spray with unbelievable stories of police brutality and resistance. Even though I couldn't be part of the action I was happy to be close to it.

I also saw the complaint for the first time and discovered that there were three informants in the WC and who they were. Many people had already thought that two of the informants, Norma Jean and Chris, were informants. They did not fit in for many reasons. Norma Jean was older than (twice the age) most of the people in the WC. She wore heavy make-up and was very quiet. She did not participate significantly in the big meetings and was not in the same subcommittee meetings as me. I did not know her well, but was not at all surprised that she was an informant.

I had had more interactions with Chris than Norma Jean. They were mostly negative. He stuck out not only because of his appearance, but also because of his actions and words.

Like Norma Jean, he did not participate in meetings very much. When he did speak out he came off as very angry and hateful. He played up hating cops, thinking that would be a way to relate to us. It didn't work. He also became very angry and hateful when talking about a past domestic assault case where he strangled his sister. I felt uncomfortable being around him. Looking back, his actions should have been enough to ask him to leave the WC whether he was an informant or not.

Andy Darst, a.k.a. Panda, was also outed as an informant at this time. I had a horrible sinking feeling when I heard that Darst was an informant. I had been his friend for about a month before we started to clash and I became convinced he was an informant. I felt horrible hearing this news because I knew that he had managed to make several friendships and that those people could be in trouble. I also felt regret. I didn't really express my concerns about him with many other people. The WC had resigned itself to the fact that there were probably informants present.

While there was a lot of debate about whether we should try to kick out potential informants, in the end no one was ever asked to leave permanently. (Chris was asked to skip a few meetings.) Looking back I'm not sure what we should have done. If we had kicked out everyone that was ever suspect we would have kicked out people who have proven themselves not to be informants and continue to make positive contributions to our communities. If we had kicked out the most likely suspects, Darst still would have been in the WC. He was trusted by many people. His appearance did not fit in much better than Chris' or Norma Jean's, but he did talk the talk a little bit better. He is an urban explorer and many people found his urban exploring stories cool and interesting. Although it took a while, he eventually gained acceptance among many.

I became suspect of Darst because of how separate he kept his family from the WC and all anarchist activities. When he stalled to get me vouches after I had asked for them, I became convinced that he was an informant. He fit in better than Chris or Norma Jean, but his life was too compartmentalized to make sense unless he was an informant.

Conspiracy to Riot

Throughout the Welcoming Committee and since the RNC, I have learned to speak up more and more. There are consequences when I let my voice be quieted. Maybe had I spoken out more loudly about my uneasiness about Darst, he would have been asked to leave and we would not be where we are today and Matthew DePalma would not be in prison. Instead, I let men whom I loved and respected tell me that I was blowing things out of proportion and talk me out of making a big deal out of it. Maybe things would have been different had I spoken out, but most likely it would have just caused another fight within the Welcoming Committee and no action.

On the second, I went to the jail vigil. When Eryn and the rest of the WC members were to be arraigned, I went inside with Carrie Feldman to see them in court. We went through the metal detectors. Sheriff Fletcher was waiting for us on the other side and arrested us both. Fletcher lectured Carrie as we started our booking process. He told us that we would be charged along with the other WC members who had been arrested.

Jail was very different this time around. It was packed with protesters. It was actually much more isolating to me the second time around. I was surrounded by people who were freaked out about getting misdemeanors and potentially missing the first week of college classes. I was facing a felony charge with a terrorist enhancement. I had a hard time relating to them.

While isolating, there was a burden taken off my shoulders once I was in jail. For the two days I was released I was in a constant state of fear. I was scared being re-arrested. I was scared that I would do something that would be construed as illegal. I was scared that I would be somewhere that would be raided. I was scared of running into the informants and of being followed. Jail was less scary. This second time around I knew what to expect.

I was arraigned with my co-defendants and ended up having the exact same charges as them. I often wonder what Fletcher was thinking when he released me. Was he thinking about not charging me? Did he think I would do something that would give them more evidence against me? Did he really think I could/would deescalate the protests? In the end I think it was probably a combination of these things. I think he was trying to mess with my head and he was successful in many regards. The day and a half in between jail was the most isolating experience I have gone through. I no longer had co-defendants, but I didn't feel free. I didn't feel like I could relate to anyone. Very few people tried to reach out me and no one got through to me. While Fletcher may have successfully messed with me, it only had a temporary effect. I now feel strength in having seven co-defendants and hundreds of supporters.

Luce Guillén-Givins

Understanding the history of state disruption and repression of resistance movements, as well as a contemporary trend of conflating anarchism with "domestic terrorism," most of us anticipated raids and arrests. Our vulnerability was increased by the fact that we had put ourselves out into the public sphere for so long prior to the RNC, giving law enforcement ample time to zero in on us as individuals, watch us, and plot their moves. But we were overwhelmed by the culmination of almost two years' worth of preparation and, unfortunately, a certain proportion of the personal precautions we could have taken in the months, weeks and days leading up to the convention fell by the wayside as we plowed ahead toward September 1st.

One of the major lessons I've taken from my experience with the RNC is in the absolute importance of taking the time to evaluate your personal vulnerability and take reasonable steps to protect yourself. For myself, I feel like I missed little things which I sincerely doubt would have fundamentally altered the legal case we face now, but they might have cushioned the fall and would have been worth the little time they would have taken from the work I was doing.

On Friday, August 29, 2008, the RNC Welcoming Committee's convergence center was raided. Almost 70 people were inside, including myself, Rob, and Garrett. The raid played out in slow motion for me: along with about 30 others, I had been on the second floor of the convergence center. I had finished my shift earlier and was supposed to be back for the overnight security shift at 10 p.m. While I was in the office upstairs in the midst of trying to wrap things up and get out of there for a few hours before having to return, I suddenly heard shouting and what sounded like a fight breaking out downstairs. Along with a few other people, I ran over to the top of the stairwell and leaned over the railing, trying to see what was going on.

Only upon seeing men in robo-cop type protective gear, carrying guns, did I realize that the "fight" was actually a police raid on the space. Strangely enough, the cops seemed to be filing into the first floor but no one was coming up the stairs, as I would have expected. Rob sprang into action and gathered everyone on the second floor into the main room, by which point I had started making phone calls to lawyers and friends to alert them to the raid. Rob did a fantastic job of getting everyone prepared—worried about potential brutality and wanting to deescalate the situation as much as possible, we were actually on the ground with our hands over our heads by the time the cops busted through the back door.

Eventually, we were cuffed and, one by one, taken into a side room and searched, mostly without incident. Though somebody obviously knew who Rob, Garrett, and I were and that we would be arrested soon, officers merely ID'ed and released us along with everyone else. I wasn't sure what to make of this that night. It seemed obvious that whatever the state was planning wouldn't end there, but I think we were all thrown off by our release. We went home, drafted a press statement for the morning press conference, and went to sleep. I don't think any of us slept more than a couple hours that night—many were woken up by raids on their own houses, and the rest of us were awoken by phone calls and text messages alerting us to those raids. My house wasn't raided, and I can only speculate as to the reasons at this point, but all of us assumed that it might be at any moment and quickly evacuated.

We've had a lot of people tell us that it was foolish to sleep in our own beds that night. I agree with this insofar as we all would have benefited from being spared the experience of the raids, but I think the assertion fails to acknowledge the bigger picture, where charges were forthcoming regardless of the circumstance of arrest. Our case is the culmination of a year-long investigation and never hinged on whatever "smoking guns" law enforcement hoped to—but didn't—find in the raids. This is evidenced by the fact that folks, like myself, who were spared from the house raids ended up in the same boat regardless. We had a choice to make in those 12 hours, and in the end I think we made the right one.

The way I see it, we could all have gone into hiding, rendering ourselves fairly useless to the organizing and infrastructure that would be necessary to pull off the protests, and in so doing we would have diverted attention and energy from the RNC protests to which we had devoted almost two years. Instead of running, it appears that most of us decided to keep our eyes on the road, as it were, proceeding with our tasks and responsibilities up until the point that we could no longer do so. I was arrested Saturday afternoon, leaving a huge meeting at a park in Minneapolis. At this meeting, I think we were able to do effective information sharing and rumor control, giving people what they needed to keep moving forward. I went to the park with the belief that I would likely be arrested at some point before the day was out, but I was intent on being useful for as long as possible, and I still feel good about my decision.

One of the most inspiring things about the RNC for me was the fact that they took eight of us out, and though the effects were felt, people stepped in to fill the void and the organizing continued. The important thing that week wasn't that every one of us stay out of jail; it was that the mobilization proceed in the manner most consistent with the goals set forth at the 2007 pReNC.

In the end, I feel like the RNC represented a victory of organizing in many ways, though we failed in the blockading strategy that had been developed through national consensus. Our two overarching goals were to "crash the convention" and "build capacity." I think we were partially successful in the former and wholly successful in the latter.

One of the most significant accomplishments of anti-

RNC organizing was the fact that we re-established anarchists as major players in the arena of mass mobilizing, a need that had been crystallized in my consciousness since the previous RNC. We were planning for the RNC as soon as anyone, and before most, and it forced people to take us seriously. Secondly and related to this, the "St. Paul Principles" were historic, and their positive effects are still felt in the Twin Cities and elsewhere. Anticipating the fallout of intergroup bickering and ideological differences, we were proactive in establishing a set of common agreements for all protest organizations that precluded this eventuality. The principles are still guiding progressives and radicals in the Twin Cities, fostering a new sense of solidarity and, especially in light of our case, keeping people strong and resistant in the face of state repression. They have also been the model for similar agreements at protests big and small across the country, a testament to their utility.

I believe the failure of the blockading strategy was due, in large part, to a lack of buy-in by many young anarchists, whose insurrectionist tendencies and obsession with rioting and outbursts of rage leave them with little interest in a strategy that called for traditional civil disobedience as much as or more than anything else. We should have been willing to put energy into more serious political and tactical discussions but were stretched too thin and worried about exerting undue influence on the direction of things, and so we sat by as plans flourished that greatly interfered with the blockading strategy. We also should have put more energy into effective outreach to non-anarchists. I believe that we had always intended to do that at some point, but we didn't prioritize it early enough and lost whatever chance we had.

The WC in its earlier days was largely preoccupied with identity and image, wanting to develop and assert an anarchist identity as a way of building a different kind of strength than we'd seen at recent mass mobilizations. It was a worthwhile endeavor, but we had in many ways succeeded by early 2008 with the development of the St. Paul Principles, and we would have better served the goal of crashing the convention by moving onto a new phase at that point in which we would have focused on cultivating investment in the blockading strategy outside of our limited anarchist scene. At 5.3, an event focused on the blockading strategy, we tried to make this shift by emphasizing that an interest in the blockades rather than identification with anarchist politics was what should determine attendance, but it was too little, too late. We managed to establish respectful relationships with the other groups organizing for the protests, but didn't push past that in a meaningful way.

Of all the aspects of our case, people often seem to be most interested in the informants. Two years later, I have some insight to offer, but the truth is that I don't think of any us has come out of this with a very complete idea of what we could have done differently, and I am reluctant to reaffirm the notion that any magical formula exists for preventing infiltration.

There are obvious things to have done differently, most notably that the county informants triggered alarms with virtually everyone they encountered and we should have kicked them out long before the RNC. But every attempt to address the issue (and there were many) was problematic in its own way, and the WC always lacked the internal trust and cohesion that would have enabled us to wade through this.

Even if we had purged the county informants and presuming that they wouldn't just have been replaced, the only informant to have gained anyone's trust was the FBI informant. This is no accident. Local cops bumble their way through political investigations because they rarely deal with them and don't have the training or mandate to do them well, but the Federal Bureau of Investigation is in the business of undermining and disrupting resistance movements, and they've honed their skills over decades. In Panda, as in so many of their informants, the Feds chose someone who had the intelligence and skills necessary to infiltrate a radical political group and gain enough trust to get close to people. Their own FBI training also gave them the ability to coach him effectively throughout the process, and he was able to manipulate people and exploit situations to such a significant extent because of the skills of the agency handling him. Though many of us were suspicious of him, we dealt with this suspicion on an individual basis.

I, for one, shielded myself quite well from all of the informants, acting on instinct and refusing to get close to any of them. Norma Jean and Chris were involved in very different areas of work than I was, and didn't seem to make much effort to spend time with or talk to me. Panda, on the other hand, did make sporadic but oddly concerted efforts to get to know me and win my approval and trust, but I didn't like him and his overtures made me uneasy, so I didn't bite. I shared my concerns about him with people I was close to. But, simultaneously, I felt guilty for not liking this person who seemed to have gained the confidence of so many—questioning my own gut feeling as criticisms I received for being unfriendly and overly judgmental echoed in my mind—and after a certain point I didn't even try to address these issues with the larger group. Because response to the issues had been so discouraging in the past, and because I knew that I was considered by some to be mean and controlling and believed that doing so would only have reinforced these perceptions of me while doing little to affect other people's opinions of him, I just didn't see any point in trying to communicate my thoughts about him.

But upon reflection, I think that if I had been willing to put myself out there anyway, at least a few people with correlating concerns might have listened. This would have helped to create the supportive atmosphere that was necessary in order to honestly and respectfully sort out the complicated dynamics that enabled Panda's manipulative presence. Though I remember clearly the internal power dynamics that kept me from doing so, I think of this frequently and deeply regret not having been more vocal and assertive about my concerns.

That the informants were mostly unknown and relatively unconnected has led a lot of people to question why we let them hang around at all. But in that way, Chris, Norma Jean, and Panda were like the majority of folks who passed through the Welcoming Committee. Most folks who joined the WC were strangers when they showed up, and for a lot of them the RNC represented their first foray into political organizing. The fact is that the WC emerged out of a void in the Twin Cities. Anarchist organizing was at a low point here when the RNC was announced, and very few people with much history in the local radical scene were willing to involve themselves in the project or any project related to the RNC at that time. The group would certainly have benefited from the participation of more people with more experience, but we worked with whoever showed up, which produced a group full of enthusiasm but where few people had pre-existing relationships to build on or any real frame of reference for each other.

Because of the presence of informants, many have criticized the very fact of our open structure and continuously public presence. It's true that these made us easy targets for surveillance and infiltration, but this need not always be the case, and these same aspects of our structure also made the successes of the RNC possible and laid the groundwork for the support we have now.

In my experience with the WC and my observation of the anarchist community in general, a major impediment to good security is the naïve perception that anything short of blindly embracing newcomers is elitist and exclusionary in a way that contradicts anarchist principles. I find this to be incredibly misguided, believing instead that as anarchists, our responsibility to care for each other actually requires that we be attentive to security, and that we not neglect the valid concerns the people we work with have about their own safety. The genuine desire to be accessible and inclusive is a positive one, but we should guard against the impulse to maintain a superficial appearance of openness while sacrificing ourselves, our comrades, and all that we work for.

It is true that a collective attitude of caution toward strangers, and acting on the knowledge that suspect individuals can pose real threats to our freedom and the success of our movement, may also repel people who aren't informants. However, we can't let this impede our better judgment. It's fair to question whether or not our movements are really strengthened by the presence of people who aren't willing to acknowledge the seriousness of what we do and the risks we run doing it. If we take our work seriously and are willing to make difficult decisions when necessary, we will attract other people who are serious about radical change and have the strength of their convictions. Likewise, by building a supportive environment in which people feel comfortable talking about the things and people that make them feel threatened and uneasy, we create the likelihood of retaining people whose commitment and sound judgment make them invaluable to our movement. And as long as education is always a component of what we do, we maintain the possibility that those non-cops and non-informants who are initially turned off by our security practices will develop their analysis enough to start coming around and contributing in a meaningful way.

In the end, there's no excuse for our collective lack of action around the informants—groups with open membership need to be willing to devote time to intentionally and organically cultivating well-founded trust—but few if any models for doing this effectively with limited time exist, and we certainly didn't create one. The State isn't going to stop sending informants and flipping former comrades, but our best defense is to cautiously build real trust and a sense of community and to be thorough as we thoughtfully and continuously evaluate interpersonal dynamics and individual behaviors.

Eryn Trimmer

Word traveled fast when the convergence center got raided. It was Friday night and the convention was scheduled to start on Monday. I was at home. The police had rushed the doors, detaining everyone, ID'ing them, and then releasing them. They searched the building, supposedly for improvised explosives and incendiary devices among other things, and took some jars and rags along with most of the thousands of pieces of literature that were there being distributed. An emergency WC meeting was called that night to try to figure out what to do. At that point, the building had been ordered boarded up and it was unclear when or if we were going to have access to it again. We ended up calling for a larger meeting the next day and eventually went home to bed.

At 7:50 the next morning, I woke up to a loud bang coming from downstairs and shouts of "Police!" followed by loud footsteps and "Get on the ground!" I made it to the hall outside of my bedroom before lying down as a large man wearing a flak jacket and carrying a large assault rifle came up the stairs. I was shaking and tense. My roommate helped calm me down as we lay face down next to each other. It was just a raid, I told myself, them trying to make our organizing less effective. Although I knew that these things happen, I really didn't think it would happen to us. The legal trainings had all been about how the officers would knock and show you the warrant before you let them in. Even if I had thought of a raid at gunpoint as a realistic possibility, I don't think I could have prepared for it psychologically—complete powerlessness, a total invasion of privacy. They identified everyone and took our pictures. One sleazy cop tried to interrogate me, taking me on to the porch and asking, "So, what's going on here?" I told him I wasn't going to answer his questions and was taken to the SUV. Garrett and Monica were also arrested.

They took us to the Hennepin County Jail in downtown Minneapolis. When I asked about my charges, they sounded unreal: conspiracy to damage property, conspiracy to cause a social disturbance and conspiracy to riot. I certainly didn't think they were real at that point;most felonies that people are charged with in protest situations get dropped. I was still scared and in shock from the raid and the unexpectedness of the situation, however, so I wasn't feeling great. After a while, we were taken to a couple of holding cells where we met up with Luce, Erik, and Nathanael. The six of us were then transferred to Ramsey County Jail, just outside of downtown St. Paul. There we were booked and I was put in a cell block that had been cleared out in anticipation of protesters getting arrested.

The feelings I had were similar to the other times I had been in Jail—an overwhelming sense of powerlessness. How can they, with the whole force of the State behind them, take away almost all of my freedom? It wasn't lonely, at least. On Monday, the jail began filling up with protesters. I was eventually transferred to a cell block with both protesters and general population.

It was nice talking to my cell mates; they made me feel a lot better about my personal situation. One cell mate was awaiting deportation to Mexico after being in the U.S. for seventeen years, and who had a wife and children here. He wasn't stressed out at all, however; perhaps he was planning on simply sneaking across the border again. Another had served twelve years for being involved with selling drugs when he was nineteen. He had been paroled and was doing great, living with his girlfriend and being steadily employed, but then he was caught having drunk a beer when his parole officer came for a surprise visit, which was a violation of his parole. He was going to lose his job. He was seriously considering asking to stay in jail for the remaining 5 months of his sentence as opposed to being paroled again and having to risk the chance that he would start his life all over again just to have it ruined when he was taken to jail again. I couldn't understand giving up that freedom, and tried to convince him that he could make it fine out there, that it was worth the risk of getting jailed again. He seemed to see his jailing as out of his control, something I suppose that comes with getting caught with one marked $20 bill in your pocket at 19 and getting sentenced to 12 years. I was starting to understand how he could feel that way.

He also, however, was quite comfortable in jail; he was used to the routine and got to see old friends from prison. He told me about the different gangs in prison and how he had eventually gotten enough respect to not be in a gang. That wasn't exactly comforting, but overall I felt like if I could find someone like him in prison to connect with, someone who was over the petty (or not so petty) squabbling, who would stick his neck out for me like I thought he would, I would be O.K.

It was odd watching the convention on the news in jail and hearing about it through the protesters who came in. I had worked for a year and a half leading up to this and now had only a vague idea of what was happening. Did the housing shortage get solved? How did the spokes-councils go? How was the convergence center running now that six (later eight) of us were arrested? How was comms working? How big was the march? How successful were the blockades? In a way it was a relief, knowing there was absolutely nothing I could do about any of it.

Of course, everyone out in the streets only knew about what they were specifically involved in, and the news barely covered the protests, so it was hard to piece together a coherent picture of events. Ironically, due to hurricane Gustav, all non-essential activities for the RNC on September 1st were canceled. Without making light of the death and destruction that the hurricane caused, we declared that nature was on our side.

One of the hardest parts of being in jail was the feeling of limbo—not knowing what was going to happen. When I first read the complaint about us, I knew that this hadn't been a simple ruse to arrest us during the convention. We were charged with conspiracy to riot in the second degree in furtherance of terrorism.[1] It had been over a year of investigation, with four undercovers and different types of surveillance. Though I knew "they were watching us," it was still mind blowing to read a couple of places that I had been followed to the previous week in the complaint. We had a bail hearing, for which bail for the eight of us with the same charge was set at $10,000 each.

Max Specktor

My seven co-defendants and I didn't make it to the protests that week. We had our convergence space and houses raided two days before it began. I wasn't at home during the raid on my house, so I found out that they were looking for me but managed to stay aloof for a couple days. I talked to a lawyer who said that there wasn't any warrant out for me because they just had my name on a probable cause hold, so I had no responsibility to turn myself in. Not actually a fugitive, I put on my sunglasses and grabbed a bag of Burger King fries (because what kind of anarchist brings fast food to the spokes-council meeting?), and went back to the convergence space to strategize about how we should respond to this preemptive strike, and what the first day of protests would look like. A few minutes into the spokes-council meeting there were a bunch of people pointing at a group of suspicious-looking folks in the back, and when those folks realized that they were holding their welcoming guides upside-down as they pretended to read, the cops gave up on their pathetic undercover operation and were escorted out of the planning meeting.

I made it home that night and managed to get a few hours of sleep before what I thought would be a busy week of organizing and trying to keep my head low. The next morning, as I was leaving my house, I got into a car with a handful of other people and a couple blocks from my house we were quickly surrounded by about a dozen law enforcement vehicles, seemingly out of nowhere. Before our car was even stopped, the lead cop pulled up to the driver window and asked, "Is Max Specktor in the car!?" to which the driver responded, "There's a lot of people in the car!" After stopping us and surrounding the car, the cops made everyone sit down with their hands up, and proceeded to put me under arrest, then ID'ed everyone else, and towed the car.

After I sat in jail for the first three days of the convention, along with hundreds of others, I was fairly confident that the charges and raids were just part of a strategy to control the media narrative, and to scare people from protesting that week. Shortly before our bail hearings, I and the other people arrested in the targeted raids were given the complaints against us. The charge against us at this point was Conspiracy to Riot in the Second Degree, in Furtherance of Terrorism. It seemed silly at first, until we read about how our group, the RNC Welcoming Committee, had been infiltrated for a year preceding the convention. We quickly pieced together who these informants and undercovers were based on the evidence included in the complaint. Three people hired by the Ramsey County Sherriff's office and one man hired by the FBI. They all attended meetings and did tasks in preparation for the protests, and some of them were even suspected at times of not being who they said they were, but at this point I was definitely surprised that the cops and feds had put this much effort into investigating our work.

Conspiracy

None of the Ramsey County undercovers were a surprise to me, as I had never fully trusted them, and their activity in the Welcoming Committee was superficial to say the least. They attended almost every meeting, but never spoke substantively during any of our intense discussions. They would help cook for events or drive people to run errands, and even formed a couple friendships with individuals in the group. The FBI undercover was the most surprising to all of us. Andrew Darst had made his first appearance at the Crimethinc. gathering in Winona, Minn. in 2006, over two years before the convention. "Panda," as people referred to Darst, was peripherally involved in the Minneapolis anarchist scene and used his credibility as an urban explorer (somebody who explores abandoned buildings and urban infrastructure) to gain trust. I never felt like I ever understood where he was coming from, or why he was into organizing against the RNC, although I had known that other anarchists many times are also avid urban explorers.

It's important to keep in mind that just because somebody is part of an underground scene or illegal activity, that it doesn't mean that they have any values or care about sending people to prison. Some people just can't care about anything more than protecting their own pathetic, comfortable lives. As far as I'm concerned, it is already horrible enough when somebody turns on their friend when they get caught for a crime or action. But it is unfathomably disgusting to me that Panda, and people like him, choose this as a line of work; leading fake lives and making fake friendships in order to learn about or manufacture a crime.

As I reflected on what this meant, or what we were going to do about it, I could only think about the interactions that I'd had with these people. The most significant amount of time spent together with any of the informants was when I got a ride with Panda to Chicago and back. We were going to give the Welcoming Committee presentation at the Bash Back! Convergence. I hadn't really gotten to know Panda before this trip, so we spent most of the time just making small talk to get to know each other. This is why it surprised me to find that a small part of our innocuous small talk on that trip made it into the criminal complaint against us. The realization that I was chatting with an FBI snitch made me feel like I would never again be able to experience a genuine social interaction, or fully trust people that I work beside. Fortunately, I am slowly gaining some of that confidence back, but it definitely left an indelible impression.

Garrett Fitzgerald

At the time of the pReNC, there were several state informants waiting in the wings to try to get involved with the RNC-WC. Marilyn Hedstrom (know to us at the time as Norma Jean Johnson) and Rachel Nieting (known to us as Amanda) had both visited the Jack Pine Community Center in the lead up to the RNC, making themselves visible and laying groundwork to later attend meetings. They picked up literature, talked to folks, and sat in on workshops. They were kept out of the strategizing session by the RNC-WC's registration/security procedure and because they were only permitted to attend "public" meetings at that time. Andrew Darst (a.k.a. "Pandy" or "Panda") made his first attempt to join up with anti-RNC organizing at the pReNC. He claimed to have shown up for an urban exploring workshop but wanted to be a part of the strategizing session as well.

I remember feeling uncertain about Darst. In truth, there were times when I felt uncertain about a lot of people. I remember he attended a workshop at the Belfry. I was around to keep the Belfry open and he stood out a bit mostly because he seemed really nervous. Others had concerns and so we worked to look into those concerns with the tools we had at our disposal, while at the same time not jumping to any conclusions that would be unfairly exclusionary. We ended up not allowing a small group of folks connected to Darst into the strategizing session. In hindsight, I think a big reason I was okay with Darst being around is because I wanted to be fair and felt bad not letting people in. I mean, how many informants were they really going to send? Yeah right.

Had I been more self-aware, I might have made a

different choice about Darst. I still think there is an important place for open public organizing, which is part of why the workshops were all open to anyone, but it's okay not to want to strategize or work with people who make you uncomfortable, even if you don't think they are snitches. Throughout my life, I have always wanted to think the best of people. I realize now that I was overly willing to rationalize away my concerns about folks to try to be friends and see the good in them.

This response to Darst is part of something I learned about myself during the whole RNC process. I tend to be overly accommodating. I've seen this in my not wanting to kick out informants, taking to heart even the most unfounded concerns hurled at the RNC-WC from outside, or taking away from the work I think is important to support the work of others that never really comes to fruition or leads to growth of the individual, the group, or the movement. In the past, my efforts have stemmed from a desire to build movement by supporting others, as well as acknowledging and being accountable to my community for the privileges I bring to the spaces I enter. Socialized male, I was encouraged to lead and to make decisions. I was told I was a good problem solver and that I would be successful at whatever I chose to do in life.

The effort is to find a balance. It is my responsibility not to take up too much space and to hold other people of privilege accountable and to really listen. It isn't my job, and is in fact arrogant, to believe I will help someone find their path to empowerment. That is a disservice to myself and that person. Likewise, trying to help a shy, awkward person from outside the movement (as I perceived Darst) get involved, while perhaps noble in some regards, ended up putting more friends at risk. Even if Darst hadn't been a snitch and had just floundered like many others, at some point the cost to the movement outweighs the gains for the individual or for the movement. (Examples of how these people take time, energy from the movement... otherwise you sound like you're not going to be supporting anyone new, awkward, or shy in the future). I always want to be kind and open, but often the wiser behavior is the harder and less popular choice; that can sometimes be a choice that hurts to make.

Chris Dugger was another informant who started coming to meetings shortly after the pReNC. He was aggressive and inarticulate and definitely looked like a cop. I approached him and tried to get to know him for a few reasons. First, I thought if I talked to him more about his reasons for coming to meetings I might have better insight into whether or not he was a cop. Secondly, if he wasn't a cop and was just out of his element, I thought it was important to be friendly and welcoming so he knew it was okay for him to be around.

Unfortunately, there is rarely a "smoking gun" that outs an informant, and I had an amazing ability to rationalize away Dugger's sketchy behavior. The more I spent time with him, the more investment I had in him as a person and the more I wanted to like him. What this ended up leading to was me putting myself at greater risk.

Dugger postured at being fairly mechanically inclined and so I invited him over to work with me on my motorcycle. One thing that was a bit of a flag at the time and continues to be notable is how Dugger was always really willing to come by and do whatever I wanted to do but, even when prompted, never wanted to choose an activity for us to do or introduce me to any of his friends or family. He came by even when he was exhausted and fell asleep while sitting on a bucket in my driveway.

With all of Dugger's aggression, he didn't have much of an analysis. This isn't a surprise in retrospect. While I tried to be understanding of his stated feelings and meet him where he was at, he spoke and acted in unacceptable ways. I worked hard to help him figure his shit out, and I realize now why he seemed so dense. I understand that Anarchist theory (and political theory in general) can get a little heady. As a movement we have also developed some of our own language to talk about the world around us. If someone doesn't have the educational privilege or access to this language, I imagine a lot of the talk that goes on can be confusing. I believed at the time that these were some of the reasons things were so hard for Dugger. Maybe I got through to him a little when, in a recent hearing, he admitted that we had extended support to him and that our ideals were much more than a philosophy but were a way of life.

Along with my own mistake in trusting Dugger I was put further at risk when, after Dugger was confronted about his aggressive behavior, Darst volunteered me to "mentor" him. I don't know how much I took on this role versus how much I simply continued on the path I was on with Dugger, but it certainly validated the bad choices I had previously made.

The State likes to depict the WC as a shadowy underground organization making secret plans for destruction. The reality is that the WC was an open group. Virtually all of the WC's activities were posted on a publicly viewable web site, including meeting times and locations, so that anyone interested could attend. The WC was not unique in that it didn't do much that was different from what has been done at past mass mobilizations.

Rather, the WC was special because it carved out a central place for anarchists/anti-authoritarians among the local and national organizing around the convention. And it was special because, as a key organizational body, the rhetoric and reasons for the organizing were from an anti-statist/revolutionary perspective.

It's how, why, and with whom the WC was organizing that made it unique. The WC wasn't organizing simply to force reform or undermine the Republican Party. I was organizing with the WC to help build a revolutionary movement. This doesn't mean I was planning on hurting people or birthing a revolution out of the RNC. I have goals beyond the RNC of which organizing with the WC was a part. I think one supporter put it well when they called the organizing "hard-edged civil disobedience." I am not loyal opposition and will not be bought off with reform. Nor will these current charges deter me from continuing to work for absolute justice.

The open nature of the WC made it easily infiltrated by government informants. There are a lot of bad choices that were made surrounding the informants, but I would disagree with some of the more common assertions. One is that the presence of informants is a reason the WC shouldn't have been an open group. There are several problems with this assertion, one of which is that most of us hardly knew each other before the WC. We were organizing out of a virtual vacuum of radical action in the Twin Cities. Had the WC been closed, it would have been an extremely small group to the exclusion of many, and likely excluding several RNC 8 codefendants.

Further, having space for open organizing, especially around heated issues, is the best way to ultimately build a stronger radical movement. If anarchist organizing is available only to those who are already anarchists and/or part of the same social scene as other anarchists, we are putting a stranglehold on our organizing, our movement, and ultimately our effectiveness. Obviously, not all groups need to be open, but I think, especially in the case of logistics for a mass mobilization that is hoping to draw from a large base, having ways for anyone in the affected community who wants to be involved to get involved (and get involved an anarchist) is important.

Secondly, folks often assert that we should have kicked out the informants at the first sign of uneasiness. While it is clear in retrospect that we would have been better off without the informants involved, it is equally important to acknowledge the fact that there was never any absolute proof of the informants until the arrests before the RNC. If we had kicked out everyone who made folks at all uncomfortable, we would have kicked out a lot of people who ended up contributing in meaningful ways.

I know I was partially blinded by the fact that the informants were not "typical" anarchists and I wanted to believe that anarchism could be meaningful for folks who weren't of the same social circles or backgrounds. However, it would obviously be even more problematic for me to respond to this incident by kicking out everyone who isn't from the same social grouping, doesn't use the same coded anarchist language, or have a developed analysis.

Kicking out everyone who doesn't have an anarchist history also clearly wouldn't stop groups from being informed upon, as is clear with the Texas group infiltrated and ratted on by Brandon Darby, an ex-activist with an impressive resumé. The fact is, the State is targeting the WC because it was an effective above-ground organizing body, and the State would likely find a reason to prosecute whether there were informants or not (which there may have been more of, if we had kicked out the ones we had). Most of the things named in the complaint against the RNC 8 are about the WC's activities that were listed on the website: the video, the informational tours, and the convergence space.

That is not to say we shouldn't resist infiltration, but we need to be able to survive it. As anarchists, without a centralization of information, leadership, or resources, we stand a better chance of minimizing the damage these infiltrators and informants can do. It also would have been easier to organize and resist incorporating informants if we were organizing from a stronger place with more confidence and skills, and with a tighter community.

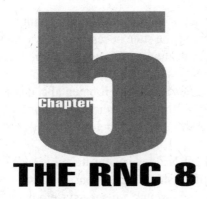

THE RNC 8

Max Specktor

As this trial drags past its second year, I am certain that this case, and the investigation leading up to it, was always about scaring people away from organizing protests in the years to come, and to control the media narrative about the dangers of anarchism more generally. What we were dealing with was a county sheriff deciding to throw 3 informants and undercover cops into the Welcoming Committee, an anarchist organizing body, while "coincidentally," the FBI had 3 informants working with anarchist groups around the country, who were preparing for the RNC.

I am able to accept this as an important reality for our movements because the state necessarily has to be threatened by us. What they are dealing with is an ever more organized element of dissent that refuses to be co-opted or recuperated. This fact is intensified by the current environmental and economic crises that are spinning further and further out of control, while the government seeks to maintain their dwindling control by any means necessary.

Since the RNC, we have watched friends struggle through grand jury fishing expeditions, witnessed countless RNC arrestees railroaded through a justice system that only cares about clearance rates and guilty pleas, and have had comrades across the country come out to support us, even though many of their communities have also been targeted by state repression. We are not the first people to experience this very blatant kind of political repression, and countless others are locked up as we speak, or are awaiting trial, for cases similar to ours.

That being said, I try to be in active solidarity with all targets of state repression, so that we can send a clear message of support to everybody who has yet to acknowledge their privilege and risk a little more with their actions, and to the people already in a place of lesser privilege who want to change that fact. If these people see a strong movement for defending us when we're in trouble, we will begin to see more and more daring actions in furtherance of liberation and a sustainable world. Unfortunately, we will also witness the state and their media generating more and more lies and attacks in furtherance of terrorism and complete control.

One task of our defense committee continues to be the de-legitimization of the repressive forces that we are engaged with. We also continue to make connections with our struggles and the struggles of other communities, including the criminal cases that may arise or have arisen from those struggles. My main hope for the trial and aftermath is that our communities feel more prepared for the next flare-up of conflict—that we show others who are now facing similar fates that our movements can handle these setbacks, while continuing the fight for justice and liberation. This should be a simple task because anti-authoritarians are the most capable of any type of organization to continue growing while under attack. They can try to crush us when and where we rear our proud heads, but like a giant game of "whack-a-mole," we will pop up somewhere else, just as strong and persistent.

Our prosecutors and investigators aren't anomalies of this system; they are the rule. There will be more of this to come, but fortunately there will also be more anarchists, anti-authoritarians, and many other individuals, ready and willing to struggle for their lives and communities. We saw this in Pittsburgh at the G20 in 2009 and in Vancouver at the Olympics in 2010, and the G20 in Toronto later that year. It's happening in classrooms across California and in forests across the country; people are going to keep fighting racism along the borders, exploitation in their workplaces, and hetero-sexism in their homes and in the streets. I am always happy to be part of such a rich tradition of struggle, and as such, it is always important to give credit where it is due. I hope that this case and the attention that it brings can be used to honor and thank all the people who have spent their lives struggling for liberation, including the ones whose hard work goes unrecognized, the ones who get away with it.

Eryn Trimmer

I got out of jail early evening of Thursday, September 4, the last day of the convention. News was that the march that was scheduled for that day had been corralled onto a bridge and was being mass-arrested. A helicopter could be seen circling downtown St. Paul. Monica and I headed home.

Those first few days after being released were a bit of a psychological whirlwind. How could this be happening? I thought it was a fairly tame project to be working with the open, logistical organizing body for a mass mobilization, and now I was all over the news as a terrorist? Friends and family were very supportive and that helped a lot. We heard the stories of how our house was rescued from being boarded-up by the city (which would have cost $10,000). People brought over food and gifts, and helped straighten up the house after the cops had turned it inside out.

Many of the people who organized for the RNC now started either doing arrestee support or working on their own legal defense. There were a lot of people from out of town stuck here dealing with their legal stuff, as well as people who stayed around after the convention to help with the aftermath.

The first two steps the eight of us took were to organize a defense committee and get lawyers. It had been assumed that we would organize collectively for our defense, and indeed that is how we proceeded. I had qualified for a public defender but wanted an activist lawyer who would understand how the eight of us wanted to approach the case better. After a bit of stress doing interviews and trying to find someone amenable to how we were going to be paying them, I settled on Barbara Nimis. Barbara does a lot of important legal work for the activist and Dakota (native people to this area) communities.

We spent the first few months after we were charged working to get the charges dropped. During this time, I felt the charges like a weight on my shoulders that I was carrying around all the time, but it was made much easier by the fact that I was going through it with seven others. We had a defense committee made up of trusted friends and allies who worked on fundraising, building us a website, setting up educational events, distributing a petition, etc.

We decided to focus on getting Susan Gaertner, the Ramsey County prosecutor, to drop the charges, since ultimately the prosecution was her choice. She was also a better target since she was running for governor as a Democrat, something that added to the political nature of the charges. We held protests outside her campaign events to try and convince her supporters to either ask her to drop the charges or stop supporting someone who prosecutes activists on trumped-up allegations.

In mid-December, soon after a successful dance party at Susan Gaertner's birthday fundraiser (during which we endorsed her campaign for governor because of her strong stance against terrorism), we received word that the State had amended the complaint against us and added three more charges: conspiracy to riot in the second degree, conspiracy to damage property in the first degree, and conspiracy to damage property in the first degree in the furtherance of terrorism.[1] So now we had essentially two different charges and then those same charges with the terrorism enhancement, all of which are felonies. Although it may seem like that would be a hard day, and it was, the addition of lesser charges told us that they had some lack of confidence in their case: they were covering their bases in case they couldn't make the terrorism enhancement stick.

Much attention has been brought to the fact that we were charged with crimes "in furtherance of terrorism," in a bill known as the Minnesota PATRIOT Act. Many people think it's ridiculous that we have been labeled with this word. I agree that we are not terrorists, and that this is a completely inaccurate and intentionally misleading description of our tactics. I am not, however, surprised or outraged that the government would label us terrorists. Throughout the whole process of organizing, the police and politicians tried to separate the radicals from the "legitimate, peaceful protesters" This was simply a continuation of that same process, an attempt by the powers that be to delegitimize the unco-optable.

I think it's more important to bring attention to the

conspiracy aspect of our charges, at least in that they are much more common and I think people would be surprised how easy they are to prosecute. All it takes is evidence of an agreement and an "overt act" that furthers the conspiracy.[2] This is dangerous for many different reasons, for revolutionaries especially, because we want to organize (i.e., conspire) to do things that are in many cases illegal, things like stopping corporations from destroying the environment, for example.

It's one thing for the government to prosecute committed illegal acts, but preemptive arrests and prosecution easily crosses the line into thought crime. We need not be accused of explicitly agreeing to do any of the crimes; the agreement may be derived from the circumstances. Also, an "overt act" need not even be illegal. In our case, the prosecution has inferred that they consider renting the convergence center an "overt act" in furtherance of the conspiracy. Essentially, our beliefs and associations with each other, and our doing anything about them, even legal actions, could be construed as a criminal conspiracy.

In April, we got an unexpected surprise: Susan Gaertner dropped the terrorism charges. She said that they "would have been a distraction in trial." This was a complete 180 from what she had said earlier—that she was under an obligation to enforce the law, even if it she didn't agree with it or it was badly written. She confirmed what we had stated all along, that the terrorism charges were completely discretionary (as are the rest of the charges). This was a huge victory for our campaign.

Of course, the real goal was to get all of the charges dropped, but it was at least circumstantial proof that our supporters and the general public had dogged her enough about this case that she felt she needed to do something about it. Dropping the terrorism charges but keeping the others would pacify many of her liberal supporters while allowing her to maintain that we were being prosecuted for serious criminal actions. This made our job of getting all the charges dropped harder, and eventually led to us backing down from that angle.

The eight of us got much better at working together. Anyone who knew how well we got along in the WC would be shocked by how well we started operating. It took a while to find a rhythm with the lawyers. I at least thought the law was much more clear-cut than it turns out to be. It was frustrating to ask an ostensibly simple question to the room of lawyers and get five different answers. Still, this whole process has only gotten easier. I no longer feel a weight on my shoulders, though I would guess that I might feel like one was taken off if we get acquitted.

Although most of the court dates up to this point have been rather banal, we did get the chance to question some of the police investigators involved in our case and two of the informants on the stand during our pretrial Florence hearing. The investigation into us started in earnest when the police saw the "We're getting ready" trailer released by the WC. Even after knowing this for almost two years, it still amazes me what the police can get away with saying on the stand with a straight face. They have the gall to call the trailer a training and recruitment video (for rioting and damage to property), and make a direct connection to the fact that two people did in fact make Molotov Cocktails when in town for the RNC.

Anyone who's seen the video would know that this is ridiculous, as it is clearly poking fun at the stereotypes of anarchists as evildoers, but between the prosecutors insinuations of our criminal natures, the police officers' "seriousness" about the law and public safety and the judge's attempts to stifle any expressions of humor or joy, the environment in court can quickly cascade into one in which obvious truths can be flipped on their heads. As lies are told about you, you are of course required to sit silently, your only means of recourse asking them questions through your legal appendage (lawyer). All in all, it's a rather disempowering and draining experience, to say the least.

When Marilyn Hedstrom, the Ramsey County officer who had gone undercover in the WC, took the stand, she couldn't point to a time when any of us had been in proximity to, talked about using, or talked about procuring a dangerous weapon for use at the RNC. She couldn't point to any plans of property destruction or anyone mentioning that they thought this was a good idea. She did say, however, that she could tell that rioting and damaging property was the real point of the group, but because of security culture no one would come out and say it. So the utter lack of evidence in fact shows that we are guilty. This is the kind of logic used by the prosecutors.

Chris Dugger's testimony was even less incriminating that Marilyn's. Besides not seeing or knowing any plans related to dangerous weapons or property destruction at the RNC, Chris admitted that Garrett took him under his wing and mentored him. Some spectators even thought they saw a tinge of regret in his eye for betraying his once-friend.

Unfortunately we couldn't question Andrew Darst, the FBI informant. The FBI is hiding his whereabouts, which is the only reason, according to the prosecutor, that he hasn't already been attacked. This also happens to make him hard to subpoena, and when we asked the judge to have her let us question him, she said no.

As of this writing members of the RNC 8 defense committee are on tour to promote the case and the upcoming trial. People are making plans to come to town and events are being planned during those weeks. Although trial is going to be long and arduous, I feel comfortable in this situation. I know what I am trying to do with my life, and I have a community to struggle with. I am still learning a ton, both about my goals and how to achieve them, and I see this process as an invaluable learning experience. I am not overly worried about what the State can and will bring to bear on us, in this trial and in the future. We fight with passion, love, and solidarity, and that is something that they can't take away from us.

Garrett Fitzgerald

The dog-and-pony show may have left town, but the RNC still isn't over. For everyone working and dealing with the aftermath, the RNC is relived over and over again as we read through evidence, go to court, sit in meetings, and organize fundraisers. It can be frustrating to be on the defensive for so long as we fight these legal battles.

Sometimes, I wonder how we can hope to make anything

happen if we are so often on the defensive, but I know our odds are worse if we don't work to take care of each other when in tight spots. A proportionately large amount of energy is spent on things like legal work and support now, but that is something we foresaw (and something that turned a lot of folks away from RNC organizing in the first place).

While it seems hard now, we have grown our capacity and some day in the future will have more capacity to organize on our own terms. Perhaps the lesson is that these events never really "end;" they just become less and less relevant until they fade from immediate memory.

Much of my time and energy in the aftermath has been spent doing legal work. I never thought of myself as gravitating toward legal work before the RNC, but with the work I was putting into my own case, it seemed logical that I could extend that work to others with minimal effort. The major State players and their "evidence" are all present in our case (as the RNC 8 are essentially being charged with organizing everything that everyone who had RNC-related charges was charged with), so I have a grasp of the big picture of RNC State repression.

For me, an important part of being a committed radical is doing the work that you are best positioned to do even if it would not be your first choice otherwise. We also can't rely on "experts" like lawyers to know the best choices for the movement. We must work to inform ourselves about our own situations and the situations affecting the position of the movement and, with this information, we must be the ones who shape it.

That's not to say that people like lawyers, who have more access to and understanding of the law, are not useful in the movement, but we must expect them to work with us and not just defer to their expert judgments. It is hard work to create relationships that give you agency over these processes, but I feel it is ultimately essential if we are to have any control over our own destinies.

There are a lot of different mobilizations and times in history that can be looked to for examples of how to organize, but ultimately, each situation is new. It is in a new location and within a new context locally, nationally, and globally, involving different relationships with different histories. It is impossible (even if it were desirable) to recreate a past event, simply because the conditions will always be different. We must all honestly and strategically evaluate where we find ourselves and make the best choices we can based on the information we have.

The anarchist movement locally was weak when we began organizing, and there were few people with experience who wanted to work on the organizing around the RNC. We spent a lot of energy trying things that didn't work out, in large part because we didn't have any sort of road map or template to follow. On the other hand, this caused us to invent some new ideas that we might not have come up with if we just followed a model.

As a movement, it would be wise to work on combating the micro-generational stratification that happens. In the WC, being "old" or "young" was a matter of five years or so. This is not a way to maintain movement history and preserve knowledge. Talking to people with experience or reading and writing zines is a great way that we pass on information. Better still, we need to find ways to keep anarchism and struggle relevant for ourselves as we move through the stages of our lives. This doesn't mean we get to lead "normal" lives, but that however we grow, we grow the struggle with us so we are around to share that experience with those who come after us.

It was definitely a success to work with non-anarchist groups, but equally as important was that we were well enough organized that we could have organized without anyone else. This meant that we had something clear that we brought to the table. I am glad that the March Coalition got a permit for the march and helped draw a lot of folks to St. Paul, but anarchists did most of the work in terms of food and housing for out-of-towners and a lot of people came to the convergence space to get these needs met who didn't identify as radicals or revolutionaries.

In 2004, anarchists at the DNC were organized, but there was a lot of hostility between Boston anarchists and other radicals and progressives. At the RNC in New York, there wasn't enough focused anarchist organizing to get behind, and the anarchists were swallowed up into other projects. I think the WC learned these lessons well by both having a strong anarchist presence and by exercising that strength in solidarity with non-anarchist organizations.

Things like the WC's Points of Unity and even to a degree the St. Paul Principles were based on the work of previous groups. I am proud to see other groups now adapting them to their work. It shows the importance of understanding our collective history and demonstrates our ability to grow and adapt lessons of the past to new situations.

The ability to do this work, both on a personal and a community level, are a success of the "capacity building" goal that came out of the pReNC. Generally, folks got out of the RNC what they put in. The folks who put in a lot and the communities that put in a lot are now stronger for it. I know that if, in the next few years, another convention or National Special Security Event comes to the Twin-Cities, it will be met with well-coordinated revolutionary resistance that will continue to build on and surpass the work done around the RNC.

As of this writing, we have been dealing with the RNC aftermath for about a year and a half, and I have been organizing around this RNC for over three years. While the RNC is and has been a major influence on my life, I also like to remember the things I have done since the RNC that have been valuable to me. I purchased a broken-down motorcycle before the RNC and spent a little time working on it with Chris Dugger. It wasn't until the summer after the RNC that I finally got it running. I have been reading up on converting it to run on alcohol and am hoping to make further headway on this project next summer.

At this point in my life, I would say motorcycle riding is at least as fun as riding trains and, as long as it doesn't break down, is faster and more reliable. I have also been playing in a band since before the RNC and we are finishing up recording a full-length album. I am continuing to teach preschool, which, as far as jobs go, is pretty mutually fulfilling. Being around children helps keep me grounded and reminds me what I'm struggling for.

A lot of folks I didn't know before the RNC became

friends afterward as they hung around town facing charges or helping others deal with theirs. It is bittersweet to know folks only in the context of repression. They end up going to jail or returning to their home communities. While here, they helped bring energy to the aftermath and keep our community feeling revitalized.

I am grateful to be part of a community that is generally supportive. It seems we will likely only get better at this sort of thing as we become a more effective part of the movement. But we are still learning and figuring it out as we go. It's not always fun work and you learn a lot about the people around you when you see how the community responds to crisis and oppression.

My family has been supportive. As our family is quite small, we are all important to each other. My mother was waiting for me when I got out of jail, and she and my sister have both come to several court appearances. I have also been especially impressed at how supportive the people at the schools I work at have been. I am still able to work as often as I can. I have both teachers and other school employees, as well as parents, ask about the case and wish me well.

Even with support, however, the legal system is brutal and slow. I have poured a lot of energy into struggling through this case that has increased my personal stress levels and reduced the amount of time and energy I have to nurture myself and my close personal relationships. The community locally has also faced strain as energy wanes and new issues arise. Most notably, two friends and comrades, Carrie Feldman and Scott DeMuth, were both summoned to an Iowa grand jury investigating an Animal Liberation Front action that took place in Iowa when Scott was seventeen and Carrie was fifteen and they were both in high school in Minneapolis. Carrie was locked up for civil contempt for four months before being released. Having been indicted on conspiracy charges, Scott has been released while awaiting trial.

Along with being responsible for our case, I have also taken on new responsibilities in my family in the past year. Since the RNC, my parents split up after almost thirty years. It might come as a surprise that I am actually quite proud of them. Things were okay enough that they could have stayed together forever, but instead they are seeking greater happiness as they approach their golden years. They are both interested in selling their house and moving out of state. I am no longer a child who can selfishly expect things from parents without responsibility. Now we all are each other's primary support and have much more mature relationships. I am proud of the way my family adapts, grows, and weathers hard times. I am proud that we all seem to be seeking the best and most meaningful lives possible for ourselves.

Back in 2002 I saw the new documentary "The Weather Underground." This spurred for me a fascination with the New Left of the '60s and '70s. Perhaps it is due to the reasonably close historical proximity, but I find myself often comparing and contrasting the state of the movement and the world now with the struggles of that era. We have lost a lot of momentum and strength that was generated around the Vietnam era. Likewise, the repression we now face is proportionately less extreme than that of the revolutionaries of the New Left. Educating myself on the histories and lives of George Jackson, Assata Shakur, David Gilbert, Angela Davis, and others keeps the repression I am facing now in perspective and should be a reminder to everyone engaged in struggle that it is going to get worse before it gets better. In spite of their years in prison members of the Back Panther Party, Weather Underground, Symbionese Liberation Army, Black Liberation Army, Revolutionary Armed Task Force, American Indian Movement, Young Patriots, Brown Berets, and other revolutionary groups continue to struggle.

In his book Revolutionary Suicide, Huey P. Newton described the term and contrasted it with "reactionary suicide." Reactionary suicide is the taking of one's own life and is usually a response to social conditions. Revolutionary suicide is a response to the same conditions but instead of taking your life, you give it over to struggle knowing that you may die. When I was a depressed high-school student I decided that instead of dying for something I wanted to live for something. In New York, when I prioritized being engaged in struggle over my artistic career, I was acting on that decision. I continue to act on that decision and am given strength by it. My life is not mine alone; it belongs to my community and the revolution. For instance, when Fred Hampton was murdered by the Chicago PD in 1968, his friend and Deputy Minister of Defense of the Illinois BPP, Bobby Rush, was asked by reporters about his personal plans. He said, "There is no personal anymore."

I don't wish to martyr myself and I have no desire to go to jail or prison, but I am proud to be a part of this radical history. This history will give me solace whatever the State does to my comrades and me. There are those for whom State repression causes a recalculation of their commitment to revolutionary struggle. There are others for whom it solidifies their resolve. I am honored to work alongside committed radicals who are facing repression head on and refusing to back down. We are strong anarchists and committed revolutionaries. They can railroad us through a kangaroo court (in a kangaroo justice system), but we won't lose as long as we continue to struggle and as long as, when we are gone or rendered ineffective, others continue on without us. It is in this spirit that we are compelled to struggle and can honestly shout from our hearts, with love and rage—WE WILL NOT BE INTIMIDATED!

Luce Guillén-Givins

On December 8, 2008, I learned that I was pregnant. I had had my suspicions for a couple weeks, but in addition to my normal full-time job, I had my hours so filled at that point that I put off addressing the situation until the first free moment I could find. The moment came between a meeting regarding support for others facing felony charges stemming from the RNC and a meeting and Christmas photo shoot with my codefendants that evening. It was cold and quite snowy, and I had been feeling exhausted and ill for days. I trudged to the bus, rode to a drug store, and bought a pregnancy test. I felt like I waited for hours for the return bus, though it was probably only a few minutes. I got home with just enough time to take the test and tell my boyfriend, Rob, before our co-defendants started arriving for our meeting.

There was never a point at which I was able to consider pregnancy apart from my legal situation. And while I was in the process of deciding what to do, our charges were quadrupled. In one day, I went from thinking about the possibility of giving birth around a trial, of being convicted, and of spending the first couple years of that child's life in prison, to thinking about spending the first twelve years locked away. Given that Rob is my co-defendant, we also had to consider that if one parent were locked away, likely enough both would be.

Several years prior, reading An Autobiography of Assata Shakur had affected me profoundly. As a final project in a fiber arts class that I was taking when I read it, I screen printed the first three stanzas of a poem by Assata Shakur onto a hand-dyed silk banner, which has hung somewhere in my various houses ever since. I replicated it many times in the years following—on gifts for friends and in the mural on the side of the Jack Pine Community Center. It reads:

> Love is contraband in Hell,
> cause love is an acid
> that eats away at bars.
>
> But you, me and tomorrow
> hold hands and make vows
> that struggle will multiply.
>
> The hacksaw has two blades,
> The shotgun has two barrels.
> We are pregnant with freedom.
> We are a conspiracy.

Assata conceived her child in a court holding cell with her codefendant while they stood trial for an alleged bank robbery. They had already lost their physical freedom, were facing much more serious consequences than we do right now, and faced real threats to their physical well-being and even their lives. And I had recited this fragment of a poem so many times in my head, thinking of it often when pondering my deepening commitment to revolutionary movement, that I couldn't help but dwell on it as I struggled with what to do.

While I grappled with the decision, I was once again incredibly fortunate to have the support of family and several close friends, in addition to Rob. My mother and my best friends all assured me that if I were sent to prison, the baby would not be lacking for people to care for it and, alternately, they offered to fly out and help me through an abortion.

Ultimately, I decided to end the pregnancy. It wasn't a decision based solely on my legal situation; I doubt that I would have felt myself ready to become a mother otherwise, but I was acutely aware throughout this process that my "freedom of choice" was curtailed quite heavily by the legal forces directed against me. I was having a really difficult time staying emotionally afloat as it was, and couldn't even consider doing so with the added stress of a pregnancy, let alone a baby, without breaking down in tears.[3] I returned over and over again to the ideas that I took from Assata's life story, recognizing that I still had agency in this situation and could find the strength to go forward however I chose, as many women have done. But I realized that in my psychological state at the time, and facing what I was, I didn't have room in my mind for any healthy vision of pregnancy and motherhood.

On December 16, I had the abortion. Less than 24 hours later, I sat in court for our first scheduling conference with a newly appointed judge. I hadn't told any of my codefendants or the attorneys, and even with Rob at my side, I felt very alone that day. While it wasn't the only factor affecting my decision, our case took a sharp turn for me at that juncture. The impact on my life now ran much deeper. Until then, the personal effects of the case had felt superficial and relatively minor, but now I actually felt that I had been robbed, a part of me severed and taken away.

The court system is designed to disempower defendants from start to finish, and my experience has been no exception to this. Though you are told that you are "innocent until proven guilty," you're definitely not treated that way. From the brute force of police busting down our doors to the authoritarian pageantry of our judge seated high above everyone else, demanding that everyone stand for her entrance and exit, every step of the legal process is a reminder that the State is immensely powerful and has seemingly infinite resources with which to do what it will. The State derives its illegitimate authority through hegemonically disenfranchising whole sectors of society and enforcing compliance and conformity under threat of violence, imprisonment, and all-out war, and there is no possibility for true justice within the confines of its own court system.

Coming into RNC work, I bore no illusions about the ways "the other side" operates, but the process has been incredibly enlightening for me in regards to limitations on the support that you can reasonably expect to receive within legal channels, even with skilled and politically aware attorneys. We've been incredibly fortunate, compared with most people navigating the legal system, in that we live in a city with enough activist attorneys willing to take on a case of this magnitude, and our supporters have fundraised enough to afford us that representation.

But dealing with our attorneys is a constant source of stress and difficulty. With a few individual exceptions, they haven't provided deep support for any of the decisions that I feel proudest of in the aftermath of the RNC. Every one of these decisions—to fight this all the way rather than pleading out; to collectivize our support structures and the disbursement of our defense fund; to push for the consolidation of our cases into one joint trial—has come through our unwillingness to budge on what we believe to be issues of principle, despite the lack of confidence and respect with which many of our attorneys treat us and our supporters.

We've had to fight to maintain the sort of defense operation that fits with the anarchist and revolutionary principles we hold, waging an uphill battle against a decidedly individualistic legal culture that produces huge egos and a trained inability to work collectively toward a common good. Though I can't imagine doing things differently, it's easy from where I stand to see why so few cases ever go to trial, even when defendants believe in their own innocence. We've only been able to do this because we are committed to being an active part of the struggle even as the State seeks to sideline us, and because we have an analysis of the implications of our decisions for the movement as a whole.

That all notwithstanding, I wouldn't say that our position is particularly bad as far as State repression goes. Even a day behind bars is too much, but in a country that holds a quarter of the world's prisoners, what we face is only a fraction of what many people deal with, and we've been relatively free to lead our lives since the RNC, compared with many radicals who've been targeted for their political work. Yet I do think that what we're going through is politically significant, a sort of flagship case in the ongoing criminalization of dissent and, in particular, the State's determination to root out anarchists and destroy our movements. This pattern of state repression isn't new and, in a strange way, our case has relatively little to do with any of us as individuals, but rather is meant as yet another cautionary tale for any would-be organizers. Through prosecuting us, the State is communicating to everyone else that organizing outside state-sanctioned avenues of "dissent" bears heavy consequences and that the only way to protect yourself and the ones you love is to lay low and stay away from anyone who doesn't.

The flip side is that the support we continue to have more than a year after the fact is setting precedent of a more positive kind, and conveys the message that folks targeted for their political work won't face repression alone. While it has been disappointing to notice absent faces, particularly from the local anarchist scene, among our supporters, my overwhelming sense has been one of pleasant surprise and gratitude. Our defense campaign brings in a diversity of people whose reasons for having our backs are varied, and I truly feel the support of an entire movement as I navigate this case. Because we have the privilege of broad support, it has been fairly easy for me to take an active role in my defense, trying to think of this time as a chance to gain skills and knowledge that will be useful to the movement beyond the confines of our case.

I wouldn't have chosen this "opportunity" of my own

free will, but neither do I want this time to be wasted. The skills I feel like I'm honing extend beyond the legal arena, as well. Though the eight of us were all a part of the same group, and contrary to the narrative the State is constructing, we weren't any sort of eight-person unit. Some of us were friends, and some of us weren't, and few of us knew any of the others before the Welcoming Committee's inception. We've had our fair share of personal differences over the past few years, and we didn't work together particularly well as a whole before the RNC. But since then, necessity has helped us learn to work with each other, and it's one of the most valuable things I've gotten out of the entire affair.

From the onset of our case, we've consciously prioritized building and maintaining an internal trust and sense of collectivity for which I'm grateful. Whatever happens at trial, I feel certain that we'll all emerge with skills in collective organizing and consensus-building that are otherwise in short supply, and I am eagerly awaiting a time when I can funnel those skills back into proactive revolutionary work.

My biggest fear coming out of the RNC is that what happened to those of us in the Welcoming Committee will frighten people away from open, public organizing. Some form of public presence is, and always has been, a necessary component of revolutionary movements. Not everyone in a struggle has to be involved in that way, just as not everyone has to be involved in clandestine activity, but it needs to be happening in order to make the very existence of a radical alternative known. Without a public and above-ground presence, movements become largely inaccessible, inhibiting their potential for growth, and history has shown time and again that movements driven underground in their entirety by State repression are often stripped of the ability to dialogue with a broader base of support and maintain their relevance and effectiveness.

These movements may still be able to carry out actions that garner attention and inspire many but they are likely to play into a culture of heroism where, as revolutionary figures are elevated and mythologized, everyday people's sense of their own ability to contribute is severely restricted. For anarchists, this is of special concern because we organize through consensus and horizontalism, and the isolation that comes with a lack of connection to public and open groups entrenches power dynamics that run counter to this, creating a movement hierarchy and inflexibility that undermine our very principles.

We seek not just the overthrow of any particular regime but the wholesale transformation of society, a process that cannot be forced along by small, isolated, underground cells. Rather, this transformation requires the active cultivation of radical consciousness and new ways of relating and interacting with each other throughout the various communities we inhabit.

I've had a lot of people ask me if the whole thing was worth it, given my current legal situation. And I've heard others say that the answer is contained in the resolution of our case, I guess meaning that if we're convicted, it wasn't worth it, and if we're acquitted, it was. But my own answer is yes, it was worth it, whatever happens at trial. I feel comfortable with the idea that, as revolutionaries, we can't measure success in terms of individual legal casualties. We have to be prepared for legal fallout, which will inevitably increase and affect more people as our movements grow in strength and size.

Our response determines the impact to our movements; if we say that convictions mean failure, or that prison will deter us, then we're agreeing to the State's terms, providing them with a clear way to control us. They can arrest and prosecute more people, and they're bound to have court victories at least some of the time, but the beauty of anarchism is that we have the means and power to build this movement, yet make ourselves replaceable on the streets and useful wherever we land. From a movement perspective, the productive and revolutionary measure of the worth of our organizing is that which assesses the collective growth we experience, and I believe the eight of us and the communities we inhabit are stronger and more capable of affecting radical change than we were before the RNC.

Monica Bicking

The last eighteen months have been a rollercoaster of both joy and pain. There is a weight on my shoulders that continues to grow. I keep wondering if this weight is what it means to be an adult.

The charges alone have been a roller coaster. It all started when we were charged with Felony Conspiracy to Riot in the Furtherance of Terrorism. I did not expect that. I had to fit prison into my vision of my future. Months later, the charges increased to four felonies, two with terrorist enhancements. How could things get worse? Fortunately not all of the charges stuck. The terrorist charges were eventually dropped, and now we are down to two felonies.

I daily cope with the realization that I am on the government's list, and that will never change because I will not roll over until they forget about me. If I do not go to jail this time, I will go next time. What does this mean? Should I never have children, a life-long dream of mine, because I cannot guarantee that I will always be there for them?

My family has had a hard eighteen months as well. My grandmother went crazy. Mean crazy. I did not have much of a relationship with her, but I do with her children. She drove them crazy, triggering the hardships of their childhood. They struggled. She died. I felt a sense of relief with her death, thinking that she could no longer hurt anyone, but my grandfather's depression deepens with her loss and the pain goes on.

In the past year, five family members have moved to Minneapolis. I never thought I would get to live in the same city as them, and my joy at their move was tremendous. I have gotten a chance to deepen my relationships with them and create new ones with a two- and three-year-old. They are joyful, rewarding relationships. It does not come without pain. The three- (almost four-) year-old has a life-threatening condition and has been in and out of surgery for more than half his life. Now that I have more of a relationship with him, my love for him has deepened and I become petrified with each surgery. Twice in the last year he has had to go for emergency surgeries. The news about the progression of his condition has been mixed. The family is constantly swinging up and down as his condition improves and worsens. He will never be like other kids, but the joy he brings to those around him is insurmountable.

One of the hardest things of the past eighteen months has been to watch a teenage family member get into an extremely abusive relationship. She has been on her own rollercoaster and those that love her have not been able to help. We tried to end the relationship, but couldn't. She loved him. She got pregnant quickly, and was pressured into an abortion by the boyfriend. She complied, only to get pregnant a month later. At this point she was starting to stand up to him and refused to have an abortion. She broke up with him. They got back together. They broke up again. I think it is permanent this time, but it does not change the fact that he is the father to her child, and she will be connected with this man forever. There is no escaping. Grief for her loss of possibilities is overwhelming. Joy for a new life with new possibilities is growing.

There have been other things, seemingly minor things or more removed things, but I can't help thinking, "Are they really minor?" She fell in the night. Was it a stroke? He has cancer. It should be treatable. She's heading to the ER. Is this a new trend? He was sent to jail. We didn't expect that, but of course he could not just get probation. She has lost hope. She has never given up before. She is drinking. When is a lot too much? He is in jail. Now he is out. Now she is in jail. Will she ever get out? Her room is so empty.

While the weight on my shoulders gets heavier, I am surprised that with each hardship I find more strength. It is a sharp contrast to how I dealt with grief in the past. I am learning. My family has grown as well as my community. I stay strong for them, lean on them, and learn from them. I have found strength in Luce's constant reminders that for every hardship we face, someone has already faced it and someone else has faced a hardship much greater with both strength and compassion.

While the State has tried to scare me and my community

away from our organizing, from our beliefs, and from our convictions, they have failed. They have only made me stronger. I no longer hold the same fear of prison. I no longer feel that I can choose to stay out of prison. I realize that the legal system has nothing to do with whether or not people did something wrong or even illegal. The laws are designed to stop dissent before it even starts. In the last year and a half I have found more strength than I ever thought I had and I now know that I will be able to handle whatever the State and life throw at me with both strength and compassion.

DEFEND THE RNC 8

COMMUNITY
SOLIDARITY
RESISTANCE

Chapter 6

AFTERTHOUGHTS

Community, Solidarity, Resistance: The Conclusion of the RNC 8 Case and Some Lessons Learned - From the RNC 8 and RNC 8 Defense Committee

After more than two years after the 2008 Republican National Convention, it appears that the last legal and political defense finally reaching a conclusion. Two years of standing together, not always in agreement, but bound by our outrage against a State that systematically destroys our supposed rights. Two years of coming to understand that we are not exceptional and that these rights do not actually exist for anyone except the richest of the rich. Two years of standing and fighting together anyway, retaining our dignity and our strength in our own separate ways.

On October 19, 2010, Max Specktor and Rob Czernik pled guilty to gross misdemeanor Conspiracy to Riot, and Garrett Fitzgerald and Nathanael Secor pled guilty to gross misdemeanor Conspiracy to Damage Property. These are all non-cooperating plea agreements; they will not be called upon to testify against anyone else. All of them received 100 hours of community service to be served over 10 months, no jail time or restitution, and a $200 fine. Max and Nathanael were sentenced to one year supervised probation; Garrett and Rob, two years. We recognize that the plea deal may come as a surprising development to supporters, especially considering that the prosecution originally branded the RNC 8 "terrorists" and was still committed to securing felony convictions for certain defendants only two weeks before the agreements.

This is not a rallying cry or a desire to spin a victory from this development in the case. There is no value now in spin, no worth in declaring victory when the situation is more complicated. Rather, this is a moment for reflection upon all the tensions and trade-offs of these last years, and a call for renewed dedication to our highest ideals.

The plea agreements that Erik, Max, Nathanael, Rob, and Garrett have accepted are an indication of the realities of the judicial system and our limitations in fighting back against its repressive maneuvers. We regret that the RNC 8, while better positioned than most to fight against this tide, still succumbed to it. The RNC 8 never asked to be placed at the center of this issue, but worked to make the best of the legal battle that they were thrust into. The 8, even at the times of greatest solidarity, had differing analyses, backgrounds, and perspectives on their positions in (or outside of) movements for revolutionary change. They brought different privileges, needs, strengths, and weaknesses to the battle.

Some may see this as a tension between the personal and political—that is, what is best for the movement might not be best for their life journeys. Others see themselves so tied to the revolutionary movement that the two are indistinguishable. The only certain truth is that there is not now, nor has there ever been, absolute agreement among the defendants in this case (or their supporters, for that matter).

There are several factors that contributed to how things ultimately played out in this case. Not everyone is in agreement on these factors, but there are clearly some tensions we can identify.

Among the defendants there was a tension between solidarity and autonomy. This tension is not unique to the RNC 8 case and, while there were breakdowns in the feelings of solidarity at times, there were also things gained when codefendants stood together and when the broader movement came together to support them. While the defendants can't claim full responsibility for the State dropping the charges against three of the eight, the majority of the defendants standing strong together certainly contributed to this outcome.

But there were times when some of the codefendants saw themselves as being in different positions based on numerous actual differences. Individual defendants' relationships to the RNC Welcoming Committee, their relationship to the State's evidence, and their differing political analyses and varying commitments to a trial made it even more difficult to navigate the already treacherous terrain with a sense of togetherness. In light of this, how can we ensure that an individual's autonomy is secure while building the strongest base of solidarity possible? When is it appropriate for an individual to remove themselves from a group? For some of us, these are lingering questions. Our experiences also lead us to ask: What is solidarity? How can we avoid "lip service solidarity" that covers up using the group to serve individual ends? How can we practice solidarity in a way that it supports both our revolutionary movement and the individual revolutionaries in our movement?

There were tensions pulling on the defendants from the outside as well. One of the most significant was the tension between political support and legal support. The political support around the RNC 8 case has been some of the most phenomenal in recent history. Part of this is because, with the hard work and at least small successes of the RNC Welcoming Committee, the RNC 8 seemed like the best anarchist pony in the race. Many, if not most, of the 8 believed this case was going to go to trial. That's what the 8 and the Defense Committee told all of you, and part of the reason we received so much support was that people believed us. And many people dedicated a lot of their time and energy to making this political support as strong and effective as it has been. We are deeply sorry for those who feel deceived or as if their pony gave up the race.

There is another component, however, that is less visible: the legal support. The official stance of the United States judicial system is that all defendants have the right to trial and to have counsel represent them at trial. However, this is rarely the case. The use of trumped-up charges, economic hardship, isolation of defendants, and fear are great tools used to bully and coerce defendants into plea deals. Part of what we have learned is that this coercion doesn't just come from the State. It's true that the State would rather folks take plea deals, but for many of the same reasons, defense lawyers also prefer them and work toward them. Lawyers at both tables are ultimately officers of the court. This situation creates a sort of Judicial-Industrial Complex in which all the suits often have a vested interest in efficiency, expediency, and getting the most amount of money for the least amount of work.

Defense attorneys' sacred mantra is to work in the best interests of their clients, but they usually perceive "best interests" in very different ways than their clients do, especially political clients. When a client puts as much or more weight on the best interests of a revolutionary movement, or makes those revolutionary interests their own, lawyers whose home turf is the system against which their client struggles can have a difficult time understanding.

The court system is also well adept at isolating defendants, even when they receive vocal and active support outside the courtroom. Defense attorneys are able to leverage defendants' need for lawyers and their specialized knowledge to separate the defendants from other people who care about them and the outcome of their cases. This is a sort of backwards way for lawyers to grab power and attempt to control defendants who are positioned at the center of the political campaign. As such, our movement needs defense attorneys who can recognize this reality and use their skills and privileges not to work out the least painful resolution but to further the struggle in dismantling the system that forces these resolutions.

We have also learned that our movement needs people who are committed to retaining their own agency as defendants and to furthering their political goals through their legal battles. Defendants must be able to set firm boundaries with their legal defense teams, support each other through the legal proceedings, and listen to and hear the advice of their friends and closest political allies as they work to make the best decisions for the movement and themselves—even if these decisions are counter to the advice they received.

Between the defendants and others working on their case/campaign, there was also a tension between support and accountability. Those of us who are anarchists (and even some who aren't) believe that, in decision making, the most weight should be given to the opinions of those who are most affected. In cases like this, it makes sense that the defendants be allowed to guide their own defense as best they are able. Affectedness, however, is a spectrum. One need not be the most affected to have a stake in a choice. If the case had been more straightforward—say, the 8 were all charged with an actual act of property destruction—the political ramifications would not have been as great and so political supporters (or the movement) would have had less at stake. But, because this case has been about taking a stand and resisting the State's ability to throw people in jail for thought crime, people beyond the defendants have something to lose. As the Defense Committee has been saying from the beginning, they are coming for the anarchists today; tomorrow it could be any of us.

Many of us draw a hard boundary on withdrawing support from snitches—folks who cooperate with the State to hurt their "friends." (Luckily, this didn't become a concern in this case.) Many of us have come to believe that there is also some grey area wherein we can ask and expect those whom we support to handle themselves with integrity and be mindful of the movement that stands behind them. This doesn't mean that support will be withdrawn or that defense committees get to make defendants' choices for them. It simply means that it is legitimate for supporters to have thoughts and feelings about the campaign they are working on and to ask that those thoughts and feelings be heard. And it means that the defendants have the responsibility to be accountable to the people supporting them.

We continue to be focused on being accountable to everyone who has supported the defendants and the work of the Defense Committee. Thank you for being there. Thank you for your donations, for your time spent in the kitchen at our community meals, for organizing and participating in rallies, fundraisers and other events. Thank you for continuing the fight around the issues that led us to resist the Republican National Convention in the first place, and thank you for raising the next generation of rebels and revolutionaries while keeping the struggle going. Thank you for standing not just with the RNC 8, but with all the RNC arrestees and with all targets of state repression. Thank you for remembering the St. Paul Principles—that despite our differences and misgivings, we are strongest when working together as one movement united for radical social change and determined to win.

Thank you for taking the high road, speaking up for true justice and liberation through the good times and the bad, demonstrating the world we will see rise from the ashes of the old. Thank you for the work you will continue to do against politics as usual, against the farce of the criminal injustice system, and against the police and prison industrial complex. And thank you for the work you will continue to do to take direct control over our lives, to fight for social and environmental justice, and to create organized dissent everywhere. In solidarity,

- The RNC 8 and the RNC 8 Defense Committee

After the hearing on Tuesday morning, October 19, 2010, members of the RNC 8 Defense Committee and defendant Garrett Fitzgerald addressed a large crowd of reporters and supporters. Here's the text of Garrett's statement to the crowd outside the courthouse on Kellogg Boulevard.

These halls are advertised as a house of justice. In reality, this is a catacomb, where cries for justice come to die. I am still strong, standing here before you, because I never simply called for justice. I knew this call would go unanswered. I demand justice, yes, but I know the courts better than to believe they would or could grant it. That is why when I stand here now I say, "I stand for justice," and I say this regardless of the court's position on the matter.

I look around this city and everything I see is made or controlled by people. Even the great river is channeled by concrete. People could have created anything; none of it is absolute, yet this is what was fabricated. This is what has been constructed and a new world will not be built upon its rotten foundation. Instead, the bricks and mortar, the ideas, the systems, all must be deconstructed.

Expressions of unrest come not from one person, or even one group of people alone, but from tumult in the social fabric. War, economic crisis, environmental devastation, that annoying boss at work—that's what brings people out into the street. And, out in the streets of St. Paul on September 1st, 2008, for a brief moment, authority lost control.

In their absence, real people began to remake the world. There were dance parties, debates, cries of pain and protest, and raw deconstruction of the old, all together in one voice rejecting this fabrication. I was in jail for those two hours when authority lost control, but if anything I did helped to bring them about—I couldn't be more proud and I would do it again in a heartbeat. In a heartbeat because my heart still beats, and until the day that it stops, I will fight for true freedom and an end to all oppression. To quote '80s pop sensation Pat Benatar:

> We can't afford to be innocent
> Stand up and face the enemy
> It's a do or die situation
> We will be invincible.

The following statement was read by Max Specktor before his sentencing at the plea hearing of October 19, 2010:

I accept total responsibility for my actions in this case, but this conspiracy is only part of the story, so I would like to share some other thoughts and plans of mine, to provide some context for these actions.

I refuse to participate in the spectacle of democracy, the idea that two parties, or three, or 100 parties, can represent all the opinions in this country. Instead, I believe in self-determination and autonomy. In practice, this means that I alone make decisions about things that only affect me. And in a group setting, we make our decisions together.

I refuse to accept the logic that our world is for sale. I don't believe that everything can be bought and sold, or that appearing happy is more important than true happiness. Instead, I choose a world that is free. In practice, this means decentralizing the power and wealth that is so concentrated in the hands of a few, and prioritizing real needs over conspicuous consumption.

I refuse to sleepwalk through life. Instead, I've chosen to celebrate life and fight to defend it. In practice, this means I am an active participant in my community, and work to provide resources to assist in supporting that community. In these hard times, I believe that communities need to learn how to support themselves and I am committed to furthering that goal.

I accept the fact that I have a lot of privilege in being able to explain my motivations today. I also owe a lot to the hard work of others for supporting me throughout this process. However, there are too many people who do not share this privilege; they lack a proscribed channel for articulating their demands. Instead, their desires and frustrations explode out of them—in the streets, on their jobs, in their homes. My only hope is that out of this chaos, we can maintain the wisdom and foresight to build the world we wish to see. These are my motivations.

The following statement was read by Nathanael Secor before his sentencing at the plea hearing of October 19, 2010:

While this case has always been about the criminalization of dissent, it would be disingenuous to characterize me as a victim of the State. I openly admit before the court and everyone assembled that I conspired to commit criminal damage to property. This decision was mine and was not swayed by the blockading strategy of the RNC Welcoming Committee, a group of which I was part but which never advocated property destruction.

Others have been similarly charged in the resolution of their cases, but there are many people and departments who will never be held accountable for the actions they have actually carried out. The Ramsey County Sheriff's Office and other cooperating agencies broke down unlocked doors and used violence and threats for the political purpose of repressing activists and agitators working to expose the injustices of colonial wars and environmental destruction. We are told this is called "keeping the peace" and was done in the name of "justice," yet when other people find it necessary to go beyond the sanctioned means of protest, they are called "terrorists." And the stakes are high—at the RNC we saw hundreds of protestors arrested and subsequent terrorism charges both used to justify a $50 million security budget and an absurd degree of social control on the part of the police.

The message is clear: there are those who make the decisions, those who enforce the rules, and if you fail to acknowledge this or if you work to change this inequitable distribution of power, there are consequences. And while some of us are able to walk away from this situation relatively unscathed, there are segments of the community and the world that the State deems it acceptable to harass and intimidate on a daily basis, who face severe consequences. For these people, survival is a political act and breaking the rules means risking routine physical violence or death. This is why struggling against this system of exploitation is so integral—because many of us as people of relative privilege are uniquely positioned to address the legacies of colonialism, hetero-patriarchy, and classism that are the sources of so much violence.

We must seize every opportunity to abolish these institutions of domination. We must be prepared to firmly face the politics of business-as-usual. And we must continue to work for nothing less than full liberation.

The following statement was read by Garrett Fitzgerald before his sentencing at the plea hearing of October 19, 2010. Without giving a reason—representative of her childish behavior all along—Judge Teresa Warner refused to allow him to quote the passage below from "The Lorax" in its entirety.

1.   Judge, I have pleaded guilty to Conspiracy to Damage Property and you are preparing to judge and sentence me. Acting in your official capacity on behalf of this system, you will stand opposed to any law being broken. But as you pass judgment, by your own rules, you are encouraged to consider my motives and character. While I'm sure I have done things in my life that you would look down on and have ideas in my head that you would disagree with, I can't help but wonder if beyond the veil of slander hung by the prosecutors and the Ramsey County Sheriff's Office, there aren't actions I have taken and paths I have chosen in my life that you may not only agree are good, but—dare I postulate—you may even find noble.

I have dedicated my life to the service of my community. As has been said often already, I work as a preschool teacher. One of the schools I teach at is for at-risk children—kids from families with histories of abuse. Children suffering from the effects of environmental racism: poisoned as infants, and even before, by lead or arsenic. Many of them lack positive male role models in their lives. I teach them that not all men hit when they're angry. I teach them that they can work out their problems together if they cooperate. I teach them to be proud of themselves and respectful of each other. As part of teaching these things, I must model them. And I promise that if any of the other teachers I work with were called upon, they would say that I do this with great commitment and integrity.

Along with working with kids, I have a long history of working in horizontally organized groups and have recently begun teaching workshops to adults in how to better share power and responsibility when working collectively.

I was back in your chambers, Judge, about a year and

a half ago while volunteering as a legal assistant on another
RNC case. I hadn't known the defendants before the RNC, but
they were in need of help and I was capable of helping them, so
I did. It wasn't a question. I wasn't paid or traded or promised
anything. It was simply the right thing to do.

Throughout my life, I have lived in voluntary poverty
in order to spend more time working to better the lives of others
around me. In the past year alone, I have been a part of serving
free meals to all who would want them, raising funds to provide
midwives for pregnant women in prison, and speaking out
against racism in my community. I am committed to a life of
sobriety; I don't drink alcohol, smoke, or do any drugs. I come
from a small family, and over the past months I have been the
closest family member in proximity to my grandmother and have
been her primary support.

I broke the law and will serve the sentence you impose.
Know, however, that my breaking of the law was not wanton or
unprincipled; rather, it is a result of my principles and work for a
better world.

2.   Throughout this case, there has been a lot of talk on
behalf of the State. From the very first reports coming out of
the Ramsey County Sheriff's Office, the approach to this case
has been exaggerated and overblown. Personally, I have never
claimed there was no illegal activity, but the State's response is
the equivalent of staking out a street corner for a week to catch a
jaywalker or setting up an FBI sting to catch a teenage shoplifter.
We openly questioned and debated the authority of the State,
and they had $50 million in federal funding to find a way to
burn us. That is what makes this case political. It's not that we
didn't break the law. It's that we were specifically targeted for
investigation because of our political beliefs.

We filed a Franks motion to draw attention to the
exaggeration in the story as told by the State and I hope that,
in spite of your not granting the motion, some bit of truth was
revealed. I have told you in the factual basis for my plea what I
am guilty of. That does not mean I am guilty of every slanderous
accusation that the State and Ramsey County Sheriff's Office

have heaped upon me.

3. I am just about finished with my remarks, but to better illustrate my position, I would like to read from one of my favorite books. I read this book with the young people I work with and I believe it is fitting for this situation. The book is *The Lorax* by Dr. Suess. To set it up briefly, a child has walked to a desolate wasteland on the outskirts of town to meet the Once-ler and hear the story of what happened to the Lorax. The Once-ler begins:

> It all started way back...
> such a long, long time back...
> Way back in the days when the grass was still
> green and the pond was still wet
> and the clouds were still clean,
> and the song of the Swomee-Swans rang out in space...
> one morning, I came to this glorious place.
> And I first saw the trees!
> The Truffula Trees!
> The bright-colored tufts of the Truffula Trees!
> Mile after mile in the fresh morning breeze.
> And, under the trees, I saw Brown Bar-ba-loots
> frisking about in their Bar-ba-loot suits
> as they played in the shade and ate Truffula
> Fruits.
> From the rippulous pond
> came the comfortable sound
> of the Humming-Fish humming
> while splashing around.
> But those trees! Those trees!
> Those Truffula Trees!
> All my life I'd been searching
> for trees such as these.
> The touch of their tufts
> was much softer than silk.
> And they had the sweet smell
> of fresh butterfly milk.

I felt a great leaping
of joy in my heart.
I knew just what I'd do!
I unloaded my cart.
In no time at all, I had built a small shop.
Then I chopped down a Truffula Tree with one chop.
And with great skillful skill and with great speedy speed,
I took the soft tuft. And I knitted a Thneed!
The instant I'd finished, I heard a ga-Zump!
I looked.
I saw something pop out of the stump
of the tree I'd chopped down. It was sort of a man.
Describe him?...That's hard. I don't know if I can.
He was shortish. And oldish.
And brownish. And mossy.
And he spoke with a voice
that was sharpish and bossy.
"Mister!" he said with a sawdusty sneeze,
"I am the Lorax. I speak for the trees.
I speak for the trees, for the trees have no tongues.
and I'm asking you, sir, at the top of my lungs"–
he was very upset as he shouted and puffed–
"What's that THING you've made out of my
Truffula tuft?"
"Look, Lorax," I said. "There's no cause for alarm.
I chopped just one tree. I am doing no harm.
I'm being quite useful. This thing is a Thneed.
A Thneed's a Fine-Something-That-All-People-Need!
It's a shirt. It's a sock. It's a glove. It's a hat.
But it has other uses. Yes, far beyond that.
You can use it for carpets. For pillows! For sheets!
Or curtains! Or covers for bicycle seats!"
The Lorax said,
"Sir! You are crazy with greed.
There is no one on earth
who would buy that fool Thneed!"
But the very next minute I proved he was wrong.
For, just at that minute, a chap came along,

and he thought that the Thneed I had knitted was great.
He happily bought it for three ninety-eight.
I laughed at the Lorax, "You poor stupid guy!
You never can tell what some people will buy."
"I repeat," cried the Lorax,
"I speak for the trees!"
"I'm busy," I told him.
"Shut up, if you please."
I rushed 'cross the room, and in no time at all,
built a radio-phone. I put in a quick call.
I called all my brothers and uncles and aunts
and I said, "Listen here! Here's a wonderful chance
for the whole Once-ler Family to get mighty rich!
Get over here fast! Take the road to North Nitch.
Turn left a Weehawken. Sharp right at South Stitch."
And, in no time at all,
in the factory I built,
the whole Once-ler Family
was working full tilt.
We were all knitting Thneeds
just as busy as bees,
to the sound of the chopping of Truffula Trees.
Then...
Oh! Baby! Oh!
How my business did grow!
Now, chopping one tree
at a time
was too slow.
So I quickly invented my Super-Axe-Hacker
which whacked off four Truffula Trees at one smacker.
We were making Thneeds
four times as fast as before!
And that Lorax?...
He didn't show up any more.
But the next week
he knocked
on my new office door.
He snapped, "I'm the Lorax who speaks for the trees

which you seem to be chopping as fast as you please.
But I'm also in charge of the Brown Bar-ba-loots
who played in the shade in their Bar-ba-loot suits
and happily lived, eating Truffula Fruits.
"NOW...thanks to your hacking my trees to the ground,
there's not enough Truffula Fruit to go 'round.
And my poor Bar-ba-loots are all getting the crummies
because they have gas, and no food, in their tummies!
"They loved living here. But I can't let them stay.
They'll have to find food. And I hope that they may.
Good luck, boys," he cried. And he sent them away.
I, the Once-ler, felt sad
as I watched them all go.
BUT...
business is business!
And business must grow
regardless of crummies in tummies, you know.
I meant no harm. I most truly did not.
But I had to grow bigger. So bigger I got.
I biggered my factory. I biggered my roads.
I biggered my wagons. I biggered the loads
of the Thneeds I shipped out. I was shipping them forth
to the South! To the East! To the West! To the North!
I went right on biggering...selling more Thneeds.
and I biggered my money, which everyone needs.
Then again he came back! I was fixing some pipes
when that old-nuisance Lorax came back with more
gripes.
"I am the Lorax," he coughed and he whiffed.
He sneezed and he snuffled. He snarggled. He sniffed.
"Once-ler!" he cried with a cruffulous croak.
"Once-ler! You're making such smogulous smoke!
My poor Swomee-Swans...why, they can't sing a note!
No one can sing who has smog in his throat.
"And so," said the Lorax,
"–please pardon my cough–
they cannot live here.
So I'm sending them off.

"Where will they go?…
I don't hopefully know.
"They may have to fly for a month…or a year…
To escape from the smog
you've smogged-up around here.
"What's more," snapped the Lorax. (His dander was up.)
"Let me say a few words about Gluppity-Glupp.
Your machinery chugs on, day and night without stop
making Gluppity-Glupp. Also Schloppity-Schlopp.
And what do you do with this leftover goo?…
I'll show you. You dirty old Once-ler man, you!
"You're glumping the pond
where the Humming-Fish hummed!
No more can they hum, for their gills are all gummed.
So I'm sending them off. Oh, their future is dreary.
They'll walk on their fins and get woefully weary
in search of some water that isn't so smeary."
And then I got mad.
I got terribly mad.
I yelled at the Lorax, "Now listen here, Dad!
All you do is yap-yap and say, 'Bad! Bad! Bad! Bad!'
Well, I have my rights, sir, and I'm telling you
I intend to go on doing just what I do!
And, for your information, you Lorax,
I'm figgering on biggering
and BIGGERING
and BIGGERING
and BIGGERING,
turning MORE Truffula Trees into Thneeds
which everyone, EVERYONE, EVERYONE needs!"
And at that very moment, we heard a loud whack!
From outside in the fields came a sickening smack
of an axe on a tree. Then we heard the tree fall.
The very last Truffula Tree of them all!
No more trees. No more Thneeds.
No more work to be done.
So, in no time, my uncles and aunts, every one,
all waved me good-bye.

They jumped into my cars
and drove away under the smoke-smuggered stars.
Now all that was left 'neath the bad-smelling sky
was my big empty factory…
the Lorax…
and I.
The Lorax said nothing. Just gave me a glance…
just gave me a very sad, sad backward glance..
as he lifted himself by the seat of his pants.
And I'll never forget the grim look on his face
when he heisted himself and took leave of this place,
through a hole in the smog, without leaving a trace.
And all that the Lorax left here in this mess
was a small pile of rocks, with the one word…
"UNLESS."
Whatever that meant, well, I just couldn't guess.
That was long, long ago.
Bur each day since that day
I've sat here and worried
and worried away.
Through the years, while my buildings
have fallen apart,
I've worried about it
with all of my heart.
"But now," says the Once-ler,
"Now that you're here,
the word of the Lorax seems perfectly clear.
UNLESS someone like you
cares a whole awful lot,
nothing is going to get better.
It's not.
"SO…
Catch!" calls the Once-ler.
He lets something fall.
"It's a Truffula Seed.
It's the last one of all!
You're in charge of the last of the Truffula Seeds.
And Truffula Trees are what everyone needs.

Plant a new Truffula. Treat it with care.
Give it clean water. And feed it fresh air.
Grow a forest. Protect it from axes that hack.
Then the Lorax
and all of his friends
may come back."

4.   The Lorax voiced protest. He asked and pleaded with the Once-ler to stop chopping down the Truffula Trees. He appealed to the Once-ler's sense of morality and ethics, but in the end, the last of the Truffula Trees still fell. The Bar-ba-loots, Swomee-Swans, and Humming-Fish all had to leave. Oh, but the Once-ler was just doing his job, making Thneeds. If the sky fills with "smogulous smoke" and the lake with Gluppity-Glup and Schloppity-Schlopp…well, it can't be his concern. What we allow and what we don't says a lot about who we are as a society. In the past few years, I have heard judges, politicians, police, and all the other Once-lers say that it isn't their job to confront systemic injustice and I have to ask, "Then whose job is it?" It's our job, and it's my job, and it's yours and yours and yours and unless someone out there cares a whole awful lot, nothing is going to get better. It's not.

Monica Bicking

When I got the phone call from my lawyer that, along with Eryn's and Luce's, my charges had been dropped I was ecstatic. I was jumping up and down and bouncy for hours. A huge weight had been lifted off my shoulders. The case had become such a normal and integral part of my life that I didn't realize the constant strain I was under until it was gone. The relief I felt was profound.

Intellectually I realized that many issues would arise for the remaining defendants with our absence, but my relief was overpowering. Prior to our charges being dropped I had discussed the possibility that Luce's and my charges could be dropped. There was very little evidence specifically about us and we had some of the most competent lawyers of the team. It seemed like it would be a strategic move on the prosecution's part because it would cause extreme inner turmoil on our end and potentially make their case easier. The prosecution saw this opportunity as well, and the outfall was not far from what we imagined.

Our relationships with the lawyers had always been rocky surrounding money and a few other issues, but I didn't envision the relationships becoming as destructive as they did. We got a glimpse of how the lawyers were going to act as trial approached a few months earlier when Erik took a plea. While we were mad at Erik, the break was cordial. The remaining seven put out a statement saying that we disagreed with his decision but hoped that people would continue to support him.

The lawyers were furious with us. They were mad that we didn't spin it as a positive and felt that we had betrayed Erik. As far as I know they jumped to all of these conclusions without ever asking Erik how he felt. Looking at how things turned out in the end, I think they were so upset because part of them was hoping that we would all take pleas and our statement made it clear that that was not our intention. They were never prepared to go to trial and a plea would and did make their job much simpler. We had argued with them before, but the tone of this argument was much nastier. They insulted our politics, what we did prior to the convention, and put themselves on a pedestal for even taking the case. It was with this same tone that arguments about whether to take a plea or not with the final four defendants occurred. Garrett's character and politics were attacked because he wanted to go to trial by attorney after attorney. Defendants' legitimate fears were used to manipulate and coerce them into taking a plea.

There are many reasons that people take pleas. The court system is designed for defendants to take pleas and for it to be their best option. Despite this, I always wanted to see the RNC 8 case go to trial. I felt that we were in the best position to do so. We had fundraised more than anyone expected and had enough money to go to trial. We had a broad array of support, from anarchists to more mainstream liberals throughout the country. The initial charges that included the terrorist enhancements and the political nature of the case were a large part of why we got so much attention and support. We had a competent and dedicated core defense committee. I wanted to go to trial to take advantage of these privileges. I wanted to go to trial because, unlike so many people, we could.

Part of why we could have gone to trial is that the consequences of a guilty verdict were minimal. We were not facing much jail time and a felony on our records would not have extremely tampered with our lives. While we would all have to shift our activities slightly with felonies I did not think that it would be that dramatic of a shift. The real damage had already been done. We are all on the government's list. We will all be harassed in future organizing efforts. We will all likely face charges again sometime, including felonies.

I did not just want to go to trial because we could and because it wasn't going to be that bad if we lost, but because I think that it is important that somebody does. Every person who goes to trial makes it easier for the next person to go to trial, giving people more choices when caught in terrible situations. Trial gives people the chance of being found not guilty. Perhaps more importantly, going to trial makes the prosecution and the State's job harder. It makes it harder for them to take us down. The prosecution wants a plea; that's why they offer it, and I was hoping we would be the case that would refuse to make their job easy for them. Ultimately we weren't. Defendants were not confident in their decisions and their lawyers did not want to take it to trial.

While I see the pleas as a loss of a project that I had been working on for two years, I gained a lot of skills. I plan to take whatever I can from this experience to better my organizing in the future and to keep fighting. This hasn't slowed me down, but rather given me the fuel to keep going.

Rob Czernik

The reader at this point will notice I haven't said anything. My life, like most, is a complicated jumble of situations and experiences that brought me to where I am today. Let me just say that I am 35 years old and have been involved in way or another in the "movement" for 18 or so of those years. I've been beaten up by cops on more than one occasion, played cat and mouse in the forests, smelled tear gas and pepper spray more than I care to recall. I've seen friends jailed and ex-friends become snitches. I've cried when I people I admired and been inspired by died way too soon, in tragic and heroic ways. I've run from cops in the streets and sat down and been dragged away in the forests.

I say this because I feel like I've given a lot of myself to the movement. I've thrown myself against the machine a lot over the years, and I will continue to until I die. It had actually been over 7 years since I had any problems with the police until our arrests began in late August of 2008. And since then, the support the eight of us received was unlike anything I had ever seen. We fought really hard for two years. And it created a situation where charges were dropped for some and the deals become an option for others. I'm not happy that Garrett felt pressure to take the deal, as he wanted to go trial, and I am saddened that I played a role in that pressure by not being more assertive in supporting his decision, and by basically attacking him for choosing to go forth. I apologize for my role in that.

Eryn Trimmer

I could have been one of the defendants who took a plea at the eleventh hour in this case. I've often been the sort of person who tags along with the group. In this case "the group" (the defendants) was all about going to trial, and then once the three of us had our charges dropped, the defendants were mostly into taking pleas.

At the beginning of our case I was scared of going to jail/prison and unsure whether or not going to trial was the best way to move forward from my values as an anarchist. I was worried that seeking any kind of "justice" through the court system, even if not only by seeking a "not guilty verdict," bordered on martyrdom or "bearing witness" as the world burns. I wasn't sure it was a battle that made sense. For the first year or so of the case, I lived with these nagging thoughts as we wrote statements that talked about fighting these precedent-setting charges all the way. I wasn't sure if going to trial was the best strategy, and I wasn't sure I wanted to make the personal sacrifices involved.

However, there came a point when I realized that I didn't want to approach this aspect of my life as simply a follower, and I decided to make a decision, and that decision was to go to trial. Once I made the decision the burden of holding thoughts that conflicted with my actions was relieved. The worries about jail and a felony lifted greatly as well. Once looked at straight on, the consequences really weren't that high at all, especially compared to what a lot of people, in a lot worse positions than me, have to face. Going to trial would expose the surveillance and repression that we faced, draw attention to non-sanctioned ways of resisting, and tell the State that they aren't going to simply intimidate anarchists into easy convictions.

The support in our case was immense, and that is one of the big reasons I am so disappointed the case ended in pleas. We were in a very good position to take this to trial. We had money, positive publicity, a well-functioning support committee, relatively large numbers of the public on our side, a legal team that was challenged (and challenging) but nonetheless who I believe would have pulled together a solid defense, almost no criminal history, supportive codefendants (we weren't in it alone), and a myriad of other privileges. Most people facing off against the legal system are lucky to have one of these things, let alone all of them. In a system that uses isolation and the threat of higher consequences to deter trials, we were in a position to be able to mitigate those consequences, no matter the verdict.

Afterthoughts

After Erik took a plea the seven of us remaining all agreed to go to trial, and we sent that agreement out to hundreds of our supporters. Apparently Rob, Max, and Nathanael hadn't really made this decision and were okay with going back on their word. Partly I would guess this is because they knew that our supporters would understand that it was their decision, since they were facing the brunt of the consequences. While this is true, this was a very destructive way of going about this decision. I feel as though we strung on hundreds of supporters for over two years about going to trial (and spent tens of thousands of their dollars in the process). I fear we damaged the credibility of future cases. The way the pleas went down was especially unfair to Garrett, the only defendant left who still wanted to go to trial. The lawyers deserve much of the blame for the bullying of Garrett, but it was with the codefendants that I felt real solidarity (and therefore had higher expectations of). I thought we had something good going on, and still think that we did, but it wasn't as strong as I thought.

Our being "in solidarity" with one another was easy when it was an easy situation; trial was somewhere in the distant future and we could simply go around raising support for our case, go through our mountains of discovery, and occasionally meet with the lawyers. This was effective to a certain degree. We were able to get the terrorism charges dropped and raise enough support to let the State know this wasn't going to be an easy battle.

While we could all easily say that we were fine with going to trial (apparently for some without it meaning much) it was no secret that we weren't all on the same page. However, we could gloss over the fact that there was a broad difference in the commitment to go to trial because there wasn't any pressure on that fissure. Except for Erik's plea, major conflicts didn't arise until the pressure of an impending trial was applied. By dropping some of our charges, the State was able to leverage the fact that we weren't really on the same page brilliantly.

This was a unique situation in some ways, being that we were chosen by the State and that we didn't get to choose who we were working with. However, given the small size of the communities many of us work in, similar situations are not uncommon. I think it is important for people to make sure they are as much on the same page as possible before extreme pressure is applied. Despite attempting to do this, by things like getting commitments from everyone that we were going to go to trial and talking about the fact that they were going to offer better plea deals at the eleventh hour, we were still not upfront with ourselves and each other about being in very different places when it came to this.

Not everyone had made the decision, in themselves, that they wanted to go to trial, but apparently had said so to please others. Saying things to please others while having doubts is something I have done many times before, and I have personal experience with the destruction it can wreak on relationships. If we are going to be able to withstand criminal charges and other onslaughts by the State (and indeed we must if we want to win), thought-through personal decisions and honest commitments must be the building blocks of our solidarity.

Max Specktor

The court is a tricky arena for political battles. Accepting a plea deal in the final days of our hectic trial preparations definitely let out a lot of the steam that our case gathered. But what would all of this heat have looked like at a trial? Certainly it would have sent a clear message to the people following our case that regardless of what the State calls us, we stand by our beliefs and our convictions. And we could have set a legal precedent that the State can't come after us for our political beliefs. We could have exposed the methods and tactics that the police used in pursuing the RNC Welcoming Committee. We also could have lost and sent a message that our political battle against the State sometimes resembles an actual war.

I, for one, never placed much weight on the idea of setting legal precedents. I wanted to set a precedent for political support for people in trouble, but I don't believe that another law will keep the State from crushing the lawless. I never prioritized, or committed enough energy to, the legal preparations for our trial. By the time it came around it seemed that our whole legal team was scrambling, and a large part of this energy was devoted to securing favorable plea deals. I never had asked my lawyers to negotiate anything on my behalf, but eventually some of our lawyers did it anyways. Staring at a deal that guaranteed no jail time, while considering the option of risking it all at trial, was no easy task.

The deciding factor for me was an acknowledgement that fighting the State is not the only fight I consider important. Anarchists and revolutionaries need to struggle everyday against systems of oppression and exploitation that run much deeper than the foundations of our city halls and county jails. The unfortunate truth is that we negotiate our way through many of these battles: accepting a shitty deal on rent with our landlord or remaining silent at work when somebody is sexually harassed. I wish to be as uncompromising as possible with my life, but I have no interest in running and hiding someplace where this might be possible.

Instead of courts and judges, I believe in accountability. As such I would like to remain accountable to the people who have helped ensure my continued freedom. Part of this accountability means that I will continue to do the work that I consider important. I am committed to dismantling the institutions and systems that divide people between criminals and citizens, immigrants and patriots, deviants and desirables, and workers and bosses. To be clear, I don't give a fuck if what I do falls within the parameters of the law, but I will of course remain law abiding during the term of my probation.

At this point, I'm a little curious to know what the investigators, the judges, and the prosecutors are thinking. Do they feel as though they've found justice? Was this just another annoying case for them to deal with until their workday was over? Or did this send a clear message that it isn't easy to fuck with strong communities of resistance? I believe they will go back to their mechanical repetitions in their justice factory, with the tiniest of itches in the backs of their heads, the smallest hint of defeat. This little itch will be a reminder that when you corner a dangerous animal, it becomes that much more aggressive, a reminder that they tried to bring us down and failed. And one day we will bring down everything, everything that holds up their petty positions of power.

Luce Guillén-Givins

Most of my reflections on our case pertain to the seven of us—Max, Garrett, Rob, Nathanael, Monica, Eryn and myself—who were actually a part of the Welcoming Committee, and who had entered into a project together and developed a sense of camaraderie over the course of it. But I want to briefly explain what happened with Erik before getting into the rest. Erik decided to take a plea agreement to gross misdemeanor conspiracy to commit criminal damage to property in August of 2010.

The rest of us weren't happy with the decision, but it was always true that Erik, while not interested in disrupting our defense campaign, was also not interested in having an active or influential role in it. His politics and interests were so different from ours that the possibility of genuine unity was always just beyond our grasp; he had chosen to work with most of us, and we him before the RNC, and we were thrown together by forces out of our control.

Yet we all agreed that it made sense to stick together and try and support each other, and I think most of us made real efforts to bridge the divides that existed between us. When he decided to take his plea, I was furious, and I find his political and personal explanations for it unconvincing. In fact, all of the remaining codefendants were upset, and we found the process of dealing with his decision so difficult that we agreed that if anyone else was going to want to take a plea at some point, it was best to do it then, with Erik, to spare the collective further turmoil.

The seven of us all agreed that we were more committed

to trial than ever, and that there was no way we'd put everyone through something like this again by taking a plea later. It was one of the only times in two years that each of us participated so enthusiastically in a group decision, the only time that everyone spoke up clearly and resolutely and on the same page.

We decided, in conversation with Erik, that at the point that he severed his case it no longer made sense for us to fundraise and organize support for him. We didn't want people to stop supporting him, but we felt it more appropriate that the circle of people he said were his actual friends and supporters— which we were clearly excluded from—and who were not contributing to our support at that point, be the ones to bottom-line his support in the final months of his case.

This decision has been criticized quite intensely by some, but I stand by it and want to firmly contradict the idea that we owed it to Erik to do more at that point. Our decision came from a place of recognition about the fact that, over the course of almost two years, the other seven of us had all made contributions of one sort or another to fundraising, support-building and media work, which he had not. While his reasons for that may have been legitimate, at the point that he was making a decision we did not support, it didn't seem fair to ask us to continue doing for him something he had never done for us. From what I was party to, the split seemed fairly amicable; we weren't out for blood, we were just setting a firm boundary for ourselves and our labor that felt like a necessary step in being able to respect his decision.

Now that the case is resolved with four more plea agreements, I've tried to reflect on my own reaction to Erik's decision. I stand by my original thoughts, and I doubt we will ever see eye to eye on anything about it, but having watched the utter breakdown of our solidarity over the subsequent two months, I do have a new appreciation for his willingness to do what he felt he needed to do in a way that didn't force anyone else onto the same path. Though it didn't feel like this at the time, his actions created far less drama and strife than what came later. While I value collectivity and the process of learning to hear, understand, and prioritize needs and desires outside of your own, I also see a lot of value in the ability to own your own decisions firmly enough that you can make them alone.

On September 16, 2010 the prosecutor dropped charges against Eryn, Monica, and me. On October 19, 2010 Rob, Max, Nathanael, and Garrett pleaded out to gross misdemeanor conspiracy charges. Since then, I've had several focal points in my reflection. I've been reviewing my own beliefs about the fight we were engaged in and my reasons for wanting to go to trial, as well as the destructive role that attorneys played in our case and the question of whether we could have done things differently with them to avoid this.

And, perhaps most importantly, I've been replaying the breakdown of internal solidarity among defendants in the weeks before the final plea hearing. Though I cannot imagine a scenario in which I would have felt that plea agreements were the best resolution to the case, it is the internal process by which they were secured that leaves me so angry and upset.

So, what did I think was going on with this case in the first place? As we've all said over and over again, Ramsey County's investigation and decision to prosecute us was politically motivated. The fact that they alleged many, various, and noticeably different conspiracies over the course of the whole thing speaks to the fact that the State never had a clear idea of what exactly they were even accusing us of doing, and of course the nature of conspiracy charges is so vague and amorphous that this didn't matter.

I can say, truthfully, that I never conspired to commit damage to property or riot at the 2008 RNC. I can also say that, in my opinion, the conversations and small actions taken by some of my codefendants that may have tended more in that direction actually amount to little more than shit-talking, posturing and pipe dreams. None of this is to say that I have any ethical opposition to the things we were accused of, or that I would have tried to disrupt such plans if I had known about them, but for strategic reasons I had no real personal interest in rioting or vandalism at the RNC.

That all said, it should be understood that going to trial was a serious risk for all eight of us. I believed that, with a good defense strategy, we had a real chance of acquittal, but there was no guarantee of that outcome. And that wasn't really what it was about for me. I refused to consider plea offers or proactively engage in plea negotiations from the beginning, resolute in my decision that I would fight this either until trial or until they dropped all the charges. This was for a number of different reasons, which I think still had merit after my own charges were dropped six weeks before trial.

First, the court system has been perfectly honed as a way of extracting pleas. The "right to a trial" doesn't exist in real terms for most defendants. Whether because they are, in fact guilty and exercising that right will only mean harsher sentencing in the end, or because they're innocent but are likely enough to get convicted anyway because of the biases of judges, prosecutors, and jurors, trials are a huge risk for individuals. Additionally, officers of the court have a vested interest in avoiding them; this includes defense attorneys, who obviously have a huge impact on a defendant's chances at trial.

In a plea hearing, a defendant is asked if they were pressured or offered anything to plead guilty. They have to answer "no" if they want the judge to accept the plea, and so they do, but this reply is of course patently false. People take pleas because they're afraid of what will happen if they don't, often because of explicit threats from prosecutors. That's how the court system is designed to work, creating a situation where cops and prosecutors rule the day, and being arrested—which can happen simply because of the color of your skin or the street you hang out on or your refusal to bend to illegitimate authority—is as good as being convicted.

This system operates at greatest expense to marginalized and oppressed communities throughout the country, and a commitment to fighting for those communities must include a commitment to pushing back at the court system itself. Not everyone facing criminal charges is in a position to resist in these circumstances, which I believe makes it all the more important that those of us with the privileges and position to resist do so. We may not have had the best chance of winning, but we had a better chance than most people ever do, and we also had enough support and resources through our movement to seriously mitigate the damage done by incarceration and any felonies on our records. I'm not naïve enough to suggest that going to trial would have turned back the tide of the State, but we've all heard that line about little drops making the mighty ocean. Rather than holding back 'til we have an ocean's worth of fight in us, I believe we should start building drop by drop now.

Second, we said all along that we were being targeted for the work that many were engaged in, and the charges were a warning to the whole movement and the public at large. Though the situation bore more immediate personal consequences for the eight of us, our prosecution was a prosecution of the movement, so our decisions were also movement-based decisions. I don't believe we can build a movement on decisions made out of self-interest. We need to take care of ourselves, but we also need to acknowledge that our actions affect other people, in particular when we have asked them to work with us and support us. We spent two years building support around the idea that our case stood out because of the insidious nature of terrorism and conspiracy charges—they present an incredible threat to any organized movement—and that we would go to trial unless all those charges were dropped because we all need to be pushing back as hard as we can.

We can't guarantee our own wins, but in seeking them we can determine how hard we make it for the government to undermine and attack us. I poured my life into the case because I believed in that fight, and people supported us because they believed in it too. In the end, what we had articulated as a bigger movement struggle was reduced to personal decisions on the part of the remaining defendants. Our movement is small and weak enough that it's totally understandable that people don't feel moved to make decisions that involve personal sacrifice, or to risk losing at trial just for the sake of putting up their best fight. But I do not believe we can build real movement strength and capacity without starting to make those decisions. So my question is, if not now, when is the right time to start acting like the movement we want to be?

Third, I believed that the worst consequences we faced,

frankly, just weren't that bad: a couple years in prison at most, and felonies on our records. If that's all it takes to stop anarchists in their tracks, then we don't have much hope. People keep telling me that felony convictions would have been a bigger deterrent to future organizing than pleading out to lesser charges. I think this is true, but my problem is that it is precisely this reality that I wanted to start to change with our case.

Is a movement of people unwilling to risk felonies and short prison sentences a movement strong enough to win? I hoped we would see acquittals at trial but, more importantly, I hoped that even if we saw convictions we would have had the opportunity to show that while we are not yet strong enough to end state repression, we can support and care for those who stand up to it. In my mind, this is part of laying the groundwork for a truly revolutionary movement.

I'm not suggesting that we should ignore the real impact of felony convictions and incarceration on individuals and movements, or that we should charge forward with reckless disregard for consequences. But I am saying that as long as mere felony convictions—which a few million people in this society manage to live with every single day—deter people, we're cheating ourselves out of the potential to win.

If the State knows that felonies are enough to hold us back, then all they have to do to kill our movements is to start levying felony charges against more and more of us. There's nothing on their side to stop them, and in an era where conspiracy charges rule the day and the public is more sympathetic to the prosecution than ever, activists who think they couldn't easily be found guilty of conspiracy are fooling themselves. We have to know that we will take knocks and sustain losses, and we have to be prepared to move forward anyway. Felonies avoided through plea bargains aren't real movement victories. They're watered-down losses for us, playing into the hands of a system that is perfectly designed to extract them. I don't want to suggest that every radical facing felonies should go to trial every time. But again, we were better positioned than most in terms of the maximum sentences we faced to fight this to trial.

Most of my codefendants who took plea agreements have said a lot of things to explain their decisions that may sound reasonable, but they are such a severe contradiction to the things they said previously and the actions they took, that I can't accept them as genuine and sincere. Among these explanations is the idea that the case changed fundamentally with the removal of Eryn, Monica, and me. The three of us always looked "less culpable" in terms of the evidence presented by the State, mostly because we had less exposure to the informants and talked less shit in meetings. A part of our trial strategy was that throwing the "least culpable" defendants in with the so-called most culpable would water down the appearance of criminality in front of a jury, increasing the chance of acquittal for those who entered with the worst chances individually.

But conspiracy law is such that if some reasonably foreseeable "overt act" was taken in furtherance of a conspiracy, you're guilty so long as you were party to the original agreement in question. There wasn't any more evidence that the remaining defendants "conspired" together than there was that the eight of us did. If we had all gone to trial, just as if the remaining four had, the prosecution would have truthfully argued to the jury that it didn't matter if we weren't all present for every conversation, it didn't matter if we didn't all know about every little thing that each other defendant or unindicted co-conspirator was doing, and it didn't matter if we were all engaged in non-criminal behavior as well.

In the end, it didn't matter how shaky the "conspiracy" was looking; if the alleged agreements existed between us, we were all guilty. Yet a jury may have been swayed by our pointing out that the initial agreements, a necessary element of each charged offense, didn't exist. The chances of this may have been better with eight of us, but they still existed with only four. What changed fundamentally a month and a half before trial was the proportion of defendants most committed to trial and all the work it entailed, not the nature of the case itself.

Another thing some of the remaining defendants have said is that, as anarchists, they were never really into the legal strategy, the trial preparation required, and the idea of fighting this through the courts in the first place. It's certainly true that the eight—or seven—of us weren't ever equally engaged in the defense, but it's not true that we only pursued the trial path because a few of the defendants wanted to, and that the rest were just begrudgingly along for the ride. We all made those decisions together. Unfortunately, the fact that there were so many of us made it possible for some people to fall back and minimize their engagement and, for the work to proceed anyway.

In being willing to do a disproportionate share of what was required to reach a collectively set goal, those of us bearing that burden helped create the environment in which others were able to divest, paving the road toward plea agreements when most of the people doing most of the work were cut out of the case. I'm also troubled by the suggestion that, because we are anarchists, it doesn't make sense for us to fight on the system's terrain, and that those people who wanted to plead out were doing so because it never made sense for anarchists to go to trial in the first place.

Not a single one of us chose to be prosecuted or wanted to deal with what would have been an incredibly difficult trial, logistically and emotionally. The courts don't offer us a level playing field, but neither do our workplaces, our cities, or for that matter, most of our personal relationships. Whether on trial or on the streets, we're never fully setting the terms, because a movement with the strength to come up against the State doesn't exist.

But I, for one, am committed to dealing with the realities around me, and while I struggle to find ethical ways of navigating a society that is fundamentally unethical, I also understand that we have to start laying the groundwork now, in our present realities, rather than opting out and waiting for better conditions. And in the end, I have trouble with the fact that the same people professing a lack of interest in the legal strategy around which we built support only did so after hundreds of hours of work and tens of thousands of dollars raised got them attractive plea bargains.

All other reasons aside, my experience and observation throughout this case has left me feeling that the single most destructive element was our legal team. In addition to my anger and resentment over the way they treated us throughout the case, I also find myself fearful that, should I ever need legal counsel again the Twin Cities, I won't have real options among the activist attorneys doing criminal defense here. I am not sure I could trust any member of our legal team again, and I am equally uncertain that, having vocally and publicly criticized the coercion and abuse that occurred behind the veil of "attorney-client privilege," any of them would willingly represent me.

For me, the whole experience of working with our legal team has been defined by patriarchy[1]. We approached the case with a minority of female defendants and didn't have a single female attorney at the onset. Over two years, two eventually came on board, but women were always a drastic minority, setting the stage for male chauvinism to underlie our entire group dynamic. I don't mean to suggest that my codefendants or most of the men I know and work with don't have a lot of work to do in terms of combating their patriarchal tendencies, but the behaviors that I personally witnessed and was subjected to by our attorneys were appalling and went far beyond what I, as a woman, expect to deal with among people who identify as progressives and radicals.

For example, when I gave a draft of my section of this book to my attorney to review from a legal perspective, he felt it appropriate to offer his personal opinion on my decision to have an abortion, which I had described in the draft. He told me that my decision was "irrational" and not based on sound reasoning and asked if my having been pregnant and hormonal was the "real" reason I had once gotten mad at him for calling me late at night to demand a payment. Additionally, he and another attorney made frequent reference to my relationship with Rob in a manner that painted me as a stereotypically nagging and controlling woman, offering him sympathy—directly and through innuendo—for having to put up with me. They were essentially reducing my role and stake in the case to being defined by my boyfriend, rather than my independent status as a defendant, someone with political agency, and a person who had devoted countless hours of hard work both to the legal team and the support committee.

Having pegged me as one sort of female archetype (the control freak pulling the strings), the lawyers also pegged Monica as another, refusing to respect her as a person with her own opinions and investment in the case. While they heard what I said with a closed mind and were quick to demonize me, they barely acknowledged Monica's existence, interrupting her as a matter of course in meetings and rarely bothering to seek her opinion on matters that pertained to her as much as to any of us.

Though I was disappointed by the failure of the female attorneys on our team to stand up to such behaviors, I was also struck by the extent to which they too were disrespected by their co-counsel: they were treated as workhorses; given small, tedious tasks that the male attorneys were unwilling to do; and never really asked for their opinions. One was told over and over again that she would do better to talk less and listen more. The list of incidents is longer than I can remember, but ranges from the examples above, to one lawyer's reference to a woman on our list of potential witnesses by her breast size, to pathological and typically patriarchal behaviors like continuously interrupting other people, cracking sexist jokes, and trying to win arguments by casting the opponents as "irrational" and minimizing emotional issues and responses.

The patriarchal propensity for coercion and heavy-handedness that permeated the legal team was of course underscored by other complicated power dynamics around money, decision-making, and their lack of interest in finding positive ways to interact as a team and share the workload equitably. Unfortunately, their behavior leaves me in a place of regret over some of the ways that we had tried to engage them in genuine dialogue around our case.

Though we always maintained that control of our defense fund rightfully belonged to us and our defense committee, in the interest of transparency and honesty, we nonetheless kept our financial books open permanently to the attorneys. Naïvely, we had thought that this would help lay a foundation of trust with the legal team. Instead, it seemed to create endless opportunities for the attorneys to lay claim to every cent we raised and take time that should have gone to trial preparation and replace it with demands that we constantly pay them.

Though generally unspoken, the implication hanging overhead was always that they wouldn't work further until they had more money in their pockets, and their demands were so disruptive that, functionally, this quickly became the reality. The majority of what we raised had gone to them for quite a while, but eventually we started setting a quarter of what we made aside in a "non-attorney" budget line, so that we would have funds available for anticipated trial costs such as expert witnesses, rush transcripts, and other forms of support that we felt a need for, like travel for family members who wouldn't be able to attend court proceedings otherwise.

We started setting this money aside because we felt like they were trying to rob us of every cent we raised, and we knew that if we let them do that, we'd be left covering other support costs out-of-pocket by the time trial came around. We and our supporters did our best to fundraise—in fact, we were incredibly successful, more than any of us imagine we would be—but I understand that the almost $10,000 apiece that the attorneys got is far less than what they might make at their regular rate.

Nonetheless, we paid them what we could, and we never lied about our inability to pay well. I find it hard to sympathize with the position, which they frequently repeated, that because of their law degrees and their years of experience, they "deserve" the $250/hour or so they usually bill. They tried to cast this as a class issue, as if we were the bosses trying to cheat them out of their hard-earned money. But of course, all eight of us live at or around the poverty line, many of us come from working-class families who struggle to get by, as do many of our supporters, and there's a huge difference between a livable wage and a standard attorney's rate. We weren't trying to cheat them out of anything; we believed that they had entered into the case understanding our financial limitations, knowing they would be donating labor, and that the best we could promise was to donate our own labor as well, which we did.

The suggestion that we had more real power in this

situation than they did, when we needed them because the State had backed us up against a wall in a court system designed by and for the ruling class, is absurd. Many of our attorneys are decent people who are trying to navigate their chosen field with political and personal integrity, but it takes a lot more than good intentions to fight the current. The result of the constant battle over payment was that the legal team was underprepared for trial as it approached, that feelings of bitterness coursed through every meeting, and that so much work was left to do that the little financial incentive we could offer wasn't enough to make trial an attractive prospect for any attorney.

The impression I'm left with is that many of our attorneys are used to situations in which their treatment of clients stays behind closed doors. Any relationship built on the isolation of a vulnerable party is fertile ground for abusive behavior, and our case was not exceptional in this way. Criminal defendants find themselves in an incredibly vulnerable position, and at the moments when it is most important to be surrounded by people whom they trust, and who truly support them, lawyers often encourage them to keep everyone else at bay and recede into the confines of attorney-client privilege.

In what was unfortunately an adversarial relationship with our attorneys, the eight of us benefited greatly from having each other as mutual support. We felt limited in our ability to reach out for needed support beyond those directly involved in the case, and we counted on our codefendants to have our backs. Unfortunately, that level of mutual support fell apart with the dropping of charges against Monica, Eryn and me. Its dissolution was greatly expedited by attorneys eager to avoid a trial and to assert control over decisions and strategy. The three of us were swiftly cut out of the work being done by attorneys and remaining defendants. The attorneys had always wanted to explore plea options, addressing our refusal to do so with condescension and exerting a constant low-level pressure in that direction.

After our charges were dropped, they swept in and encircled the remaining four, taking what they saw as a golden opportunity to finally steer the case toward a non-trial resolution.

They did so with more enthusiasm than they ever displayed in trial preparation, writing email after email pontificating on the "political victory" to be had through a plea bargain and expounding on their reasons for thinking that going to trial was foolish and politically unjustified.

It was clear at this point that Rob, Max and Nathanael were interested in a non-felony plea but that Garrett still wanted very much to proceed to trial, even if he had to do it alone. Rather than respecting this and offering their dedicated trial support to him—which they could have done even as they secured plea bargains for Max, Nathanael, and Rob—the attorneys closed in around him, berating him for being "egotistical" and "selfish" and making it clear that most of them, including the most skilled and experienced attorneys, would not stick around to help out at trial if their respective clients pled out.

Obviously, a defendant going to trial with attorneys who've been dragged there kicking and screaming has a pretty poor shot at acquittal, particularly when the weeks that should have been devoted to trial prep were squandered on infighting and plea negotiations instead. All four of the defendants eventually decided for themselves that taking the plea agreement was the best of several bad options, but the attorneys played a significant and active role in making a trial the worst option on the list. The invectives directed at Garrett in the final weeks leaves me unable to believe that genuine concern for the well-being of the defendants individually or as a group played any role in the legal team's dedication to avoiding the trial.

Ultimately, though, I consider the final resolution of the case to be a failure in our ability to enact anarchist principles. We failed to find a common path forward through consensus and, on the other hand, failed to find ways to move forward on separate but mutually respectful paths. In what I thought at the time was the end of my contribution to this book, I said, "From the onset of our case, we've consciously prioritized building and maintaining an internal trust and sense of collectivity for which I'm grateful. Whatever happens at trial, I feel certain that we'll all emerge with skills in collective organizing and consensus-building that are otherwise in short supply."

Afterthoughts

In the weeks leading up to the end, and the in the days right afterwards, I felt like I watched the trust and solidarity I'd helped build over two years get torn apart from the inside. Where only a few months prior I had felt immensely positive about the relationships I'd built with codefendants, I suddenly found myself so enraged and hurt by the behavior of a few of them that I questioned whether I would ever be able to work with them again.

While I felt enormous relief when my charges were dropped, it came with a fair amount of "survivor's guilt" and was overshadowed by a gut feeling that the next development in the case wouldn't be such a cause for celebration. In fact, many of us had discussed this possible turn of event months prior, agreeing that it would affect the group dynamics in a profoundly negative way. As I tried to balance my own sense of relief with serious concern for Garrett, Rob, Max, and Nathanael, I struggled to find a way to retain some positive role in the case.

I felt especially alienated as I dealt with bewilderment from so many supporters who saw the dropping of our charges as a pure, if partial, victory. Dropped charges don't mean I'll get these two years of my life back. I don't get to just cross my name off the government watch lists now that I'm free of this case. Every time I cross the border to visit my family, I have to consider the possibility that I'll be detained and searched for hours upon return, and I have to think about the fact that I am subjecting my family to that as well. I felt a weight lifted when charges were dropped, and I stopped having nightmares, which had been a nightly occurrence for months. And for the first time in what seemed like forever, I was able to call my mom with good news, rather than adding to her list of things to worry about. But I also understand that I benefited from a strategic move on the part of the prosecution, and what others see as a "win" feels more like the mere end to a bad streak to me.

As I've explained, I don't agree that taking plea deals amounts to any sort of victory for us, and this would likely have been my reaction regardless of the deal itself. But I could come to terms with the personal decisions some of my former codefendants felt compelled to make if not for the coercion that they employed to get there. At the end of the day, the only thing we can do is act with integrity and with a level of care and respect toward our fellow people that this system has sought to make impossible. In fact, this task often does seem impossible, and it is because we were so close to finishing this case in keeping with that goal that it so hard to accept the breakdown.

Nathanael, Max, and Rob had the option of taking their plea agreements and still supporting Garrett through his trial. They could have weighed in on Garrett's side, refusing to let their own decisions be used as fodder in the attorney onslaught against him and affirming as much as necessary, loudly and clearly, to him, to the legal team, and to supporters, that a decision to proceed to trial was a respectable decision for him to make. They didn't, and eventually Garrett found himself in a position where taking the plea made more sense than anything else.

An important concept to me, as an anarchist, is that power and privilege and coercion exist all around us, and within us, and that unless we are actively opposing these forces, we are silently complicit in them. One of my hopes in building our support campaign was that we would begin to construct a new way of doing this sort of support, moving away from the models I've seen of uncritical deference to the person or people receiving support, toward a model where accountability runs both ways, and where we demand a certain level of integrity and thoughtfulness from the people we support. For anarchists, especially, it seems essential to do this work, as one way of dismantling the power structures we oppose while moving forward. I am still committed to this idea, and despite my frustrations, the work around our case has also given me the opportunity to build and deepen relationships with other people who share this vision.

Looking back over those two years, I see powerful examples of the things that we can achieve through collective solidarity. Forcing the government into a position where it was prudent to drop the original terrorism charges, ruining any shot that Susan Gaertner had at becoming governor, and getting the charges against three of us dropped entirely, these were significant events brought about by our hard work. And the broad diversity of supporters that we brought together around our case still amazes me today. Living in the Twin Cities and watching new instances of State repression unfold all the time, it is evident to me that we've made leaps in building a culture of resistance here, and I'm proud to know that I have played a role in that. More than two years after the start of our case, I find myself at a point that I thought about many times, but never knew how to prepare for. The word "grief" comes to mind, and I think best describes the sum of my feelings about the final developments in the case. I have already moved beyond my initial feelings of intense anger and sadness, but I feel like it will be a long time before I am able to rebuild the bonds I saw shattered in the plea process.

With some codefendants, and a great number of supporters, I still feel a level of camaraderie and trust that I am fortunate to have and, despite the tumultuous ending, the process of dealing with our case has been enlightening and, in many ways, empowering. This is the first time in those two years that I have really allowed myself to think about what I might do next, and while I give myself some time and space to figure that out, I do feel more committed than ever to living as a revolutionary and as an anarchist.

Garrett Fitzgerald

Walking upstream, waist deep in a river, one fights for every step. The stronger the current, the harder it is to gain each inch. Even holding position takes effort. With all the work to fight the current, the moment you give in, any gain in ground can be undone in an instant. The same goes for fighting the momentum carried by systems of repression. They have such well-established currents that to do nothing means being swept away. Change comes with constant struggle and can be largely undone if the struggle is relented. For this reason, I greatly value building sustainable communities that foster a culture of resistance.

What does it mean to build a culture of resistance? I believe that a key part is placing social value on positioning oneself in opposition to the momentum of systems of coercion. The slaves who rise up and risk death for a narrow chance at freedom, the tree sitters who make it that much harder to clear cut old-growth forests, all choose to struggle against the current. Often the odds are stacked against those who choose to resist, but for those who dream of a better world, doing nothing is a greater tragedy than fighting and failing.

The whole of the RNC 8 criminal case was born out of our desire and willingness to resist. Whatever it was that people went to the 2008 RNC wanting to fight, no one could have believed that on September 1st we were going to put an end to capitalism, fascism, and imperialism. No one could have believed we were going to deconstruct the most formidable military, economic, and global governmental/political power in history.

Resistance leads to friction. Friction wears on the social order. And so our resistance to the RNC put us in the crosshairs and led to our facing charges. Our resistance to the State and their charges for two years brought us a lot of support and helped build the movement. We helped put forward a clear abolitionist analysis of the Prison Industrial Complex and how it affects all people, not just activists. We built connections and solidarity with political prisoners and others facing charges, anti-fascist organizers, immigrant rights activists, labor groups, and many others, to demonstrate that we are part of one movement for social justice and an end to coercive government and social practices. We offered free meals, co-hosted speakers and other educational events, and held joint fundraisers to share resources and support.

Building the movement around our case is part of what forced the State to make tactical sacrifices—dropping terrorism enhancements and dropping charges completely on three of the eight of us. Still the State continued to push back with the whole apparatus of the court system. The courts, with a force that is low intensity and largely psychological, are isolating, threatening, grating—Kafkaesque with centuries of refinement. Still, for me the effort was to resist, even when all the strength I could muster just meant holding my ground and not being swept away by the current.

As the case was resolving with a plea deal, all I could think about is all the ground that folks fought to gain over those two years and how so much of it ended up being swept away. While hopefully many of the connections we built and analysis we put forward will remain, the great loss will be to the energy we built through our commitment to struggle. I had hoped that taking our case to trial could be part of a shift in how radicals handled charges like ours. Much like how I, as part of the RNC-WC, wanted to encourage anarchists to think bigger and more strategically, I wanted our case to demonstrate another way to challenge the systems of control we stand opposed to. I feel that, because we put that forward as such a key part of our objective, we lost credibility on that issue and demoralized supporters who were standing by us because they shared this understanding. I also think, with all of our relative privilege, we lost credibility as allies by refusing to sacrifice some privilege to confront the systems that subjugate those with less than us.

There is clearly a place in struggle for strategic retreat, but I don't believe this was one of those times. I believe that the way we built the movement over the past two years was not dependent on the defendants winning at trial, but was built on the presumption that we were fighting for something more than ourselves and that we would fight to the end. I wanted to fight all the way through because I believe resistance should be the default, even when the stakes are high. That doesn't mean there aren't times for strategic retreat, but that we value struggle and desire to see our efforts through.

Ultimately, the reasons argued for taking a plea in our case fall into two categories. One was unwillingness by the defendants to sacrifice personal privileges (i.e., the risk of felony charges and the resulting restrictions on future plans). The lawyers trumped up those sacrifices and used the fear of felonies to encourage plea deals. The other was a misplaced responsibility and inflation of the risks to the movement without acknowledging the true potential for movement growth. Those who wanted to see the plea happen (namely, the lawyers) were paternalistic and patronizing, choosing to believe that people who said they would testify didn't really want to or didn't understand what they were doing, that people who gave money would rather it went to something else, and that no one would benefit from our choosing to struggle if we didn't win in the courts. Treating people as naïve was a way of silencing those who believed in the struggle through trial.

So how, in the face of my criticisms of the plea deal, did it come to be that I was a part of it? To understand how it happened, it is first important to acknowledge and name the pressures at play and the directions in which they all were pushing. The most obvious, and therefore the one that takes the least thought and explanation, is the State. There were also pressures beyond those of the State that were caused, effected, or driven internally by members of the legal team and by my codefendants as a unit (or units), as well as individually.

Part of the pressure from the system comes because putting people in jail is big business. The prison system funnels money from civil funds to private industry through contracts to build and maintain prisons and jails. When slavery was abolished, a prison exception was written in, allowing for a free labor pool inside the prison. There are businesses built around extorting prisoners and their families by charging $1.50 a minute for phone calls or $2 for what on the outside would be a 25-cent pack of dried soup.

The business of putting people in jail/prison is greatly expedited by plea agreements. Trials are costly both in terms of money and time. Ramsey County, where we were prosecuted, budgets for only a handful of trials but still manages to put large numbers of people in prison/jail each year. Prosecutors overcharge to pressure people into deals. The system could not work the way it does if plea deals weren't a part of it or if, in mass, people stopped taking them.

Another pressure at play, which turned out to be one of the hardest currents to struggle against, was from our own lawyers. When someone becomes a lawyer, they are sworn to act as an officer of the court. To maintain their ability to practice, they must operate within those constraints. That is the first compromise. Because being a lawyer is a position that the normative American culture values, it is a life path that is less precarious than, say, taking up arms with the Black Liberation Army.

Since lawyers are compromised in the revolutionary work they can do and receiving spoils from their normative status, I believe it is important for lawyers who see themselves as revolutionaries or part of a people's struggle to first and foremost acknowledge these things and humble themselves to the movement. I have met a few lawyers who I believe do this and do it well, and in return have not just won my respect, but have created a relationship with some communality. I can feel that we have different roles in a shared struggle. The lawyers who do it well don't demand accolades for their sacrifices and share as best they can the privileges their position in society has granted.

As a movement for liberation, it is fair for us to expect lawyers who claim to be working for the movement to be accountable to that movement. What often happens, however, and what happened in our case, is that the lawyers involved foster a culture among themselves that is self-congratulatory and unaccountable to others. Instead of looking around the movement at their would-be peers in struggle, they compare themselves to other professional lawyers, who, by contrast, make them seem humble, righteous, and sacrificial. From their perspective, they are doing more important work for less status and financial gain than their non-movement counterparts. The question they should be asking themselves is, "Am I a lawyer who tries to help people out of the goodness of my heart, or am I a peer to others in this common struggle?"

The pressures brought to bear among codefendants can be the hardest to talk about. Rarely were codefendants overtly malicious. Over the course of the first year after the RNC, we worked to build the movement. A feeling of togetherness and solidarity was fostered, although to say such things paints broadly over the detail of what was going on. As lawyers were complaining about money and not doing the work that they had agreed to do, they also grabbed for power and control. I believe they are used to their clients being made vulnerable by the legal system, ceding all their agency over to their lawyers and allowing them to run the show. Each of the defendants was putting in unequal amounts of time and effort into the case, which also led to strained relationships and power disparities. Those of us who were stuck in it and who felt compelled to pour energy into working on the case were few, but we were strong enough together to hold enough power over our own fates to guide the process in a way that we found ethical and movement-building. But we were constantly battling the tensions and currents that surrounded us.

These tensions existed steadily within us defendants as a group and were another pressure at play that led up to the plea agreement. Holding together even the appearance of solidarity among the codefendants was hard at times. We are all different people in different places in our lives, with different political leanings. We all had other things going on in our lives outside the case: different family troubles, different relationship issues, different work situations, and different health concerns. In some ways, our lives were on hold for the case, but the world still spun.

Issues that had been below the surface finally bubbled out when Erik decided to pursue and later accept a plea deal independent from the rest of our work. I was frustrated with Erik. He had been absent for some time from both the legal and political work around our case. My other codefendants and I had worked to include him and, in his absence, be mindful of him; I saw his taking a deal as a blow on all fronts. Other codefendants were angry as well, but we worked not to respond too emotionally and to do right by him. Because Erik had other friends outside the sphere of our local political support who agreed with his decision, he assured us that they would be his base of support as he served his jail time so that the supporters who had been rallying around us to fight the charges and go to trial could have their energy go toward trial support.

The legal team showed some of their agenda and chastised the seven of us remaining defendants for "abandoning"

Erik. They didn't, however, talk to him about what he wanted or how he felt, nor did they acknowledge that it was Erik who had chosen to go in a new direction from the rest of us and how his choice would affect both the legal and political work we were engaged in.

The remaining seven codefendants all expressed frustration with the new situation and everyone agreed that, even if they might consider taking a deal, they wouldn't do it unless everyone agreed to it. Most of us, however, were fully committed to trial and it seemed highly unlikely the prosecutors would offer a deal that even a handful of us would be interested in accepting.

In hindsight, while I would have been upset about it at the time, I think a more genuine expression of true solidarity might have been for Nathanael, Max, and Rob to negotiate alongside Erik to get a deal they all would be interested in. That way, Erik may have gotten a better deal and Nathanael, Max, and Rob could likely have gotten a similar deal to the one they ultimately got. Most importantly, they would have been able to move toward an end that was more in keeping with what they actually wanted rather than allowing themselves to be dragged around for a few more weeks. It would have been easier on Erik politically and, likely, emotionally; and it would not have left him as isolated.

It also would have been better for the remaining four defendants who wanted to see a trial happen. Likely, we four would have gone to trial together, or I may have had my charges dropped along with the other three. Even in a scenario in which they kept the charges on me and just dropped them on the other three, it would have cut down on the animosity between myself and the legal team.

While I believe that Nathanael, Max, and Rob should have taken the deal with Erik and that it was ultimately their responsibility to think through, speak to, and actualize their desires in a way that would cause the least trouble to others, it is important for me to acknowledge that a likely part of why they didn't was that they were pushed to make decisions before they were ready and that efforts to revisit decisions were met with frustration. Further, when anger was clearly expressed concerning Erik's choice to take a deal, that created a disincentive for others who might have some agreement with him to speak or act accordingly.

The problem is that accommodating the needs of those who weren't able to think through and follow their true desires punishes those who work to be more thoughtful and decisive. This approach also devalues the feelings of those who felt strongly by asking them to foreground the feelings of those who were less invested over their own.

Should we have kept our outrage about Erik to ourselves so as to not pressure others? I don't think that's fair, and I think it's important that everyone knew how their actions were affecting everyone else. The State forced us into a position in which we had to be decisive. Should those who were able to be more decisive have sacrificed that advantage in order to accommodate those who, after two years, still had not taken the time to think through their situation to the end? Had that happened, I think things would have ended worse, sooner, and with less movement built.

About a month after Erik took his plea deal, the prosecution made what was its smartest strategic move in the whole two-year process by dropping the charges on three of the remaining seven codefendants. On one level, the people working on the case rejoiced that not all eight were still facing felonies, but some of us knew that it wasn't all good. The three whose charges were dropped and I had been at the center of the work around the case from the beginning. There were often defendant meetings at which only the four of us attended. We had the truest solidarity with each other because it was built on mutual respect and joined efforts. Once the charges were dropped, all my closest allies were marginalized.

When meeting with the legal team shortly after the charges were dropped, the lawyers all smiled and talked about how great it was, but they shared sideways glances and a glint in their eyes. With three strong personalities marginalized, it was easier for the lawyers to run the show. During a discussion on moving forward, one of the lawyers professed that I was "all alone now." I found out later that there were plea discussions with the three other remaining codefendants and some lawyers without me present during which it was asserted that if they worked out a plea deal, I would "come around to it."

Among the remaining four codefendants, internal tensions flared up. I felt things unfolding just like they did during the worst parts of the Welcoming Committee but didn't know how to stop it. If I relented, I didn't trust that smart decisions would be made, especially with the redoubled pressure from the lawyers to take over steering the direction of the case. I also knew from what happened with the RNC-WC that if I had to fight over every decision, I wouldn't have energy left to do the work. At a meeting just a few weeks after the charges had been dropped, I rose out of my seat as a codefendant and I yelled back and forth over each other. It was a nightmare.

On Wednesday, October 6, I was working on case narratives for a mock trial we were spending a good chunk of our defense fund on to organize through the National Jury Project. I received an email from a lawyer saying that he had engaged the prosecutor in negotiations about a plea deal and that we could all plead guilty to gross misdemeanors instead of felonies, which the State had been insisting on for some of the defendants for the past two years. According to the email, the lawyer had been instructed by his client to engage in these negotiations. This was the first I had heard of it, I had certainly not been asked, and I would have said that I did not want it to happen had I been asked.

I talked to some of my codefendants as well as other supporters. Hoping that nothing would come of it, I continued to prepare for the mock trial on October 16 and helped prepare witness information for our investigator. I met with the other three remaining codefendants Thursday night. We had a meeting with the lawyers on Friday morning, so we talked and decided that we would all go to the meeting with the lawyers on Friday and tell them we didn't want the deal and, if we were going to negotiate (which I spoke against), that we only accept all four of us getting misdemeanors. It seemed like we were all on the same page and relatively resolute in this position.

The next morning, the lawyers, with great enthusiasm,

asked that the plea deal be at the top of the agenda. We stated our position, which was angrily dismissed. The lawyers asked, "So what do you want to come back with when they reject that offer?" I stood by our position and said that I wouldn't take anything more than a misdemeanor, that I didn't even want to take a deal and would rather go to trial, but if this case was going to settle, that's what they needed to get for me. I also suggested that if the others were desperate to get out of it, they could take a deal without me, but I wanted to fight.

As the conversation closed, I tried to rally some excitement and asked if there was anyone else who wanted to fight. I said that I was willing to put my neck on the chopping block, knowing we could lose, and that all I wanted was for one lawyer in the room to stand up and say, "Yes, if you are willing to put yourself at risk to resist, I will happily fight all the way, not just for you, but because it is a powerful and meaningful way to struggle." The closest I got, with all my pleadings, was, "It's our job to fight and we can trick ourselves into being enthusiastic if it comes to that."

Throughout the rest of the meeting, no other agenda item involving trial preparation received nearly the enthusiasm as the plea discussions. I met with my lawyers alone after the meeting. I had two relatively inexperienced lawyers. One was young and had never tried a criminal case; the other was more experienced in the courtroom but was licensed in Wisconsin and didn't have a solid grasp of the finer points of Minnesota law. They told me that they didn't feel like they could take me to trial by themselves and, if I wanted to fight the charges, I would need to get other lawyers to help.

Over the next few days, I received a new email or phone call every 30 minutes concerning the plea deal. The lawyer leading the negotiations had effectively cut me out of them by putting on the table right away that the others would take the gross misdemeanor deal without me. My lawyers took turns calling me, telling me how I was stupid not to take the deal, how in their professional opinion it doesn't get any better than this, and that they didn't understand why I would ever want to go to trial, especially by myself. I was told that I would appear narcissistic and would lose support from all but my most hard-core supporters. I knew that this was untrue, but I heard it over and over again as the lawyers' echo chamber fed back the same baseless analysis of the situation.

As things became harder and harder, I was lucky to have the help of a handful of friends and close supporters. I couldn't have held out as long as I did, and it would have been harder to even entertain the idea of going to trial alone without help. My partner, my former codefendants, and close supporters in the defense committee saw that I was in crisis and made themselves available. There were several times when I felt shaken and needed a comrade. I received immediate support that was deep, based not just on care for me, but on a belief that I was working to do the right thing. This included an amount of respect that I wasn't getting anywhere else.

Still, the negotiations moved forward, taking more energy from trial prep. There was a meeting of the Defense Committee that Sunday, and I told them what was going on. They were super supportive of my wanting to go to trial. They agreed that the defendants owed some consideration to the effect their choices would have on the people who spent so much time supporting them. Some of them said they would talk to the other codefendants, none of whom had come to the meeting, and see if they could persuade them to stay the course.

The next night, I talked to my codefendants. The one who had initiated the plea discussions, justifying them by saying he was trying to get better deals for others, said that he was going to take a deal no matter what the rest of us chose to do. He told me that I "was not a Black Panther" and that my ego was a primary reason he was deciding to take a deal. Another said he would consider not taking the deal now, but that he would take one by himself later if we didn't take one soon. The third said he would take the deal if I did, but didn't want to leave me high and dry.

Throughout these days, there was a lot of waffling and changing of minds, and even this meeting was not the end of it, but I feel like it really demonstrated where people were. Some folks might be dragged kicking and screaming through a trial, but at least one was trying to get out ASAP and the other two were shaky and non-committal at best.

The lawyers used the waffling to counter attack, saying that having folks change their positions was wreaking havoc on their professional credibility and the good faith they had built with the prosecutors in the negotiations. Although I was the most unwavering, I was attacked for "manipulating the others away from the choice that was in their best interest." The negotiating lawyer said that they had negotiated instead of doing the work they had agreed to do on the mock trial and said that he now was not going to work on the mock trial at all and was going to walk away from the case as soon as he got his client off. No one offered to step in and take his place on the mock trial.

As I struggled to hold my ground, my life was constantly at a point of great stress—some of the greatest stress I have ever felt, and it never let up. I was nauseated all the time and could hardly eat. I couldn't drink coffee (my greatest love) because my nerves were so shot. I couldn't turn my head past 45 degrees without pain. I barely slept, waking up early in the morning with my heart racing with a mix of panic and dread.

I got more calls from my lawyers and from other lawyers on the legal team asking me to reconsider. Finally, I blew up at my lawyer and told him not to call me to talk about it anymore, that I had told him my position and that was that. He told me he was coming to town and would like to talk.

My two lawyers and I met at a conference room at another lawyer's office. They laid it out, all the same baseless analysis that had been echoing around among the lawyers. My lawyer told me that he was about to hit me over the head with a flashlight. I was told that if I kept doing this sort of work, I was probably going to need a lawyer again someday, but would have a hard time finding a lawyer in this town if I took the case to trial.

They told me that there was a "unanimous consensus" among the lawyers that I was being egomaniacal. That they didn't have enough experience to take me to trial themselves. That they didn't want to go to trial, that they thought we would lose, and things would be worse. That when I lost, I wouldn't be able to teach kids. When I mentioned feeling that the situation was coercive, one lawyer burst out, "I'm not coercing you! How am I coercing you? It's my job to counsel you. I'm counseling you."

At the same time, we heard that the prosecution wasn't willing to extend the offer they had made to just one defendant. At least three people had to take it or they wouldn't offer it. This news caused the other two codefendants to reconsider their previous decision and commitments once again.

I left and took a walk around the block. I called my closest supporters, former codefendants, and other people I knew wanted to see the case go to trial. I cried. I told them I was losing. That I couldn't keep fighting the whole legal team and resist the current that my remaining codefendants were hoping to ride out of the case. That I was sorry. That I never thought I would break like this. That I never thought I would have to fight against so many people who were supposed to be on my side.

In the past four years, I had never "blocked" consensus on a decision for the RNC-WC or for the RNC 8. Now, when I tried to assert myself and not go along with the will of the lawyers and the preferences of my codefendants, I was having all my other options stripped away.

I went back into the office. I said I would take the deal but that I would rather do jail time and "sentence to serve" (a county-run community service program) than pay fines or be on probation. In a final example of how the lawyers failed to understand how anyone could see the world differently from them, they celebrated getting us no jail time but leaving fines and probation up to the judge.

So I took a deal, feeling stripped of all the tools I had worked to develop in order to fight. I have had a lot of friends and supporters tell me that it is okay, that they still care about me and still appreciate the fight. While their support is meaningful, I want people to feel that it's okay to be pissed, that it's okay for them to say, "Damn, I really wanted to see you go to trial, even if you lost."

It's okay, because I feel the same way. I don't feel good about the way the case ended, and I never will. I'm angry. I feel betrayed and let down. How is it that I can be willing to put my freedom on the line, and I can't even find one lawyer in a room of ten who is excited to take a month to fight when all they have to sacrifice is a few weeks of work?

I am embarrassed when I think about other liberation movements that I have expressed solidarity with, who face much greater risks and have paid a much greater price. I regret that I was not strong enough to hold myself together, nor insightful enough to see this outcome on the horizon and do more work to prevent it.

Could I have had my charges dropped, or had at least had a better shot at trial, if I would have encouraged Max, Rob, and Nathanael to take a deal with Erik? What if I had drawn a harder line refusing to negotiate and given more encouragement for the three of them to take the deal without me? Could I have then focused on getting more lawyers on board with trial and avoided being cast as "manipulative"? These sorts of "what ifs" will be things that I will always wonder.

Looking back, if I had known or planned on taking a plea deal, there are plenty of things I would have done differently. With the deal, I feel like I lost integrity. I wouldn't have said so clearly that I was going to go to trial. I wouldn't have asked for the same sort of support or as much of it. I probably would have put more time into other projects and worried less about the case.

The pouring through discovery, the meetings with the lawyers, the court dates; they may have given me new information and new ways to grow, but that is not enough to make them feel worthwhile. After two years of time and energy invested, it feels like a net negative return. Movement was built, but it could have been built around fighting foreclosures, police brutality, xenophobia, or any of dozens of other fights worth fighting.

Still, the work was not for nothing. I believe the movement is better off than when we started. Personally, I learned a lot about the judicial system and its inner workings. I was well positioned to aid other RNC arrestees, worked closely on the cases of four other RNC defendants, and assisted several others by helping them understand their options, offering them places to stay and extending emotional support.

The same skills continued to be useful when Carrie Feldman and Scott DeMuth were subpoenaed to the grand jury in Iowa, which later indicted Scott. Much of the "evidence" used to indict him was taken from his home during a raid prior to the RNC, and so I was able to lend insight based on my knowledge of the raids. Even more recently, several local activists who had worked on organizing the large anti-war march on the first day of the RNC had their homes raided by the FBI. It seems unlikely that the FBI investigation is directly tied to the RNC, but having built a broad local support network, the community was able to move swiftly to respond. Further, we were able to use our case as a way to expand the understanding of what political State repression looks like and give perspective to these new raids and grand jury subpoenas.

As I continue to reflect on the past four years, it is important to identify why I choose to organize the way I do and what pitfalls exist in the models I use. A lot of the "New Left" era radicals whom I admire believed in and experimented with vanguardist movement-building models. That is, if they pushed and escalated struggle, others would fill in behind them, inspired by their advanced action. While some people were inspired and there was some movement, the response was never nearly the scope that the "vanguard" hoped. They were left hanging, isolated.

On the other hand, there have been many groups through history that have focused on organizing "the masses," hoping to gain clout by winning over the hearts and minds of a critical mass of the citizenry. They then hoped to leverage general strikes, boycotts, and mass divestment to win demands. The problem is that, in the face of immediate life issues, it is hard to get people on board for some abstract action set out in the future. Further, when people are asked en masse to silence their individuality for group cohesion, it can begin to feel like choices are being made outside their control. This, in turn, leads to dropping out.

What I see as the current political reality is work that

falls both outside and in between these two models. It is not prudent or historically effective for the most committed radicals to self-isolate and try to teach the "correct" way to struggle. Rather, I believe the movement will be grown by people who are at varying places in their journeys coming together to struggle to meet their immediate needs with an eye toward the future and the world they wish to create together. Together, we push each other to be better people and better revolutionaries. However, we are humans working with other humans. Sometimes, when we push ourselves, we still come up short.

Not everyone is going to live up to our hopes, and that is a great frustration of anti-authoritarianism. At the end of the day, we can't force those we work with to make the choices we think they should. At the RNC, anarchists, virtually across the board, showed up with fewer comrades and less thought-out plans than they had projected they would bring. People who said their town was sending dozens of folks came with only one or two cars full. This was disappointing and could have been remedied by folks being more honest with themselves about where they were and not just expressing their best-case fantasies.

I feel the same thing happened with this case. Some codefendants and lawyers wanted to be committed to trial and said they were committed to trial, even when they weren't. They weren't so much lying as they were fooling themselves and not confronting or being honest about their fears or concerns. Encouraging honesty and allowing space for self-examination might help better forecast how things will play out. However, when one is working within a group and pushing that group, not everyone is always going to live up to every hope or expectation, and that is simply the reality of this style of organizing. It is always disappointing, but it cannot be allowed to discourage us from continuing to push to be the best we can and to grow the movement we want to see and be a part of.

Personally, I have grown to realize that the times I am most proud of the choices I make are the times when I imagine the kind of person I would most like to have in this movement and work to be that person. This means shooting beyond where I know I can reach but being honest about my shortcomings. It means working to meet and even go beyond the work done by my greatest heroes. It means taking stances in order to inspire myself. It doesn't mean posturing (we aren't lacking for that), but making decisions with integrity and pride, being forthright and honest, and working hard even when things are difficult. I think over the past four years, I have gained a clearer picture of the kind of person, the kind of revolutionary, I want to be. Having that picture is a necessary step toward getting there.

Endnotes

Chapter One

1.   Quaker worship can be divided into programmed and unprogrammed. Unprogrammed meetings have no formal leader and worship by gathering in silence out of which anyone can speak. Programmed meetings generally include a sermon from a Pastor.

2.   The "Abraham Lincoln Brigade," part of the Communist Party's "International Brigades," was comprised of several thousand Americans who volunteered to go to Spain and fight against General Franco and his nationalist army in the Spanish Civil War. Though several years later the U.S. itself joined the war against fascism, in the late 30s this was considered a break with American policy, the US having refused to back the Republicans and anti-fascists against Franco even as he received immense support from Nazi Germany. Many members of the ALB were labeled "anti-American" and targeted for harassment and persecution in the subsequent decades, even as some of them continued to fight fascism as members of the US military in World War II.

3.   In fact, my grandpa's hatred of communists was strong enough that, in the McCarthy era, he cooperated when called to make a brief testimony before the House Un-American Activities Committee (HUAC) about a former acquaintance.

4.   The Catholic Worker movement was a movement founded by Dorothy Day and Peter Maurin in the 1930s. Catholic Workers advocate "personalism," decentralism, and a "green revolution." They also commit to nonviolence, works of mercy, manual labor, and voluntary poverty. Catholic Worker Houses all over the country provide various direct services, including food and shelter, to the poor, needy and forsaken, and the movement is anarchist in structure and practice. (http://www.catholicworker.org).

5.   Volunteers In Service To America (VISTA) is a national service project geared towards fighting domestic poverty.

6.   "Sanctuary" was a faith-based movement of people and churches across the country who dedicated themselves to helping refugees from then-war-torn Central America find safe haven across the US.

7.   In March of 1982, Tucson's Southside Presbyterian Church was declared a "sanctuary for political refugees fleeing civil war and death squads in Central America. Ultimately, 600-700 churches and synagogues across the country followed suit." Many of those involved were eventually indicted on and convicted of smuggling and other charges. (http://www.southsidepresbyterian.org)

8.   The modern Mexican ejido was a part of the post-revolutionary land reforms enacted throughout Mexico, but "the repartition of land in most of Mexico did not begin until Lázaro Cárdenas became president in 1934...The typical procedure for the establishment of an ejido involved the following steps: (1) landless farmers who leased lands from wealthy landlords would petition the federal government for the creation of an ejido in their general area; (2) the federal government would consult with the landlord; (3) the land would be expropriated from the landlords if the government approved the ejido; and (4) an ejido would be established and the original petitioners would be designated as ejidatarios with certain cultivation/use rights. Ejidatarios did not actually own the land, but were allowed to use their alloted parcels indefinitely as long as they did not fail to use the land for more than two years. They could even pass their rights on to their children. In 1991, Mexican President Carlos Salinas de Gortari eliminated the constitutional right to ejidos, citing the "low productivity" of communally owned land.[1] Since then some of the ejido land has been sold to corporations, although most of it is still in the hands of farmers." (source: Wikipedia, "Ejido," 6 Oct 2009)

9.   Literally, the storming of the lands, which took place on January 27, 1937, and is celebrated annually.

10.   The housing complex has since been demolished, for these reasons.

11.   Spanish for mixed, the word mestiza specifically invokes the mixed racial heritage — a combination of Spanish and indigenous bloodlines — and resultant national identity that distinguish European conquest and colonialism as it played out in Mexico from that which played out in the United States, where indigenous populations were decimated and then isolated rather than integrated into colonial society.

12.   Liberation theology is a Catholic theology informed by Marxism that emphasizes justice for the poor and oppressed. It emerged in the late '60s and was an important force in revolutionary struggles throughout Latin America.

Chapter Two

1.   Not real name
2.   Attachment disorder is cause by a baby / young child's needs not being met, and therefore never developing trust with caregivers, resulting in an inability to form healthy, trusting, relationships.
3.   Ricardo Flores Magón is a famous Mexican anarchist involved in the Mexican Revolution.
4.   Over the past decade, more than 2,000 bodies have been recovered in Arizona alone, according to Derechos Humanos (http://www.derechoshumanosaz.net). The vastness of the desert and the increased speed with which bodies decompose in the harsh summer conditions, makes it a certainty that many more bodies will never be found.
5.   The rise of Liberation Theology was directly tied to popular revolutionary groups of the era, a fact that cost many clergymen and women their lives throughout Latin America.
6.   In addition to "Pacifism as Pathology," I'd recommend "How Non-Violence Protects the State" by Peter Gelderloos.
7.   The AWC is a local, women-led group affiliated with Freedom Road Socialist Organization. They recently celebrated their tenth anniversary and are one of the most consistently active groups in the Twin Cities, regularly organizing demonstrations and civil disobedience actions that get new people involved in local activism.
8.   Free Trade Area of the Americas, a proposed expansion of NAFTA (North American Free Trade Agreement) to include all Latin American countries besides Cuba.
9.   Only five years later, St. Paul and Denver were granted $50 million apiece for convention security.
10.   The 2003 FTAA summit ended in stalemate as leaders of several Latin American countries refused to cooperate in a process that would only decrease the quality of life of their citizens.
11.   The Coca-Cola Corporation, in addition to various other atrocities, has engaged in brutal union-busting activities at its Colombian factories. The company has contracted with paramilitary organizations and is responsible for beatings, kidnappings and murders of many union organizers there. United Steelworkers sponsored a campaign focusing on US college campuses, trying to get them to break exclusive contracts with Coca-Cola as the first step in a national boycott.
12.   Ronald W. Reagan, bad actor, worse president, had died the summer before the 2004 RNC. He was beloved by rich conservatives

and hated by anyone with a modicum of genuine concern for poor and working people here and the world over.

13.   John Hinckley attempted to assassinate then-president Reagan in a crazed attempt to get the attention of actress Jodie Foster. For you humorless law-enforcement types out there, note that I clearly state that this banner was satirical.

14.   So-called because people used pots and pans (cacerolas) as noisemakers during the demonstrations.

15.   Members of the MTD are also called "piqueteros" because of their common use of militant pickets and road blockades to demand jobs and specific welfare packages from the government.

16.   The workers of the largest recuperated factory in the hemisphere, a ceramic factory called FaSinPat (Fábrica Sin Patrón, or Factory Without a Boss), formerly Zanón, recently won a years-long legal battle and were granted full legal ownership of the factory that they took over and transformed after being locked out in a prolonged labor dispute in 2001.

17.   Though originally intended to keep prosecutors in check, grand juries are a secretive and powerful tool at the prosecutor's disposal. The quick rundown of how they function is this: grand juries are convened as a regular matter of course, and a prosecutor can bring evidence before one in an attempt to gain indictments for crimes believed to have been committed. To this end, the prosecutor can get court subpoenas for individuals, legally compelling them to appear before the grand jury on the given date to testify. The prosecutor doesn't have to inform the individual of what they will be questioned about, and the individual is not allowed to have counsel present in front of the grand jury. The proceedings are not open to the public and records are sealed. Refusal to testify can result in a finding of contempt of court, and the individual under subpoena can be jailed for up to 18 months at a time.

18.   Scott is the seventh person nationally to be indicted under the AETA, which qualifies interference with animal enterprises (e.g., fur farms, research labs, meatpacking plants, etc.) as acts of terrorism.

Chapter Three

1.   "Critical Mass is a monthly bicycle ride to celebrate cycling and to assert cyclists' right to the road" (source: http://critical-mass. info). Critical Mass rides are organized autonomously all over the world and vary in size, attitude and the responses they receive, but a

typical ride consists of dozens of bicyclists riding in a group, taking up multiple lanes of traffic.

2.   Urban exploring is an activity which at minimum requires criminal trespass and often more serious crimes; it basically involves things like exploring abandoned buildings, tunnels and sewer systems. Panda was, and probably still is, a serious urban explorer, all while being paid thousands by the FBI. He even wrote an article about urban exploring for an issue of the CrimethInc. publication, Rolling Thunder.

3.   We had initially had three tiers, with tier one being most important and the other two supplementary and meant to be filled if numbers permitted.

4.   Darby was responsible for ensnaring Bradley Crowder and David McKay in a half-assed plot to use Molotov cocktails at the RNC. The Molotovs were never used—many of us believe they never would have been—but despite the fact that Darby, an older activist whom they had emulated, clearly entrapped them, Crowder and McKay both ended up pleading guilty and serving time in federal prison.

5.   The Minnehaha Free State was a historic, 16 month occupation of land in south Minneapolis blocking the reroute of Highway 55.

Chapter Four

1.   From Minnesota Statute 609.71 "When three or more persons assembled disturb the public peace by an intentional act or threat of unlawful force or violence to person or property, each participant who is armed with a dangerous weapon or knows that any other participant is armed with a dangerous weapon is guilty of riot second degree."

From Minnesota Statute 609.714: "…a crime is committed to 'further terrorism' if the crime is a felony and is a premeditated act involving violence to persons or property that is intended to: (1) terrorize, intimidate, or coerce a considerable number of members of the public in addition to the direct victims of the act; and (2) significantly disrupt or interfere with the lawful exercise, operation, or conduct of government, lawful commerce, or the right of lawful assembly. "

Chapter Five

1.   From Minnesota Statute 609.595: Criminal damage to property in the first degree:
"Whoever intentionally causes damage to physical property of another without the latter's consent may be sentenced to imprisonment for not more than five years or to payment of a fine of not more than $10,000, or both, if:
(1) the damage to the property caused a reasonably foreseeable risk of bodily harm; or…the damage reduces the value of the property by more than $1,000 measured by the cost of repair and replacement…"

2.   From Minnesota Statute 609.175:
"…Whoever conspires with another to commit a crime and in furtherance of the conspiracy one or more of the parties does some overt act in furtherance of such conspiracy" is guilty of conspiracy for that crime."

3.   I don't mean to suggest that most women have greater freedom in this area; poverty, racism, and any number of other social forces always transpire in a manner that inhibits genuine freedom for women, crowding out any room for consideration of one's true wants and needs. It is this understanding, in fact, that has led me to view the "pro-choice" movement with great distrust, as it tends toward single-issue liberalism at the expense of a systemic analysis, prioritizing access to abortion over measures that might actually create real and diverse options for women.

Chapter Six

1.   In *The Will to Change: Men, Masculinity and Love*, Bell Hooks defines patriarchy as "a political-social system that insists that males are inherently dominating, superior to everything and everyone deemed weak, especially females, and endowed with the right to dominate and rule over the weak and to maintain that dominance through various forms of psychological terrorism and violence."

DEFEND THE RNC 8

OR YOU'RE NEXT.

www.rnc8.org